Rural Housing and Economic Development

Housing is crucial to the quality of life and wellbeing for individuals and families, but the availability of adequate or affordable housing also plays a vital role in community economic development. Rural areas face a substantial disadvantage compared to urban areas in regard to housing, and this book explores these issues.

Rural Housing and Economic Development includes chapters from nationally known experts from throughout the U.S. to provide insight to help understand and address the difficult housing concerns within rural areas. The chapters cover a variety of issues including housing for rural minorities, the extent of and problems associated with mobile home dwelling, the extent to which affordable rental housing is available in rural areas, the rapidly growing elderly population and the housing consequences of rapid population and economic growth associated with energy development. The authors not only describe various housing problems, but also suggest policy approaches to more effectively address them.

This book will be a vital resource to policymakers at the local, state or national level as they grapple with difficult rural housing problems. Researchers and professionals dealing with housing issues will also benefit from the insights of these experts, while the book will also be appropriate for upper-level undergraduates or graduate students in courses on housing or economic development.

Don E. Albrecht is the Director of the Western Rural Development Center, Utah State University, USA.

Scott Loveridge is a Professor in the Department of Agricultural, Food, and Resource Economics at Michigan State University, USA.

Stephan Goetz is the Director of the Northeast Regional Center for Rural Development and Professor of Agricultural and Regional Economics at Pennsylvania State University, USA.

Rachel Welborn is a Program Manager at the Southern Rural Development Center, Mississippi State University, USA.

Routledge Advances in Regional Economics, Science and Policy

For a full list of titles in this series, please visit www.routledge.com/series/RAIRESP

Rural Housing and Economic Development

Edited by Don E. Albrecht,
Scott Loveridge, Stephan Goetz
and Rachel Welborn

Routledge
Taylor & Francis Group

LONDON AND NEW YORK

First published 2018
by Routledge

2 Park Square, Milton Park, Abingdon, Oxfordshire OX14 4RN
52 Vanderbilt Avenue, New York, NY 10017

Routledge is an imprint of the Taylor & Francis Group, an informa business

First issued in paperback 2019

British Library Cataloguing-in-Publication Data
A catalogue record for this book is available from the British Library

Library of Congress Cataloging-in-Publication Data
A catalog record for this book has been requested

ISBN: 978-1-138-04019-9 (hbk)
ISBN: 978-0-367-88877-0 (pbk)

Typeset in Bembo
by Apex CoVantage, LLC

Contents

Contributors

Don E. Albrecht, Western Rural Development Center, Utah State University, USA

John Cromartie, Economic Research Service, USDA, USA

Surabhi Dabir, Rural Housing Service, USDA, USA

William Dyar, North Central Regional Center for Rural Development, Michigan State University, USA

Felix Fernando, University of Dayton, USA

Lynette Flage, North Dakota State University, USA

Tiffany W. Franklin, Southern University Agricultural Land Grant College, USA

Lance George, Housing Assistance Council, USA

Stephan Goetz, Northeast Regional Center for Rural Development, Pennsylvania State University, USA

Brandn Green, Center for Behavioral Health Statistics and Quality, USA

Leslie T. Grover, Southern University and Agricultural & Mechanical College, USA

Peter Han, Economic Research Service, USDA, USA

Robert Hearne, North Dakota State University, USA

Eric Horent, Louisiana Department of Children and Family Services, USA

Jeffrey Jacquet, Ohio State University, USA

Anne Junod, Ohio State University, USA

Han Bum Lee, Department of Agricultural and Consumer Economics, University of Illinois at Urbana-Champaign, USA

Carlos V. Licón, Department of Landscape Architecture and Environmental Planning, Utah State University, USA

Jungmin Lim, North Central Regional Center for Rural Development, Michigan State University, USA

David Lipsetz, Housing Assistance Council, USA

Scott Loveridge, Department of Agricultural, Food, and Resource Economics, Michigan State University, USA

Paul E. McNamara, Department of Agricultural and Consumer Economics, University of Illinois at Urbana-Champaign, USA

Ebunoluwa Odeyemi, University of Georgia, USA

Stephanie A. Pink-Harper, Department of Political Science, Southern Illinois University Carbondale, USA

Ignacio San Martín, Urban Design and Ecological Urbanism, School of Architecture, College of Design, University of Minnesota, USA

Corianne Payton Scally, Urban Institute, USA

Mark Skidmore, North Central Regional Center for Rural Development, Michigan State University, USA

Kim Skobba, University of Georgia, USA

Karen Tinsley, University of Georgia, USA

Haoying Wang, Department of Management, New Mexico Tech, USA

Russell Weaver, Department of Geography, Texas State University, USA

Rachel Welborn, Southern Rural Development Center, Mississippi State University, USA

Keith Wiley, Housing Assistance Council, USA

1 Rural housing and economic development

Don E. Albrecht, Scott Loveridge, Stephan Goetz and Rachel Welborn

Introduction

A person's home is among the most important features of his or her life. Not only is housing essential for basic needs such as shelter and safety, it is also closely related to other aspects of quality of life, such as privacy and comfort. Additionally, many people use their home as a way of presenting their personal identity (Clapham 2005). Often, a home is an important source of wealth that can be used to start a business, help children with their education or for numerous other uses. Social services agencies are increasingly relying on "housing first" approaches to help the homeless and addicted because a stable living situation is key to successfully addressing other issues for the vulnerable (Tsemberis et al. 2004).

In addition to the relevance of housing to individual and family quality of life and wellbeing, the availability of adequate or affordable housing plays a vital role in community economic development. For community economic development efforts to succeed, adequate and affordable housing is essential to attract new businesses and their employees. If housing is inadequate, the business or industry may simply choose to go elsewhere (Leigh and Blakely 2013).

Homes are where significant proportions of energy, water and other resources are consumed. From a national and global perspective, home size and the quality of construction have major implications for Greenhouse Gas Emissions and climate change trends, as well as the extent to which other resources are used (Choguill 2007). Average home sizes have increased in recent decades, while the average household size has declined. The result is an increase in the number of housing units and greater total resource consumption (McKibbon 2008). A study in arid Arizona, for example, found that water consumption was strongly related to home and lot size, regardless of views and attitudes about conservation and sustainability (Harlan et al. 2009).

Three major rural housing concerns have prompted the development of this book.

Housing programs and policies and rural wellbeing

Rural communities tend to be economically disadvantaged to begin with (Albrecht 2014), and housing concerns often magnify these disadvantages. Problems appear exacerbated by federal policies and programs that funnel disproportionate resources to urban areas (Belden and Wiener 1999; Housing Assistance Council 2012), and these rural disadvantages have existed for decades (Malpass and Murie 1994).

In rural areas, homes values tend to be substantially lower, which reduces wealth accumulation (Potepan 1996). The data in Table 1.1 show that nationwide in 2014, the median value of owner-occupied homes in non-metro counties was $114,500,

Table 1.1 Median Value of Owner-Occupied Homes and Percent of Homes Owner-Occupied by State and Metro–Non-Metro Status, 2014

State	Median Value of Owner-Occupied Homes			Percent Owner-Occupied		
	Total	*Metro*	*Non-metro*	*Total*	*Metro*	*Non-metro*
Alabama	181,200	199,300	114,500	63.1	61.7	70.8
Alaska	125,600	137,900	92,100	67.7	67.0	69.7
Arizona	176,700	181,400	109,500	61.1	60.8	69.0
Arkansas	112,500	131,700	86,000	65.8	63.2	69.7
California	412,700	420,300	246,300	53.7	53.4	66.4
Colorado	255,200	259,200	219,600	63.9	63.2	69.7
Connecticut	267,200	268,000	255,900	66.4	65.8	75.4
Delaware	230,500	230,500	–	70.3	70.3	–
District of Colombia	486,900	486,900	–	40.6	40.6	–
Florida	162,700	164,600	90,700	64.1	63.8	72.2
Georgia	147,900	158,100	96,500	62.2	61.6	65.1
Hawaii	528,000	583,000	352,300	56.7	54.8	64.3
Idaho	165,300	170,000	153,400	68.0	68.2	67.6
Illinois	171,900	188,700	92,100	65.5	64.4	73.6
Indiana	124,300	132,100	102,300	68.6	66.8	74.5
Iowa	133,100	153,500	105,200	70.9	68.5	74.1
Kansas	132,100	157,000	89,100	66.6	65.2	69.5
Kentucky	123,800	149,600	91,600	66.1	63.4	69.8
Louisiana	143,600	153,700	87,500	64.4	64.0	66.8
Maine	174,800	203,500	146,400	71.3	69.4	74.0
Maryland	288,500	290,600	218,000	65.9	65.8	70.0
Massachusetts	338,900	339,800	274,100	61.6	61.5	70.2
Michigan	125,700	131,500	109,200	70.2	68.5	77.7
Minnesota	188,300	203,100	143,800	71.7	70.2	76.5
Mississippi	104,000	133,000	84,200	67.7	66.9	68.3
Missouri	138,500	150,500	102,200	66.9	66.1	69.4
Montana	196,800	202,200	192,700	66.4	64.0	67.7
Nebraska	133,800	147,900	102,400	65.9	63.6	69.9
Nevada	192,100	197,400	160,500	53.6	51.8	70.5
New Hampshire	236,400	254,600	205,100	70.2	69.7	71.0
New Jersey	313,200	313,200	–	63.3	63.3	–
New Mexico	158,400	171,800	117,700	66.9	65.6	69.8
New York	279,100	310,200	109,700	53.0	51.5	71.3

State	Median Value of Owner-Occupied Homes			Percent Owner-Occupied		
	Total	*Metro*	*Non-metro*	*Total*	*Metro*	*Non-metro*
North Carolina	155,000	164,200	117,900	64.2	63.0	68.5
North Dakota	161,800	180,900	139,700	63.8	58.6	69.1
Ohio	129,100	135,500	109,900	65.3	64.0	70.5
Oklahoma	119,800	134,000	93,700	65.1	64.0	67.3
Oregon	239,800	252,900	172,500	60.7	59.9	64.9
Pennsylvania	165,400	173,000	107,300	68.8	68.0	74.5
Rhode Island	236,000	236,000	–	58.8	58.8	–
South Carolina	140,000	148,500	85,800	68.0	67.4	71.6
South Dakota	142,300	163,500	114,500	68.2	67.5	68.7
Tennessee	142,900	154,500	104,100	66.1	64.7	71.0
Texas	139,800	147,000	86,700	61.2	60.6	70.6
Utah	223,200	226,700	188,400	69.2	68.6	72.8
Vermont	214,600	254,400	195,300	70.0	67.1	71.5
Virginia	247,800	274,100	123,500	65.3	64.3	72.1
Washington	266,200	274,500	200,700	61.7	61.3	65.8
West Virginia	103,900	114,200	89,000	72.2	69.9	76.0
Wisconsin	164,700	172,300	145,800	66.6	64.0	73.7
Wyoming	201,000	203,400	199,700	66.9	65.6	67.5

compared to $199,300 in metro counties. In every state in the nation, home values are greater in metro compared to non-metro counties. Housing prices in rural areas also failed to recover from the Great Recession as quickly or completely as in urban areas (Mian and Sufi 2015).

As a result of lower housing prices, a higher proportion of non-metro households own their home rather than rent. Table 1.1 shows that 70.8 percent of non-metro households live in owner-occupied homes compared to 61.7 percent of metro households. Idaho was the only state where the proportion of owner-occupied homes was greater in metro counties than in non-metro counties. Related to lower home values, rural residents are much more likely than urban residents to live in mobile homes. The data in Table 1.2 show that 13.7 percent of non-metro households reside in mobile homes compared to 4.4 percent of metro residents. Mobile homes tend to lose value rather than build equity.

Creative policies are needed to meet these problems and concerns. The first five chapters have been written to provide insights and analysis on these concerns.

Housing needs of disadvantaged populations

Adequate housing for vulnerable and disadvantaged populations has long been a significant concern. Housing for minority and elderly populations is especially relevant. With respect to the elderly, major socio-demographic changes are leading to a

Table 1.2 Comparison of Metro and Non-Metro Counties on Types of Housing Structures, 2014

	Metro	Non-metro
1 – Detached	61.0	72.5
1 – Attached	6.7	1.9
2 – Apartments	3.8	2.8
3 – 4 Apartments	4.6	3.0
5 – 9 Apartments	5.1	2.5
10 + Apartments	14.4	3.5
Mobile Home	4.4	13.7

Table 1.3 Gross Rent as a Percentage of Household Income, 2014

Less than 15	*12.0*
15–19.9	12.3
20–24.9	12.6
25–29.9	11.4
30–34.9	9.2
35 or More	42.6

mismatch between the current rural housing stock and future housing needs. With the aging of the baby-boom generation, for instance, the need for housing conducive to elderly populations increases. By 2030 it is expected that about 40 percent of non-metro households will include elderly persons. Most current homes are not structured in a way to make them conducive to the needs of the elderly. Housing not favorable to the needs of the elderly makes it less likely that they can "age in place." The social and economic benefits to individuals and society if people can age in their own home are significant (Wacker and Roberto 2013).

Another housing problem resulting from socio–demographic change results from growing levels of inequality. In recent decades, a high proportion of income growth has gone to the very wealthy (Piketty 2014). At the same time, large numbers of individuals and families have static or declining incomes and consequently struggle to find affordable housing that is adequate (Amato et al. 2015). In 2014, more than 40 percent of U.S. households were paying more than 35 percent of their household income for housing (Table 1.3). Finding ways to provide adequate housing for low-income persons is of vital concern, especially in rural areas, where a lack of multiunit dwellings provides substantial obstacles to efforts to meet housing needs of the economically disadvantaged. Chapters 7 through 10 are intended to help address these concerns.

Housing and rural economic development

Adequate and affordable housing provides significant obstacles to economic development in rural communities. To begin with, rural areas generally have much less capacity than urban communities to react and adjust to growth and change. Consequently, economic development opportunities are lost because adequate housing is unavailable or unaffordable. For example, where major energy development projects occur and large numbers of workers move to an area, a lack of housing makes already difficult circumstances much worse. By contrast, urban communities with a much larger initial housing stock can deal with increased demand as a matter of course. Another example where adjustment is difficult is in high-amenity rural communities. In these communities, high demand has resulted in housing costs skyrocketing, making it extremely difficult for anyone but the very wealthy to afford to live in the community (Marcouiller et al. 2011). As a consequence, unaffordable housing places a heavy burden on low- and middle-income persons who work in the community but often have to live elsewhere. The final four chapters address these issues.

Plan of the book

The book consists of this introductory chapter and 13 additional chapters written by rural housing experts with a wide range of expertise and from a variety of organizations and agencies from throughout the nation. The chapters are organized into three sections corresponding to the major concerns that are addressed. Our goal is to inform policymakers with the hope that policies will be developed more likely to successfully address significant housing concerns. Additionally, our goal is to advance research on these important topics.

References

Albrecht, D. E. (2014). *Rethinking rural*. Pullman: Washington State University Press.

Amato, P. R., Booth, A., McHale, S. M., & Van Hook, J. (Eds.) (2015). *Families in an era of increasing inequality*. New York: Springer.

Belden, J. N., & Wiener, R. J. (Eds.) (1999). *Housing in rural America: Building affordable and inclusive communities*. Thousand Oaks, CA: Sage Publications.

Choguill, C. (2007). The search for policies to support sustainable housing. *Habitat International*, *31*(1), 143–149.

Clapham, D. F. (2005). *The meaning of housing: A pathways approach*. Bristol, CN: Policy Press.

Harlan, S. L., Yabiku, S. T., Larsen, L., & Brazel, A. J. (2009). House-hold water consumption in an arid city: Affluence, affordance, and attitudes. *Society and Natural Resources, 22*, 691–709.

Housing Assistance Council. (2012). *Taking stock: Rural people, poverty, and housing in the 21st century*. Washington DC: Housing Assistance Council.

Leigh, N. G., & Blakely, E. J. (2013). *Planning local economic development*. London: Sage Publications.

Malpass, P., & Murie, A. (1994). *Housing policy and practice*. New York: Macmillan.

Marcouiller, D., Lapping, M., & Furuseth, O. (Eds.) (2011). *Rural housing, exurbanization, and amenity-driven development: Contrasting the 'haves' and the 'have nots'*. London: Routledge.

McKibbon, B. (2008). *Deep economy*. New York: Henry Holt and Co.

Mian, A., & Sufi, A. (2015). *House of debt*. Chicago: University of Chicago Press.

Piketty, T. (2014). *Capital in the twenty-first century*. Cambridge, MA: Harvard University Press.

Potepan, M. J. (1996). Explaining intermetropolitan variation in housing prices, rents and land prices. *Real Estate Economics, 24*(2), 219–245.

Tsemberis, S., Gulcur, L., & Nakae, M. (2004). Housing first, consumer choice, and harm reduction for homeless individuals with a dual diagnosis. *American Journal of Public Health, 94*(4), 651–656.

Wacker, R. R., & Roberto, K. A. (2013). *Community resources for older adults*. Washington, DC: Sage Publications.

2 The role of housing in rural behavioral health

Brandn Green

Introduction

Housing is an essential component of rural behavioral health care systems. Safe and secure housing provides stability and a foundation for developing the community ties necessary for individuals to successfully manage their behavioral health care needs. Conversely, inadequate housing risks undermining stability, increasing stress, and exacerbating daily challenges for those same individuals. Understanding the relationship between housing and behavioral health is a complex enterprise, as the home is not a simple or singular influence in the life of the individual. A home can be the location where one receives mental health care through the efforts of an in-home nurse, the site of danger in the event of natural disasters or the goal for an individual who is homeless. Variation in the role of home corresponds to variation in the influence housing has on behavioral health. Examining this relationship through a rural frame requires a strategy for linking the experiences of the individual and the home to the community setting. This chapter examines the scholarship on housing and behavioral health in rural areas as well as the financial aid mechanisms and strategies taken by federal and state governments to facilitate stable housing and access to behavioral health care in rural communities.

This chapter is intended to encourage continued expansion of research on the relationship between housing and behavioral health in rural communities. Rather than a comprehensive accounting of funding programs, federal investment is used as a marker of concepts about the role residence has in behavioral health throughout the life course. As there has been relatively little research done specifically about the relationship between housing and behavioral health in rural communities, I overview and combine research completed in behavioral health, public health and rural sociology to depict and conceptualize how housing informs behavioral health in rural settings. The chapter concludes with a set of research questions intended to structure a prospective research agenda on the relationship between housing and behavioral health in rural communities.

Federal investment in housing and behavioral health

Behavioral health is defined by the federal agency tasked with supporting behavioral health services as the "state of mental/emotional well-being and/or choices and actions that affect wellness" (SAMHSA 2013). Historically, this broad understanding has been separated into the two domain areas of substance abuse and mental health. Current trends both in the academic community and among service providers and government agencies working to remediate social burden and individual disease link together these two domain areas and the systems that address them (CDC 2011). Integration of care delivery systems within states and local jurisdictions has been unfolding at different rates, meaning that some government units have behavioral health systems that are well integrated with health and human service divisions, while others remain separated. For the purposes of this chapter, behavioral health is used as the most inclusive term and refers to the entire system of substance abuse care and mental health care. Substance abuse rates and care systems and mental health prevalence rates and care systems will be referred to specifically, as different funding streams provide different types of linkages between housing and care for substance users and those with diagnosed serious mental illness (SMI) (HHS 2014a; HHS 2015).

Behavioral health care is supported by the federal government through multiple administrations, mainly from within the Department of Health and Human Services. The Substance Abuse and Mental Health Services Administration (SAMHSA) is the largest provider of funding to enhance the wellbeing of American citizens' behavioral health. In addition to SAMHSA, the Administration for Children and Families, Centers for Medicaid and Medicare Services and the Veteran's Administration fund a wide array and variety of efforts aimed at improving the behavioral health of American citizens. The scope of the federal investment in housing makes a catalogue of services difficult to complete. Rural communities present an additional layer of complexity, as there is currently no simple method for establishing the amount and nature of federal and state investment improving housing to individuals with behavioral health needs in rural places (GAO 2006). Being unable to ascertain the extent and geography of federal investment is the product of differential definitions of rural/urban distinctions by federal agencies and differences in grant reporting requirements (GAO 2006). This data limitation has consequences for presenting a straight forward accounting of the role federal agencies play in providing housing as a component to the rural behavioral health care system. State-level housing funding systems and variation in the utilization of federal programs such as Medicaid contribute an additional layer of complexity (TAC 2014).

Across 20 agencies, the federal government administers 160 programs, tax expenditures and assistance strategies intended to increase homeownership and access to affordable rental housing (GAO 2015a). These programs are diverse, and they provide incentives and direct financial support to both low- and middle-income citizens for housing (CBO 2015). Since the 1937 Housing Act initiated a policy for providing housing assistance for the poor, the central tenet of housing funding has been that the provision of housing is the provision of a stabilizing force in the day-to-day lives of all people (Kyle and Dunn 2008; Newman 2008). Stable housing has been imprecisely used in empirical work on housing (Frederick et al. 2014). In this chapter, stable housing is used to reference housing that is constant, reliable and persistent. Rather than being a definition that can serve an empirical investigation, it is a definition that is consistent with language used across federal housing agencies providing support for housing services (CBO 2015). In contrast, unstable housing is used to reference housing that is uncertain, varied and episodic.

The nature of access to housing service program incentives and benefits explicitly linked to improving behavioral health varies by funding agency and program type. Each funding program must follow restrictions and limitations that correspond to the stated goals and missions of the funding agencies and authorizing legislation. For example, federal funding provided by SAMHSA through their Projects for Assistance in Transition from Homelessness (PATH) can be used to give services to homeless or imminently at risk of being homeless people with an SMI. The definition includes those with co-occurring substance use disorders. Funding from PATH can be used by states to provide a range of services, including outreach, rehabilitation, community mental health services and staff training, but cannot be used fund the construction of new housing (SAMHSA 2015). The multidimensional nature of federal funding mechanisms requires states and local providers to link together different federal programs to provide complete behavioral health care to individuals also struggling with their housing. With the expansion of Medicaid through the Affordable Care Act (ACA), some states have begun to provide reimbursement for care coordination and care management, which serves to improve the quality of coordination across behavioral health and housing services (HHS 2015).

Priorities and strategies for accomplishing congressionally mandated responsibilities for federal agencies to provide housing and behavioral health services shift and change over time as understandings of social mechanisms shift and change. Since 1999, two major strategy shifts have significantly informed the approach taken by federal agencies providing housing funding. Actions taken by the largest housing funding agency, Housing and Urban Development (HUD), has encouraged strategic, data-informed and integrated service delivery through the implementation of Continuums of Care (HUD 1999). This strategy promotes the utilization of data collection and reporting to enable geographically bounded planning and service delivery regions across the country. One strength of this approach is that it enhances local capacity to leverage multiple funding sources to provide integrated services that link housing with substance abuse treatment needs or mental illness care. Increased integration of data tracking systems across human services agencies as a component of the Continuum model has also sought to limit the ability of specific individuals to take advantage of the systems or gain inappropriate access to multiple services (HHS 2009). A second recent change has been the federal strategy to homelessness by shifting away from program structure requiring enrollment in behavioral health treatment to access housing toward housing first models that provide housing to the homeless free from conditions of abstaining from substance use (SAMHSA 2010).

Behavioral health of rural geographies

The prevalence of substance abuse and mental illness are comparable across rural and urban geographies (HHS 2005). Differences become apparent when exploring the intersectionality of geography and demographics of subpopulations that tend to reside in rural areas. American Indians residing in rural areas have higher rates of alcohol-attributable mortality; non-Hispanic Whites tend to have higher rates of opioid usage, and non-Hispanic White females tend to have higher rates of depression than the same groups in urban areas (Compton et al. 2007; Willging et al. 2013; HHS 2014b; Haegerich et al. 2014). SMI prevalence rates do not differ substantially between rural and urban settings (HHS 2005).

A substantial difference exists between rural and urban in access to behavioral health services (Chipp et al. 2008). A rural resident is less likely to utilize behavioral health care, is less likely to remain in treatment once a treatment program is initiated and is more likely to live in a medically underserved area than his or her urban counterpart (Sawyer et al. 2006; Sundararaman 2009; Robinson et al. 2012). Rural residents are much more likely to receive their mental health care directly from a primary care physician, even when the primary care physician is without any professional training in mental health (Williams et al. 2015). Practical challenges for accessing behavioral health care extend beyond care system infrastructure, as the distances to care in many rural places, and the associated stigma and social proximity of small communities, act as disincentives for the pursuit of mental health care (Boyd and Parr 2008).

In the midst of the diversity and unique qualities of individual rural communities, many rural places reflect a set of common traits. A basic survey of the literature within rural sociology, as well as within the fields of rural public and community health, identifies some of these characteristics. They include: aging infrastructure, limited technological advances, dense social relationships with ambiguous impacts, limited but increasingly innovative employment opportunities, an aging and increasingly racially diverse population and under representativeness in non-agricultural national policies (Hartley 2004; Brown and Schafft 2011). These shared characteristics impact rural livelihoods and health care differently for different regions of the country and for different population groups within those places. These are not only challenges or limitations to overcome in the provision of mental health care; they are also elements of rural life that many residents find to be compelling.

Behavioral health care systems can best provide culturally appropriate care in rural settings by recognizing that challenges are produced by the benefits of rural life. Housing systems that enhance behavioral health in the rural context must reflect rural preferences while providing care in line with the current state of the science. By examining the ways that housing is linked to behavioral health, and by linking these to funding programs offered by federal agencies, local service providers can retrofit old models and create new systems of care for rural residents with behavioral health needs.

Housing and behavioral health in rural geographies

Homes are complex sites of social interaction that defy simplistic definitions (Evans et al. 2002; Leff et al. 2009). A home can be a site of stability upon which one rebuilds her life after a jail sentence for using illicit drugs. A home can be a site of instability because of domestic violence or financial insecurity. Housing interventions seek to provide stable and safe shelter for those in need of assistance, but even these programs, for example, homeless shelters, can be sites of violence and trauma (Folsom et al. 2005). Fundamentally, the underlying theory driving federal investment in housing as an element of behavioral health is the idea that stability is essential for recovery and overall well-being. Instability in an element of life as basic as housing means that an individual is unable to structure his or her life in a manner that allows them to manage their mental illness or substance dependence or abuse (SAMHSA 2010).

I surveyed the current state of the research on housing and behavioral health and examined the federal policies and funding programs aimed at supportive housing and have identified five mechanisms for how a home or housing is linked with behavioral health. This review refrained from exploring the ample literature on well-being and the built environment (Evans 2001). Each category corresponds to a set of posited mechanisms currently influencing or shaping funding priorities of different federal agencies. The five categories are organized around the framing of housing as: care, family, danger, distress and foundation. Each of these reflects a conceptualization that can be extended to understand housing as a dynamic and multifaceted component to rural behavioral health.

Housing as care

The most direct way housing overlaps with behavioral health is as the location where one receives treatment or mental health care. In a range of settings, including, but not exhaustively catalogued, residential treatment centers, transitional living spaces, institutions and in-home care, reveal the home as the setting for behavioral health care. Often, these settings have a mixture of formal and informal strategies connecting continued access to housing with that of continuation with treatment (Reif et al. 2014).

In the case of individuals with SMI, supportive housing through group homes and long-term care locations within communities marked a shift away from government-run institutionalization (Leff et al. 2009). The community setting is believed to provide palliative effects and to be the more humane care location for individuals in need of significant assistance for daily living. This shift has been unfolding across the country since the late 1960s and has been highlighted as being in need of much greater financial support. Multiple commentators have argued that one potential outcome of underfunding for housing individuals with mental illness has been that jails and prisons have unintentionally been functioning as the most significant sites of mental health care for many (Dumont et al. 2012).

Prisons are disproportionally located in rural counties, and jails in rural areas are often in the greatest need for mental health care providers (Hooks et al. 2004; Sawyer et al. 2006). If prisons are understood to be places where individuals are housed, and if they are sites where mental health care is accessed, then they are an element to housing and behavioral health care in rural settings. Prisons house individuals within community settings that are from other communities. One understudied and ancillary product of the prison system is concern about the effects working in prison systems has on employees (Dumont et al. 2012). In the ways that these potentially untreated mental health needs follow employees to their homes, they present a potential interaction between two types of housing that directly engage with the behavioral health needs of residents in rural spaces.

The rural population is more elderly than that in urban areas (Brown and Schafft 2011). As an individual ages, and ages in place, mental health needs shift and change. Medicare funding can be used to cover the costs of much in-home care for elderly residents, and there is some evidence that changes to the health care system through the ACA have also increased in-home care opportunities for non-Medicare-eligible rural residents (Sorocco et al. 2013). Telemedicine has been highlighted as a potential pathway for rural residents of all ages to access mental health care in their homes (Chipp et al. 2008). Questions remain if this care delivery mechanism will be accessible to elderly residents of rural regions who may lack the technological infrastructure and skill necessary to take advantage of the expansion of these programs.

By understanding the home, be it in an institutional setting or as a site of in-home professional medical care, as a locus of care, the home is conceptualized as a context for receiving health care. The treatment center model removes the individual from his or her community setting for a defined period of time to help them focus on the pursuit of wellbeing. The home as a care setting model replaces the individual in his or her community. The institution places individuals from extra-local communities in rural places and those who are incarcerated are affected by the potential lack of services and health care access. Rural communities function as both the foreground and background in which behavioral health care occurs in residential spaces. Prisons and some treatment centers only engage with the local setting through the local residents who comprise the staff. In-home care and telemedicine are strategies for overcoming the geographic challenges and lack of service providers rural communities present to residents. In all versions of housing as care, the individual or family receives services on top of a stable residential setting.

Housing as family

As children, we lack the ability to choose where we are going to live. In acute situations, children become homeless due to circumstances entirely beyond their control. Or, potentially more severely, they find themselves trying to make sense of the stress from housing instability or domestic violence they absorb from their home of origin. Conversely, healthy families are foundational to healthy mental health development and the acquisition of healthy substance utilization behaviors (Compton and Shim 2015). Prevention programs and family educational programs aim to assist parents in making a healthier household specifically target improvement of inner-home dynamics for children and adults (Newman 2008). These efforts assume the presence of a house, do not necessarily connect user to housing services and focus attention on the quality of the social dynamics within the home setting for all family members.

Psychologists and public health officials have begun to understand that the impact of trauma in childhood is a major predictor of mental illness and substance abusive behavior in adults (SAMHSA 2014). The housing as family theory views the house as the locus of private influences that are less controlled by government agencies or private health care providers. In this space, the complex dynamics of parenting, sibling relationships and coming of age unfold and overlap. If the physical structure of the home is unsafe or if the loss of a home occurs during childhood, the developmental process is negatively affected (Leventhal and Newman 2010). In the most severe situations of danger, child and protective services remove the child from the home, thereby protecting him or her from the adverse impacts of the family system.

Emotional danger exists in a home where there is abuse, partners engaging in adverse substance usage or when informal care taking exacts an emotional tone on household caregivers. In these scenarios, the home may become a place to flee and avoid. The trauma enacted within the home may adversely impact the mental health of the individual who may, in response, increase or change the nature of their substance usage. Rural settings add an additional layer of geographic isolation to the home that may exacerbate or create mental illness in situations of trauma (Jones et al. 2014).

Images of the home as the location of family are pervasive in popular culture. It is a motif that highlights the psychological, or soft, impacts that homes have in the American psyche (Shaw 2004). These impacts are less well studied and tend to be conceptualized outside of health disciplines. Rural homes and rural family structures have historically been structured by labor. As the rural economy has shifted away from farm based economic systems toward economic systems requiring off-farm labor, the role of the home as the locus for family life has also begun to shift (Lobao and Meyer 2001). An inability to meet the expectations that individuals who live in rural communities have about how an ideal family, and therefore an ideal home, are constructed may exacerbate stress stemming from economic pressures. Much more research needs to be undertaken to develop clearer understandings about the potential impacts to individual psychological development shifting and changing symbols of home and to identify if there are different symbolic pressures between urban and rural spaces (Shaw 2004).

As a locus for the family, the physical residence is viewed as the locus for psychological development within a social space, the family. The composition of the family unit is less relevant to the theory than the underlying principle that the space of a home impacts the individual through the actions of others in said space. The home as family is a recognition that for the vast majority of people, our first experiences of being housed are social.

Housing as danger

The physical characteristics of the home, be they lead paint, rickety stairs or a lack of sunlight, present a wide array of physical danger when the quality of the home is substandard. These risks might be heightened in rural contexts where ramshackle housing is more likely to remain classified as usable property, rather than being con-demned, due to a lack of oversight and difficulty in viewing rural properties (GAO 2000). In traumatic situations where the home is destroyed through the forces of fire or water, the home itself becomes life threatening. Long-term emotional trauma from these events is well documented and an important consideration in rural areas where homes are exposed to danger from natural disasters (North and Pfefferbaum 2013).

One burgeoning area of research explores the relationship between the physi-cal design of the housing unit and the predilection to mental illness. This research area has largely focused on spaces with high density, like office buildings and public housing in urban spaces (Bambra et al. 2010). However, the underlying concepts that drive this research would also apply to the rural context. Do certain types of housing that are common in rural communities have an independent effect on individual wellbeing? Research in this domain is limited by ethical concerns, but some work has been done in situations with natural experiments when changes to public housing policy have created opportunities for large populations with similar demographic characteristics to be placed in new and different types of housing (Sanbonmatsu et al. 2011). Once again, most of this research has taken place in urban settings and reflects an opportunity for additional work in the rural context.

One element of housing as danger that is distinctive in rural areas is concerns about the quality of housing made available to migrating farmworkers (GAO 2000). This housing is often found to be substandard and to present significant physical risk to those who are given this type of shelter (Holmes 2006). This example is part of a broader point about housing as tied to labor production and how that varies across rural and urban settings.

In the ways that physical danger enhances stress, it runs the risk of having a del-eterious effect on mental health. The fundamental assumption in this classification of housing and behavioral health is that the exposure to physical risks increases stress. One additional concern is that exposure to environmental hazards might cre-ate or exacerbate mental illness, especially in children (Compton and Shim 2015). By improving understanding about the role the physical properties of the home shape mental health, federal funding and state funding programs aimed at improv-ing the quality of existing homes can be utilized to help improve physical comfort and mental well-being for the diverse populations that call rural America home.

Housing as distress

A systematic review of all studies examining the impact home foreclosures had on mental health found that those with a personal experience of home foreclosure had higher levels of depression, anxiety, alcohol use, psychological distress and suicide (Tsai 2015). Extending foreclosure beyond the home and to property, including farm land, the effects of economic downturns and mental health crises remind us of the 1980s farm crisis and the suicide clusters of farmers (Stark and Riordan 2011). Individuals who become overleveraged on their mortgage or debts display higher degrees of substance use and poorer measures of mental health than those with smaller personal debt amounts (Tsai 2015). The home itself and the stress associated with trying to keep the home exacerbate preexisting mental health conditions and tend to worsen substance usage patterns.

Housing as distress may also adversely impact the mental health and overall well-being of individuals who feel pressure to meet specific expectations of the home as a manifestation of conspicuous consumption (Schnittker and McLeod 2005). Although research among high-income earners and their mental wellbeing is much less common than that of research among low-income earners, work in this area has shown higher levels of psychic pressure emanating from the pressure to consume than the inability to consume (Rahman Khan 2012). It is unclear how this impact would unfold differently in rural communities. It might be that the style of conspicuous consumption differs or it might be that it is less present. However, as rural communities with natural resource amenities continue to increase in population, and increase the localized economic pressures, one might expect these pressures to be more of an influence in well-being in seemingly idyllic rural settings.

Renters, who are less prevalent proportionally in rural communities than in urban, face the potential stress of eviction (Suglia et al. 2011). In situations where natural resource booms shift or change the housing dynamics in rural communities, loss of housing through dramatic rent increases has been found to place the housing insecure at the greatest risk (Schafft et al. 2014). Renters in rural areas may also have a higher likelihood to be in substandard housing that is not monitored or routinely assessed by local zoning officers. When a renter can be more easily removed from her residence, stress of housing loss may have deleterious mental health effects.

Rural residents tend to utilize behavioral health services less readily and often than urban residents (Williams et al. 2015). In times of financial hardship, mental wellbeing and an increased likelihood to engage in adverse substance abuse behavior can be exacerbated by a lack of behavioral health care. Conceptualizing housing as the primary source of emotional distress, when it is an accurate reflection of personal need, shifts the nature of psychological care beyond counseling and to advising patients about debt relief options (Compton and Shim 2015). Rural area mental health providers may be better equipped to link together services in this way, as research has found that they tend to be more integrated with social service programming than urban providers (Chipp et al. 2008).

Housing as foundation

Being homeless is a significant risk factor for all forms of health, including behavioral health (Hernwood et al. 2013). The concept of the housing first model is to provide housing to the homeless before asking them to participate in substance abuse treatment programs. The state of New Mexico was the first state to orient their attempt to address homelessness around the provision of housing. Early evaluations of this work have shown a positive effect on the presence of homelessness in Albuquerque (Guerin 2007). This model has been implemented in a wide range of locations and is receiving wide-spread support among federal and state agencies tasked with providing care for the homeless.

Many homeless individuals may have had to leave situations of being housed for reasons listed in another causal process for behavioral health and housing. However one ends up being homeless, the need to restore a steady home that is safe and secure has become tantamount to increasing the likelihood of wellbeing and health. Research demonstrates convincing results that housing first models improve housing stability, reduce homelessness and increase the utilization of services. The results of reviews of the effect on substance use or psychological symptoms are less definitive but tend to produce evidence of a small, positive effect on wellbeing (SAMHSA 2010; Rog et al. 2014).

Permanent housing models are the most widely utilized form of federal funding, especially through Section 8 housing vouchers (HUD 2008). These programs provide long-term, community-based housing without a designated length of stay. Permanent supportive housing provides the same undesignated length of stay and provides support services for individuals with a diagnosed SMI who receive disability (Bengtsson-Tops et al. 2014). Concerns exist about the level of funding that is provided for these individuals, as a recent analysis has concluded that there is not a single housing market in the United States where an individual on disability could find affordable housing when affordable housing is defined as 30% of overall household income (GAO 2015b).

For vulnerable populations, be they homeless, transitioning out of an institutional setting or veterans, the pursuit of housing and the need to negotiate between shelters and doubled-up living arrangements while navigating the public assistance system can result in extended periods of uncertainty and housing insecurity (TAC 2001). In this situation, especially in rural communities, where transportation costs and arrangements can be harder to manage, housing first models have begun to highlight how stable, reliable, no-strings-attached housing is necessary for wellbeing. It is the foundation upon which an individual can move toward independent living and mental health. Linking services to this foundation through Medicaid programs has proven to increase the effectiveness of housing first models (HHS 2014a). Mobile mental health units and telemedicine equipped housing units for those involved in housing first models can link care to rural residents more effectively than reliance upon central places for service acquisition (Chipp et al. 2008). If housing is found, behavioral health care can begin.

Summary of types

Housing does not have a bimodal effect on physical or mental health, as the research reviewed in this chapter and elsewhere has demonstrated that the home can be a source of both security and risk (Shaw 2004). Federal and state funding programs aim to decrease the negative effects of inadequate or insecure housing by providing incentives and assistance for the acquisition of stable and safe housing. By identifying the physical, social and psychological influences that unfold within housing settings, the influence of shelter on behavioral health can be more clearly understood and theorized. However, each site of shelter occurs within a broader context, and these typologies may have different types of effects once the community context of housing is added to the models of influence.

Each of the five types identified in this chapter might assert both independent and combined effects on the behavioral health of a rural resident. The nature and extent of these effects varies across regions, demographic categories, cultural contexts and individual differences in degree of mental illness (GAO 2006). The physical context of the home, both in location and materials, can be a direct and indirect hazard to mental health. The physical residential setting, be it a home or an institution, is a social space where treatment can occur or where emotional traumas can lead to substance abuse behaviors. The nesting of effects of residence and behavioral health make the process of teasing out uniquely rural effects very complicated. More generally, research has found that the rural setting and the limits to the behavioral health care workforce and treatment capacity of rural communities are the most significant relationships between behavioral health and housing. However, by taking a nested understanding to the nature of influence on behavioral health, rural location can be understood as one layer of nested influence that will have varied effects across different types of rural places for different types of rural residents (Newman 2001).

Housing in context

No literature review or meta-analysis examined in the development of this chapter included rural/urban as a demographic variable in their evaluations of the impacts of housing on behavioral health (Leff et al. 2009). This gap was produced because few studies include these elements in reports or publications. The lack of focus on context, both geography and neighborhood characteristics, is one of the large gaps in our understanding of the relationship between housing and behavioral health (Newman 2001; Shaw 2004; Leff et al. 2009).

States vary greatly in both the ways they manage specific federal programs and in the extent to which they have developed state specific supported funding for housing programs (TAC 2014). Housing costs also vary state to state and community to community, so that federal standards for housing subsidy amounts may not accurately reflect conditions in local rental markets. Small towns and small cities in rural counties tend to have lower rent prices than metro areas (NCD 2010). This lower cost of living is one reason why retirees chose to settle in rural, amenity-rich communities (McGranahan et al. 2011). Available rural housing stock may present an opportunity for individuals who are able to access federal funding subsidies. However, the understaffing of agencies at the county level with staff who may be able to provide recommendations about specific program opportunities often creates an insurmountable barrier for residents of many rural areas (McCauley et al. 2015).

The link between housing and behavioral health is complicated by the lack of behavioral health providers in most rural counties (Sawyer et al. 2006). Supportive services for individuals with housing who are also looking to enroll in therapy or to receive counseling are severely limited in rural locations. This may present a complex choice for an individual between moving to a non-rural area that is not connected to their social networks to pursue treatment and to receive housing. In some cases, in the event an individual is on parole or probation and cannot leave a state, the lack of rural behavioral health care ensures that he or she will be unable to receive care during an important transition time (Ditton 1999).

To take one example, a nested understanding of housing programs produces a surfeit of questions to investigate about the effect of context on housing first models. Do individuals who receive housing out of their neighborhood of origin tend to do better or worse on behavioral health outcomes? Does the amount and character of staff support provided to individuals in supportive housing shape outcomes? Do rural and urban residents differ in their preferences for types of housing? Do housing models vary in effectiveness across racial, ethnic, gendered, or income level? How do housing first models compare to short-term doubled-up living arrangements? Do these differ between rural/urban settings? These questions are examples of the lack of systematically collected knowledge we collectively have about the context of housing interventions, especially in rural communities.

A proposed research agenda for improving understanding about the impact of housing on behavioral health in rural America

The state of research on the effect of housing on behavioral health can be improved through increased collaboration and data quality concerns from federal agencies providing grants to communities (GAO 2012). The open data initiative of the Obama Administration pushes federal agencies to increase access to data collected by federal agencies. A thoughtful assessment of the data elements across agencies providing funding for programs linking housing and behavioral health care would be an important step toward improving the quality and usefulness of data being generated through federal systems.

The United States Interagency Council on Homeless marks an important cross-agency collaboration aimed at improving the quality and content of data systems used to understand the services provided to the homeless population. This is a model that can be used to continue to enhance collaboration around data. Rural areas have been identified as producing estimates of homelessness that are almost certainly under-counts of the true population (USICH 2015). This same data collection challenge extends to housing programs and behavioral health care service utilization, but it has a different cause. Underreporting of homeless in rural areas is a byproduct of geography, as the counting methodology developed by HUD tends to miss hard to find individuals (HCH 2001). Data collection for programs in rural areas is limited by the technological capacity and geography of rural service provision systems. It is not the case that there is no count of housing provided to individuals with behavioral health needs in rural areas, it is the case that there is not an effective system for aggregating and disseminating this data (GAO 2010).

With an improved openness and integration of data systems by federal and state agencies tasked with providing housing, scholars will be able to more easily investigate an array of relationships between housing and behavioral health. In particular, research should focus on five content areas. These content areas reflect themes from the categories used in the overview of the research and underlying concepts of federal investments in housing that support behavioral health or they reflect broader research questions identified in the housing as context section of the chapter.

1　How is funding allocated across geographies when federal, state, and private monies intended for supportive housing of any type? Where are these facilities located, and do the locations correspond to characteristics of the population of users or to the characteristics of local real estate markets?

2　How does housing differentially impact individuals over the life course? Are there essential gaps when inadequate housing has the most significant impact on mental health?

3　Are there rural/urban differences in neighborhood effects? For example, if one lives in a block group that has been identified as heavily blighted through the HUD assessment tool, does it make more or less of a difference on individual wellbeing if it is a small town or a large urban space?

4　When an individual transitions from being housing insecure to homeless, how often is this precipitated by a mental health or substance usage issue? Are they less likely to become homeless if there are specific types of support or intervention services in the community? If so, what do these look like for rural places and how can rural social service agencies work together to provide services across large geographic areas?

5　What are the internal migration patterns of the housing insecure in different regions of the country? Does this impact utilization of behavioral health care services, and how does this differ by class, insurance status and state of residence?

All of these research areas will require the continued elaboration of theory about why housing would be a key variable for positive health outcomes in the individual. Identifying differences and similarities across the rural/urban gradient are essential to refining our understanding and seeing if the theoretical mechanisms posited in each geographic location carry over to another.

Conclusion

Supported housing in rural communities is subsidized by state and federal agencies with specific priorities and theories of change. Each of these different conceptual models determines how access to services unfolds and what characteristics an individual must have to gain access to financial supports. A general movement toward housing first models of care, aimed predominately at the remediation of homelessness, is one of the current shifts in service delivery by federal agencies. The nature of how funding unfolds and how funding can be tracked will shift and change as priorities within administrations shift and change over time. Increasing the careful data collection, evaluation research agenda and openness of federal funding programs will enable improved and specific understandings about the role of housing in the behavioral health of rural residents.

References

Bambra, C., Gibson, M., Sowden, A., Wright, K., Whitehead, M., & Petticrew, M. (2010). Tackling the wider social determinants of health and health inequalities: Evidence from systematic reviews. *Journal of Epidemiology & Community Health, 64*(4), 284–291.

Bengtsson-Tops, A., Ericsson, U., & Ehliasson, K. (2014). Living in supportive housing for people with serious mental illness: A paradoxical everyday life. *International Journal of Mental Health Nursing, 23*(5), 409–418.

Boyd, C. P., & Parr, H. (2008). Social geography and rural mental health research. *Rural and Remote Health, 8*, 804–809.

Brown, D. L., & Schafft, K. A. (2011). *Rural people & communities in the 21st century*. Malden, MA: Polity Press.

CBO. (2015). *Federal housing assistance for low-income households*. Washington, DC: United States Congressional Budget Office.

CDC. (2011). *Public health action plan to integrate mental health promotion and mental illness prevention with chronic disease prevention, 2011–2015*. Atlanta, GA: United States Centers for Disease Control and Prevention.

Chipp, C. L., Johnson, M. E., Brems, C., Warner, T. D., & Roberts, L. W. (2008). Adaptations to health care barriers as reported by rural and urban providers. *Journal of Health Care for the Poor and Underserved, 19*(2), 532–549.

Compton, M. T., & Shim, R. S. (2015). *The social determinants of mental health*. Arlington, VA: American Psychiatric Publishing.

Compton, W., Thomas, Y., Stinson, F., & Grant, B. (2007). Prevalence, correlates, disability, and comorbidity of DSM-IV drug abuse and dependence in the United States. *Archives of General Psychiatry, 64*(5), 566–576.

Ditton, P. M. (1999). *Mental health and treatment of inmates and probationers*. NCJ 174463. Washington, DC: United States Department of Justice.

Dumont, D. M., Brockmann, B., Dickman, S., Alexander, N., & Rich, J. D. (2012). Public health and the epidemic of incarceration. *Annual Review of Public Health, 33*, 325–339.

Evans, G. (2001). Environmental stress and health. In A. Baum, T. Revenson, & J. Singer (Eds.), *Handbook of health psychology* (pp. 365–385). Mahwah, NJ: Erlbaum.

Evans, G., Wells, N., & Moch, A. (2002). Housing and mental health: A review of the evidence and a methodological and conceptual critique. *Journal of Social Issues, 59*(3), 475–500.

Folsom, D. P., Hawthorne, W., Lindamer, L., Gilmer, T., Bailey, A., Golshan, S. . . . Jeste, D. V. (2005). Prevalence and risk factors for homelessness and utilization of mental health services among 10,240 patients with serious mental illness in a large public mental health system. *American Journal of Psychiatry, 162*, 370–376.

Frederick, T. J., Chwalek, M., Hughes, J., Karabano, J., & Kidd, S. (2014). How stable is stable? Defining and measuring housing stability. *Journal of Community Psychology, 42*(8), 964–979.

GAO. (2000). *Rural housing: Options for optimizing the federal role in rural housing development*. Washington, DC: United States Government Accountability Office.

GAO. (2006). *Rural housing service: Overview of program issues*. Washington, DC: United States Government Accountability Office.

GAO. (2010). *Homelessness: A common vocabulary could help agencies collabore more and collect more consistent data*. Washington, DC: United State Government Accountability Office.

GAO. (2012). *Housing assistance: Opportunities exist to increase collaboration and consider consolidation*. Washington, DC: United State Government Accountability Office.

GAO. (2015a). *Affordable rental housing: Assistance is provided by federal, state, and local programs, but there is incomplete information on collective performance*. Washington, DC: United State Government Accountability Office.

GAO. (2015b). *Mental health: HHS leadership needed to coordinate federal efforts related to SMI*. Washington, DC: United State Government Accountability Office.

Guerin, P. (2007). *City of Albuquerque housing first program evaluation report*. Albuquerque, NM: Institute for Social Research, University of New Mexico.

Haegerich, T., Paulozzi, L., Manns, B., & Jones, C. (2014). What we know, and don't know, about the impact of state policy and systems-level interventions on prescription drug overdose. *Drug and Alcohol Dependence, 145,* 34–47.

Hartley, D. (2004). Rural health disparities, population health, and rural culture. *American Journal of Public Health, 94,* 1675–1678.

HCH. (2001). Hard to reach: Rural homelessness & health care. *Healing Hands: A Publication of the Health Care for the Homeless Clinicians' Network, 5*(5), 1–3.

Hernwood, B. F., Cabassa, L. J., Craig, C. M., & Padgett, D. K. (2013). Permanent supportive housing: Addressing homelessness and health disparities? *American Journal of Public Health, 103*(S2), 188–194.

HHS. (2005). *Mental health and rural America: 1994–2005*. Washington, DC: United States Health and Human Services.

HHS. (2009). *Homelessness data in health and human services mainstream programs*. Washington, DC: United States Health and Human Services.

HHS. (2014a). *A primer on using medicaid for people experiencing chronic homelessness and tenants in permanent supportive housing*. Washington, DC: United States Health and Human Services.

HHS. (2014b). *Trends in Indian health: 2014 edition*. Washington, DC: Indian Health Service, United States Department of Health and Human Services.

HHS. (2015). *State strategies for coordinating medicaid services and housing for adults with behavioral health conditions*. Washington, DC: Office of the Assistant Secretary for Planning and Evaluatoin, United States Department of Health and Human Services.

Holmes, S. M. (2006). An ethnographic study of the social context of migrant health in the United States. *PLoS Medicine, 3*(10), 1776–1793.

Hooks, G., Mosher, C., Rotolo, R., & Lobao, L. (2004). The prison industry: Carceral expansion and employment in the U.S. counties, 1969–1994. *Social Science Quarterly, 85*(1), 37–57.

HUD. (1999). *Guide to continuum of care planning and implementation*. Washington, DC: HUD Exchange, United States Department of Housing and Urban Development.

HUD. (2008). *Supportive housing program desk guide*. Washington, DC: United States Department of Housing and Urban Development.

Jones, R., Reupert, A., Sutton, K., & Maybery, D. (2014). The interplay of rural issues, mental illness, substance use and housing problems. *Journal of Mental Health, 23*(6), 317–322.

Kyle, T., & Dunn, J. R. (2008). Effects of housing circumstances on health, quality of life and healthcare use for people with severe mental illness: A review. *Health & Social Care in the Community, 16*(1), 1–15.

Leff, H. S., Chow, C. M., Pepin, R., Conley, J., Allen, I. E., & Seaman, C. A. (2009). Does one size fit all? What we can and can't learn from a meta-analysis of housing models for persons with mental illness. *Psychiatric Services, 60*(4), 473–482.

Leventhal, T., & Newman, S. (2010). Housing and child development. *Children and Youth Services Review, 32*(9), 1165–1174.

Lobao, L., & Meyer, K. (2001). The great agricultural transition: Crisis, change, and social consequences of twentieth century US farming. *Annual Review of Sociology, 27*, 103–124.

McCauley, K., Montgomery, P., Mossey, S., & Bailey, P. (2015). Canadian community mental health workers' perceived priorities for supportive housing services in northern and rural contexts. *Health & Social Care in the Community, 23*(6), 632–641.

McGranahan, D. A., Wojan, T. R., & Lambert, D. M. (2011). The rural growth trifecta: Outdoor amenities, creative class and entrepreneurial context. *Journal of Economic Geography, 11*(3), 529–557.

NCD. (2010). *The state of housing in America in the 21st century: A disability perspective.* Washington, DC: United States National Council on Disability.

Newman, S. J. (2001). Housing attributes and serious mental illness: Implications for research and practice. *Psychiatric Services, 52*, 1309–1317.

Newman, S. J. (2008). Does housing matter for poor families? A critical summary of research and issues still to be resolved. *Journal of Policy Analysis and Management, 27*(4), 895–925.

North, C. S., & Pfefferbaum, B. (2013). Mental health response to community disasters: A systematic review. *Journal of the American Medical Association, 310*(5), 507–518.

Rahman Khan, S. (2012). The sociology of elites. *Annual Review of Sociology, 38*(1), 361–377.

Reif, S., George, P., Braude, L., Dougherty, R. H., Daniels, A. S., Ghose, S. S., & Delphin-Rittmon, M. E. (2014). Residential treatment for individuals with substance use disorders: assessing the evidence. *Psychiatric Services, 65*(3), 301–312.

Robinson, W. D., Springer, P. R., Bischoff, R., Geske, J., Backer, E., Olson, M. . . . Swinton, J. (2012). Rural experiences with mental illness: Through the eyes of patients and their families. *Families Systems & Health, 30*(4), 308–321.

Rog, D. J., Marshall, T., Dougherty, R. H., George, P., Daniels, A. S., Ghose, S. S., & Delphin-Rittmon, M. E. (2014). Permanent supportive housing: Assessing the evidence. *Psychiatric Services, 65*(3), 287–294.

SAMHSA. (2010). *Permanent support housing: The evidence.* Rockville, MD: Substance Abuse and Mental Health Services Administration, United States Department of Health and Human Services.

SAMHSA. (2013). *Behavioral health treatment needs assessment toolkit for states.* Rockville, MD: Substance Abuse and Mental Health Services Administration, United States Department of Health and Human Services.

SAMHSA. (2014). *Trauma informed care in behavioral health service.* Rockville, MD: Substance Abuse and Mental Health Services Administration, United States Department of Health and Human Services.

SAMHSA. (2015). Projects for assistance in transition from homelessness (PATH). *Substance Abuse and Mental Health Services Administration, United States Department of Health and Human Services.* Retrieved from www.samhsa.gov/homelessness-programs-resources/grant-programs-services/path

Sanbonmatsu, L., Ludwig, J., Katz, L., Gennetian, L., Duncan, G. J., Kessler, R. C., . . . Lindau, S. T. (2011). *Moving to opportunity for fair housing demonstration program.* Washington, DC: United States Department of Housing and Urban Development.

Sawyer, D., Gale, J., & Lambert, D. (2006). *Rural and frontier mental and behavioral health care: Barriers, effective policy strategies, best practices.* Washington, DC: National Association for Rural Mental Health.

Schafft, K. A., Glenna, L. L., Green, B. Q., & Borlu, Y. (2014). Local impacts of uconventional gas drilling within Pennsylvania's Marcellus Shale Region: Gauging boomtown development through the perspectives of educational administrators. *Society & Natural Resources, 27*(4), 389–404.

Schnittker, J., & McLeod, J. D. (2005). The social psychology of health disparities. *Annual Review of Sociology*, *31*(1), 75–103.

Shaw, M. (2004). Housing and public health. *Annual Review of Public Health*, *25*, 397–418.

Sorocco, K. H., Bratkovich, K. L., Wingo, R., Qureshi, S. M., & Mason, P. J. (2013). Integrating care coordination home telehealth and home based primary care in rural Oklahoma: A pilot study. *Psychological Services*, *10*(3), 350–352.

Stark, C., & Riordan, V. (2011). *Rurality and suicide*. Oxford, UK: Blackwell Science.

Suglia, S., Duarte, C. S., & Sandel, M. (2011). Housing quality, housing instability, and maternal mental health. *Journal of Urban Health*, *88*(6), 1105–1116.

Sundararaman, R. (2009). *The U.S. mental health delivery system infrastructure: A primer*. Washington, DC: United States Congressional Research Service.

TAC. (2001). *A housing toolkit: Information to help the public mental health community meet the housing needs of people with mental illnesses*. Boston, MA: Technical Assistance Collaborative, Inc.

TAC. (2014). *State funded housing assistance programs*. Boston, MA: Technical Assistance Collaborative, Inc.

Tsai, A. C. (2015). Home foreclosure, health, and mental health: A systematic review of individual, aggregate, and contextual associations. *PLoS One*, *10*(4), e0123182.

USICH. (2015). *Opening doors: Federal strategic plan to prevent and end homelessness*. Washington, DC: United States Interagency Council on Homelessness.

Willging, C., Malcone, L., Cyr, S., Zywiak, W., & Lapham, S. (2013). Behavioral health and social correlates of reincarceration among hispanic, native American, and white rural women. *Psychiatric Services*, *64*, 590–593.

Williams, D., Eckstrom, J., Avery, M., & Unutzer, J. (2015). Perspectives of behavioral health clinicians in a rural integrated primary care/mental health program. *Journal of Rural Health*, *31*(4), 346–353.

3 Are rural areas underserved by HUD's subsidy programs?

Paul E. McNamara and Han Bum Lee

Introduction

A federally funded rental subsidy program, managed by the U.S. Department of Housing and Urban Development (HUD) in the United States, primarily provides housing subsidies to the elderly, persons with disabilities and low-income families who face a probable risk of falling into poverty in the absence of the subsidy. In recent years, HUD has served approximately five million eligible low-income families each year, devoting around $40 billion annually, which is over two-thirds of federal spending on the Earned Income Tax Credit (EITC) and twice what is spent on the Temporary Assistance for Needy Families (TANF) (Spar and Falk 2016). Because of its national scale of regulatory intervention and governance and the large federal contribution, an extensive research literature exists concerning the effectiveness of the federal rental subsidy program in assisting vulnerable people and reducing spatial poverty concentration, as well as helping people move toward employment and breaking the poverty cycle (i.e., Wilson 1987; Currie and Yelowitz 2000; Katz et al. 2001; Goetz 2003; Jacob 2004; Jacob and Ludwig 2012). However, most research efforts have concentrated on understanding the effects of public provision of subsidized housing opportunities in urban areas, especially large cities, under the urban antipoverty political agenda, and very little research exists concerning the spatial distribution of federal rental subsidy programs across rural and urban areas.

The research question we explore in this chapter is, does a rural-urban bias exist in the current HUD rental subsidy programs? We use a multilevel modeling approach structuring a two-level model with counties (local governments) at the lower level grouped within the states at the higher level. It enables us to investigate the level of variation in the percent of people in poverty who received HUD's rental subsidy programs by a rural-urban geographic basis in different geographic levels. The main data set used in this chapter is HUD's 2013 Picture of Subsidized Households (PSH) merged with the five-year (2009–2013) American Community Survey (ACS) data at the county level. Also, we adopt two rural-urban geographical classifications using the Economic Research Service's (ERS) 2013 Rural-Urban Continuum Codes and HUD's definition of rurality.

The remainder of the chapter proceeds as follow: It begins by describing poverty in a rural context and addressing its critical needs for adequate rental subsidy programs in rural areas. Then, the chapter discusses the background information of the federally funded rental subsidy programs. The next section presents data on the geographical distribution of the rental subsidy programs and then compares selected rural-urban characteristics based on defined rural-urban geographical classifications. The following section details the empirical strategy, discusses the regression results and performs robustness checks of the results. Lastly, the chapter closes with concluding remarks.

Poverty in rural America

Rural America has long suffered a disproportionate share of the nation's poverty population (Tickamyer and Duncan 1990; Albrecht and Albrecht 2000; Duncan and Coles 2000). Poverty is more prevalent among women, racial and ethnic minority groups, people with low-socioeconomic status and single-parent families. Because these phenomena are often presented as the nation's urban problems, most of us tend to think of poverty as being associated with metropolitan areas; however, in reality, nearly 16.5 percent of non-metropolitan residents were impoverished, which is two percentage points higher than in metropolitan areas. Also, a recent ERS report shows that there exists 353 persistently poor counties in the U.S., and about 85 percent of those counties are in non-metropolitan areas (Farrigan 2015).[1]

Severity and persistence of poverty in rural areas are often linked to a limited opportunity structure – mainly derived from past social and economic development policies targeting economic areas with promising higher returns and agricultural industrialization – associated with insufficient and unstable jobs (significant decrease in share of agricultural employment), challenges in geographic and income mobility, and limited access to health care and affordable housing, as well as narrow investment for community development and diversity in economic and other social institutions (Albrecht 1998; Brown, Swanson, and Barton 2003; Conger and Elder 1994; Duncan and Coles 2000; Irwin et al. 2010; Ricketts 1999). Moreover, according to the 2012 Housing Assistance Council (HAC) report, there were approximately 7.1 million renter-occupied units (or 28.4 percent of the rural housing stock, which was eight percentage points lower than national levels), and single-family homes and manufactured homes were more prevalent for rural renter-occupied units. Also, the incidence of rural residents experiencing housing affordability problems increased by six percentage points between 2000 and 2010, with nearly half (47 percent) of all rural renters cost-burdened (spending 30 percent or more of their monthly income) and about half of these households paying more than 50 percent of their monthly income toward housing (HAC 2012). Without access to rental housing assistance, these people have very few options for affordable housing, rendering them vulnerable toward homelessness.

The provision of federally funded rental subsidy programs

HUD's rental subsidy programs can be broadly divided into three major programs – public housing (publicly owned housing), Section 8 Housing Choice Voucher (HCV) (privately owned housing), and Section 8 Project-Based Voucher (PBV) programs (privately owned, subsidized housing). Eligibility for HUD's rental subsidy programs is limited to physically and financially disadvantaged people, determined by applicants' demographic status (elderly or disability status) and gross annual income adjusted by family size.

Public housing was the first federal housing subsidy program, established by the Housing Act of 1937, aimed at clearing slum-dwelling poor, especially in large cities, to create a better living environment believed to improve their economic mobility (Hoffman 1996; Hoffman 2012). Rents for public housing tenants are limited to 30 percent of income, with public housing authorities receiving federal operating subsidies intended to cover the difference between rental income and operating costs. By 1950, the government had begun or completed construction of about 150,000 public housing units nationally. Through the next two decades of rapid expansion, the stock of public housing units peaked at 1.4 million in 1991 (Schwartz 2014). However, as the public housing program grew, emerging issues (i.e., obsolete building conditions, inefficient utility costs, racial and economic segregation) led to a policy shift to the tenant-based rental subsidy programs, gradually diminishing the stock of public housing (Jencks and Mayer 1990; Massey and Kanaiaupuni 1993; Wilson 1987).

Since the mid-1970s, the Section 8 HCV program has received greater attention as an alternative public housing policy to resolve pre-existing problems, particularly the issue of low-income minorities' poverty concentration around public housing developments (i.e., Devine et al. 2003; Newman and Schnare 1997; Goering et al. 1995; Pendall 2000; Lens et al. 2011; Turner 1998). In contrast to the downward trend of public housing units, the HCV program has grown to represent the nation's largest housing subsidy program, serving more than 2.2 million low-income families in conjunction with over 3,000 local public housing authorities. Uniquely, the HCV program allows recipients to rent privately owned housing in any neighborhood within the jurisdiction of the local public housing authority, giving recipients more flexibility about where to live. Section 8 housing voucher holders are generally obliged to pay the Total Tenant Payment (TTP), which is 30 percent of their monthly income towards housing; however, the HCV program exceptionally allows an additional 10 percent of voucher holders' income in situations where the gross rent exceeds the locally designated payment standard representing the maximum allowable rent subsidy. HUD pays the subsidy to the landlord of the unit selected by the tenant, provided the unit meets certain quality inspection standards.

The Section 8 PBV program, which emerged in the 1960s, relies on a public-private partnership in which federal government enters into contracts with private owners to provide affordable housing for a specified number of years, after which the housing is converted to market rate by owners' decisions. Specifically, unlike the HCV program renewing the rental contract every year, the PBV program provides owners with a guaranteed rental contract (a long-term contract of ten years) as long as the property remains in the assisted program. Recently, the PBV program served nearly 1.3 million low-income families, mostly elderly or disabled head of households; however, this stock of housing is in danger of being permanently lost because of owners opting out or physical deterioration of property (Newman 2005; Rice 2009). Therefore, a key challenge for this housing program is to incentivize existing owners to remain under contract, as well as increase new owners' program participation, to maintain the stock of affordable housing for low-income families.

Data set

The data set used in this study is HUD's 2013 Picture of Subsidized Households (PSH) merged with the five-year (2009–2013) American Community Survey (ACS) data at the county level. Specifically, the PSH provides the total number of HUD's rental subsidies including public housing, Section 8 HCV, Section 8 PBV, Section 8 New Construction/Substantial Rehabilitation, Section 236 and Multi-family rental subsidy programs. Also, the five-year ACS data set provides more reliable estimates of demographic and socioeconomic characteristics at smaller geographic boundaries than one-year and three-year estimates (Census Bureau 2008). We use the five-year ACS data to obtain the number of households with income below the poverty threshold to calculate the percent of poor who receive HUD's rental subsidy programs. Other county-level and state-level variables are obtained from the five-year ACS data and 2013 Annual Survey of State Government Finances.

We consolidate the data to the county level because HUD's rental subsidy programs are administered by local PHAs, distributed across more than 3,000 counties in the 48 contiguous states of the United States.[2] For the purpose of this analysis, we adopt the ERS's 2013 Rural-Urban Continuum Code scheme, defining a county as rural if it belongs to categories "Completely rural or less than 2,500 urban population." According to the ERS geographical classification, there are 3,106 counties including 626 completely rural counties in non-metropolitan areas and 2,480 urban counties in metropolitan and non-metropolitan areas.[3] Also, for a sensitivity analysis, we replicate the analysis with a different definition of rurality using HUD's rural geographic definition – a county with a population of 20,000 inhabitants or less and not located in a Metropolitan Statistical Area. According to HUD's rurality definition, there are 1,464 urban counties and 1,645 rural counties.[4] Since the PSH contains observations that list the number of rental subsidies with no geographic identifier for each state, we exclude a total of 6,060 housing subsidies – 5,860 housing subsidies in New York state (about one percent of the allocated housing subsidies in New York state) and 200 housing subsidies for the rest of the 47 states.[5]

Regional characteristics and descriptive statistics

Since the late 1970s, state and local governments have had an increasingly more important role than the federal government in implementing programs and providing services more closely attuned to the needs of specific communities and populations. In order to capture distinct effects of the components determining the *recipients-poor ratio* at different geographical levels, we construct the following state- and county-level variables.

County-level variables: We measure *poverty rates* by dividing the number of persons with income below the poverty threshold by the total number of persons in the county, and the *recipients-poor ratio* represents the percent of persons in poverty who received HUD's rental subsidies. *Rural* is a binary variable – 1 for rural and 0 for urban counties. *Sex ratio* indicates the number of males per 100 females (divided by 100); *elderly dependency ratio* is the number of persons 65 and older to every 100 persons of traditional working ages 15–64 (divided by 100); *population-housing ratio* represents the average number of persons in a housing unit; and *population density* represents the average number of people living in a unit of an area (mile). *Percent rental housing* measures the level of availability of rental housing units for HUD's rental subsidy programs. Also, *percent Black population*, *percent Hispanic population*, *percent disabled population*; *percent single-parent family*, *median income* and *median rent* are included as county-level control variables to increase the precision of the estimates in the regression.

State-level variables: We measure *public welfare expenditure* by dividing the state's public welfare expenditures (Medicaid, Supplementary Security Income and TANF; and other welfare services) by the number of persons in poverty in the state.[6] Also, we include the state's intergovernmental expenditures, since rural communities depend heavily on such transfers from the states to provide local services (Felix and Henderson 2010). *Intergovernmental expenditure* is measured by the total amounts paid to local governments – "as fiscal aid in the form of shared revenues and grants-in-aid, as reimbursements for performance of general government activities and for specific services for the paying government, or in lieu of taxes" (State Government Finances n.d.) – divided by the number of counties within the state. This represents the average amount of the state's transfers to each local government if all conditions are identical; however, in reality, it is more likely that a larger share of transfers happens in metropolitan areas and large cities potentially due to high population density (high demand for local services) and economic returns. The state-level variables do not necessarily indicate the exact amount transferred to the local governments, but they explain the specific state effect related to those expenditures on the *recipients-poor ratio* in the regression, and the story of the rural effect conditioned on such expenditures can be explained by the interactions with those variables with the *rural* variable. These state-level variables are designed to capture state efforts – financial supports and means-tested assistance programs dedicated to poverty alleviation and administration of general activities and programs related, but not limited to, housing and community development on specific places and populations in need – on the provision of HUD's rental subsidy programs at the local government level.

For a more detailed comparison between rural and urban counties across the 48 contiguous states, Table 3.1 presents descriptive statistics for the selected rural and urban characteristics. We observe that overall *poverty rates* are higher in rural areas, and the gap of mean poverty rates between rural and urban areas becomes greater using HUD's rurality definition, while on average the *recipients-poor ratio* in rural areas tends to be smaller than in urban areas (the absolute mean difference

Table 3.1 Descriptive Statistics of Regional Characteristics by the ERS and HUD's Rural-Urban Classifications Included in Multilevel Model Regressions of Rural-Urban Bias of HUD's Rental Subsidy Programs

	All counties	ERS		HUD	
		Rural	Urban	Rural	Urban
Poverty rates	0.159	0.165	0.157	0.171	0.146
	(0.060)	(0.067)	(0.058)	(0.063)	(0.054)
Recipients-poor ratio	0.222	0.155	0.239	0.193	0.255
	(0.150)	(0.138)	(0.148)	(0.138)	(0.157)
County-level variables					
Sex ratio	1.004	1.034	0.997	1.024	0.982
	(0.109)	(0.143)	(0.097)	(0.129)	(0.074)
Elderly dependent ratio	0.275	0.348	0.256	0.310	0.236
	(0.086)	(0.094)	(0.072)	(0.083)	(0.069)
Percent Black population	0.091	0.061	0.098	0.078	0.104
	(0.146)	(0.145)	(0.145)	(0.153)	(0.136)
Percent Hispanic population	0.085	0.059	0.092	0.078	0.093
	(0.134)	(0.111)	(0.139)	(0.138)	(0.129)
Percent disabled population	0.140	0.154	0.136	0.154	0.125
	(0.052)	(0.063)	(0.049)	(0.056)	(0.042)
Percent single-parent family	0.300	0.272	0.307	0.300	0.303
	(0.102)	(0.125)	(0.094)	(0.111)	(0.090)
Population-housing ratio	2.165	1.864	2.240	2.025	2.321
	(0.371)	(0.395)	(0.323)	(0.382)	(0.287)
Population density	219.012	14.305	270.684	32.404	428.850
	(1245.180)	(15.491)	(1388.768)	(92.871)	(1789.466)
Percent rental housing	0.277	0.242	0.286	0.259	0.297
	(0.078)	(0.067)	(0.079)	(0.063)	(0.089)
Median income ($/10^4$)	4.575	4.135	4.687	4.135	5.071
	(1.180)	(0.872)	(1.221)	(0.850)	(1.296)
Median rent ($/10^2$)	6.786	5.563	7.094	5.883	7.800
	(1.847)	(1.135)	(1.865)	(1.118)	(1.975)
State-level variables					
Public welfare expenditure	10.393	9.951	10.505	10.112	10.709
(/ persons in poverty)	(3.613)	(2.611)	(3.817)	(2.962)	(4.206)
Intergovernmental	1.565	0.845	1.747	1.113	2.074
expenditure	(2.512)	(1.404)	(2.692)	(1.771)	(3.066)
(/ number of counties in state; $/10^6$)					
N	3,106	626	2,480	1,644	1,462

Note: Standard deviations are in parenthesis.

of the *recipients-poor ratio* is greater with the ERS definition). The results suggest that, although rural areas have higher percentages of people living in poverty than metropolitan-non-metropolitan urban areas, HUD underprovides rental subsidy programs in rural areas. Also, rural areas tend to have a greater ratio of elderly to working-age population, and the proportion of disabled people is higher than in urban areas. On the other hand, rural areas tend to have a lower proportion of minorities (Black and Hispanic population), single-parent families, and rental housing units, as well as a lower level of median income and median rent than those in urban areas. Moreover, the results show a distinct difference between rural and urban areas in *population density* and *population-housing ratio* variables. For the state-level characteristics, we observe that rural areas tend to be in states with a relatively lower level of public welfare (adjusted by the number of persons in poverty) and intergovernmental expenditures (adjusted by the number of counties in the state) than more urbanized states.

Conceptual model

Multilevel models, also referred to as linear random coefficient and hierarchical models, have long been applied in the social sciences. The distinctive feature of the model is to capture regional random effects (heterogeneous state effects), while also accounting for the correlation between counties nested within the same state (non-independently identically distributed). Additionally, the multilevel models address potential issues of spatial heterogeneity, assuming that the effect of an explanatory variable can be different in each geographical level. For instance, in some states, rural counties may be more strongly associated with the outcome variable than in others, indicating that the slope would vary from one state to another. In this study, we structure a two-level model in which county-level variables explain county (lower level) variation within a state, and state-specific variables explain state (higher level) variance between states. If we denote by y_{ij} the outcome variable in county i, in state j ($i = 1, \ldots n_j; j = 1, \ldots, J$), the following equations show a simple, two-level linear model:

$$Y_{ij} = \beta_{0j} + \beta_{1j}R_{ij} + \beta_{2j}X_{ij} + \varepsilon_{ij} \tag{1}$$

$$\beta_{0j} = \gamma_{00} + \gamma_{01}C_j + u_{0j}. \tag{2}$$

In Eq. (1), the outcome variable, y_{ij}, can be modeled as a function of the mean outcome variable for state j (β_{0j}), rural-urban binary variable (R_{ij}), county-level control variables (X_{ij}) and county-level errors (ε_{ij}) that assume to be independent and normally distributed with a mean of 0 and a variance of σ_e^2 within each state. In Eq. (2), the state mean of the outcome variable, (β_{0j}), is modeled as a function of a state-mean outcome variable (γ_{00}), state-level variable (C_j) and state-level errors (u_{0j}), which are assumed to be normally distributed with mean 0 and variance of σ_{u0}^2.[7] Substituting Eq. (2) into Eq. (1) yields the two-level multilevel model shown as:

$$Y_{ij} = \gamma_{00} + \beta_{1j}R_{ij} + \beta_{2j}X_{ij} + \gamma_{01}C_j + u_{0j} + \varepsilon_{ij}. \tag{3}$$

Relaxing the assumption of the fixed coefficient in the Eq. (3) yields the random slope model, in which, of particular relevance to our study, we allow rural-urban binary variable (R_{ij}) to vary randomly across states, shown as the following equation:

$$\beta_{1j} = \gamma_{10} + \gamma_{11}C_j + u_{1j}. \tag{4}$$

In Eq. (4), (β_{1j}) (the regression coefficient of the effect of (R_{ij}) on y_{ij}) can be modeled as mean slope (γ_{10}), state-specific variable (C_j) and state-level errors (u_{1j}), which represent the deviation of the slope within each state from the overall slope (γ_{10}) after accounting for the effect of (C_j). Substituting Eq. (4) into Eq. (3) yields the two-level random slope model shown as:

$$Y_{ij} = \gamma_{00} + \gamma_{10}R_{ij} + \beta_{2j}X_{ij} + \gamma_{01}C_j + \gamma_{11}C_jR_{ij} + u_{1j}R_{ij} + u_{0j} + \varepsilon_{ij}. \tag{5}$$

The state-level errors u_{0j} and u_{1j} are assumed to have a multivariate normal distribution with expectation 0, and to be independent from the county-level residual errors (εij). The variance of the residual errors u_{1j} is specified as σ_{u0}^2. Also, covariance between u_{0j} and u_{1j} denote by σ_{u2}^2 (for example, if is positive, as the intercept increases the slope increases). Eq. (5) includes the fixed coefficients for county-level variables, state-level variables and interaction terms; as well, it has a complex error structure, including random intercept component and a random slope and individual-level errors.

Results

Table 3.2 presents the results of three multilevel models for the geographical distribution of HUD's rental subsidy programs. Column (1) presents the unconditional model that only includes the intercept varying across states, and the results confirm that the two-level structure provides a better fit to the data.[8] Columns (2) and (3) report the results of the random intercept models with an inclusion of the *rural* variable and the set of county-level control variables based on the two rural-urban geographical classifications. With the exception of the *percent Hispanic population* variable, all coefficients exhibit high levels of statistical significance. The negative coefficient of the *rural* variable indicates that rural residents in poverty are less likely to receive HUD's rental subsidies by approximately 6.4 percentage points and 2.7 percentage points than in urban areas using the ERS and HUD rurality definitions, respectively. Also, the results show that the *elderly dependent ratio* and the proportion of minorities (Black and Hispanic population), disabled people and single-parent family are positively associated with the *recipients-poor ratio*. We also find that an increase in the proportion of rental housing units in the county increases public provision of subsidized housing opportunities. Moreover, *population-housing ratio*, *population density* and *median income* positively correlate, while *sex ratio* and *median rent* negatively associate with the *recipients-poor ratio*.

Based on the estimates of the random intercept model, we can predict the states' random effects (unobserved heterogeneity) to examine the extent to which the state attenuates or amplifies the effects of the current federal rental subsidy programs. Since we predict a random effect for each state without state-level predictors in this model specification, the interpretation of the results is straightforward.[9] Figure 3.1 describes the predicted states' random effects, and it shows that, based

Table 3.2 Multilevel Model Regression Results: Unconditional and Random Intercept Models of Rural-Urban Bias of HUD's Rental Subsidy Programs by the ERS and HUD's Rural-Urban Classifications

	Unconditional	Random intercept			
	(Dependent variable: recipients-poor ratio)				
	(1)	*ERS (2)*	*HUD (3)*	*ERS (4)*	*HUD (5)*
Rural		−0.0635***	−0.0265***	−0.0633***	−0.0265***
		(0.0064)	(0.0057)	(0.0064)	(0.0057)
Intercept	0.2514***	0.4297***	0.3783***	0.3565***	0.3031***
	(0.0167)	(0.1162)	(0.1200)	(0.1163)	(0.1201)
County-level characteristics					
Sex ratio		−0.0571***	−0.0708***	−0.0591***	−0.0729***
		(0.0209)	(0.0213)	(0.0209)	(0.0213)
Elderly dependent ratio		0.0037***	0.0035***	0.0037***	0.0034***
		(0.0004)	(0.0004)	(0.0004)	(0.0004)
Percent Black population		0.1834***	0.1658***	0.1807***	0.1630***
		(0.0259)	(0.0261)	(0.0257)	(0.0260)
Percent Hispanic population		0.0368	0.0318	0.0317	0.0264
		(0.0246)	(0.0249)	(0.0245)	(0.0248)
Percent disabled population		0.2971***	0.2992***	0.2923***	0.2941***
		(0.0622)	(0.0630)	(0.0622)	(0.0630)
Percent single-parent family		0.2448***	0.2652***	0.2412***	0.2616***
		(0.0332)	(0.0335)	(0.0332)	(0.0335)
Population-housing ratio		0.0369***	0.0481***	0.0376***	0.0487***
		(0.0086)	(0.0087)	(0.0087)	(0.0087)
Population density		0.0093***	0.0084***	0.0087***	0.0077***
		(0.0019)	(0.0019)	(0.0019)	(0.0019)
Percent rental housing		0.7005***	0.7058***	0.6956***	0.7002***
		(0.0407)	(0.0413)	(0.0407)	(0.0412)
Median income[a]		0.2901***	0.2747***	0.2891***	0.2737***
		(0.0212)	(0.0216)	(0.0211)	(0.0216)
Median rent[a]		−0.1630***	−0.1526***	−0.1663***	−0.1560***
		(0.0185)	(0.0189)	(0.0185)	(0.0189)
State-level variables					
Public welfare expenditure				0.0065***	0.0067***
				(0.0014)	(0.0014)
Intergovernmental expenditure				0.0411**	0.0424**
				(0.0193)	(0.0192)
Estimated variances					
State $\left(\sigma_{u0}^2\right)$	0.0129	0.0109	0.0110	0.0060	0.0059
	(0.0029)	(0.0025)	(0.0025)	(0.0017)	(0.0016)
County $\left(\sigma_e^2\right)$	0.0177	0.0130	0.0133	0.0130	0.0134
	(0.0005)	(0.0003)	(0.0003)	(0.0003)	(0.0003)
N	3,106	3,106	3,106	3,106	3,106

a Denotes variable measured in natural logarithms. Standard errors are in parenthesis.
* Denotes significance at 10 pct., ** at 5 pct., and *** at 1 pct. level.

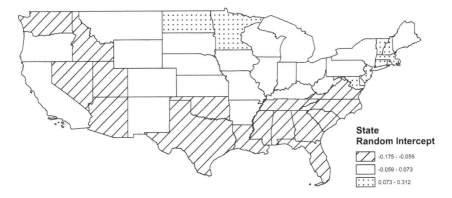

Figure 3.1 Predicted States' Random Effects on the Percent of Persons in Poverty Who Received HUD's Rental Subsidies

on the ERS rural–urban definition, most states in the South region (i.e., Florida, Georgia, Mississippi, South Carolina and Texas) and some states in the West region (i.e., Arizona and Nevada) are predicted to have a relatively lower level of the *recipients-poor ratio* among 48 contiguous states, while some states in the Northeast region (i.e., Connecticut, Massachusetts, New Hampshire, New Jersey and Rhode Island) and the Midwest region (South Dakota and Minnesota) are more likely to have a higher level of the *recipients-poor ratio*.[10] In columns (4) and (5), we add state-level variables into the random intercept models. The results show that state-level variables – the *public welfare expenditure* (per person in poverty) and *intergovernmental expenditure* (adjusted by the number of counties within state) – are positively associated with the *recipients-poor ratio*, but it does not change the effect size of the *rural* variable.[11]

Then, we allow the *rural* variable to vary randomly across states in addition to state-level random intercepts (Table 3.3). As we discussed in Eq. (5), we add the interaction terms between *rural* variable (random slope variable) and state-level variables into the regressions. In column (1), the results show that rural residents in poverty are less likely to receive the rental subsidies by 8.7 percentage points after accounting for the interaction terms (fixed effects) and random effects (random intercept and random slope); however, using HUD's rurality definition, the rural effects are absorbed into interaction terms (lose its statistical significance). Also, we find that the interaction term between rural and intergovernmental expenditure variables is negatively correlated with the *recipients-poor ratio*, indicating that rural areas tend to have a lower level of the *recipients-poor ratio* compared to the urban areas with the same level of the intergovernmental expenditures. Specifically, if the state's expenditures on intergovernmental transfers to local governments are concentrated in particular urban areas, it does not necessarily alleviate poverty nor increase the number of rental subsidies in rural areas. Indeed, in this case, rural poverty and inequality of the provision of federal rental subsidies between rural and urban areas would become more severe. This story is plausible based on findings in

Table 3.3 Multilevel Model Regression Results: Random Slope Models of Rural-Urban Bias of HUD's Rental Subsidy Programs by the ERS and HUD's Rural-Urban Classifications

	(Dependent variable: recipients-poor ratio)	
	ERS (1)	*HUD (2)*
Rural	−0.0870***	−0.0103
	(0.0298)	(0.0221)
Intercept	0.4085***	0.3116***
	(0.1165)	(0.1200)
County-level characteristics		
Sex ratio	−0.0498**	−0.0783***
	(0.0211)	(0.0213)
Elderly dependent ratio	0.0037***	0.0033***
	(0.0004)	(0.0004)
Percent Black population	0.1825***	0.1570***
	(0.0256)	(0.0258)
Percent Hispanic population	0.0350	0.0205
	(0.0243)	(0.0246)
Percent disabled population	0.2834***	0.2874***
	(0.0620)	(0.0627)
Percent single-parent family	0.2390***	0.2575***
	(0.0332)	(0.0334)
Population-housing ratio	0.0338***	0.0482***
	(0.0089)	(0.0088)
Population density	0.0086***	0.0074***
	(0.0019)	(0.0019)
Percent rental housing	0.6763***	0.6923***
	(0.0408)	(0.0412)
Median income[a]	0.2802***	0.2678***
	(0.0212)	(0.0216)
Median rent[a]	−0.1684***	−0.1496***
	(0.0185)	(0.0189)
State-level variables		
Public welfare expenditure	0.0060***	0.0061***
	(0.0014)	(0.0014)
Intergovernmental expenditure	0.0086**	0.0058
	(0.0041)	(0.0047)
Interaction variables		
Public welfare expenditure × Rural	0.0020	−0.0020
	(0.0027)	(0.0020)
Intergovernmental expenditure × Rural	−0.0078***	−0.0046
	(0.0018)	(0.0030)
Estimated variances		
State $\left(\sigma_{u0}^2\right)$	0.0069 (0.0019)	0.0077 (0.0022)
State $\left(\sigma_{u1}^2\right)$	0.0020 (0.0011)	0.0015 (0.0011)
COV $\left(\sigma_{u0}^2, \sigma_{u1}^2\right)$	−0.0026 (0.0014)	−0.0023 (0.0017)
County $\left(\sigma_{e}^2\right)$	0.0128 (0.0003)	0.0131 (0.0003)
N	3,106	3,106

a   Denotes variable measured in natural logarithms. Standard errors are in parenthesis.
*   Denotes significance at 10 pct., **at 5 pct., and ***at 1 pct. level.

the previous literature. Rural local governments may have insufficient professionals, administrative capacity and experience to obtain block grants and undertake housing and community development initiatives (Reeder 1996; Brown, Swanson and Barton 2003). Also, from the perspective of economic returns, "federal funds are increasingly disbursed in the form of block grants to the states, which can then decide whether they will invest in lagging rural communities or in more economically vibrant communities that can serve as engines of economic growth" (Brown, Swanson and Barton 2003, p. 254). Under block grants, with less redistributing within a state, rural local governments may fall even more behind.

Robustness check

As discussed in the data section, the PSH data contain 6,060 observations that list the number of HUD's rental subsidies with no geographic identifier for each state, and 97 percent of these missing observations are from New York State. Therefore, we run the same multilevel model specifications (random intercept and random slope models), developed in previous sections, without the New York State observations. The results listed in the columns (1)–(4) in Table 3.4 are quite consistent in terms of the sign, level of statistical significance and the magnitude of the *rural* variable coefficient, except the magnitude of random slope estimates in columns (3) and (4). Specifically, if a majority of the rental subsidies were missing from rural counties, the *recipients-poor ratio* in rural counties would be lower, resulting in an upward bias of the rural effect estimate, because this creates a greater gap of the *recipients-poor ratio* between rural and urban counties. On the other hand, if a majority were missing from urban counties, the *recipients-poor ratio* in urban areas would decrease, resulting in a downward bias of the rural effect estimate. As seen from column (3), using the random slope model specifications, the absolute value of the rural coefficient increases, indicating that the inclusion of the New York State observations tends to reduce differences in the *recipients-poor ratio* between rural and urban counties; however, since these missing rental subsidies occupy only about 1 percent of all allocated rental subsidies in New York State, potential bias in estimates of the measurement errors may not be huge. Additionally, we also perform a transformation of the dependent variable taking the square root of the *recipients-poor ratio*.[12] The results in columns (5)–(8) in Table 3.4 show different magnitudes of the coefficients because of the dependent variable transformation but still maintain the same sign and similar levels of statistical significance.

Discussion

This chapter uses multilevel modeling to analyze the extent of rural-urban spatial disproportionality in the current federal rental subsidy programs across all counties in the 48 contiguous states. Our primary findings show a statistically significant program bias in the HUD public housing subsidy programs against poor rural people. While 2.7–8.7 percentage points may not appear to be a large effect size, the bias against poor rural people that we measure implies between 4,000 and 10,000

Table 3.4 Robustness Check Regression Results of Rural–Urban Bias of HUD's Rental Subsidy Programs

(Dependent variable: recipients-poor ratio)

	Without New York State observations				Transformation of dependent variable			
	Random intercept		Random slope		Random intercept		Random slope	
	ERS (1)	HUD (2)	ERS (3)	HUD (4)	ERS (5)	HUD (6)	ERS (7)	HUD (8)
Rural	-0.0667***	-0.0275***	-0.0985***	-0.0221**	-0.0936***	-0.0324***	-0.1110***	0.0036
	(0.0064)	(0.0057)	(0.0303)	(0.0240)	(0.0075)	(0.0067)	(0.0377)	(0.0257)
Intercept	0.5207***	0.4482***	0.5707***	0.6923***	0.6386***	0.5210***	0.7105***	0.5363***
	(0.1192)	(0.1232)	(0.1193)	(0.1247)	(0.1361)	(0.1417)	(0.1365)	(0.1414)
Estimated variances:								
State (σ^2_{u0})	0.0074	0.0073	0.0082	0.0091	0.0066	0.0065	0.0021	0.0060
	(0.0021)	(0.0020)	(0.0022)	(0.0025)	(0.0019)	(0.0019)	(0.0010)	(0.0020)
State (σ^2_{u1})			0.0024	0.0020			0.0061	0.0011
			(0.0013)	(0.0015)			(0.0018)	(0.0006)
COV $(\sigma^2_{u0}, \sigma^2_{u1})$			-0.0033	-0.0031			0.0006	0.0008
			(0.0017)	(0.0021)			(0.0016)	(0.0012)
County (σ^2_{e})	0.0129	0.0133	0.0127	0.0130	0.0180	0.0188	0.0177	0.0185
	(0.0003)	(0.0003)	(0.0003)	(0.0003)	(0.0005)	(0.0005)	(0.0005)	(0.0005)
N	3,043	3,043	3,043	3,043	3,106	3,106	3,106	3,106

Standard errors are in parenthesis. * denotes significance at 10 pct., ** at 5 pct., and *** at 1 pct. level.

rural poor families do not receive services under the current program implementation compared to a subsidized housing program implementation where rural people are treated similarly to urban people. We also find that the states in the South region (Mississippi, South Carolina, Florida, Georgia and Texas) tend to have a lower level of the *recipients-poor ratio*, even after accounting for rural-urban effect and other plausible factors, and, according to the 2012 HAC report, these are states where more than half of rural residents reside in poverty. On the other hand, some states in the Northeast region (Connecticut, Massachusetts, New Hampshire, New Jersey and Rhode Island) are more likely to provide housing subsidies to persons in poverty, which provide state-level evidence of spatial inequality of federally funded housing subsidy programs. These results suggest several possible implications for public housing policy. First, greater attention and tracking should be placed on potential inequities in public housing programs across rural and urban areas by the degree of rurality. Care should be taken to consider alternative definitions of rurality to track spatial patterns of public housing program provisions that vary across space. Specific efforts to measure and assess the variations in housing programs across space should be built into the law and public policy so that rural communities and people receive an equal opportunity to participate in public housing programs. Along with measurement and tracking, rural public housing authorities may require targeted support and outreach efforts to help them benefit from HUD programs. Further, some program innovations, such as the Moving to Work Program of HUD, should build in special analysis and learning efforts to study the rural-specific dimensions of the program on access to housing and opportunity for self-sufficiency of rural public housing program participants.

Another dimension of these findings that should not be overlooked is that the rental housing stock is largely and positively correlated with an increase in HUD's rental subsidies that provide significant insight into a policy encouraging an increase in rental-housing stock for low-income households. In particular, rural areas have limited rental housing opportunities, and because HUD rental subsidy programs might fit better for urban/suburban areas with a lot of rental housing units, poor, rural residents do not benefit as much as urban poor people. The within HUD housing program differential points to the importance of the USDA housing and rental assistance programs, such as the Section 521 Rental Assistance Program and the Section 515 financing program for developments that include low-income households. Despite their importance as part of the rural housing safety net, these USDA programs have experienced lower funding levels recently, with reductions for the Section 521 Program in 2013 totaling 7.5% of the previous year's funding level (HAC n.d.).

Because of the presence of USDA's rural housing programs, our estimates represent an upper bound on the size of the overall urban bias in public housing in the United States. That said, significant variation in rural housing services exists at the state level, and public housing in general faces a difficult financial future. These results should be confirmed and tested with data from other years, as well as alternative types of data available at the individual and household level, as well as, at the housing authority level and county level. It may be possible that alternative econometric approaches yield different findings or provide estimates of different effect sizes from our analysis. All of these reasons point to the need for continued monitoring and measurement of access to affordable housing in rural areas of the United States.

Notes

1 The study defines persistent poverty as at least higher than 20 percent poverty rates in each U.S. Census 1980, 1990, 2000 and ACS five-year estimates 2007–2011.

2 Some PHAs manage public provision of the rental subsidy programs in city area rather than county (i.e., Chicago Housing Authority, Housing Authority of Baltimore City etc.). In order to run a county-level analysis, we incorporate city-based PHAs into the county-based housing authority.

3 The 2013 Rural-Urban Continuum Code has nine categories, in which the first three categories belong to metropolitan counties and the latter six categories belong to non-metropolitan counties. The 2013 Rural-Urban Continuum Code scheme includes a total of 1,167 metropolitan counties and 1,976 non-metropolitan counties. Among categories under non-metropolitan counties, we define a rural county based on the eighth and ninth categories defined as "Completely rural or less than 2,500 urban population, adjacent to a metro area" and "Completely rural or less than 2,500 urban population, not adjacent to a metro area," respectively.

4 HUD defines rural in three ways: (*i*) a place having fewer than 2,500 inhabitants; (*ii*) a county or parish with an urban population of 20,000 inhabitants or less and (*iii*) any place with a population not in excess of 20,000 inhabitants and not located in a Metropolitan Statistical Area. Since HUD's first rural definition is the same as ours using the ERS's rural definition, we focus on the latter two definitions. We define rural as a county with a population not in excess of 20,000 inhabitants in non-metropolitan areas, comprising the latter four (6–9) categories of the ERS's Rural-Urban Continuum codes.

5 New York State consists of 62 counties with 49 urban counties (or 79 percent). Excluding 5,860 rental subsidies in New York State may decrease the *recipients-poor ratio* of a certain county. For example, if majority of the rental subsidies were missing from rural counties, it will decrease the *recipients-poor ratio* in rural counties which result in upward bias of the rural effect estimate because this will create a greater gap of the *recipients-poor ratio* between rural and urban counties. On the other hand, if majority were missing from urban counties, it will decrease the *recipients-poor ratio* in urban areas resulting in a downward bias of the rural effect estimate. We first regress with all observed counties, and then regress without New York state observations in order to see how the estimates (sign, statistical significance and the magnitude) change.

6 See State Government Finances glossary, Census Bureau, for a detailed metric of public welfare expenditures.

7 Specifically, u_{0j} measures a state-specific deviation from the state-mean outcome (γ_{00}) after accounting for the effect of state-specific variable (C_j). Variance of the residual errors of (εij) is specified as σ_e^2.

8 This preliminary information is useful in providing an Intraclass Correlation (ICC) coefficient estimated by the ratio of variance between states (σ_{u0}^2) to the total variance $(\sigma_{u0}^2 + \sigma_e^2)$. As can be seen in the column (1), the estimated variance, σ_e^2, is 0.0177 at county level and at the level of states equals, (σ_{u0}^2), 0.0129. The ICC is approximately 42.2 percent, and the remaining variation is at the county level (57.8 percent).

9 Because the state random effect (u_{0j}) measures a state-specific deviation from the state-mean outcome after accounting for the effects of state-specific variables, the inclusion of additional state-level variables make the interpretation difficult.

10 We observe very similar results of the predicted state effects (random intercepts) using HUD's rural definition except slight changes in the magnitude of coefficients in South Dakota, Kansas and Kentucky states.
11 The inclusion of state-level variables explains about an additional 14 percent of variation in ICC coefficient at the state level.
12 Since the data have some observations with 0 value of the recipients-poor ratio, we decided that a log-transformation of the dependent variable is not appropriate.

References

Albrecht, D. E. (1998). The industrial transformation of farm communities: Implications for family structure and socioeconomic conditions. *Rural Sociology*, *63*(1), 51–64.

Albrecht, D. E., & Albrecht, S. L. (2000). Poverty in non-metropolitan America: Impacts of industrial, employment, and family structure variables. *Rural Sociology*, *65*(1), 87–103.

Brown, D. L., Swanson, L. E., & Barton, A. W. (2003). Challenges for rural America in the twenty-first century. *Rural Studies Series/Rural Sociological Society*.

Conger, R. D., & Elder Jr., G. H. (1994). *Families in troubled times: Adapting to change in rural America: Social institutions and social change*. New York: Walter de Gruyter, Inc.

Currie, J., & Yelowitz, A. (2000). Are public housing projects good for kids? *Journal of Public Economics*, *75*(1), 99–124.

Devine, D. J., Gray, R. W., Rubin, L., & Taghavi, L. B. (2003). *Housing choice voucher location patterns: Implications for participant and neighborhood welfare*. Washington, DC: U.S. Department of Housing and Urban Development. Retrieved from www.huduser.gov/publications/pdf/location_paper.pdf

Duncan, C. M., & Coles, R. (2000). *Worlds apart: Why poverty persists in rural America*. New Haven, CT: Yale University Press.

Farrigan, T. (2015). Geography of poverty. *Economic Research Service (ERS), United States Department of Agriculture (USDA)*. Retrieved from www.ers.usda.gov/topics/rural-economy-population/rural-poverty-well-being.aspx

Felix, A., & Henderson, J. (2010). Rural America's fiscal challenge. *Federal Reserve Bank of Kansas City*. Retrieved from http://kansascityfed.org/publicat/mse/MSE_0310.pdf

Goering, J. M., Stebbins, H., & Siewert, M. (1995). *Promoting housing choice in HUD's rental assistance programs: Report to Congress*. Washington DC: US Department of Housing and Urban Development, Office of Policy Development and Research.

Goetz, E. G. (2003). *Clearing the way: Deconcentrating the poor in urban America*. Washington DC: The Urban Institute.

Housing Assistance Council. (n.d.). USDA Rural Development notifies rural rental housing borrowers regarding section 521 rental assistance shortfall. Retrieved from www.ruralhome.org/whats-new/mn-whats-new/45-announcements/726-usda-rural-development-notifies-rural-rental-housing-borrowers-regarding-section-521-rental-assistance-shortfall

Housing Assistance Council. (2012). *Taking Stock: Rural People, Poverty, and Housing in the 21st Century*. Washington DC: Housing Assistance Council.

Irwin, E. G., Isserman, A. M., Kilkenny, M., & Partridge, M. D. (2010). A century of research on rural development and regional issues. *American Journal of Agricultural Economics*, *92*(2), 522–553.

Jacob, B. A. (2004). Public housing, housing vouchers, and student achievement: Evidence from public housing demolitions in Chicago. *American Economic Review*, 233–258.

Jacob, B. A., & Ludwig, J. (2012). The effects of housing assistance on labor supply: Evidence from a voucher lottery. *The American Economic Review*, 272–304.

Jencks, C., & Mayer, S. E. (1990). The social consequences of growing up in a poor neighborhood. *Inner-city poverty in the United States, 111,* 186.

Katz, L. F., Kling, J. R., & Liebman, J. B. (2001). Moving to opportunity in Boston: Early results of a randomized mobility experiment. *Quarterly Journal of Economics,* 607–654.

Lens, M. C., Ellen, I. G., & O'Regan, K. (2011). Do vouchers help low-income households live in safer neighborhoods? Evidence on the housing choice voucher program. *Cityscape,* 135–159.

Massey, D. S., & Kanaiaupuni, S. M. (1993). Public housing and the concentration of poverty. *Social Science Quarterly, 74*(1), 109–122.

Newman, S. J. (2005). Low-end rental housing: The forgotten story in Baltimore's housing boom. *Urban Institute.* Retrieved from www.urban.org/research/publication/low-end-rental-housing

Newman, S. J., & Schnare, A. B. (1997). . . . And a suitable living environment: The failure of housing programs to deliver on neighborhood quality. *Housing Policy Debate, 8*(4), 703–741.

Pendall, R. (2000). Why voucher and certificate users live in distressed neighborhoods. *Housing Policy Debate, 11*(4), 881–910.

Reeder, R. J. (1996). *How would rural areas fare under Block Grants?* (No. 33609). United States Department of Agriculture, Economic Research Service.

Rice, D., & Obama's, W. P. (2009). What to look for in HUD's 2010 budget for low-income housing. *Center on Budget and Policy Priorities, 5.*

Ricketts, T. C. (1999). *Rural health in the United States.* New York: Oxford University Press.

Schwartz, A. F. (2014). *Housing policy in the United States.* New York: Routledge.

Spar, K., & Falk, G. (2016). Federal benefits and services for people with low-income: Overview of spending trends, FY2008-FY2015. *Congressional Research Service (CRS), United States Congress.* Retrieved from www.fas.org/sgp/crs/misc/R44574.pdf

Tickamyer, A. R., & Duncan, C. M. (1990). Poverty and opportunity structure in rural America. *Annual Review of Sociology,* 67–86.

Turner, M. A. (1998). Moving out of poverty: Expanding mobility and choice through tenant-based housing assistance. *Housing Policy Debate, 9*(2), 373–394.

U.S. Bureau of Census. (n.d.). State Government finances. Retrieved December 15, 2015 from www.census.gov/govs/state/

U.S. Bureau of Census. (2008). A compass for understanding and using American Community Survey data: What general data users need to know. *Census Bureau.* Retrieved from http://www.census.gov/content/dam/Census/library/publications/2008/acs/ACSGernealHandbook.pdf

Von Hoffman, A. (1996). High ambitions: The past and future of American low-income housing policy. *Housing Policy Debate, 7*(3), 423–446.

Von Hoffman, A. (2012). History lessons for today's housing policy: The politics of low-income housing. *Housing Policy Debate, 22*(3), 321–376.

Wilson, W. J. (1987). *The truly disadvantaged: The inner city, the underclass, and public policy.* Chicago: University of Chicago Press.

4 What drives spatial variation in housing cost-burden among rural low- and moderate-income renters?

John Cromartie and Peter Han

Introduction

The long-standing struggle among low- and moderate-income households to secure affordable housing in this country has in this decade expanded to historically unprecedented levels. Nearly seven million Americans lost their homes to foreclosure during the housing mortgage crisis and Great Recession that followed (CoreLogic 2015). Depressed wages and constrained credit placed the dream of homeownership further out of reach and triggered a ten-year decline in homeownership rates, from 69 percent in 2004 to 63 percent in 2015 (U.S. Census Bureau 2016). As a result of these economic shocks combined with demographic trends, growth in renter households nationally is averaging 1,000,000 per year since 2010, compared with less than 400,000 per year during the 2000s. (JCHS 2015). The current surge in demand for rental housing is fueled in large part by demographic groups and income brackets that in the past were more likely to be homeowners: middle income, non-Hispanic White, middle-age and retiree households. They have put a squeeze on affordable housing for the rapidly rising population of traditional renters: low-income, minority and young, newly-forming households.

Economic and demographic drivers of this ongoing crisis have been identified mostly along broad geographic contours, often limited to national-level statistics. For instance, we know that half of all renter households in the U.S. are now considered cost-burdened (paying 30 percent or more of their income on rent) and that rental housing costs increased 3 times faster than median household incomes between 2007 and 2013 (PAHRC 2015). Another national-level study based on demographic projections found that the aging of the baby boom generation alone will add over 2 million renters over age 65 by 2025 (JCHS 2015). At the same time, renter households headed by members of the millennial generation (currently 10–30 years old) will double in number from 11 to 22 million, with roughly half headed by Hispanics. Other studies provide similarly important baseline statistics on the housing affordability crisis but with little or no geographic detail (Goodman et al. 2015; Charette et al. 2015; Terwilliger 2011). When geographic analysis is provided, it is most often limited to differences among states or large metropolitan areas. With a few notable exceptions (NRHC 2014; HAC 2012), little is known about housing affordability trends in rural and small town America.

This chapter helps close this knowledge gap by examining two aspects of increasing cost-burden among low- and moderate-income renters. First, we use annual data from the Census Bureau's American Community Survey (ACS) to compare increases in cost-burden from 2005 to 2014.[1] We analyze differences between metropolitan (metro) and non-metropolitan (non-metro) areas, as well as differences among non-metro areas by state. The growth in renter households and its spatial variability are also documented. The increase in renters without a corresponding increase in the supply of rental units, especially for lower-income households, has been the primary driver of rental cost-burden increases (NRHC 2014; JCHS 2015). Second, we use 5-year ACS aggregate data to examine local variation in housing cost-burden. Regression analysis is employed to identify county-level characteristics associated with high cost-burden among low- and moderate-income renters and to show how these associations vary between metro and non-metro areas.

The housing affordability crisis has placed a spotlight on the need for adequate housing in rural America, at a time when many rural communities are at risk of losing federally subsidized rental properties (HAC 2013). For individuals and families, housing cost-burden is a fundamental challenge and a growing impediment to upward mobility. For rural communities, unmet housing needs are a drag on future employment growth and fiscal health. Evidence is mounting that declining homeownership and higher rents exacerbate income and wealth inequalities among low- and high-income households and communities (Foster and Kleit 2015). This study builds on recent efforts to expand research on rural housing affordability (Ziebarth 2014). It is meant to provide housing advocates and program administrators with knowledge about how this continuing crisis affects rural people and places and how it has played out differently across the country.

Background

Since the housing mortgage crisis in the mid-2000s, demand for affordable rental housing has sharply increased, especially for low- and moderate- income households. The supply of new rental housing has been slow to catch up with this new demand. The resulting increase in rental prices, coupled with a decline in household income since the Great Recession, caused a sharp increase in housing cost-burden in the U.S. Several national-level reports provide detailed demographic and economic analysis of this growing crisis but contain little or no information on rural conditions or trends (Goodman 2015; JCHS 2015; Leopold et al. 2015; PAHRC 2015).

Several economic and demographic factors that contributed to the crowding of the rental market and increased housing cost-burden nationwide are known to have impacted rural areas as well. First, foreclosures since 2007 displaced millions of homeowners and forced them back onto the rental market. The unprecedented rise in subprime lending that helped trigger the foreclosure crisis affected rural communities as much as if not more than large cities (Nelson and Cromartie 2014). Second, the Great Recession increased unemployment and lowered the portion of household budgets available for housing, and these conditions persisted longer in rural areas (U.S. Department of Agriculture 2015). Third, with the collapse of the housing market in 2007, credit was severely constrained, especially impacting rural mortgage access. Home purchase loan applications in rural areas declined by more than 50 percent between 2003 and 2010 (HAC 2012). As a result of these economic shocks combined with demographic trends, we expect our results to show increased crowding in the rural rental housing market, especially at the lower end of the income scale.

The annual rate of growth in rental households more than doubled nationally from 2000–2010 to 2010–2015 (JCHS 2015). At the same time, construction of multifamily housing dropped to a 50-year low of approximately 100,000 units in 2010. Despite a significant recovery in multifamily construction (more than 300,000 units started construction in 2015), rental housing supply has fallen far short of demand (JCHS 2015). Also, most new multifamily rental housing construction is designed and located to serve relatively high-income renters, at a time when low- and moderate-income renters face unprecedented housing cost-burdens.

Far fewer multifamily housing options exist in rural areas to absorb the newly renting population (HAC 2013). Furthermore, high out-migration of young people from rural areas has left a large aging population, most of whom are dependent on fixed or no income. As their rents increased, the housing cost-burden on elderly populations also increased (HAC 2014). Coupled with remaining Gen Xers (born between 1970 and 1985) opting to rent instead and the very large "Millennial" cohort (born between 1985 and 2005) just entering their 20's, the future demand for rental housing in rural America is expected to increase substantially (JCHS 2015). Increased immigration and the long-term trend of persistent rural poverty have exacerbated housing challenges in particular states since the Great Recession, as the share of housing costs in most household budgets was already high in both immigrant destination communities and high-poverty areas. These unique characteristics of rural residents are likely compounding the housing challenges faced by the general population.

There are two competing economic models associated with housing costs and wages that can be extended to rural areas. On the one hand, the quality-of-life literature suggests that interregional differences in amenities cause labor and households to relocate to maximize well-being (Roback 1982; Bloomquist et al. 1988). As a result, real rents and wages readjust across different regions to reach spatial equilibrium in line with the levels of amenities available in different places. Higher urban housing costs reflect the higher concentration of amenities, including cheaper transportation, higher-paying jobs, better schools and more options for leisure-time activity.

On the other hand, the spatial mismatch literature suggests that low- and moderate- income households encounter barriers to their mobility, and the market prices for rents and wages do not readjust to compensate for interregional amenity differences (Holzer 1982; Kain 1992). As a result, poorer households are more likely to face higher-than-market rents for their housing options, worsening their housing cost-burden. Barriers to mobility include continuing racial and ethnic segregation and discrimination, lack of information about options elsewhere, local zoning laws and age and maintenance of local housing stock. In this chapter, we find evidence of lower rural housing costs reflecting quality-of-life differences but follow the spatial mismatch approach to analyze the geography of housing cost-burden faced by low- and moderate-income households. We expect to find differences between metro and non-metro counties, and among different non-metro regions, related to economic, geographic and demographic characteristics.

Data and methods

Data from a wide array of surveys and other sources are used to document housing trends at the national level but are not large enough or geographically coded to provide detailed information on rural (non-metro) areas.[2] For instance, Housing Vacancy Surveys and Current Population Surveys (both from the U.S. Census Bureau) are used to track homeownership rates and renter household growth among demographic groups (JCHS 2015). Both can be used to track annual non-metro trends for the nation as a whole, but their relatively small sample sizes make them less useful for deriving accurate estimates for smaller geographic areas or demographic groups. Here we use the much larger American Community Survey, which started in 2005 and was meant to replace decennial Census sample data as the primary source for detailed population and housing data. Over two million household interviews are completed every year, enough to provide annual estimates for non-metro areas by state. For smaller geographic units such as counties, the Census Bureau aggregates five years of annual surveys and provides estimates that represent the average for those five years. This study uses one-year data from 2005 to 2014 and the most recent five-year aggregate data, covering 2010–14.

ACS data for this study come from summary tables providing information on renter households (U.S. Census Bureau 2015). The number of renter households paying more than 30 percent of their gross income (before taxes) on gross rent (rent and utilities) is available for different income groups. This ratio approach for defining cost-burden is commonly used in research and the 30 percent threshold has long been the defining metric for identifying cost-burdened households in both research and federal housing programs. Its limitations as an accurate measure of cost-burden have been extensively documented (Belsky et al. 2005). For example, it cannot distinguish budget-constrained households from those with a preference for expensive neighborhoods. Here we calculate the percent of cost-burdened renter households in a given area for low-income and moderate-income households only, thus reducing this discrepancy in our findings. Low-income households earn less than $20,000 per year and moderate income households earn between $20,000 and $50,000. In addition, summary tables provide information on rentership rates (the inverse of homeownership rates) and change in the number of renter households by age groups and by race-ethnicity.

One-year ACS data is used to track non-metro trends in renter cost-burden at the state level starting in 2005, the first year of full ACS implementation. Some of the time trends are reported through 2014, using the most recent ACS data available. However, metro and non-metro areas changed in 2013 (with updates based on the 2010 decennial census), thus the state-level spatial analysis is limited to change between 2005 and 2012. Five-year ACS data is used to help explain county-level variation in renter cost-burden among low- and moderate-income families. Standard OLS regression analysis is used to identify county characteristics strongly associated with high cost-burden.

Findings

Non-metro renter households grew by over 300,000 between 2005 and 2012, from 5.2 to 5.5 million, a 5.7 percent increase compared with total household growth of only 0.3 percent. As a result, the non-metro rentership rate increased from 27 to 28.5 percent (Figure 4.1). An initial increase occurred in response to the mortgage crisis of 2007 as home values plummeted, credit disappeared and foreclosures threw thousands of rural homeowners onto the rental market. Renter household growth was further bolstered by a stalled rural economy following the Great Recession. The decline in the number of renter households seen between 2012 and 2013 resulted strictly from the loss of roughly 100 non-metro counties to reclassification as metro. Growth in renter households continued in counties that remained non-metro, from 2013 to 2014, and the non-metro rentership rate increased to 29.1 percent.

Metro-non-metro differences in cost-burden

Rising demand for rental housing combined with stagnant wages drove up housing cost-burdens for low- and moderate-income renters in both metro and non-metro areas (Figure 4.2). The percent of households paying more than 30 percent of income on rents is generally higher in urban areas, but primarily because

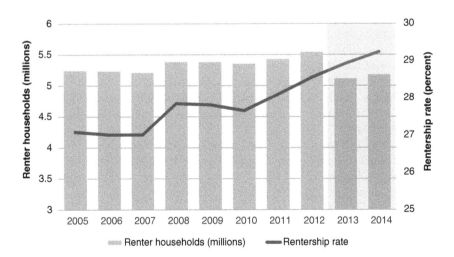

Figure 4.1 Renter Households and Rentership Rates in Non-Metro Areas, 2005–2014

Note: Non-metro classification used in the ACS changed after 2012 (highlighted in gray).

Source: USDA-ERS using data from U.S. Census Bureau, ACS one-year data, 2005–2014.

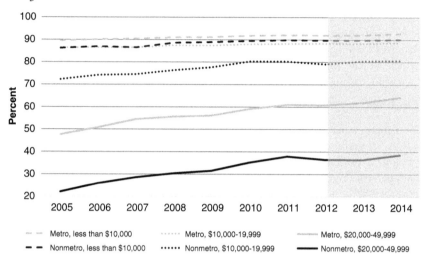

Figure 4.2 Cost-Burden among Low- and Moderate-Income Renters by Residence, 2005–2014

Note: Cost-burdened households spend more than 30 percent of gross income on gross rent.

Metro-non-metro classification used in the ACS changed after 2012 (highlighted in gray).

Source: USDA-ERS using data from U.S. Census Bureau, ACS one-year data, 2005–2014.

higher-income households pay higher urban rents in exchange for better access to jobs, school and services. For those who do not have room in their budget to consider these trade-offs, cost-burdens are quite similar across the rural-urban hierarchy. Cost-burdens for households earning less than $10,000 per year approached 90 percent in 2005 regardless of residence and rose to slightly above 90 percent in 2014. For the next-lowest income group – those earning between $10,000 and $20,000 per year – the rise in cost-burden was much steeper for non-metro households, from 62 to 77 percent. Metro households in this income category did not see a corresponding increase in cost-burden; thus, the metro-non-metro gap decreased by half.[3]

The largest increase in cost-burden among non-metro income groups occurred for households with moderate incomes, earning between $20,000 and $50,000. Over 285,000 additional households in this group were cost-burdened in 2012, with the share nearly doubling from 22 to 39 percent. Renter cost-burden is increasingly a middle-class problem in metro areas as well, with cost-burdens among this group rising from 47 to 64 percent. The higher level of cost-burden for metro renters, resulting from the housing-amenities trade-off, can be seen in the 25 percentage point difference for this group. This metro-non-metro gap persists among higher-income groups (not shown). For instance, 22 percent of metro renters earning between $50,000 and $75,000 are cost-burdened compared with just 5 percent of non-metro renters.

State differences in non-metro cost-burden

The emergence of high cost-burden among moderate-income renters likely had an impact on the geography of housing affordability in rural America. We expect to see significant spatial variation in housing cost-burden given the diverse demographic make-up, economic structure and financial well-being of rural communities. Cost-burden among moderate-income renters was 37 percent for non-metro areas as a whole in 2012, but state-to-state variation ranged from 24 percent in South Dakota up to 69 percent in Hawaii (Figures 4.3 and 4.4).

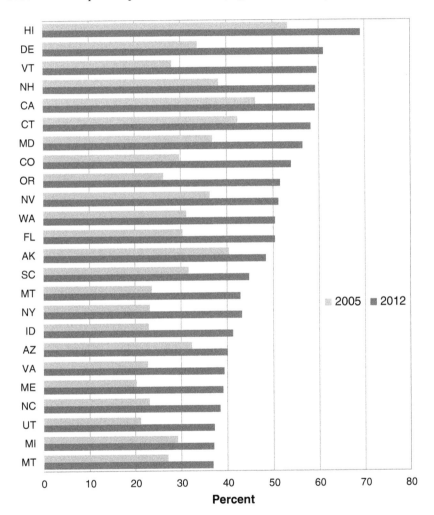

Figure 4.3 States with the Highest Housing Cost-Burden Rates among Non-Metro Moderate-Income Renters, 2012, with Comparison to 2005

Note: Cost-burdened households spend more than 30 percent of gross income on gross rent.

Moderate-income households earn between $20,000 and $50,000 per year.

Source: USDA-ERS using data from U.S. Census Bureau, ACS one-year data, 2005 and 2012.

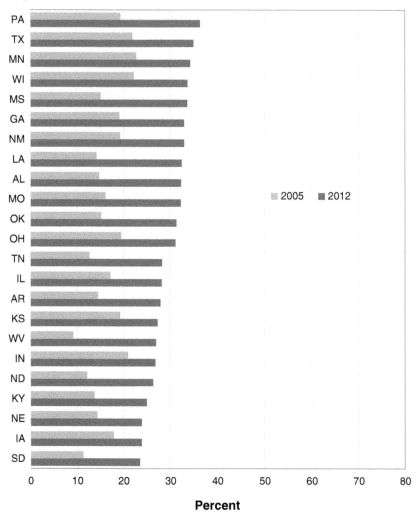

Figure 4.4 States with the Lowest Housing Cost-Burden Rates among Non-Metro Moderate-
Income Renters, 2012, with Comparison to 2005

Note: Cost-burdened households spend more than 30 percent of gross income on gross rent.

Moderate-income households earn between $20,000 and $50,000 per year.

Source: USDA-ERS using data from U.S. Census Bureau, ACS one-year data, 2005 and 2012.

Most states with the highest levels of cost-burden share an abundance of scenic
landscapes or other recreational resources that attracted new residents and spurred
economic growth up through the mid-2000s. Non-metro areas in states such as
New Hampshire, Connecticut, Maryland and Florida combined scenic amenities
with proximity to expanding metro regions, which added to rapid population

growth prior to the 2008 recession. The loss of home equity and the foreclosure crisis hit hard in these types of high-growth, high-amenity locations. As a result, many of these states experienced higher-than-average increases in cost-burden between 2005 and 2012, including Delaware, Vermont, Colorado and Oregon (Figure 4.3).

Most states with the lowest cost-burdens are in the Great Plains and other regions marked by persistent out-migration and aging populations, including the 3 lowest: South Dakota, Iowa and Nebraska (Figure 4.4). Chronic out-migration coupled with high unemployment and low wages characterize other states with low cost-burden, such as Kentucky, West Virginia and Arkansas. The sharpest increases in rural cost-burden occurred in high-poverty states: West Virginia, Alabama, Mississippi and Louisiana. In all four cases, cost-burden more than doubled from relatively low rates in 2005. Other states experiencing higher-than-average increases in rental cost-burden participated in the oil-and-gas energy boom, which attracted thousands of workers and brought housing shortages to remote areas of North Dakota, Nebraska, Oklahoma and Pennsylvania.

Change in renter households

These findings show that increasing rentership rates and the concomitant rise in rental cost-burden is taking place throughout rural and small town America, but under diverse circumstances and for different reasons. One way to document these differences is to divide the change in the number of renter households occurring in a particular area into the portion that can be attributed to overall household growth and the remaining portion caused by an increase in rentership rates (Figure 4.5). Two states with the highest numeric increases in non-metro

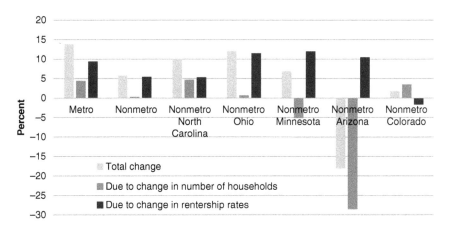

Figure 4.5 Renter Household Change, Metro-Non-Metro and Selected Non-Metro Areas by State, 2005–12

Source: USDA-ERS using data from U.S. Census Bureau, ACS one-year summary data, 2005 and 2012.

renter households (North Carolina and Ohio) show different growth patterns. Half of the increase in North Carolina was due to overall population growth, while almost all the increase in renter households in non-metro Ohio came from an increase in rentership rates. For other Midwestern states, such as Minnesota, renter households grew rapidly despite an overall decline in non-metro households. The same pattern is seen in Michigan, Illinois, Iowa and Missouri. Finally, Arizona is one of six states with fewer renter households in 2012 compared with 2005. In all six cases, the decrease was smaller due to an increase in rentership rates. Only one state, Colorado, showed a decline in non-metro rentership rates during this period, but the number of renter households increased because of sufficient overall population growth.

County-level variation in cost-burden

The most recent five-year ACS data release provides county-level estimates that represent the average level of housing cost-burden during 2010–14. Here we employ Ordinary Least Squares (OLS) regression to document spatial variation in rural cost-burden among low- and moderate-income renters. Specifically, we identify the most important geographic, economic, and demographic characteristics of counties associated with high cost-burden. County-level cost-burden indicators are combined with data from ACS and other data sources, the decennial Census, USDA-ERS and BLS (Table 4.1). Metro-non-metro differences for all the summary

Table 4.1 Description and Sources of County-Level Indicators

Name	Description	Source
Dependent variables		
Low-income cost-burden	Percent of low-income households spending more than 30 percent of income on rent	5-year ACS, 2010–14
Moderate-income cost-burden	Percent of moderate-income households spending more than 30 percent of income on rent	5-year ACS, 2010–14
Demographic characteristics		
Population 65 plus	Percent of population 65 years or older	Decennial census, 2010
Black	Percent population Black	Decennial census, 2010
Hispanic	Percent population Hispanic	Decennial census, 2010
College grads	Percent 25–64 with a college degree	5-year ACS, 2010–14
Net migration	Percent population change from net migration	Census estimates, 2010 to 2014

Name	Description	Source
Geographic characteristics		
Density	Population per square mile	Decennial census, 2010
Metro commute	Percent of workers commuting non-metro to metro	5-year ACS, 2010–14
Natural amenities	Index of climate and landscape amenities	USDA-ERS
Housing market		
Average rent	Mean gross rent	5-year ACS, 2010–14
Multifamily renters	Percent of renters living in multifamily rental properties	5-year ACS, 2010–14
Owner-renter income gap	Mean renter income as a percent of mean owner income	5-year ACS, 2010–14
Labor market		
Employment rate	Percent civilian labor force employed	5-year ACS, 2010–14
Household income	Median household income	5-year ACS, 2010–14
Deep poverty	Percent with incomes below half of the poverty threshold	5-year ACS, 2010–14

Source: USDA-ERS.

statistics except one were significant at the 1 percent level (Table 4.2). In general, there were higher proportions of cost-burdened households in metro counties than in non-metro counties, with a greater gap between low- and moderate-income households in non-metro counties. A higher percentage of elderly and a lower percentage of Blacks resided in non-metro counties compared to metro counties. There was a greater proportion of 24–64 year olds with a college degree in metro counties. Between 2009 and 2014, there was an average out-migration of 0.96 percent for non-metro counties, whereas metro counties on average increased in population by 0.85 percent due to migration. Furthermore, metro counties were not only much more densely populated, but also tended to be disproportionately located in regions of the country with high natural amenities.

As predicted by the quality-of-life theory, average rents were lower in non-metro counties by approximately $210 and median household incomes were lower by $10,400. Deep poverty, measured in terms of the share of population earning below half of the poverty threshold, was higher on average in non-metro counties. Income inequality between renters and homeowners was lower in non-metro counties along with the employment rate. There were also lower shares of multifamily housing units. These statistics suggest that even with lower rents, non-metro residents could be at a greater risk of being housing cost-burdened.

Table 4.2 Descriptive Statistics

Variables	Metro (N=1158)		Non-metro (N=1945)	
	Mean	*Std.Dev.*	*Mean*	*Std.Dev.*
Dependent variables				
Low-income cost-burden	87.66	7.252	81.41	10.90
Moderate-income cost-burden	50.37	16.56	32.09	14.78
Demographic characteristics				
Population 65 plus	13.76	3.522	17.13	4.045
Black	10.71	13.46	7.59	14.84
Hispanic	8.94	12.16	7.90	13.75
College grads	25.86	10.93	18.23	6.897
Net migration	0.85	3.221	-0.96	3.447
Geographic characteristics				
Density	625.65	2791	42.83	94.96
Metro commute	0.00	0	8.93	11.13
Natural amenities	0.28	2.301	-0.08	2.255
Housing market				
Average rent	869.40	226.1	655.87	135.4
Multifamily renters	45.70	18.79	32.81	14.16
Owner-renter income gap	51.15	7.141	55.56	10.70
Labor market				
Employment rate	56.59	6.910	52.89	8.688
Household income	53093.56	13553	42678.85	9140
Deep poverty	6.51	2.949	7.23	3.523

Source: USDA-ERS.

OLS regression results describe the degree to which these indicators account for county-level variation in the percentage of cost-burdened renter households. The relationship between high cost-burden on the one hand, and demographic, geographic, housing-market and labor-market conditions on the other is expected to vary between non-metro and metro counties, given the unique qualities of rural housing markets. Results are shown separately for low-income and moderate-income households (Tables 4.3 and 4.4, respectively).

Among demographic characteristics, the percentage of population that is Black had a significant effect on housing cost-burden, especially among moderate-income households. In non-metro counties, a 1 percent increase in the Black population increased the cost-burden by 0.04 percent among low-income households and

Table 4.3 OLS Regression on Low-Income Cost-Burdened Households

Variables	All counties	Metro	Non-metro
Demographic characteristics			
Population 65 plus	−0.402***	−0.307***	−0.442***
	(−0.163)	(−0.147)	(−0.160)
Black	0.0356***	0.0445**	0.0383**
	(0.0508)	(0.0827)	(0.0527)
Hispanic	0.00447	0.00192	0.0148
	(0.00580)	(0.00323)	(0.0187)
College grads	0.178***	0.0829**	0.295***
	(0.164)	(0.124)	(0.186)
Net migration	−0.000238	0.402***	−0.144
	(−8.09e-05)	(0.178)	(−0.0451)
Geographic characteristics			
Density (logged)	2.182***	1.318***	2.462***
	(0.367)	(0.271)	(0.297)
Metro commute	0.000832		0.0178
	(0.000807)		(0.0182)
Natural amenities	0.774***	0.501***	0.790***
	(0.174)	(0.158)	(0.164)
Housing market			
Multifamily renters	−0.155***	−0.0762***	−0.181***
	(−0.261)	(−0.197)	(−0.233)
Owner-renter income gap	0.00143	0.0219	0.000280
	(0.00133)	(0.0213)	(0.000265)
Labor market			
Employment rate	0.0296	−0.0401	0.0141
	(0.0239)	(−0.0381)	(0.0111)
Deep poverty	−0.0143	0.100	−0.102
	(−0.00469)	(0.0407)	(−0.0329)
Constant	81.84***	86.23***	81.31***
Observations	3,097	1,157	1,940
R-squared	0.242	0.227	0.173

Robust standard errors in parentheses.

*** p<0.01, ** p<0.05, * p<0.1.

Source: USDA-ERS.

0.11 percent among moderate-income households. This effect is independent of other characteristics included in the model, such as deep poverty and inequality. Following spatial mismatch theory, this suggests that housing demand in predominantly Black neighborhoods increases due to racial segregation and restricted

Table 4.4 OLS Regression on Moderate-Income Cost-Burdened Households

Variables	All counties	Metro	Non-metro
	Demographic characteristics		
Population 65 plus	−0.455***	−0.609***	−0.170
	(−0.106)	(−0.128)	(−0.0458)
Black	0.148***	0.203***	0.110***
	(0.121)	(0.166)	(0.113)
Hispanic	0.0670***	0.184***	0.0436
	(0.0498)	(0.135)	(0.0411)
College grads	0.553***	0.590***	0.522***
	(0.291)	(0.388)	(0.246)
Net migration	0.321***	0.181	0.280***
	(0.0628)	(0.0353)	(0.0660)
	Geographic characteristics		
Density (logged)	4.214***	3.422***	3.696***
	(0.407)	(0.309)	(0.335)
Metro commute	0.00972		0.101***
	(0.00540)		(0.0773)
Natural amenities	2.343***	1.927***	2.496***
	(0.301)	(0.268)	(0.386)
	Housing market		
Multifamily renters	0.00512	−0.0173	0.0756***
	(0.00495)	(−0.0197)	(0.0728)
Owner-renter income gap	0.0442	0.147**	0.0315
	(0.0237)	(0.0634)	(0.0223)
	Labor market		
Employment rate	−0.159***	−0.323***	−0.107*
	(−0.0736)	(−0.135)	(−0.0629)
Deep poverty	−0.986***	−1.565***	−0.546***
	(−0.185)	(−0.279)	(−0.132)
Constant	29.24***	43.39***	17.75***
Observations	3,103	1,158	1,945
R-squared	0.576	0.624	0.330

Robust standard errors in parentheses.

*** $p<0.01$, ** $p<0.05$, * $p<0.1$.

Source: USDA-ERS.

mobility among low- and moderate-income households, resulting in higher cost-burden. A similar but much smaller increase is associated with higher Hispanic population shares, but is only significant in metro counties.

High education levels among 25–64 year olds also increase cost-burden, likely for quality-of-life reasons. For low-income households, a 1 percent increase in the share with college degrees increases cost-burden by 0.3 percent. Most households at low- and moderate-income levels have lower education but face increased housing competition from higher-income households in counties with higher-quality schools. As new housing construction is slow to respond to increased demand for better housing, the current housing stock is often renovated to meet this demand and owners are able to charge higher rents. As a result, low- and moderate-income households experience an additional cost-burden. Surprisingly, as the share of elderly population increases, the percentage of cost-burdened households decreases. We expected a positive relationship, since many elderly rely on fixed incomes and are unable to cope effectively with increases in rent. However, homeownership rates are high among elderly rural residents and the demand for rental housing is not increasing as fast in counties with high elderly shares.

The effect of net migration was statistically significant for low-income households in metro counties and for moderate-income households in non-metro counties. From general migration patterns in the U.S., we know that migrants from non-metro to metro counties mainly consist of low-income households, especially young adults seeking their first entrance into the job market. Older and more financially secure households dominate moves from metro to non-metro counties. Therefore, in metro counties, the demand for low-income housing would increase, and the rent would also increase, resulting in a higher cost-burden for low-income households. In non-metro counties, the demand for moderate-income housing would increase, resulting in a higher cost-burden for moderate-income households.

Among geographic characteristics, population density uniformly increases housing demand and rent, contributing to higher cost-burden among both low- and moderate-income households. This is in line with quality-of-life perspectives, as are results indicating high cost-burden in areas with high scenic amenities. However, the effect of density is greater in non-metro counties, especially for low-income households: A 1 percent increase in population density increased the percentage of the cost-burden by 2.46 percent in non-metro areas but only 1.3 percent in metro areas. As the rental housing stock is smaller in non-metro areas, population increases would negatively affect housing cost-burden more severely. Also, as the share of workers commuting from non-metro to metro increased, the cost-burden on moderate-income households increased. A higher share of workers commuting to a metro area indicates how closely a non-metro county is located to a metro county. Therefore, workers who earn moderate wages and who can afford to commute to but not to live in a metro county would choose to live in a nearby non-metro county, increasing housing demand and rent for moderate-income households.

As the share of multifamily housing increases in non-metro areas, it alleviates the cost-burden among low-income households but increases the cost-burden among moderate-income households. Multifamily homes are built to serve more densely-settled, lower-income neighborhoods, especially in non-metro counties. Therefore, a higher proportion of multifamily units increases housing supply options for low-income households but could increase cost-burden among moderate-income households if they are more interested in single-family housing options.

The effects of county characteristics associated with changes in household income were not statistically significant for low-income households. While an increase in employment rate did not affect cost-burden among low-income households in metro and non-metro counties, it decreased the proportion of cost-burdened households among moderate-income households. The effect was greater and more statistically significant in metro counties. Furthermore, increased deep poverty did not affect cost-burden among low-income households and actually lowered it among moderate-income households in both metro and in non-metro counties. When a larger proportion of the county is in deep poverty, the demand for housing suitable for moderate-income households might be lower, resulting in lower rents. However, it is less clear why this would not increase the cost-burden among low-income households.

In summary, housing cost-burden increases with density in line with quality-of-life arguments that find households trading higher housing costs for urban-based amenities. In addition, we did not find a statistically significant effect of employment increase on cost-burden among low-income households. However, there are significant racial, educational and housing-market components related to high housing cost-burden in rural areas, confirming expectations based on spatial mismatch theory. Households in counties with high Black populations appear to be especially challenged by mobility constraints or other factors contributing to high housing cost-burden. Finally, in terms of potential policy implications, the proportion of multifamily housing in rental markets was positively associated with alleviating cost-burden among low-income households.

Conclusion

Finding affordable housing has always been a challenge for low-income families but has become increasingly difficult in the last ten years. Nationwide statistics show an unprecedented reduction in homeownership and a corresponding increase in costs associated with renting, especially for low- and middle-income families and individuals. This study confirms testimony from rural housing experts and reports from advocacy groups that rentership rates and rental cost-burdens are also increasing in rural communities. As in urban areas, rural cost-burden is increasing due to a combination of housing-market turmoil, economic shocks and demographic change in favor of groups with high rentership rates.

Rural areas differ in terms of their housing needs and the resources they possess to address them. Housing costs are lower in rural areas generally, but mostly because higher-income urban households pay higher rents in return for urban amenities. Little rural-urban difference in cost-burden is evident among very low-income households: In both types of areas, over 90 percent of households earning less than $10,000 now pay more than 30 percent of their incomes on rent. The metro-non-metro gap has begun to close as well for households earning between $10,000 and $20,000. However, the increase in rural cost-burden is most evident among moderate-income renters, earning between $20,000 and $50,000. The share of these renters that are cost-burdened almost doubled from 22 to 39 percent between 2005 and 2012.

The geography of rural housing affordability is shifting along with the demographic and economic profiles of cost-burdened households. The large increase in cost-burden among moderate-income households occurred in all states, but was particularly pronounced in three types of rural areas. First, in high-amenity Sunbelt and East Coast locations, where cost-burdens were already higher than average, rapidly developing towns and small cities were particularly hard hit by the housing-market crash. Second, high-poverty areas in the South and Southwest experienced increased unemployment and reduced wages, increasing the cost-burdens for moderate-income households where they had been lower than average. Third, in areas exposed to the oil-and-gas energy boom, rapid in-migration of workers created perhaps temporary housing shortages.

Regression results confirm these regional differences in cost-burden, at least for high-amenity areas and high-poverty areas in the South. Quality-of-life theory is confirmed by findings that show an increased cost-burden associated with high-amenity scenic counties, more urban higher-density counties and counties with higher education levels. However, evidence also exists to support spatial mismatch theory, in particular the persistence of mobility constraints among those living in predominantly Black rural counties.

Taking these findings into account may help increase the effectiveness of federal housing assistance programs, especially programs designed to increase the availability of affordable rental housing. For instance, the different types of rural regions most affected by increasing cost-burden may require different strategies to help expand affordable housing. Federal housing assistance programs rely heavily on public-private partnerships, providing incentives to private investors through tax credits, low-interest mortgage loans and rental subsidies. Such strategies are likely more successful in wealthier and higher-density areas that can attract and support private investment, such as the high-amenity Sunbelt and East Coast locations adjacent to metro areas. Other approaches to building affordable housing may be required in more remote locations, such as the high-poverty areas in the South and Southwest or in states participating in the oil-and-gas energy boom. Policymakers and housing advocates also may consider the rapid increase in cost-burden among working families with incomes between $20,000 and $50,000. Such households may not currently be eligible for rent subsidies due to income thresholds. Ongoing changes in the rural housing market caused by economic and demographic forces, especially the changing balance between owners and renters that is expected to continue, will require intense scrutiny of rural housing policy options in the years to come.

Notes

1 Analysis is limited to 2005–12 in some of our reported findings due to a change in metro-non-metro classification in the ACS.

2 The terms "non-metro" and "rural" are used interchangeably in this chapter. They refer to counties and populations outside of Metropolitan Statistical Areas, which include cities of 50,000 or more and counties connected to these cities through commuting. For further

discussion, see www.ers.usda.gov/topics/rural-economy-population/rural-classifications/what-is-rural.aspx.

3 In the next section, these two income groups are combined to form a single "low-income" category earning less than $20,000.

References

Belsky, E. et al. (2005). *Measuring the Nation's rental housing affordability problems*. Cambridge, MA: Joint Center for Housing Studies Harvard University. Retrieved February 19, 2016 from www.jchs.harvard.edu/sites/jchs.harvard.edu/files/rd05-1_measuring_rental_affordability05.pdf

Bloomquist, G., Berger, M., & Hoehn, J. (1988). New estimates of quality of life in urban areas. *The American Economic Review, 78*, 89–107.

Charette, A. et al. (2015). *Projecting trends in severely cost-burdened renters: 2015–2025*. Columbia, MD: Enterprise Community Partners, Inc. Retrieved February 19, 2016 from https://s3.amazonaws.com/KSPProd/ERC_Upload/0100886.pdf

CoreLogic. (2015). *CoreLogic National foreclosure report*. Irvine, CA: Author.

Foster, T. B., & Kleit, R. G. (2015). The changing relationship between housing and inequality, 1980–2010. *Housing Policy Debate, 25*(1), 16–40, DOI: 10.1080/10511482.2014.933118

Goodman, L. (2015). *The demographics of demand*. Retrieved February 19, 2016 from www.urban.org/sites/default/files/alfresco/publication-pdfs/2000491-The-Demographics-of-Demand.pdf (Reprinted from Mortgage Bankers Association, October 1, 2015).

Goodman, L. et al. (2015). *Headship and homeownership: What does the future hold?* Washington, DC: Urban Institute. Retrieved February 19, 2016 from www.urban.org/sites/default/files/2000257-headship-and-homeownership-what-does-the-future-hold.pdf

Holzer, H. (1991). The spatial mismatch hypothesis: What has the evidence shown? *Urban Studies, 28*(1), 105–122.

Housing Assistance Council. (2012). *Taking stock: Rural people, poverty, and housing in the 21st century*. Retrieved February 19, 2016 from www.ruralhome.org/storage/documents/ts2010/ts_full_report.pdf

Housing Assistance Council. (2013). *Rural research note: Rental housing in rural America*. Retrieved February 19, 2016 from www.ruralhome.org/storage/research_notes/rrn_rural_rental_housing.pdf

Housing Assistance Council. (2014). *Housing an aging rural America: Rural seniors and their homes*. Retrieved February 19, 2016 from www.ruralhome.org/storage/documents/publications/rrreports/ruralseniors2014.pdf

Joint Center for Housing Studies of Harvard University. (2015). *America's rental housing: Expanding options for diverse and growing demand*. Retrieved February 19, 2016 from www.jchs.harvard.edu/sites/jchs.harvard.edu/files/americas_rental_housing_2015_web.pdf

Kain, J. (1992). The spatial mismatch hypothesis: Three decades later. *Housing Policy Debate, 3*(2), 371–460.

Leopold, J. et al. (2015). *The housing affordability gap for extremely low-income renters in 2013*. Washington, DC: Urban Institute. Retrieved February 19, 2016 from www.urban.org/sites/default/files/alfresco/publication-pdfs/2000260-The-Housing-Affordability-Gap-for-Extremely-Low-Income-Renters-2013.pdf

National Rural Housing Coalition. (2014). *Rural America's rental housing crisis: Federal strategies to preserve access to affordable rental housing in rural communities*. Retrieved February 19, 2016 from http://ruralhousingcoalition.org/wp-content/uploads/2014/07/NRHC-Rural-America-Rental-Housing-Crisis_FINALV2.compressed.pdf

Nelson, P., & Cromartie, J. (2014). Subprime lending and its impacts on rural housing markets. *Housing and Society*, *41*(2), 145–176.

Public and Affordable Housing Research Corporation. (2015). *Value of Home: 2015 PAHRC Report*. Retrieved February 19, 2016 from www.pahrc.org/studies/2015PAHRCReport.pdf

Roback, J. (1982). Wages, rents, and the quality of life. *The Journal of Political Economy*, *90*, 1257–1278.

Terwilliger, R. J. (2011). *America's housing policy-the missing piece: Affordable workplace rentals*. Washington, DC: Urban Land Institute.

U.S. Census Bureau. (2015). *ACS summary file technical documentation: 2014 ACS 1-year and 2010–2014 ACS 5-year data releases*. Washington, DC: American Community Survey Office.

U.S. Census Bureau. (2016). *Residential vacancies and homeownership in the fourth quarter 2015*. Retrieved February 19, 2016 from www.census.gov/housing/hvs/files/currenthvspress.pdf

U.S. Department of Agriculture, Economic Research Service. (2015). *Rural America at a glance: 2015 edition*. Retrieved February 19, 2016 from www.ers.usda.gov/media/1952235/eib145.pdf

Ziebarth, A. (2014). Introduction to the special issue: Housing in the countryside. *Housing and Society*, *41*(2), 105–118.

5 Reinvesting in rural America through affordable mortgage finance

Keith Wiley and Lance George

Introduction

Changes in the financial and mortgage lending landscape over the past three decades have impacted rural communities and consumers. Bank and financial institution mergers have occurred at a fast pace, transforming the rural mortgage marketplace. The decreasing numbers of financial institutions potentially limits credit options available to rural borrowers. Bank mergers and consolidations may impact rural communities in other ways as well. Large banks serving places far from their home offices may not be as attached to the communities they serve as smaller, local banks would. As a result, large banks do not fully know their new customer base, and they may make fewer loans and be less involved in the community.

This research investigates rural mortgage finance activity and lending institutions using time series analyses from ten years of Home Mortgage Disclosure Act (HMDA) data and regulatory reporting from the FDIC, the Federal Reserve and the Office the Comptroller of the Currency (OCC). Specific strategies presented from the analyses include expansion and increased inclusion of rural "assessment" areas for financial investment through the Community Reinvestment Act (CRA) and enactment of rural-specific "Duty to Serve" requirements and efforts by Government Sponsored Entities (GSEs – Fannie Mae and Freddie Mac). The ultimate goal of this research is to inform policymakers and practitioners about efforts to enhance the availability of affordable, high-quality mortgage products and avenues – especially to low-income rural borrowers.

Background

Decline in number of banks

Since the 1980s, the number of chartered banks and savings and thrifts, which totaled approximately 18,000 institutions in 1985, declined over 60 percent by 2013 (Figure 5.1). Industry consolidation, along with bank closings and relatively few new charters, reduced lender numbers every year during the last 30 years. The decline is concentrated in small institutions, lenders with assets totaling less than $100 million, whose numbers dropped by 85 percent over the last three decades.[1]

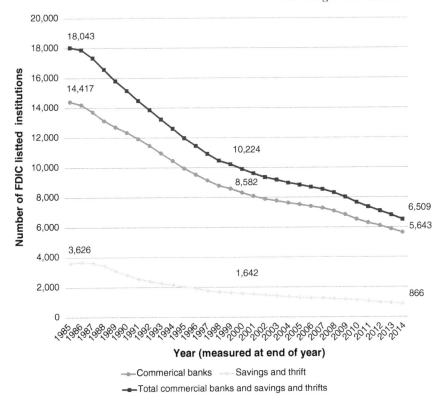

Figure 5.1 Commerical Banks and Savings and Thrifts 1985 to 2014

Source: Author analysis of FDIC historical bank and savings and thrifts data accessed 2/14/16 from FDIC website https://www5.fdic.gov/hsob/SelectRpt.asp?EntryTyp=10&Header=1.

At the same time, assets have become more concentrated among the largest lenders. The five largest banks held just 17 percent of all assets in 1970, but by 2010, that figure had grown to more than half.[2]

Possible impact on rural credit markets

As Figure 5.2 shows, the number of banks and savings and thrifts headquartered in rural areas declined at a similar percentage to those headquartered in suburban/exurban areas and actually at a lower rate than urban-based institutions. Because a majority of lenders are headquartered in rural communities, however, the decline in rural based lenders, in absolute terms, is large and touches many communities.

The reduction in charters often result from bank acquisitions/mergers. In the cases where a larger, multistate bank acquires a small, rural institution, the acquisition can sever the direct corporate connection to the community. These large banks may not fully know their new customer base, and they may make fewer loans and

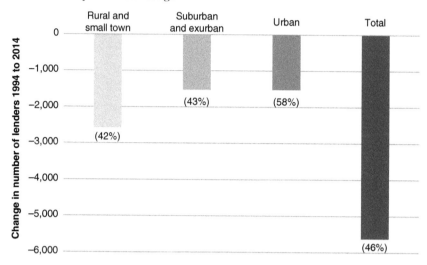

Figure 5.2 Change in Commercial Banks and Savings and Thrifts By Headquarters Location 1994 to 2014★

★Geography based on Housing Assistance Council's rural-suburban-urban classification. Information on this measure: Percentages in parentheses represent within geography change. For example, 42 percent decline in banks and savings and thrifts headquartered in rural and small town geographies.

Source: Author analysis of bank and savings and thrifts. Summary of Deposit data accessed 2/14/16 from FDIC website https://www5.fdic.gov/idasp/advSearch_warp_download_all.asp?intTab=4:.

be less involved in the community. This is in addition to the reduction in credit options and competition in local credit markets which can result from an acquisition or closing of a bank.[3] Research has indicated that rural businesses must now turn to faraway bank officials when seeking funding for their projects because of the loss of local lenders.[4]

Access to credit and economic distress

Access to credit is an important part of any vibrant community. One aspect of credit is the critical role financial services play in creating a stable housing market, which is a major part of most successful communities. As others have noted, access to affordable home financing, and the homeownership it supports, provides families not only with a safe place to live and a source of long-term savings, but also confers benefits to the community as a whole due to economic growth (construction jobs, real estate and financial services etc.) and stability.[5]

Limited access to affordable credit largely reflects the economic distress that is a common condition for many rural and small town areas. For example, the American Community Survey estimates an 18.2 percent poverty rate for counties located outside of a metropolitan area (often used as proxy for rural) – three percentage points higher than the metropolitan area. Similarly, the outside metropolitan median household income is 23 percent less than the metropolitan area median.

Eighty-five percent of counties experiencing persistent poverty – 20 percent or higher poverty rates for four decades – are located outside of metropolitan areas, and these counties represent 15 percent of all outside metropolitan counties.[6] The outside metropolitan area population estimates, for the first time ever, declined for the last four years while the rest of the nation's population grew.[7] An estimated six in ten outside metropolitan area counties lost population during the 2010 to 2013 period.[8]

Economic and credit access problems are most acute in high need rural areas, such as Central Appalachia, the Border Colonias, the Lower Mississippi Delta region and Native American Lands and among rural minorities. Research has found elevated denial and high-cost mortgage lending in these regions and among rural minorities in particular.[9] For example, nationally, 5 percent of all HMDA mortgage originations were classified high-cost[10] in 2009 compared to 22 percent for rural African-Americans living in the Lower Mississippi Delta region.[11]

Review

Rural banking

The academic literature exploring rural banking primarily addresses the impact of industry and demographic changes on lender competitiveness/viability. Walser and Anderlik's 2004 research, exploring depopulation and community banks, provides an example.[12] The authors focus on the Great Plains, a region generally experiencing depopulation, and analyze the demographic and economic conditions of depopulating, rural counties, along with the community banks serving them. The study indicated that bank profitability was not related to service area depopulation, and that banks located in depopulating areas did not experience elevated rates of decline when compared to metropolitan area and population growing counties.

Keeton's 1998 study of rural banking in Midwest explores sluggish growth in rural deposits and lender actions.[13] The author finds that slow deposit growth is an issue which does create funding pressure on banks – something that Walser and Anderlik noted in their study – but that this is a problem for small banks in general, not just rural-headquartered institutions.[14] More recent research has found that the decline in depository institutions over the last several decades is almost universally related to small-asset banks.[15] Since most small-asset banks are located in rural areas, this might explain why the decline in associated with geography.[16]

Several other papers explore more closely how access to credit might be altered as a result of industry consolidation. Gilbert's 1997 paper, exploring the possible impact of allowing nationwide bank branching on rural lending, reviews the academic literature to see if a consensus exists on the impact of increased involvement of large, multistate lenders in rural credit markets. The research generally supports the idea that the laws expanding access increases the presence of multistate banks in rural counties, possibly leading to a dominant role in for such lenders in rural credit markets. Research used variations in state laws to analyze the impact, and the findings generally match the overall trend in banking of a decline in small lenders and an increase in large banks discussed earlier.[17]

While Gilbert found that most research suggested an expansion of multistate lenders in rural counties would result in less lending, particularly small business lending, findings were not in agreement and data sources limited. The author concludes that the risk to small, rural-based lenders is significant and the role they play important enough that policymakers should consider limiting regulatory burdens on them to ensure they are able to perform their role. Walser and Anderlik, in their 2004 study of rural depopulation and banking, also note that easing regulations may help small-asset rural lenders.[18]

Tolbert et al.'s 2014 paper evaluates the degree to which industry consolidation and the loss of locally owned small banks limits small business access to credit in rural communities. Rural small business owners previously relied on local loan officers and relation lending to obtain credit. Relational lending involves local loan officers, who live in a community and have extensive information about the residents, taking into account non-quantitative borrower characteristics, such as standing in community and reputation, in deciding credit access. The relationship between the borrower and local bank is the key factor.[19]

The authors find that during the 1976 to 2007 study period the consolidation in banking has diminished the number of locally controlled lenders, particularly in rural counties. These non-local lenders rely more on standardized approaches that don't consider relational aspects. In addition, these larger banks often avoid small business loans as a way of ameliorating risk.

Interviews with rural, Texas small business owners supplement the research and highlight the difficulties that now exist with obtaining credit for small business activities. The business owners point to a reliance on standardized practices in deciding credit access and a desire on the part of large lenders to avoid risky, small business loans. Lending to larger big box stores or to people with stellar credit histories is preferred. A reduction in credit accessibility for small business in turn greatly impacts rural communities where such businesses play a large role in stimulating growth and community development.

Although research usually finds that rural banks remain profitable, even in depopulating areas, risks, as noted in the Tolbert 2014 study, are significant. As bank service area residents and economic activity decline, which is inevitable in areas experiencing chronic depopulation, banks have an increased reliance on the remaining elderly population. This means "as many elderly customers also carry large deposit balances, their passing may result in a major loss of funding that may be difficult for many small banks to withstand" (pg. 80). How the industry and policymakers respond to such challenges will be important to ensure access to affordable credit continues.

Rural home mortgage activity

Most discussion of rural credit markets derive from regulatory agencies and focuses on efforts to expand access. For example, the Consumer Finance Protection Bureau recently eased rules increasing the number of financial institutions able to offer certain mortgages in rural and underserved areas. The concern is that new rules designed to protect consumers might limit lending activity by small rural based institutions.[20] Given the many discussions and policies that impact lending in rural communities, one would expect to find a considerable amount of research and analysis on rural lending activity.

There is a dearth of academic research specifically exploring rural mortgage lending and credit markets. At least part of the reason for the limited amount of research is the lack of high quality data on rural lending activity. For example, the HMDA, which is the premier public source of mortgage lending, does not include data from small-asset lenders and lenders operating entirely outside of metropolitan areas.[21] While the degree to which these exemptions restrict rural coverage is unknown – some believe they represent a significant limitation,[22] and others suggest a smaller impact[23] – the fact that specific data exclusions exist raises concerns. Information regarding rural loan delinquencies and foreclosures is even more questionable with more than a quarter of all counties sparsely populated, rural jurisdictions, not included in widely used data sources.[24]

Despite the data limitations, some analysis of rural mortgage lending exists. This analysis, usually confined to a single year, consistently finds an increased prevalence of denials and high cost lending for rural applicants.[25] For example, 15 percent of all rural HMDA originations were high cost compared to 11 and 12 percent for suburban and urban borrowers respectively.[26] Studies have also pointed to the elevated high cost lending rates associated with manufactured home loans which are disproportionately originated to rural borrowers. A 1998 Carsey Institute paper found that 17 percent of all rural HMDA originations were high cost in 2004 compare to 51 percent for rural manufactured home loans. This report also highlighted the prevalence of high cost lending in Central Appalachia, Lower Mississippi Delta, Border Colonias and Native American Lands.[27] Other reports have noted that rural African American's in the Lower Mississippi Delta had a high cost lending rate of 22 percent compared to 5 percent for the nation using HMDA 2009 data.[28]

Even with the exclusions, the HMDA data presented in these reports suggest that among reporting institutions, which includes all major lenders, rural loan applications were more often denied, and if originated, the loans were more often high cost. Further exploration is needed.

Approach

Questions for consideration

As noted in the literature review, research on rural lending and on policies designed to ensure access to credit and rural communities is limited. Most focus is on larger urban and suburban markets. For example, since the Great Recession and the mortgage foreclosure crisis (2007–2009), which generated considerable academic focus in the literature, particularly on hard-hit areas such as Las Vegas, there has been little written about how rural housing markets fared during economic turmoil and now recovery. A better understanding of rural markets and how policies work in such areas could help policymakers better tailor policies to effectively help areas of trouble. This chapter hopes to begin that work.

This chapter has two parts. The first part discusses rural mortgage lending to provide a better understanding of rural credit markets. The following questions will guide this analysis:

1   What have been the trends in rural mortgage lending over the last ten years, and how does rural activity compare to suburban and urban lending?
2   What, if any, are the problem areas (high-cost loans, denials etc.), and has this been the case over the study period?

The second section investigates federal mortgage policies, specifically the CRA and the degree to which they serve rural communities and how their lending activity related to their lender-defined assessment areas for which they are evaluated on. The following research questions will guide this analysis:

3   To what degree do CRA-regulated lenders serve rural communities, and how much of this activity involves small-asset, rural-headquartered lenders?
4   To what degree do CRA assessment areas include rural communities, and do these assessment areas accurately reflect rural lending activity?

This study provides a descriptive analysis of both rural mortgage lending and CRA regulated lender actions in rural areas. For the review of rural mortgage lending, the analysis looks at HMDA reported activity occurring over the 2005 to 2014 period. Loan applications are labeled as rural, suburban and exurban, or urban, depending on the geography of the applicant. The analysis explores trends in lending patterns concentrating on loan type, purpose and actions taken. Comparisons of rural to both suburban and exurban and urban activity are made to identify rural specific trends.

The mortgage lending analysis explores more closely loan denials and high-cost lending. The focus is on differences by property type (single family versus manu- factured home) and borrower race and ethnicity. Comparisons highlight where rural activity differs from suburban and exurban and urban lending. The analysis, once again, looked at the trends over the ten-year period. Geographic areas of concentrated high denial and high-cost lending rates are identified. The underlying economic and demographic characteristics of these communities will be described.

The second part of the research considers CRA-regulated institutions and their involvement in rural areas. The analysis describes CRA-regulated institutions both by asset size and main office headquarters geography. The main focus is on rural- headquartered lenders and their characteristics. The analysis includes an estimate of CRA regulated lender activity by geography (rural, suburban and exurban, and urban) over the study period.

This analysis includes an estimate of CRA assessment areas and the degree to which they include rural areas and encompass rural mortgage lending activity. Lender assessment areas include all counties containing a deposit-taking branch office. This approach is similar to the one used by the Federal Reserve in their annual report on HMDA data.[29] For those lenders reporting HMDA mortgage loan data, rural lending activity is described as to its inclusion in the assessment area. The analysis explores lender assessment areas as they existed for the 2012 to 2014 period and only considered rural activity.

As noted, HMDA data has limitations, particularly when it comes to rural data. HMDA exemptions exclude from filing small-asset institutions (less than $44 million in total assets) and lenders operating entirely outside of metropolitan areas. While these exemptions certainly mean some rural lending activity is missing, the HMDA data includes large-asset and high volume lenders who originate a majority of home loans. For the HMDA filing lenders, the coverage is comprehensive in that it does not exclude or provide less thorough rural information. The geographic information provided is specific enough to allow for relatively precise classification (go beyond a less precise county-level analysis to the tract level). So while the data are less than perfect and may understate small lender activity, they do provide important information that should improve our understanding of rural markets.

Data[30]

The study uses publicly available data from both the Federal Financial Institutions Examination Council (FFIEC) and Federal Deposit Insurance Corporation (FDIC). The FFIEC provides the HMDA, which is the source for all mortgage lending information. HMDA data include information on borrower location, down to the census tract level, allowing for relatively precise geographic identification of activity as rural, suburban and exurban and urban. Records without a state, county and census tract FIPs codes and Puerto Rico records were excluded from research.[31]

The FDIC, based on Summary of Deposits and Call Reports, provides bank office/branch location and lender background characteristics information. This research used the FDIC data to estimate CRA assessment areas and to classify lenders. Lender geographic classifications, as rural, suburban and exurban, or urban, are based on the main office location. This analysis links the FDIC provided lender information to HMDA mortgage data to explore lending patterns.

The ACS 2010–14 five-year estimate data provides population estimates. The analysis uses the USDA, ERS persistent poverty classification to identify chronically poor areas.[32]

Home lending in rural America

What is the current state of rural credit availability and markets? Before policymakers can tailor policies to better serve communities, they need to fully understand where the problems may exist. A review of mortgage lending data helps provide this insight.

Rural mortgage accessibility and affordability

Rural mortgage originations (home purchase, refinance and home improvement), over the 2005 to 2014 period, have consistently represented between 14 and

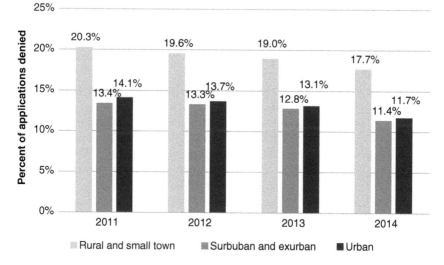

Figure 5.3 HMDA Home Purchase Applications Denied 2011 to 2014

16 percent of all U.S. mortgage activity annually, which is several percentage points below the rural share of the population (approximately 20 percent). Restricting the analysis to only first lien, home purchase originations, the rural percentages are similar. While the data suggest a slightly under-representative amount of lending in rural areas, it is important to remember HMDA filing exemptions and unreported loans might account for some of the difference.

Related to these low levels of lending, rural loan applicants experience high denial rates. For example, as shown in Figure 5.3, lenders denied 18 percent of rural, home purchase applications in 2014 compared to 11 and 12 percent for suburban and urban applications, respectively.[33] This large difference is not just a one-time event. Denial rates for rural home purchase loans have exceeded suburban and urban rates by five percentage points or more for every year since 2011.

In addition to the elevated denials rates, rural applicants who were able to successfully navigate the mortgage lending process more often receive a so-called "high-cost" loan. Since 2007 and the onset of the Great Recession, the percent of rural originations classified as high cost has always exceeded suburban and urban levels. For example, 15 percent of rural home purchase loans were high cost compared to 11 and 12 percent for suburban and exurban borrowers in 2014.[34]

The high cost of manufactured home loans

A major reason for the elevated rural denial and high cost lending rates is the high prevalence of loans involving manufactured homes. While manufactured home originations make up a small proportion of lending activity in all geographies, they are considerably more common in rural areas, making up 5 percent of all originations over the 2010 to 2014 period compared to one percent for suburban originations. Approximately half of home purchase loans involving a manufactured home were high cost in 2014, a percentage that was consistent over the previous five years and is seven times the percent for loans involving one to four family units (7 percent).

It is not that a higher percentage of rural borrowers purchasing a manufactured home obtain a high cost loan, but rather, that such a high proportion of rural borrowers are involved in these loans. Rural borrowers originated over half of all manufactured home loans for each year during the 2005 to 2014 period.

Taking into account loans involving manufactured homes, a higher percentage of rural loans were classified as high cost. The percentage of rural originations involving one to four family dwellings that were high cost was consistently 1 to 2 percentage points above the suburban and urban percentages.

Rural minorities

Among the populations most affected by both the relatively high percentage of denial and high cost loans are rural minorities. Rural African-Americans in particular consistently experienced the highest denial rates, when looking at lending activity by race/ethnicity group and geography, over the 2005 to 2014 period. In 2014, lenders denied 35 percent of rural African-American applications involving a first lien, home purchase loan, and, of those who received loans, 30 percent were high cost, both percentages that were twice as high as those for rural, White non-Hispanic applicants (Figure 5.4).

Rural high cost lending rates, for almost all races and ethnicities over the last ten years, also exceed suburban and urban rates. Since 2012, the proportion of loans classified as high cost, across all racial and ethnicity categories and geographies, increased substantially as mortgage lending markets have stabilized.

CRA and rural finance

The Community Reinvestment Act

Access to affordable, quality housing along with the credit necessary to finance and maintain it are an important part of any community's economic viability and success. Recognizing this need, Congress established policies to ensure lenders serve all parts of their service area, particularly those areas which are often distressed and underserved. This legislation recognizes an obligation for lenders that essentially says, in exchange for a charter allowing them to take part in the government-supported banking system (FDIC insurance etc.), lenders must fulfill, in a safe and sound manner, the credit needs of their entire service area.[35] The CRA shoulders a large part of these efforts.[36]

The CRA, enacted in 1977, requires all federally insured depository institutions provide access to credit to all areas where the institution takes in deposits and/or does significant banking activity. The CRA charges federal bank regulators[37] with

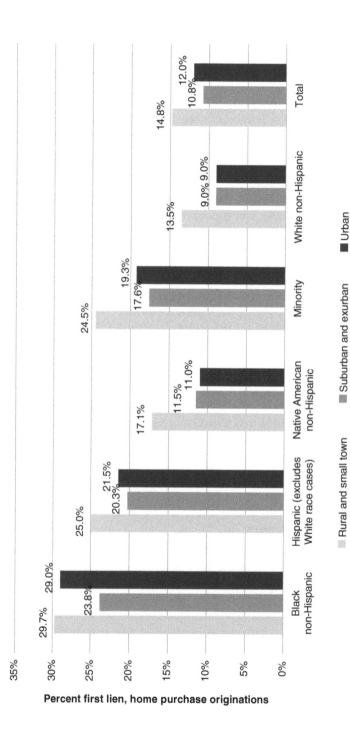

Figure 5.4 HMDA 2014 High-Cost Home Purchase Originations by Select Race/Ethnicity

periodically (two to five years) evaluating lenders on the degree to which they are fulfilling these requirements. CRA examinations vary largely based on lender asset size, with the largest-asset lenders having the most extensive requirements.[38]

CRA examinations explore, to varying degrees, retail lending, service availability and community investment efforts. Close attention is paid to activity, or the lack there of, in low- and moderate-income, economically distressed and underserved portions of a lender's service or, as it is officially known, "assessment" area. CRA exams, which involve an on-site visit by regulators and an extensive review of records and data, can take considerable time, several months, to complete.[39] All examinations are made public weeks before they begin and the public encouraged to comment and provide information.

At the end of the CRA examination, the regulator awards the lender one of four ratings: Outstanding; Satisfactory; Needs to Improve; and Substantial Non-Compliance. Regulators can use earning one of the latter two ratings as a reason for denying a bank application for such things as opening a new branch or merging with another institution. After each examination, a full report is released which includes the rating and a description of how it was derived.

Challenges exist for policymakers when it comes to rural areas, though, and this chapter specifically explores the degree to which assessment areas both include rural communities and reflect rural lending patterns.

Review

Most CRA studies, particularly of late, focus on the degree to which CRA regulations promote risky lending and contributed to the Great Recession.[40] Likely related to the policy's creation in 1977 as a response to disinvestment in primarily urban neighborhoods, these CRA studies usually focus on metropolitan areas and urban/suburban communities. Research specifically exploring the CRA in rural communities is rare; however, a few papers provide insight.

HAC's 2015 report, entitled, "The Community Reinvestment Act and Mortgage Lending in Rural Communities," is the only paper to specifically analyze CRA regulated lender activity in rural communities.[41] The study finds that the CRA regulated lenders play a non-trivial role in many rural credit markets. Lenders headquartered in rural and small town communities actually represent a majority of lenders regulated by the CRA, and lenders subject to CRA regulations originated a majority of rural home loans in 2012. While most CRA regulated lenders are rural, small-asset institutions, large-asset lenders originated a majority of home loans in rural, suburban and urban geographies. The analysis uses main office locations to classify lenders as rural, suburban or urban.

The Federal Reserve, in their annual review of the soon to be released HMDA data, includes a brief evaluation of CRA regulated lender activity. The review specifically explores the volume of CRA lending and the degree to which this activity occurs in assessment areas. While these reviews do not specifically discuss rural communities, the author's method of estimating lender CRA assessments area is helpful. The authors define lender assessment areas as consisting of counties where a lender operates a deposit-taking bank branch. Once assessment areas are defined, the research evaluates the degree to which these areas capture lending activity. The 2014 review found that small-asset lenders originated over 40 percent of their loans outside of their CRA assessment areas.[42]

A 2005 Federal Reserve study explored two proposed changes to the CRA focusing on their possible impact on outside metropolitan areas.[43] The study first evaluated the then proposed (and now implemented) reductions to CRA examination requirements for moderate asset size lenders. The authors estimated that many mid-sized lenders would be subjected to the less frequent and less demanding intermediate, small-bank CRA exam instead of the large-bank exam. The analysis found that the change would impact a disproportionate number of rural-headquartered lenders.

The second part of the analysis explored the possible effect of expanding what constituted a credited community development project to include projects in an economically distressed or underserved census tracts located outside of a metropolitan area. The proposal sought to encourage more community development activity outside of metropolitan areas by changing the CRA low- or moderate-income ("CRA-eligible") census tract classification to include outside metropolitan areas experiencing high poverty, high unemployment and population loss. Previously, only community development occurring in low- and moderate-income census tracts qualified for CRA credit. The Federal Reserve analysis predicted this change was unlikely to alter lender behavior, but that it would expand outside of metropolitan area CRA-eligible tracts.

Policy discussion of the CRA and rural banking often focus on efforts to increase lender CRA-related activity in rural communities. As Thomas Curry, Comptroller of the Currency, noted when describing comments to a proposed rule change:

> some observers noted that banks tended to take the safe route and concentrate their community development activities where CRA consideration would be assured. In many cases that will leave CRA activities concentrated in metropolitan areas where banks' assessment areas are located, creating or perpetuating an imbalance in community development activities between metropolitan and rural non-metropolitan areas.[44]
>
> (p. 3)

The policy challenge is to overcome these problems and expand lending to rural areas while at the same time ensuring that the expanded credit is affordable and safe. Particularly for economically distressed and isolated rural areas, increased access to credit is an important step towards establishing a vibrant community. A first step in this process is to better understand both rural credit conditions and policies such as the CRA.

CRA lending activity

The CRA provides oversight to a large segment of rural mortgage lending. CRA-regulated lenders, throughout the 2005 to 2014 period, consistently originated a higher percentage of mortgage loans in rural and small town areas compared to suburban and urban communities. In 2014, for example, CRA regulated lenders originated 57 percent of all HMDA reported, first lien, home purchase loans to rural and small town borrowers compared to 46 percent for suburban/urban areas. CRA regulated lenders, in 2014, originated a majority of home purchase loans in approximately 72 percent of rural counties, a testament to the CRA's broad reach in rural areas.[45] Even with the relatively large role depository institutions play in rural mortgage lending, local credit markets vary. Credit unions or independent mortgage companies originated a majority of home purchase loans in 300 rural counties.

As highlighted in Figure 5.5, over the last seven years, the role of CRA regulated lenders in mortgage lending has declined. CRA regulated lenders originated almost 80 percent of rural first lien home purchase loans in 2007, but by 2014, the proportion declined to less than 60 percent. The decline was even greater for the nation as a whole, where CRA-regulated institutions no longer originated a majority of first lien, home purchase loans in 2014. Bhutta, et al. note, in their 2015 *Federal Reserve Bulletin* article exploring the 2014 HMDA lending data, that non-CRA regulated lenders "now account for a historically large share of mortgage lending."[46] The role of non-depository lenders in mortgage lending fluctuates though with non CRA-regulated lenders engaging in a large share of mortgage originations in the late 1990s.[47] As the role of non-depository institution grows, CRA's ability to provide credit market oversight declines. In such cases, the GSE duty serve would shoulder

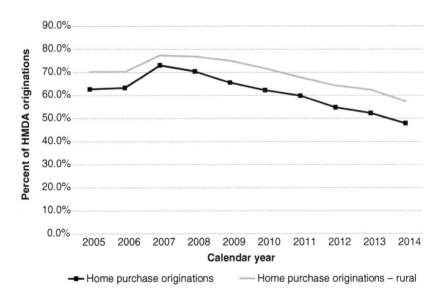

Figure 5.5 CRA-Covered Lender Activity as a Percent of all Mortgage Lending Activity 2005–2014★

★All commerical banks and savings and thrifts make up CRA-covered lenders. The data also include their affiliates. The HMDA mortgage data include all originations for which loan location data was provided (state, county and census tract fips). The data includes only first lien, home purchase loans.

the primary responsibility of ensuring credit access to often overlooked or under-served areas.

Large- and small-asset lenders

Large-asset institutions, identified in this report as those with assets exceeding the CRA large bank exam threshold, originated, for each study year, a majority of all CRA-regulated lender, home purchase originations for both rural areas and the nation as a whole. On average, during the 2005 to 2014 period, large-asset lenders represented just 14 percent of CRA-regulated lenders making loans to rural borrowers; however, these lenders accounted for 60 percent or more of all CRA-regulated institution home purchase lending.

The role of large-asset lenders in CRA lending declined over the study period; however, dropping 10 percentage points from 2007 to 2014 for the nation as a whole and almost 15 percentage points for rural and small town areas specifically. This decline coincides with the overall drop off in proportion of mortgage lending activity attributable to CRA-regulated lenders. Other research has also noted this decline in all lending among large-asset institutions.[48] At least in part due to this drop off, large-asset CRA-regulated lenders accounted for 50 percent or more of all HMDA reported loans in just 18 percent of rural counties in 2014.[49]

There was also variation in lender activity by geography related to asset size. Large-asset lenders consistently originated about 10 percentage points more CRA home purchase loans in suburban/urban areas than rural areas. The exact opposite occurred for small-asset lenders and rural activity suggesting that, although they account for a small portion of the home purchase activity – less than 16 percent of rural CRA lending in 2014, small-assets lenders play a larger role in rural credit markets in comparison to urban/suburban areas. This is to be expected, given that a majority of lenders headquartered in rural communities are small-asset.[50,51]

CRA assessment areas

One of the most important, if not the most important, elements of the CRA is the lender-identified service or, as it is known, "assessment" area. CRA examiners evaluate lenders *only* on their activities, or lack thereof, in these assessment areas. CRA regulations requires lender assessment areas to include:

> geographies where the institution has its main office, branches, and deposit-taking ATMs, as well as the surrounding geographies in which the institution originated or purchased a substantial portion of its loans.[52]

(p. 3)

Assessment areas consist of relatively large geographies, such as metropolitan statistical areas, towns and counties. Lenders refine these larger areas, using the smaller census tract geography, to more accurately reflect their service areas. In the process, refined assessment areas must be contiguous, and they cannot exclude low- to moderate-income geographies.[53]

Rural assessment area coverage

Using the presence of an office in a county to define assessment areas, a majority of lenders – an estimated 85 percent – include some rural population in their assessment areas (Figure 5.6). Approximately 40 percent of lenders have a majority rural population assessment area. This represents approximately 2,600 banks and thrifts. These are overwhelmingly small-asset lenders. For example, institutions with an estimated majority rural assessment area population held just 3 percent of all assets reported by FDIC-insured institutions. The largest-asset lenders commonly included some rural population in their assessment areas, but these populations were relatively small, less than 25 percent.

An estimated 72 percent of rural- and small-town-headquartered institutions identified majority rural population assessment areas.[54] Most of these lenders, about 88 percent in 2014, were small-asset institutions, as defined by the CRA small bank examination threshold, and a majority operated in only one county. A similar type of lender makes up the majority of institutions with no rural assessment area population; small-asset institutions that often operate in only one county, but this time, it is urban or suburban areas.

Larger-asset lenders, on the other hand, serve more communities and encompass more geographically diverse populations. These large-asset lenders are primarily (86 percent in 2014) urban and suburban headquartered. While more than 85 percent of these lenders consistently have rural assessment area populations, rural residents represent less than 25 percent of the total assessment area population for approximately 90 percent of large-asset lenders. The relative small proportion of rural assessment area population may mean limited funding efforts

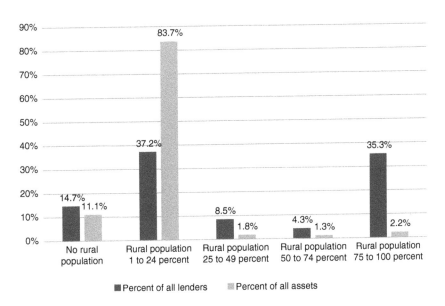

Figure 5.6 CRA-Regulated Lenders 2010–12 Estimated

for rural projects when compared to the more numerous suburban and urban opportunities.

Regulators scrutinize large-asset lenders more thoroughly and regularly, as seen by the differences between small bank and large bank CRA examination requirements. The large bank examination, which occurs every one or two years compared to every three to five years for the small bank examination, reviews not only the retail lending activity-only test for small bank examination, but also service availability and provision and community investment activity. Small bank lenders are not required to make community investments, so one would not expect them to engage in as many of those activities.

Assessment area lending

In aggregate, assessment areas, as defined by lender office locations, are estimated to contain 66 percent of all lender originations and 60 percent of rural activity. For a comparison, an estimated 67 percent of suburban/urban originations occurred in lender assessment areas. Large-asset lenders, on average during the 2012 to 2014 period, originated approximately 59 percent of all CRA covered rural loans, with about three-quarters of them coming from suburban/urban headquartered institutions. Reviewing individual lender activity is the best approach for evaluating CRA assessment area lending, since a few large lenders can shape aggregate numbers.

Eighty-three percent of all lenders are estimated to have originated a majority of their loans in their assessment area, with an estimated 60 percent originating 75 percent or more in their assessment area. Percentages for rural loans are considerably lower with 58 percent of lenders originating a majority of rural loans in their assessment area and only 41 percent of lenders with 75 percent or more in their assessment area. The low rural assessment area coverage rates do not vary based on lender size as is the case when looking at all geographies together, where large lenders are more likely than small lenders to include loans in their assessment area.

Rural-headquartered lenders originate a much higher percentage of their rural loans in their assessment area. Specifically, an estimated 74 percent of rural-headquartered lenders in 2014 originated three-quarters or more of their rural loans in their assessment area, but only 25 percent of suburban-urban headquartered lenders reached that threshold. These big differences hold regardless of the lender asset size and for all three study years.

This may at first seem in error, given that rural lenders make up over 60 percent of all FDIC-insured small-asset lenders. This is the case, however, because many of the small-asset rural banks do not report HMDA loans. The analysis includes, on average, 4,000 to 4,200 each year out of a 6,700 to 7,200 FDIC-insured institutions. Rural small-asset lenders represent approximately 45 percent of all small-asset lenders originating and reporting an HMDA rural loan.

An estimated 25 percent of lenders that originated loans to rural borrowers did not have a rural assessment area population. While the majority of these cases involved lenders who originated an extremely small number of rural loans, about 5 percent of these institutions, or roughly 60 lenders, who lacked a rural assessment originated 50 or more rural loans. Such cases suggest that assessment areas might, at times, be off considerably.

CRA distressed and underserved census tracts

What are they?

To ensure lenders fulfill their CRA obligation to make credit accessible to all portions of their service area, regulators specifically look for and highly rate safe and sound lender activity occurring in low- and moderate-income, economically distressed or underserved assessment area census tracts. These CRA-eligible census tracts represent areas that might otherwise receive less than adequate access to credit.[55] Providing services to these communities then exemplifies fulfilling the CRA obligations.

CRA-eligible areas initially consisted of only low- and moderate-income census tracts. These census tracts have a median family income which is less than 80 percent of the area median family income. In an effort to encourage activity in economically struggling rural areas,[56] regulators added the, outside OMB defined, metropolitan areas, distressed and underserved census tract categories in 2005.[57] Economic distress reflects having one of the following: an unemployment rate 1.5 times the national rate, a poverty rate of 20 percent or more, or a population loss of at least 5 percent during the 2005 to 2010 period, or 10 percent during the 2000 to 2010 period. Underserved census tracts are "low density" areas identified using the USDA, ERS Urban Influence Codes.[58] The Federal Financial Institution Examination Council (FFIEC) updates the list of census tracts annually.

Where are they located?

Approximately 43 percent of all rural census tracts, representing 41 percent of the rural population, were CRA-eligible annually during the 2012 to 2014 period. Figure 5.7 highlights these CRA-eligible census tracts in 2014. This is similar to urban census tract and population coverage and about twice as much as suburban coverage.[59] Over half of the rural CRA-eligible census tracts were distressed and underserved classifications. Without the 2005 expansion, a relatively small percentage of rural census tracts would have qualified. Every state, with the exception of Rhode Island, had at least one rural CRA-eligible tract with areas of concentration in high poverty areas like Central Appalachia, the Lower Mississippi Delta and the Border Colonias region. This coverage includes 88 percent of the population living in rural persistent-poverty counties. CRA-eligible census tracts then include many of the at-risk and in-need-of-credit-access rural areas and populations.

Inclusion in assessment areas

Approximately 42 percent of all lenders were estimated to have a rural CRA-eligible census tract in their assessment area, which is higher than the 33 percent for suburban/exurban CRA-eligible census tract. This largely reflects the fact that

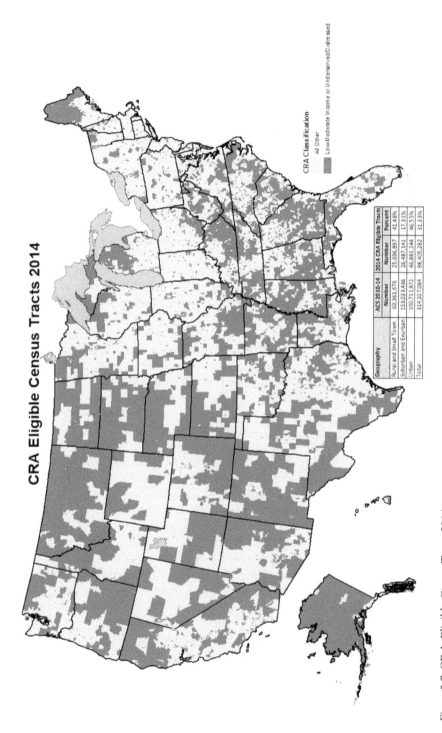

CRA Eligible Census Tracts 2014

Geography	ACS 2010-14 Number	2014 CRA Eligible Tracts Number	Percent
Rural and Small Town	60,361,676	25,036,897	41.48%
Suburban and Exurban	153,033,436	26,487,141	17.31%
Urban	100,711,972	46,881,244	46.55%
Total	314,107,084	98,405,282	31.33%

CRA Classification
  All Other
  Low-Moderate Income or Underserved/Distressed

Figure 5.7 CRA-Eligible Census Tracts 2014

rural-headquartered lenders, which represent an estimated 82 percent of the lenders with a rural CRA-eligible census tract, make up a majority of all depository institutions. In addition to being rural-headquartered, 60 percent of lenders with a rural CRA-eligible tract were small-asset institutions.

Rural CRA-eligible populations were relatively small, representing less than 25 percent of assessment area populations, for three-quarters of lenders. This was particular the case for intermediate and large-asset banks, where the rural CRA-eligible portion of the overall assessment area population was estimated to be less than 10 percent for 86 percent of the institutions. These lenders usually serve multiple counties and states, operating primarily in suburban and urban markets.

There were a few lenders with a majority rural CRA-eligible assessment area. Approximately 250 to 260, or about 4 percent of all depository institutions annually, had an estimated majority assessment population living in rural CRA-eligible census tracts. These majority rural CRA-eligible assessment area lenders were small-asset, rural-headquartered institutions serving a single county.

Mortgage lending in CRA-eligible areas

Approximately two-thirds of lenders reporting HMDA loans (home purchase, refinance or home improvement) in 2014 originated a loan in a rural CRA-eligible census tract. Lending to these areas was relatively widespread; however, the activity made up a small percentage of most lender's total originations. For over half (58 percent) the lenders making at least one loan in a rural CRA-eligible census tract, these loans constituted less than 10 percent of all lending activity. This compares to 80 percent of all lenders originating more than 10 percent of their mortgage loans in suburban and urban CRA-eligible census tracts.[60] While almost half of the lenders reporting a mortgage loan to a rural CRA-eligible census tract where small-asset institutions; large-asset banks, who made up just 14 percent of lenders originating rural CRA-eligible loans, were responsible for 58 percent of all such originations.

While a majority (63 percent) of all rural loans occurring in low- or moderate-income, distressed or undeserved areas were located in an estimated lender assessment area, there is great variability among lenders. Approximately 40 percent of lenders with loans in rural CRA-eligible census tracts originated 75 percent or more of them inside their assessment area. These lenders accounted for 44 percent of all loans occurring in a rural CRA-eligible census tract and 70 percent of such loans occurring in a lender's assessment area. A majority of these lenders were intermediate, small and large-asset banks (52 percent) who were responsible for 80% of the loans. Overall, 55 percent of lenders reporting loans in a CRA-eligible census tract made a majority of them in an estimated assessment area census tract. These loans would be subject to regulatory scrutiny.

At the other extreme, approximately 36 percent of lenders originating rural CRA-eligible loans originated all of them to borrowers located outside of their estimated assessment area. These, lenders were primarily small-asset-55 percent, headquartered in a suburban or urban area-83 percent. Almost all them (96 percent) did not have any rural CRA-eligible census tracts in their assessment area. While on average these lenders were involved in few rural CRA-eligible loans annually, an average of 15 per lender, in total they originated about 9 percent of all loans going to a rural CRA-eligible census tract. These loans and similar activity would not be subject to regulatory scrutiny.

A "Duty to Serve" rural communities

The 2008 Housing and Economic Recovery Act established a duty for the Federal National Mortgage Association (Fannie Mae) and the Federal Home Loan Mortgage Corporation (Freddie Mac) (collectively, Enterprises) to serve underserved markets. Specifically, the Enterprises are tasked to address three specific underserved markets – manufactured housing, affordable housing preservation and rural housing – in order to increase the liquidity of mortgage investments and improve the distribution of investment capital available for mortgage financing in those markets.

The Duty to Serve mandate was enacted roughly eight years ago, but it has yet to be implemented due largely to the Enterprises' status of conservatorship by their regulator the Federal Housing Finance Agency (FHFA). While the enterprises are still in conservatorship, they have largely returned to profitability, and FHFA has reissued a proposed rule for open for comment on the Enterprises' role in serving underserved markets. In the rural-specific components of the plan, the Enterprises are to be rated on the level of their activity related to the purchase of loans from low- and moderate-income borrowers in specified "rural areas." Additionally, under the rural Duty to Serve, the Enterprises will also be evaluated on their activities in traditionally high-need rural regions and populations such as "Middle" Appalachia, the Lower Mississippi Delta, Border Colonias communities, Native American Lands and Migrant and seasonal farmworkers.

The Duty to Serve regulation has yet to be fully implemented, and its future is uncertain, but the federal mandate for Fannie Mae and Freddie Mac (two of the largest players in the mortgage markets) to specifically address rural communities is important. While all three of the identified underserved markets in the "Duty to Serve" mandate are prevalent in rural areas, the specific mandate for the Enterprises to serve rural markets is potentially impactful.

Discussion

The United States is emerging from one of the most extensive and painful economic crises in memory. It is well established that housing markets are at the heart of this crisis, and millions of American households continue to have difficulties meeting their mortgage payments or rents. Changes in the financial and mortgage lending landscape over the last two decades have also impacted rural communities. Bank and financial institution mergers continue a long trend and the impacts of bank consolidations are also evident in home mortgage activity within rural communities. While problems from the recent housing crisis are not to be overlooked, far too many rural residents have struggled with access to decent mortgage credit and inadequacies for years, if not decades, before the national housing crisis hit.

Despite prevailing assumptions, CRA does play a role in rural and small town lending markets. CRA enforcement suffers from limited coverage, a less than critical assessment, and an outdated service area identification process. In addition, many mortgage lenders – such as credit unions, mortgage brokers, and manufactured home lenders – are excluded from CRA oversight, although they originated roughly one-third of all mortgages and at other times, reported a majority of all home loans. These gaps are particularly problematic in rural and small town communities, where a single lender might be the only source of credit, and a failure to evaluate that lender is a failure to evaluate the entire market. There should be some way to ensure that all credit markets, even the most remote and sparsely populated, receive at least some level of oversight.

Some regulators have also raised concerns about the effectiveness of the CRA to promote community development lending in rural high-need areas. While this study addresses primarily mortgage lending, a review of the available FDIC-regulated lender assessment area data indicates that few rural high-credit-need census tracts are included in most lenders' assessment areas. This likely reflects the overall makeup of the credit markets of many large banks, not some blatant disregard on their part. Regulators should specifically recognize more rural and small town lending efforts to encourage involvement. Efforts have been underway to expand consideration for CRA-qualified activities to recognize more rural communities outside of metropolitan areas – even if they are not in defined assessment areas.[61]

Lender assessment area identification criteria could also benefit from more oversight and expansion to ensure they accurately reflect current lending practices. It does appear that, in at least a few cases, lender-identified assessment areas do not match actual home lending activity. A potential response might be for the CRA evaluation to note any discrepancies. In some instances, this could benefit the institution being evaluated. Given that lending is not limited by the proximity of an office, as the HMDA data show with almost 25 percent of reported rural and small town mortgage loans occurring outside assessment areas, it might be necessary to modify the criteria to include a larger role for actual lender activity in defining assessment areas.

Although potential changes could improve it in the rural context, CRA is clearly a valuable policy tool. CRA does touch many rural and small town lenders and works to ensure that these lenders consider the overlooked portions of their service areas. CRA places a positive value on serving these communities, something that otherwise might not exist. CRA is far from perfect, and changes to broaden coverage and improve available information would certainly make it more effective for its intent of improving credit availability for all consumers – urban and rural.

Policy responses

The mortgage and CRA review highlight several areas of concern for policymakers:

> *The Need for Data Improvements.* Improved data on mortgage lending activity. HMDA filing exemptions create uncertainty particular with regards to rural activity since most exempt lenders likely operate in rural locations. Similarly, CRA data need substantial improvements to make it usable for the public. Important information on lender assessment area census tracts, for example, is not available for all lenders in a single location. In its current form, one would have to read thousands of CRA examination reports to collect this data. Better HMDA and CRA data would empower the public to provide more effective oversight.

> *More Access to Conventional Mortgages for Manufactured Home Lending.* Given the extremely elevated denial and high-cost lending rates, lending terms and practices associated with manufactured homes need to evaluated. Policies need to focus on lowering the fees and changing the onerous terms of manufactured home loans. Loans involving manufactured home loans are usually considered private property or chattel, and, as a result, the loan terms are more onerous than a standard home mortgage. Industry practices have also been criticized for taking advantage of customers and even discrimination. Because this may be only option in many rural communities with limited incomes, policies need to work to make sure the market is affordable. The Duty to Serve, with one of its focuses being manufactured homes, can potentially help address this problem.

> *Reassessing CRA Assessment Areas.* The lender-identified CRA assessment area is an important part of the program. The assessment essentially identifies what part of a lender's market will be subject to critical evaluation. The system, set up at time when banking was done at a brick-n-mortar office, creates a few challenges for rural communities. For most large-asset lenders, rural service areas are relatively tiny part of their service area. These assessment areas, in many case, reflects the distribution of rural lending activity which is often limited; however, this likely results in limited rural activity particularly with regards to community investment lending which is only required of large bank lenders.

> Lenders have more opportunities to fulfill these CRA obligations in suburban and urban and areas and the likely do so which is reflected in the claims of limited rural community investments. The lenders for which rural communities make up a majority of their assessment area are usually small rural-headquartered banks which do not have the same CRA requirements as large banks.

Change in lending market

As the last two decades have shown, home financing markets are not static. Sometimes, large, depository institutions are the primary source of mortgage credit, and other times, it is independent mortgage companies. Currently, lenders regulated do not make a majority of loans for the nation as a whole and slightly more than 50 percent of rural lending. This means that the CRA regulatory oversight is not applying to all markets. The Duty to Serve regulations can hopefully address these CRA coverage limitations. Regardless of the changes, it is certain that the circumstances surrounding rural mortgage lending will constantly be changing and in need of review.

Notes

1 Backup, Benjamin and Richard Brown. 2014. Community Banks Remain Resilient Amid Industry Consolidation. *FDIC Quarterly*, 8(2): 33–43. Article accessed 1/5/16 at the following url: www.fdic.gov/bank/analytical/quarterly/2014_vol8_2/article.pdf

2 Federal Reserve Bank of Dallas. 2011. *Choosing the Road to Prosperity: Why We Must End Too Big to Fail – Now, 2011 Annual Report, Federal Reserve Bank of Dallas*. Report accessed 12/1/15 at the following url: http://dallasfed.org/assets/documents/fed/annual/2011/ar11.pdf

3 In 2014, four or fewer lenders originated all home purchase loans in 95 counties, all of which each had a majority rural population. If two lenders merged in these markets, for example, there would only be three providers. In more populated areas, the options are likely greater to begin with, so a consolidation or closure might not have the same impact.

4 Tolbert, Charles M., C. Mencken, Jing Li, and Lynn Riggs. 2014. Traditional and Alternative Financial Institutions in Rural America. *Rural Sociology*, 79(3): 355–379.

5 Levitin, Adam J., and Janneke H. Ratcliffe. 2013. *Rethinking Duties to Serve in Housing Finance*. Joint Center for Housing Studies, Harvard University Paper HBTL-12. Paper accessed 12/27/15 at the following url: www.jchs.harvard.edu/sites/jchs.harvard.edu/files/hbtl-12.pdf

6 The USDA, Economic Research Service (ERS) created the persistent-poverty classification. In the most recent iteration, a persistent-poverty classification means a county experienced poverty rates of 20 percent or more for the last four decades as measured by the 1980, 1990 and 2000 Census and the 2007–11 American Community Survey (ACS), which replaced the decennial Census long form, used in place of the 2010 Census. For more details, see the following url accessed 1/5/16 : www.ers.usda.gov/topics/rural-economy-population/rural-poverty-well-being/geography-of-poverty.aspx

7 Cromartie, John. 2013. Non-metro Areas as a Whole Experience First Period of Population Loss. *Amber Waves*. May 6, 2013. Article accessed 1/5/16 at the following url: www.ers.usda.gov/amber-waves/2013-may/non-metro-areas-as-a-whole-experience-first-period-of-population-loss.aspx#.VsOgY4-cFu0

8 Frey, William H. 2014. *A Population Slowdown in Small Town America*. Brookings Institute, Opinion Piece. March 31, 2014. Article accessed 12/15/15 at the following url: www.brookings.edu/research/opinions/2014/03/31-population-slowdown-small-town-america-frey

9 Singleton, Theresa, Lance George, Carla Dickstein, and Hannah Thomas. 2006. *Subprime and Predatory Lending in Rural America: Mortgage Lending Practices that can trap Low-Income Rural People*. Carsey Institute, Policy Brief No. 4 Fall 2006.

10 A high-cost loan is a loan which has an interest rate that substantially exceeds what the prime rate would be for a similar loan. The method of determining when a loan meets the high-cost threshold has changed over the years. At the time of the research cited here, high-cost loans were: 1) first lien loans with an interest rate that exceeded the average prime rate offer for a comparable transaction by 1.5 percentage points and 2) second lien loans exceeding the average prime rate by 3.5 percentage points.

11 Housing Assistance Council. 2012. *Taking Stock: Rural People, Poverty, and Housing in the 21st Century*. Washington, DC: Author. Publication accessed 12/1/16 at the following url: www.ruralhome.org/storage/documents/ts2010/ts_full_report.pdf

12 Walser, Jeffrey and John Anderlik. 2004. The Future of Banking in American: Rural Depopulation: What does it Mean for the Economic Health of Rural Areas and the

Community Banks that Support Them? *FDIC Banking Review*, 16(3):57–95 Article accessed 12/10/15 at the following url: http://citeseerx.ist.psu.edu/viewdoc/summary?doi=10.1.1.159.3768

13 Keeton, William. 1998. Are Rural Banks Facing Increased Funding Pressures? Evidence from Tenth District States. *Economic Review* (2nd Quarter): 43–67.

14 Walser, Jeffrey and John Anderlik. 2004. The Future of Banking in American: Rural Depopulation: What does it Mean for the Economic Health of Rural Areas and the Community Banks that Support Them? *FDIC Banking Review*, 16(3):57–95
    Article accessed 12/10/15 at the following url: http://citeseerx.ist.psu.edu/viewdoc/summary?doi=10.1.1.159.3768

15 John, Anderlik and Richard Cofer. 2014. Community Banks Remain Resilient Amid Industry Consolidation. *FDIC Quarterly*, 8(2): 33–59. Article accessed 1/10/16 at the following url: www.fdic.gov/bank/analytical/quarterly/2014_vol8_2/article2.pdf?source=govdelivery

16 Sixty-three percent of all small-asset depository institutions (CRA examination threshold) in 2014 were rural headquartered.

17 Gilbert, R. Alton. 1997. Implications of Banking Consolidation for the Financing of Rural America. In *Financing Rural America*. Kansas City, MO: Kansas City Federal Reserve.

18 Walser, Jeffrey and John Anderlik. 2004. The Future of Banking in American: Rural Depopulation: What does it mean for the Economic Health of Rural Areas and the Community Banks that Support Them? *FDIC Banking Review*, 16(3): 57–95. Article accessed 12/10/15 at the following url: http://citeseerx.ist.psu.edu/viewdoc/summary?doi=10.1.1.159.3768

19 Tolbert, Charles. M., F. Carson Mencken, T. Lynn Riggs, and Jing Li. 2014. Restructuring of the Financial Industry: The Disappearance of Locally Owned Traditional Financial Services in Rural America. *Rural Sociology*, 79(3): 355–379.

20 Credit Union National Association. 2015. *New: CFPB Eases Rural and Underserved Credit Access*. Webpage article written 9/21/2015 from the following url: http://news.cuna.org/articles/107629-new-cfpb-eases-rural-and-underserved-credit-access

21 The HMDA data filing asset threshold was $44 million for 2015. The threshold is adjusted for inflation annually.

22 Avery, Robert B., Kenneth P. Brevoort, and Glen B. Canner. 2007. Opportunities and issues in using HMDA data. *The Journal of Real Estate Research*, 29(4): 352–379.

23 Wiley, Keith. 2009. *What Are We Missing? HMDA Asset-Excluded Filers*. Housing Assistance Council Report. Report accessible at the following url: www.ruralhome.org/storage/documents/smallbanklending.pdf

24 Bishop, Bill. 2009. *Foreclosures in Rural America? Who Knows!!!* Daily Yonder Blog, October 16, 2009. This article was accessed 12/5/15 at the following url: www.dailyyonder.com/foreclosures-rural-america-who-knows/2009/10/16/2398/

25 Housing Assistance Council. 2014. *Rural Mortgage Activity Declines. Home Purchase Are up, but So Are High Costs Loans*. Rural Research Note. October 2014. The report accessed 12/6/15 at the following url: www.ruralhome.org/storage/documents/publications/rrnotes/rrn-rural-mortgages.pdf. Housing Assistance Council. 2008. Mortgage Lending in Rural Communities. March 2008. This report accessed 12/6/15 at the following url: www.ruralhome.org/storage/documents/hmda.pdf

26 Wiley, Keith. 2015. *Rural Home-Purchase Loans Grow at Faster Rate Than Urban*. Daily Yonder Blog, October 6, 2015. See the following url: www.dailyyonder.com/rural-new-sales-mortgage-starts-increase-at-greater-rate-than-urban/2015/10/06/8874/

27 Singleton, Theresa, Lance George, Carla Dickstein, and Hannah Thomas. 2006. *Subprime and Predatory Lending in Rural America: Mortgage Lending Practices That Can Trap Low-Income Rural People*. Carsey Institute, Policy Brief No. 4 Fall 2006.

28 Housing Assistance Council. 2012. *Taking Stock: Rural People, Poverty, and Housing in the 21st Century*. Washington, DC: Author. Publication accessed 12/1/16 at the following url: www.ruralhome.org/storage/documents/ts2010/ts_full_report.pdf

29 Bhutta, Neil, Jack Popper, and Daniel R. Ringo. 2015. The 2014 Home Mortgage Disclosure Act Data. *Federal Reserve Bulletin*, 101(4): 1–43. Article accessed 12/15/15 at the following url: www.federal.reserve.gov/pubs/bulletin/2015/pdf/2014_HMDA.pdf

    This the latest version of the annual Federal Bulletin article that the Federal Reserve does upon the release of the HMDA data. Each paper uses a similar approach to their analysis.

30 This study uses the Housing Assistance Council's (HAC's) rural and small town classification system. The HAC approach uses the census tract as its unit of analysis and classifies census tracts according to housing density and computing patterns. This classification was chosen because it uses a relatively small unit of analysis (census tract as opposed to county) and includes a suburban and exurban category as opposed to just a dichotomous rural-urban distinction. The analysis uses the HAC classification for both 2010 and 2000 census tracts, since the study period includes data based on both geographies.

31 Excluded cases without a state, county and census tract FIPs code because they could not be located and classified geographically. This represents less than 2 percent of HMDA records for all years. The Puerto Rico exclusion reflects the fact this analysis covers only the 50 states and the District of Columbia.

32 The USDA, ERS measure classifies as persistent poverty counties experiencing poverty rates of 20 percent or more for each of the last four decades. Poverty rates are measured using the 1980, 1990 and 2000 Census along with the ACS 2006–10 five-year estimates (and longer decennial Census estimates). See the following url (accessed 1/1/16) for more information: www.ers.usda.gov/topics/rural-economy-population/rural-poverty-well-being/geography-of-poverty.aspx

33 Home purchase loans for this analysis refer to first lien, home purchase originations alone. Second lien records are removed to avoid double counting of so-called piggyback loans.

34 The specific thresholds and even method of measuring high-cost loans changed over the last decade. These changes limit the ability of the user to compare figures over time, but comparisons of differences within the same year by geography would be justified.

35 Levitin, Adam J., and Janneke H. Ratcliffe. 2013. *Rethinking Duties to Serve in Housing Finance*. Joint Center for Housing Studies, Harvard University Paper HBTL-12. Paper accessed 12/27/15 at the following url: www.jchs.harvard.edu/sites/jchs.harvard.edu/files/hbtl-12.pdf

36 The other element of "Duty to Serve" involves the Government Services Enterprises – Fannie Mae and Freddie Mac.

37 The Federal Reserve Board, Office of Comptroller of the Currency and Federal Depository Insurance Corporation perform CRA examinations. The agency with oversight authority over a given lender, which is based on the institution's charter, performs its CRA examination.

38 Over 95 percent of CRA examinations are one of the following three: Small Bank, Intermediate, Small Bank and Large Bank. The categories are determined by lender asset size, with a lender that exceeds a threshold for two years being subject to that exam. The thresholds are updated for inflation annually. The December 2016 thresholds were less than $304 million (small bank exam), between $304 million and less than $1.216 billion (intermediate, small bank exam) and $1.216 billion or more (large bank exam).

39 Agarwal, Sumit, Efraim Benmelech, Nittai Bergman, and Amit Seru. 2012. *Did the Community Reinvestment Act (CRA) Lead to Risky Lending?* National Bureau of Economic Research Working Paper 18609.

40 For example, see the following articles. Agarwal, Sumit, Efraim Benmelech, Nittai Bergman, and Amit Seru. 2012. Did the Community Investment Act (CRA) Lead to Risky Lending. NBER Working Paper No. 18609; Raymond H. Brescia. 2014. The Community Reinvestment Act: Guilty, But Not as Charged. Albany Law School Research Paper No 23 for 2012– 2013; and Avery, Robert B., and Kenneth P. Brevoort. 2015. The Subprime Crisis: Is Government Housing Policy to Blame? *Review of Economics and Statistics* 97(2): 352–336.

41 Housing Assistance Council. 2015. *CRA in Rural America: The Community Reinvestment Act and Mortgage Lending in Rural Communities.* Report accessed 12/5/15 at the following url: www.ruralhome.org/storage/documents/publications/rrreports/rrr-cra-in-rural-america.pdf

42 Bhutta, Neil, Jack Popper, and Daniel R. Ringo. 2015. The 2014 Home Mortgage Disclosure Act Data. *Federal Reserve Bulletin*, 101(4): 1–43. Article accessed 12/15/15 at the following url: www.federal.reserve.gov/pubs/bulletin/2015/pdf/2014_HMDA.pdf
    This the latest version of the annual Federal Bulletin article that the Federal Reserve does upon the release of the HMDA data. Each paper uses a similar approach to their analysis.

43 Avery, Robert B., Glenn B. Canner, Shannon C. Mok, Dan S. Sokolov, and Onka L. Tenkean. 2005. Community Bankks and Rural Development: Research Relating to Proposals to Revise the Regulations that Implemented the Community Reinvestment Act. *Federal Reserve Bulletin*, 91 (2205): 202–235.

44 Curry, Thomas J. 2014. *Remarks before the National Community Reinvestment Coalition, March 12, 2014.* The speech transcripts were accessed 10/27/17 at the following url: www.occ.gov/news-issuances/speeches/2014/pub-speech-2014-38.pdf

45 Rural counties are defined as counties with over 50 percent of the population living in rural and small town census tracts. There are 2,208 rural and small town counties, and credit unions and/or independent mortgage companies made a majority of home purchase loans in 306 of them.

46 Bhutta, Neil, Jack Popper, and Daniel R. Ringo. 2015. The 2014 Home Mortgage Disclosure Act Data. *Federal Reserve Bulletin*, 101(4): 1–43. Article accessed 12/15/15 at the following url: www.federal.reserve.gov/pubs/bulletin/2015/pdf/2014_HMDA.pdf

47 Park, Keven. 2008. *Subprime Lending and the Community Reinvestment Act.* Harvard University, Joint Center for Housing Studies Paper, N08–2. Paper accessed 1/5/16 at the following url: www.jchs.harvard.edu/sites/jchs.harvard.edu/files/n08-2_park.pdf

48 Bhutta, Neil, Jack Popper, and Daniel R. Ringo. 2015. The 2014 Home Mortgage Disclosure Act Data. *Federal Reserve Bulletin*, 101(4): 1–43. Author accessed the article 12/15/15 at the following url: www.federal.reserve.gov/pubs/bulletin/2015/pdf/2014_HMDA.pdf

49 The key here is "large-asset" CRA lender as opposed to *all* CRA lenders who, as noted earlier, originated over half of all loans in most rural counties.

50 These number are likely an undercount as well, given HMDA data restrictions that limit small bank reporters.

51 Housing Assistance Council. 2015. *CRA in Rural America: The Community Reinvestment Act and Mortgage Lending in Rural Communities.* Report accessed 12/5/15 at the following url: www.ruralhome.org/storage/documents/publications/rrreports/rrr-cra-in-rural-america.pdf

52 FFIEC. 2007. Community Reinvestment Act: Examination Procedures for Small Institutions. July 2007 Small Institution CRA Examination Procedures Guide. Document accessed 1/4/16 from the following url: www.ffiec.gov/cra/pdf/cra_exsmall.pdf

53 Housing Assistance Council. 2015. *CRA in Rural America: The Community Reinvestment Act and Mortgage Lending in Rural Communities.* Report accessed 12/5/15 at the following url: www.ruralhome.org/storage/documents/publications/rrreports/rrr-cra-in-rural-america.pdf

54 Rural-headquartered lenders made up 97 percent of institutions with majority rural assessment area population.

55 Crandall, Kristin. 2013. 2013 CRA Eligibility Status Data Update. Policy Map data availability update posted 8/2/2103. www.policymap.com/blog/2013/08/2013-community-reinvestment-act-cra-eligibility-status-data-update/

56 The low- and moderate-income threshold is a less than perfect measure for identifying economically distressed rural areas, because the area median family incomes in many rural areas for which census tracts medians are compared are often extremely low due to widespread economic distress. This means it is nearly impossible to be less than

80 percent of an area median if, for example, the area median is less than $15,000. The inclusion of the distressed and underserved categories was an effort to include the areas not identified with the median family income measure.

57 Caputo, Stephanie. 2006. 2005 CRA Revisions: How banks and examiners are implementing the new rule. OCC Community Developments. http://occ.gov/static/community-affairs/community-developments-investments/summer06/newcrahelp.html

58 Underserved census tracts are those tracts receiving a USDA, ERS Urban Influence Code of 7, 10, 11 and 12.

59 Low- and moderate-income census tracts, on average during the 2012–14 period, made up approximately 47 percent of both urban census tracts and population compared to 21 and 17 percent for suburban census tracts and population, respectively.

60 The majority of lenders, 70 percent, made between 10 and 50 percent of their loans in suburban and urban CRA-eligible census tracts. They were more commonly part of a lender's portfolio than a loan in a rural CRA-eligible census tract.

61 Thomas J. Curry. 2014. *Remarks before the National Community Reinvestment Coalition, March 12, 2014.* The speech transcripts accessed 10/24/17 at the following url: www.occ.gov/news-issuances/speeches/2014/pub-speech-2014-38.pdf

In this speech, Mr. Curry mentions that dearth of community development/investment spending in rural areas and efforts that were done and continue to be done to increase such assistance through the CRA.

6 National rural housing policy and programs

Opportunities and challenges

Corianne Payton Scally with Surabhi Dabir and David Lipsetz[1]

Introduction

Rural America is changing, and so are its housing needs. Demographic and economic shifts over the last several decades have significantly affected rural opportunities and prosperity (Bailey et al. 2014). While some rural communities have prospered – as recreational areas, amenity communities and suburbanizing areas – others struggle with persistent poverty or high out-migration (Marcouiller et al. 2011; McGranahan et al. 2010). These divergent rural realities have led to increasing income inequality driven by declining incomes, particularly among poor households (Hertz and Farrigan 2016).

For low-income rural households, the struggle to access safe, quality, affordable housing is real (Belden and Wiener 1999). Incomes are too low to afford the limited housing stock that is available, which can be old, poorly maintained and lack basic plumbing in historically marginalized communities. Aging rural residents face additional problems, such as the difficulty and cost of retrofitting older homes for full accessibility by those facing mobility impairments or other types of disabilities.

Since the market downturn during the post-2007 recession, rural housing options have become even more limited. After reaching historically high home-ownership rates, rural homeowners have been hit harder than their urban counterparts (Nelson and Cromartie 2014), and access to mortgage credit for home purchase remains a significant problem (MacTavish et al. 2014). Multifamily rental opportunities are sparse in many rural communities, and significant financing and investment challenges thwart the construction of new apartments and the rehabilitation of existing ones (Housing Assistance Council 2013a).

Low incomes can result in high housing cost-burdens and the need for subsidies to put quality housing and other community necessities within reach of rural families (Belden and Wiener 1999; Kropczynski and Dyk 2012). The U.S. Department of Agriculture's (USDA) Rural Development agency provides significant subsidies and assistance through its Rural Housing Service (RHS), with over $145.8 billion of active investments in rural homeownership, rental housing and community facilities (U.S. Department of Agriculture [USDA] Rural Development 2016). RHS is currently assisting over 1.2 million homeowners with affordable mortgages (USDA Rural Development 2016) and over 400,000 households with quality, affordable rental housing (USDA Rural Housing Service 2016). Since 2009, RHS has also invested over $9.6 billion to support thousands of essential community facilities in rural America, including healthcare, safety, education, public infrastructure, cultural resources and other community needs (USDA Rural Development 2016). In the midst of changing rural fortunes, these programs continue to be a critical source of investment, but they also face challenges in serving future rural housing and community economic development needs.

This chapter will highlight some of the key national trends in rural housing, provide an updated overview of the USDA RHS program portfolio and characteristics and highlight the opportunities and challenges for the RHS and other partners in meeting rural needs for housing and community facilities.

Rural changes and impacts on housing

There have been many shifts in rural America in recent years that affect the availability of affordable, adequate rural homeownership and rental opportunities. One significant driver is geographic shifts in population, and the resulting changing characteristics of rural populations. Recently, rural areas have been experiencing small but steady population loss, including an absolute population loss since 2010 for the first time in recorded history (USDA Economic Research Services [ERS] 2015a). However, some areas – particularly where recreational amenities and energy-related activities are high – have gained population during this time. These shifts affect local housing markets and their ability to provide quality units at affordable prices for lower-income households. In declining areas, housing may be affordable, but quality may decline as the buildings age and maintenance and energy-efficiency challenges increase. In growing areas, housing supply may not keep up with new demand, causing prices to rise even as quality may improve through renovation and new construction.

Population shifts have changed the demographic characteristics of the rural population. This population is aging as young adults move away from rural areas while older adults remain behind to age in place or retire to rural communities (U.S. Department of Agriculture Economic Research Service [USDA ERS] 2015a). Additionally, rural poverty peaked during the recent recession, while child poverty rates continued climbing, reaching 25 percent in 2014 (USDA ERS 2015a). Poverty rates for minority racial and ethnic groups are even higher, with African Americans experiencing rates above 35 percent, followed by Native Americans and Alaskans at 33 percent and Hispanics at 27.5 percent (USDA ERS 2015a). Many rural communities – approximately 85 percent of non-metro counties – also face persistent poverty, generally defined as at least three decades with poverty rates of over 20 percent (USDA ERS 2015b). Some communities are building and expanding wealth through recreational development and energy extraction, but often at the cost of widening inequality (Marcouiller et al. 2011).

Rural housing markets face unique challenges as a result of both recent shifts and long-term trends. Historically, rural homeownership rates are much higher than national rates, over 71 percent in 2010 compared to just over 65 percent nationally (HAC 2012). As homeowners age, they accrue equity in their homes, but not as much as urban homeowners. They also face difficulties in home modification and repairs to allow increased accessibility for aging in place (HAC 2012). Renters are more racially and ethnically diverse and are more likely than homeowners to be cost-burdened, or paying more than 30 percent of their income toward housing costs (HAC 2013a). Since the majority of rural housing stock is single-family homes, almost half of rural renters live in this type of structure, with manufactured housing as the second most common rental unit type; multiunit structures are much less common (HAC 2013a). Another unique characteristic of rural housing are higher vacancy rates – around 18 percent – over half of which can be attributed to seasonal vacancies in recreational amenity communities (HAC 2012). This can pose challenges to communities by artificially constricting housing supply and exacerbating affordability issues.

USDA Rural Housing Service

USDA was first authorized to provide loans to farmworkers for housing purposes in 1937. This authority was subsequently expanded through the Housing Act of 1949 and amended in the 1960s to include nonfarm single-family and multifamily properties (Collings 1999). Originally called the Farmers Home Administration (FmHA), USDA RHS is responsible for implementing the Housing Act of 1949 in rural communities with the goal of safe, decent, sanitary housing for every American family. Its community facilities program also provides affordable access to credit for the financing of essential rural community facilities, including hospitals, libraries and schools.

Eligibility criteria for RHS loans, guarantees and grants vary slightly across programs but share some key characteristics. First, all properties for which funding is sought must be located in an eligible rural area. While the definition of rural has changed slightly over time, RHS housing programs are generally restricted to communities of 35,000 people or less,[2] while community facilities is restricted to serving communities of 20,000 or less.[3] Second, programs are means-tested, meaning that borrowers must be at or below a certain income threshold in order to qualify for housing funds, or facilities should serve low-income communities in order to score higher on community facility funding applications. This helps target limited resources to the neediest populations. Third, RHS tries to serve as a lender of last resort, providing access to credit to rural people and places where the private sector is not sufficiently meeting the need. Finally, RHS programs have a variety of protocols and tools to help borrowers succeed when they encounter repayment difficulties. Through a variety of mechanisms such as loan deferrals, refinancing and additional loans or grants, RHS can work with borrowers to develop long-term solutions to keep people in their homes and apartments and essential facilities operating within their communities.

Single-family housing

The goal of the USDA RHS single-family division is to provide affordable homeownership opportunities to low and moderate income households purchasing modest homes in rural communities who otherwise lack access to credit. It accomplishes this task by providing direct mortgage loans to borrowers (Section 502 Direct), guaranteed loans made through qualified lenders (Section 502 Guaranteed) and home repair loans and grants to very low-income rural homeowners (Section 504). The Mutual Self-Help Housing program (Section 523) also funds technical assistance to groups contributing sweat equity to help build one another's homes. Since the 2009 federal fiscal year,[4] the single-family programs have assisted 140,000 to 170,000 borrowers annually with purchasing a home and another 7,000 to 11,000 existing homeowners per year in making home repairs (see Figure 6.1 below).

The Section 502 Direct program has assisted around 88,000 home purchases for low- and very low income households in total since 2007, generally ranging from 7,000 to 12,000 per year, with the exception of additional households served by American Recovery and Reinvestment Act funding in 2009 and 2010 (see Figure 6.2 below). These loans can cover up to 100 percent of the home value with terms up to 33 years and can be used to buy, improve, repair or rehabilitate a home within an eligible rural area. Forty percent of all loans are targeted to very low income households earning at or below 50 percent of area median income (AMI), while the remainder can serve any low-income households earning at or below 80 percent of area median income. The average loan amount for a very low income household in 2015 was $113,483; it was $135,092 for a low-income household.

The Section 502 Guaranteed program provides a government guarantee on a private lender-issued mortgage to pay up to 90% of the loan amount back to the lender in the event the borrower defaults on payment. This allows for more affordable mortgage terms to be offered to the borrower while requiring less total subsidy from the federal government than had the government issued the entire mortgage directly. This program serves households purchasing homes in eligible rural areas that earn up to 115 percent of area median income. As reflected in Figure 6.3, this

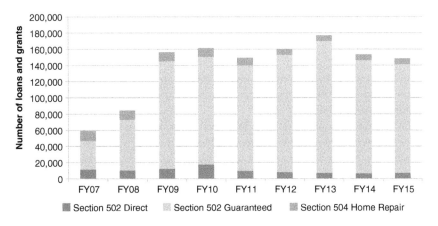

Figure 6.1 Number of Loans and Grants by Single-Family Program by Fiscal Year, 2009–2015

Source: USDA Rural Development, various years, Annual Progress Report.

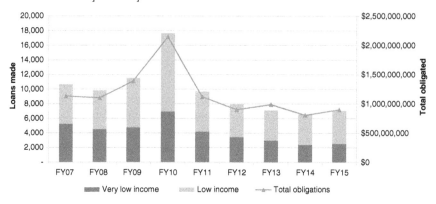

Figure 6.2 Number of Section 502 Direct Home Purchase Loans and Total Obligated Amount by Buyer Income Group by Fiscal Year, 2007–2015

Source: USDA Rural Housing Service, various years, unpublished data.

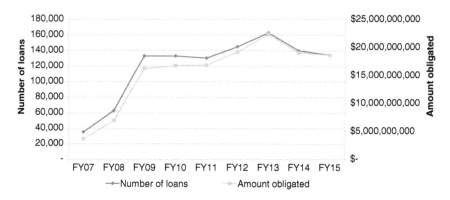

Figure 6.3 Number of Section 502 Guaranteed Loans and Amount Obligated by Fiscal Year, 2007–2015

Source: USDA Rural Development, various years, Annual Progress Report.

program grew significantly beginning in 2009 and currently guarantees between 133,000 and 163,000 home purchase loans per year representing $16–22 billion of guaranteed investments.

The Section 504 program provides either grants or loans to low-income home-owners to perform needed home repairs. The loans can be provided to any eligible homeowner falling within income and geographic guidelines, whereas grants are limited to homeowners age 62 or older. Loan amounts up to $20,000 are eligible, although the average amount is much smaller: $6,027 for 504 Loans in 2015, and $6,133 for 504 Grants. The total amount obligated has declined over the past dec-ade, from over $73.3 million in 2007 to a low of just over $40.3 million in 2012 (see Figure 6.4 below). By 2015, it had risen again to $55 million but was still reaching

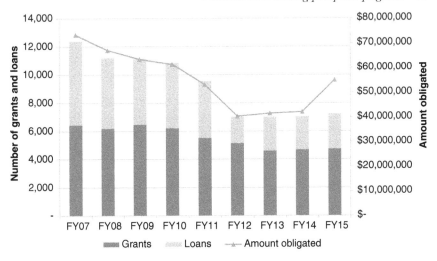

Figure 6.4 Number of Section 504 Home Repair Grants and Loans and Obligated Amount by Fiscal Year, 2007–2015

Source: USDA Rural Housing Service, various years, unpublished data.

fewer households. The number of annual grants has decreased 27 percent since 2007, while the number of loans has decreased by 58 percent.

The Section 523 Mutual Self-Help program funds technical assistance for rural communities that gather together to contribute sweat equity to the construction of one another's homes. These homeowners accumulate equity through contributing their labor to the construction of the homes and can qualify for Section 502 Direct mortgages. From 2007 through 2015, more than 10,200 Section 523 participants received Section 502 Direct mortgages (see Figure 6.5). In 2015, the average loan value was $144,600. This program celebrated its fiftieth year of operation in 2015 by reaching the significant milestone of 50,000 homes built.

Multifamily housing

The multifamily housing program at USDA RHS offers direct loans to owners (Section 515 and Section 514 Farm Labor Housing), guaranteed loans made by approved lenders (Section 538) and a small amount of grants for repair (Section 533) and farm labor housing projects (Section 516). Together, these programs currently fund over 14,770 properties, providing more than 400,000 affordable rental units for rural American households. Rental Assistance (Section 521) also helps two out of every three tenant households to keep their rental payments to no more than 30 percent of their household income.

Over 403,000 households, made up of over 673,000 people, live in RHS-financed rental housing (USDA RHS 2016). These households are generally small, with a high proportion of elderly and disabled residents, as well as very low-income residents. As highlighted in Table 6.1 below, average household size is 1.67 people,

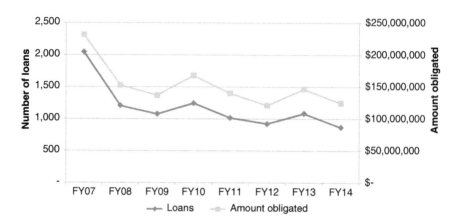

Figure 6.5 Number of Section 502 Direct Home Purchase Loans to Section 523 Mutual Self-Help Program Participants and Amount Obligated by Fiscal Year, 2007–2014

Source: USDA Rural Development, various years, unpublished data.

Table 6.1 Characteristics of Tenant Households in Section 515 and Section 514 Multifamily Properties, 2015

	Number	Percent
Total Households	403,389	100%
Total Household Members	673,681	100%
Household composition		
Average Household Size	1.67	NA
Elderly, Disabled or Handicapped Households	244,565	60.6%
Elderly	126,809	31.4%
Disabled	101,935	25.3%
Handicapped	15,821	3.9%
Female-Headed Households	287,128	71.2%
Single female	166,946	41.4%
Multiperson female	120,182	29.8%
Male-Headed Households		
Single male	76,092	18.9%
Multiperson male head of household	40,169	10.0%
Race/ethnicity		
White, Non-Hispanic	268,402	66.5%
Non-White, Non-Hispanic	134,987	21.8%
Black	77,717	19.3%
Asian/Pacific Islander	2,967	0.7%
American Indian/Alaskan Native	6,326	1.6%
Non-Designated/Multiple Races	2,079	0.5%
Hispanic/Latino, Any Race	45,898	11.4%

	Number	*Percent*
Income		
Average Household Income	$12,729	NA
Households with very low incomes (at or below 50% area median income)	372,110	92.2%
Households with low incomes (between 50–80% of area median income)	26,574	6.6%
Households with moderate incomes (between 80–120% of area median income)	2,534	0.6%
Households with above moderate incomes (above 120% of area median income)	2,171	0.5%
Rent-burdened households		
Households paying 30–40% of income for rent	21,207	5.3%
Household paying 41–50% of income for rent	13,306	3.3%
Households paying 51% or more of income for rent	19,658	4.9%
Total Rent-burdened Households	*54,171*	*13.4%*
Rental subsidies		
USDA Rental Assistance	270,879	67.2%
Other Rental Assistance	54780	13.6%
No Subsidy	77730	19.3%

Source: USDA Rural Housing Service 2016 and 2015 Annual Fair Housing Occupancy Report.

with over 60 percent of households made up of just a single individual. Over 60 percent of resident households identify as elderly (age 62 or older) or disabled. Most households are non-Hispanic White, but one out of every three RHS tenant households is a racial or ethnic minority, with around 20 percent African-American and 11 percent Hispanic. Over 90 percent of tenant households earn less than 50 percent of their area's median income, with average household income of only $12,700 annually. Thanks to rental assistance programs – highlighted in Figure 6.6 – only a small proportion (13 percent) of tenant households are rent-burdened, or paying more than 30 percent of their income toward rent. Two out of every three tenant households receive USDA Rental Assistance with another 13 percent receiving other types of public and private rent subsidies. Less than 20 percent of tenant households receive no rental assistance.

The largest portfolio, Section 515, consists of a large but aging housing stock. Characterized by low-interest, long-term loans, many of these properties are over 30 years old and are concentrated in the Northeastern, Midwestern and Southern U.S. Most properties are owned by private owners, with the exception of about 16 percent that are owned by nonprofit organizations. Sixty-three percent of the almost 14,000 properties are built as family housing, while 35 percent of the properties are age-restricted to heads of households that are 62 years or older or persons

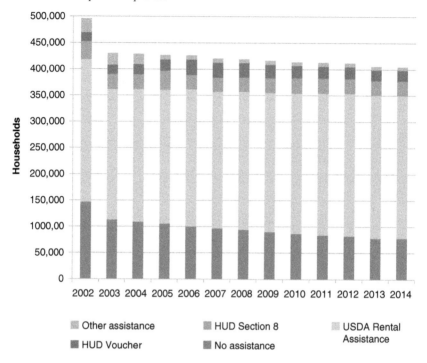

Figure 6.6 Tenant Households in USDA RHS Direct Multifamily Loan Program Properties, By Type of Rental Assistance Received, 2002–2015

Notes: Not all numbers reported line up with fiscal year reporting.

Source: USDA Rural Housing Service, various years, Annual Fair Housing Occupancy Reports.

with disabilities of any age. Eighty percent of the properties contain studio, one- and two-bedroom apartments only, while the remainder include some larger apartments.

The number of properties and households served through USDA RHS direct loan properties has steadily decreased over recent years as owners pay the final payment due on their loan. As shown in Figure 6.7, between 2002 and 2014, almost 3,000 properties, or 17 percent, exited the portfolio, resulting in almost 91,000 fewer households housed in RHS-financed properties by 2015. At the same time, some properties have been successfully preserved to continue to provide affordable rental housing for a longer term. As of June 2015,[5] over 2,300 properties have been transferred to a new owner who agreed to extend the restricted use of the property as affordable rental housing. Over 650 properties have been consolidated in order to realize economies of scale in operations and management to keep the units affordable to low-income households.

Community facilities

Access to affordable housing is an important determinant of where households choose to call home. However, providing necessary infrastructure and community services to

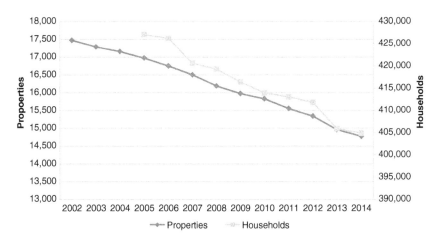

Figure 6.7 Properties and Households Served Through USDA RHS Direct Multifamily Loan Programs, 2002–2014

Note: Not all numbers reported line up with fiscal year reporting.

Source: USDA Rural Housing Service, various years, Annual Fair Housing Occupancy Reports.

support resident needs and promote a high quality of life is just as important to creating sustainable rural communities. To this end, the USDA RHS community facilities division provides loans, guarantees, and grants to public, nonprofit or tribal entities to finance essential community facilities. Funding can go toward the purchase, construction or improvement of facilities, as well as toward equipment purchase. Eligible facility types include, but are not limited to, health care, childcare centers, public safety buildings and equipment, schools, libraries, town halls, community centers and local food distribution and preparation facilities. Funding priorities are given to small communities with populations of 5,500 or less and to low-income communities.

Between 2009 and 2015, over 10,300 community facilities were funded through RHS, led by fire, rescue and public safety facilities, followed by cultural and education facilities, public buildings and improvements and health care (see Figure 6.8). Overall, the Communities Facilities (CF) program invested over $8.1 billion dollars in rural communities during this seven-year period, of which approximately $6.4 billion was loans and the remainder grants. According to applicant estimates at the time of the funding request, these investments saved almost 29,500 jobs while creating over 28,600 new ones within rural communities, with almost 50 percent of these generated via health care investments.

Beginning in 2012, the CF program saw a substantial increase in appropriations to make new Direct loans. As recently as 2007, CF received less than $200,000 in annual appropriations from Congress for its Direct Loan program. Figure 6.9 illustrates that this amount has grown to $2.2 billion annually – an aggressive target – with $1.6 billion successfully obligated in 2015. The number of loans made annually has stayed relatively stable since 2011 at around 1,300.

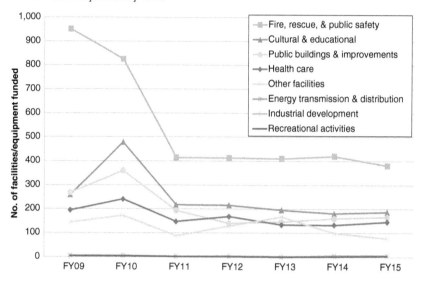

Figure 6.8 Number of Facilities/Equipment Funded by Type by Fiscal Year, 2009–2015

Source: USDA Rural Housing Service, various years, unpublished data.

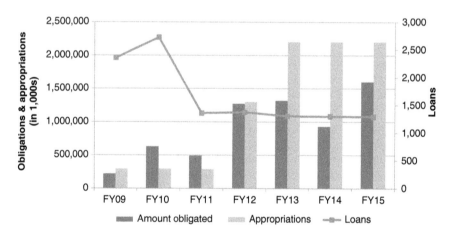

Figure 6.9 Community Facilities Obligations, Appropriations and Number of Loans by Fiscal Year, 2009–2015

Sources: USDA Rural Development, various years, Annual Progress Reports; USDA Rural Housing Service, various years, unpublished data.

Opportunities and challenges

Given the great housing needs of rural America and the current state of USDA RHS programs and portfolios, there are both opportunities and challenges to developing and implementing solutions. On the one hand, the opportunities for federal, state and local collaboration on meeting rural housing needs have never been greater. On the other hand, changes in rural America have left some communities far behind, deepening the difficulty of the work required to promote sustainable affordable housing solutions.

Diversity of demand

Rural demographic and economic shifts have important consequences for national rural housing policy and programs (HAC 2012). For example, with the simultaneous growth in older adults with fixed incomes and the percent of children in poverty, there is a high need for affordable housing solutions for both those aging in place and for poor families with young children. The diversity of rural markets – from those experiencing rapid or intensifying growth and development, to others showing steady declines in jobs and populations – make them difficult to serve with one-size-fits-all policy solutions. This means a range of housing options are needed in rural communities, from quality rental units – both large and small – to first-time homebuyer opportunities, to home repair and modification resources for homeowners aging in place.

Hard-to-serve people and places

Rural housing policy and programs have historically recognized populations and communities that are harder to serve than other rural areas. These include low-income households, the elderly and disabled, and farmworkers, as well as tribal lands, colonias, Central Appalachia, the Mississippi Delta region and persistent-poverty areas (Belden and Wiener 1999). These people and places have often received funding priority through set asides, as well as targeted designations and technical assistance to enhance their access to RHS, other USDA Rural Development programs and resources from other partner agencies, including HUD, the U.S. Environmental Protection Agency and the U.S. Department of Transportation (Partnership for Sustainable Communities 2012). These include a variety of place-based investment initiatives, such as rural Empowerment Zones[6] (1993–2014) and rural Promise Zones[7] (2013–ongoing), as well as regional planning initiatives to help neighboring communities work together on charting a sustainable economic future, including HUD's Sustainable Communities Initiative[8] (2009–ongoing) and USDA Rural Development's Stronger Economies Together[9] program (2009–ongoing). Despite these targeted investments there are still significant obstacles to serving these parts of rural America, but also some growing opportunities.

Many rural households lack access to affordable housing opportunities due to limited incomes and other circumstances that restrict their housing options. Low-income households have a reduced ability to pay for their housing costs and face additional barriers that lead to greater housing instability through unaffordable housing, overcrowding, frequent moves and homelessness (Kleit, Kang, & Scally 2016). This requires deep financial subsidies to put housing in reach, such as no-down payment and zero-interest home mortgages, and below-market rents and government rental assistance for tenants in rental homes. In addition to potentially having low or fixed incomes, the elderly and disabled can face accessibility challenges within the rural housing stock, as well as constraints in connecting to necessary services due to the unavailability of services or lack of transportation options (HAC 2014a). Historically, farmworkers have faced particular housing difficulties, including a lack of quality housing options near where they work, high housing costs compared to the wages they earn and more seasonal employment forcing regular moves (Peck 1999; HAC 2013b).

Aside from households, entire regions can be hard to serve due to a combination of difficult to serve populations and specific market characteristics. For example, Native Americans that live on tribal lands face underdeveloped community infrastructure and lack access to credit based on differing standards of property ownership (Dewees 2014). The Central Appalachia region – consisting of all of West Virginia and portions of Ohio, Kentucky, Tennessee, Virginia and North Carolina – has historically lacked jobs and adequate housing, problems exacerbated in the past few decades by the decline of the natural resource extraction industry in the area (HAC 2013c). The Mississippi Delta region – which includes more than half of the states of Mississippi, Louisiana and Arkansas, and portions of Missouri, Illinois, Kentucky and Tennessee – faces deep pockets of poverty and racial inequality and has been hit by a number of significant disasters further hindering economic growth and access to credit (HAC 2013d). Finally, the border colonias along the U.S.-Mexico border often lack adequate public infrastructure, including water and road access, as well as stable land tenure and safe housing opportunities (HAC 2013e). Often, these areas and their residents need targeted assistance, in addition to housing counseling to understand their housing opportunities and prepare to take proper advantage of them (Tighe 2013).

Preserving and expanding affordable rural rental housing

The USDA multifamily portfolio is aging, and many properties are in need of physical revitalization, as well as preservation tools to keep them in the affordable rural rental housing programs. A number of strategies have been employed to preserve units as affordable rental housing, as well as to improve their quality through renovation. These include providing additional loans, re-amortizing loans to extend the term on the remaining principal amount due and deferring existing debt payments. The Multifamily Preservation and Revitalization Demonstration Program (MPR) was specifically developed as a way to recapitalize aging Section 515 properties and pay for renovations while keeping them within the use restrictions of the program without raising rents. It provides a variety of tools for lowering existing debt by 1) modifying existing loans, 2) providing a new 0% interest loan, 3) providing a new 1% interest loan with deferred payments on debt or 4) giving grants to nonprofits for emergency health and safety-related repairs. In 2004, it was estimated that the Section 515 portfolio required $2.4 billion to meet capital needs over the next 20 years. An estimate from 2015 suggests that the 20-year deficit across all USDA rental housing programs stands at over $4 billion. Since MPR was launched in 2005, the program has obligated over $780 million to assist over 27,000 units with renovations (see Figure 6.10), falling short of the investment pace and scale needed to meet portfolio-wide capital needs. However,

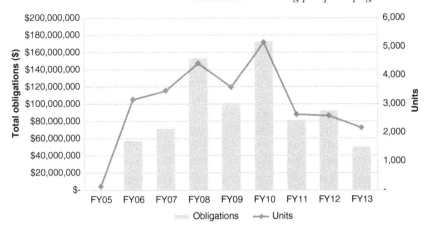

Figure 6.10 Multifamily Preservation and Revitalization (MPR) Demonstration Program Total Obligations and Total Assisted Units by Fiscal Year, 2005–2013

Source: USDA Rural Housing Service, various years, unpublished data.

the most recent capital needs assessment found MPR properties on better physical and financial footing than Section 515 and 514 properties that have not yet benefited from the program.

There is also a need for new construction of rural rental housing in order to replace the aging stock where it is still needed, as well as to serve new rural markets where a severe shortage of affordable rental housing has emerged. The Section 515 program has not supported significant new unit construction since the mid-1990s, with new construction dollars zeroed out since the 2012 fiscal year (HAC 2014b). The newer Section 538 guaranteed loan program has helped finance over 34,500 newly constructed units so far between fiscal years 1996 and 2013 (HAC 2014b), but layered financing makes deals complex, and tenants of these new units are not eligible to receive USDA Rental Assistance – since it is only available for eligible Section 515 and 514 properties – and may find rents difficult to afford.

The most significant source of funding for multifamily new construction and preservation is the federal Low Income Housing Tax Credit (LIHTC) program (Schwartz 2014). Authorized in 1986, LIHTC provides a federal income tax credit to investors who make qualified equity investments in affordable rental housing projects. The program exists within the federal tax code, but is implemented by state housing finance agencies (HFAs) and monitored by the U.S. Department of Housing and Urban Development. HFAs receive an annual allocation of competitive 9 percent tax credits based on population size which they distribute according to a Qualified Allocation Plan (QAP) published each year. Within the QAP, they specify criteria for scoring project applications according to state priorities and set-asides. Properties that can qualify for public bond financing also have access to 4 percent tax credits, which are non-competitive but provide less equity and are costlier, which can result in higher rents for low-income tenants without an additional source of rental assistance.

As of 2013, approximately 8,830 or 22 percent of all existing LIHTC-financed projects were located in non-metropolitan census tracts (U.S. Department of Housing and Urban Development 2013). These projects represented just under 300,000 affordable units for low-income households, or around 13 percent of all LIHTC units. Approximately 4,350 LIHTC projects containing 135,500 low-income units also have current USDA Section 515 loans, and a smaller number – 34 properties with 1,975 low-income units – have USDA Section 514 farm labor loans.

There are specific challenges to accessing LIHTC financing for rural rental housing. In order to be competitive with larger urban development projects in the state for the more lucrative 9% tax credits, rural priorities or set-asides are needed within state Qualified Allocation Plans. In 2013, 22 states had rural and tribal set-asides; nine states set aside at least 20 percent of their tax credits for rural projects, and eight specifically targeted preserving USDA-financed units (National Council of State Housing Agencies 2015). While this is indeed a positive sign, these states and set-asides do not necessarily align with where the bulk of USDA loans are maturing, or where current rural housing needs are greatest. Another challenge concerns the misalignment of USDA RHS funding models with typical LIHTC project financing. Historically, USDA multifamily loans were structured as single-source funding for capital debt and, if eligible, operating subsidies through Rental Assistance. This model is being replaced by complex layered financing for preservation and new construction of rural rental housing, but the laws and regulations guiding USDA programs can be different from those governing other funding sources. At the same time, USDA has also had flexibility over the years to work with borrowers and properties experiencing difficulties, and to protect tenants, in a way that may be jeopardized by layered deals with multiple funders and competing regulatory frameworks.

Access to credit for housing

No matter how well-delineated the housing demand, new construction or preservation needs are, unless capital is flowing to fund the needs, they cannot be adequately met. Access to mortgage credit for home purchase, as well as multifamily construction and permanent loans, remains a key issue in encouraging the demand for and supply of safe, decent, affordable housing in rural communities. The rural market has still not recovered from the 2007–2009 mortgage crisis, with home purchase activity still less than half of what is was in 2006, while high-cost mortgages continue to proliferate in some rural communities (HAC 2014c).

There are several mechanisms for encouraging private sector lenders to provide access to credit in rural areas. Since the 1930s, government guarantees against loan default have encouraged private lenders to reach underserved populations such as low-income households and veterans (Schwarz 2014). While the RHS Section 502 single-family and Section 538 multifamily guaranteed programs discussed above are limited to property purchases in rural areas serving low-income households, other federal agencies such as the Federal Housing Administration and the Department of Veterans Affairs are not limited to rural locations or households with earning below certain incomes.

Another key mechanism for encouraging access to credit through private lenders is the Community Reinvestment Act of 1977 (CRA) which requires federally insured depository institutions to provide access to credit within their service areas (Immergluck 2004). This can include originating the government-insured loans mentioned above, as well as other loans including those purchased by the Government-Sponsored Enterprises Fannie Mae and Freddie Mac to maintain the liquidity of lender capital. However, the rural CRA landscape is not straightforward (HAC 2015). Many regulated CRA lenders are not based in rural communities, and even this number is shrinking. It is difficult to track the impact of CRA-based lending in rural communities, since small banks with assets under $43 million or that only operate in non-metropolitan areas are exempt from reporting on their loan activity (HAC 2015).

New statutory requirements and proposed rules provide another opportunity to expand access to housing credit to underserved rural communities. Along with other financial regulations released post-2007 housing crisis, the Housing and Economic Recovery Act of 2008 took new national responsibility for encouraging the flow of private sector housing credit to underserved markets. It established a requirement for the government-sponsored enterprises Fannie Mae and Freddie Mac – institutions that purchase loans, pool them together and repackage them for investors – to serve three underserved markets: rural, preservation of affordable housing and manufactured housing. Targeted rural populations and markets include some of the hardest to reach, including farmworkers, Native American/Alaskans, Middle Appalachia, colonias and the Mississippi Delta. The proposed rule issued in December 2015 by the Federal Housing Finance Agency provides an opportunity to expand access to credit to these hard to serve areas by creating incentives for more rural single-family and multifamily home loan purchases, new housing finance product innovations and greater private lender participation in meeting the needs of rural America.

Next steps: more evidence for improved policies

In order to bring appropriate resources to rural communities, existing demographic and economic analyses and forecasts need to include analyses of housing market dynamics and public policy and programs to consider how best to serve diverse, dynamic rural populations and markets. In order for RHS and other federal housing resources to effectively target the people and places with the greatest needs, more comprehensive and detailed analyses are required to promote evidence-based decisions on future investments. Deeper analyses about local supply and demand dynamics could help with strategic decision-making around important questions, such as where there is growing unmet demand for affordable home purchase mortgages and/or rental units and what types of policy and program innovations are needed to reach persistently underserved markets.

To this end, RHS embarked on a new release of public data in 2016 across all three of their program areas, providing unprecedented information on their housing and community facility investments in rural America.[10] Researchers can now bring together data on RHS-financed properties, loans, borrowers and tenants with other data on housing markets and consumers to answer critical questions about federal rural housing strategies: past, present and future (Scally and Lipsetz 2017). These include general questions, such as what share of rural market demand is served by RHS, and what difference has RHS investments made in rural communities? These data also allow for more program-specific examination, such as where has RHS been successful in preserving multifamily properties, and what are the characteristics of these properties – their location, the tenants, the funding – that may have contributed to such success? How do borrowers and loans in the RHS Section 502 Direct Loan program compare to other rural home mortgages made through private lenders?

Having basic administrative data publicly available to help answer questions about past investments paves the way for more complex and strategic questions to shape future policy decisions. Where is rural America underserved by RHS investments, why and what is necessary to improve this in the future? How can RHS adjust its policies and programs to ensure they continue to reach the hardest-to-serve people and places amid shifting demographics and markets? What other types of resources are necessary for the success of rural communities – employment opportunities, educational institutions, social services, transportation infrastructure, broadband and more – and who are the partners needed to plan, finance and provide these resources alongside RHS investments? These questions require evidence-based answers to ensure the continued evolution and effectiveness of national rural housing policies and programs.

Conclusion

There is a growing set of national policies and programs to address rural housing needs, and more data are available than ever before to understand past investments, current needs and future demand for and delivery of housing programs. At the same time, rural housing needs are shifting and growing in new ways, making it an increasingly diverse and challenging market to serve. Over the past 80 years, USDA Rural Housing Service has met the needs of millions of rural renters and homeowners for safe, decent affordable housing. Yet significant parts of the rural population still need assistance. Given the changing needs of rural America and the increasing complexity of housing markets and finance, meeting future needs requires greater partnerships with other private and nonprofit lenders and property owners to preserve and expand the supply of safe, affordable units. It also entails deeper coordination with other federal and state agencies that control funding or influence other rural housing investments. Finally, private sector capital is needed to leverage limited public funds, making them stretch further and reach deeper. Working together, the changing needs of rural America – including those of people and places that are hardest to serve – can be addressed.

Notes

1 The authors were all employed by the U.S. Department of Agriculture (USDA) Rural Housing Service (RHS) at the time of this writing. The contents do not reflect the position of USDA, RHS or the Administration.

2 As of this writing, the current definition of rural for RHS housing programs is contained in Section 520 of the Housing Act of 1949 as amended by the Agricultural Act of 2014 (Farm Bill): "Any open country, or any place, town, village, or city which is not part of or associated with an urban area and (1) has a population not is excess of 2,500 inhabitants, or (2) has a population is excess of 2,500 but not in excess of 10,000 if it is rural in character, or (3) has a population in excess of 10,000 but not in excess of but not in excess of 10,000 if it is rural in character, or (3) has a population in excess of 10,000 but not in excess of 20,000, and (A) is not contained within a standard metropolitan statistical area, and (B) has a serious lack of mortgage credit for lower and moderate-income families, as determined by the Secretary and the Secretary of Housing and Urban Development. For purposes of this subchapter, any area classified as 'rural' or a 'rural area' prior to October 1, 1990, and determined not to be 'rural' or a 'rural area' as a result of data received from or after the 1990, 2000, or 2010 decennial census, and any area deemed to be a 'rural area' for purposes of this subchapter under any other provision of law at any time during the period beginning January 1, 2000, and ending December 31, 2010, shall continue to be so classified until the receipt of data from the decennial census in the year 2020, if such area has a population in excess of 10,000 but not in excess of 35,000, is rural in character, and has a serious lack of mortgage credit for lower and moderate-income families."

3 The Consolidated Farm and Rural Development Act of 1991 authorized the following definitions for RHS community facility programs: "the terms 'rural' and 'rural area' mean any area other than a city, town, or unincorporated area that has a population of greater of 20,000 inhabitants." The population count source is the most recent decennial census.

4 Unless otherwise noted, all RHS program data discussed in the remainder of the paper are provided according to the federal fiscal year, which runs from October 1st through September 30th of the following calendar year.

5 Data on property preservations are current as of June 2015.

6 For the history of HUD's Empowerment Zone program and its outcomes, see: http://portal.hud.gov/hudportal/HUD?src=/program_offices/comm_planning/economicdevelopment/programs/rc

7 For the program description and details on rural Enterprise Zones – jointly coordinated by HUD and USDA Rural Development – see: www.hudexchange.info/programs/promise-zones/.

8 For program description and details on HUD's Sustainable Communities Initiative, see: www.hudexchange.info/programs/sci/. A list of rural-focused resources is available here: www.sustainablecommunities.gov/partnership-resources/rural-communities.

9 For an overview of USDA Rural Development's Stronger Economies Together program, see www.rd.usda.gov/about-rd/initiatives/stronger-economies-together and http://srdc.msstate.edu/set/home.

10 The USDA Rural Development Datasets website is located here: www.sc.egov.usda.gov/data/data_files.html. These data are also available via data.gov.

References

Bailey, C., Jensen, L., & Ransom, E. (Eds.) (2014). *Rural America in a globalizing world: Problems and prospects for the 2010s*. Morgantown, VA: West Virginia University Press.

Belden, J. N., & Wiener, R. J. (Eds.) (1999). *Housing in rural America: Building affordable and inclusive communities*. Thousand Oaks, CA: Sage.

Collings, A. (1999). The role of federal rural housing programs. In J. N. Belden & R. J. Wiener (Eds.), *Housing in rural America: Building affordable and inclusive communities* (pp. 101–109). Thousand Oaks, CA: Sage.

Dewees, S. (2014). Native nations in a changing global economy. In C. Bailey, L. Jensen, & E. Ransom (Eds.), *Rural America in a globalizing world* (pp. 471–488). Morgantown, VA: West Virginia Press.

Hertz, T., & Farrigan, T. (2016). *Understanding the rise in rural child poverty, 2003–2014.* Washington, DC: U.S. Department of Agriculture, Economic Research Service.

Housing Assistance Council [HAC]. (2012). *Taking Stock: Rural people, poverty, and housing in the 21st century.* Washington, DC: Author.

Housing Assistance Council [HAC]. (2013a). Rental housing in rural America. Retrieved from www.ruralhome.org/sct-information/mn-hac-research/rural-rrb/654-rrn-rural-rental-housing

Housing Assistance Council [HAC]. (2013b). *Housing conditions for farmworkers.* Washington, DC: Author.

Housing Assistance Council [HAC]. (2013c). *Housing in Central Appalachia.* Washington, DC: Author.

Housing Assistance Council [HAC]. (2013d). *Housing in the Lower Mississippi Delta.* Washington, DC: Author.

Housing Assistance Council [HAC]. (2013e). *Housing in the border Colonias.* Washington, DC: Author.

Housing Assistance Council [HAC]. (2014a). *Housing an aging rural America: Rural seniors and their homes.* Washington, DC: Author.

Housing Assistance Council [HAC]. (2014b). *USDA RD historic activity through FY2013.* Retrieved January 20, 2016 from www.ruralhome.org/sct-information/usda-housing-program-data/rd-annual-obs/189-historic-activity

Housing Assistance Council [HAC]. (2014c). *Rural mortgage activity declines; home mortgage purchases are up, but so are high cost loans.* Washington, DC: Author.

Housing Assistance Council [HAC]. (2015). *CRA in rural America: The Community Reinvestment Act and mortgage lending in rural communities.* Washington, DC: Author.

Immergluck, D. (2004). *Credit to the community: Community reinvestment and fair lending policy in the United States.* New York, NY: Routledge.

Kleit, R. G., Kang, S., & Scally, C. P. (2016). Why do housing mobility programs fail in moving households to better neighborhoods? *Housing Policy Debate, 26*(1), 188–209.

Kropczynski, J., & Dyk, P. (2012). Insights into housing affordability for rural low-income families. *Housing and Society, 39*(2), 125–148.

MacTavish, K., Ziebarth, A., & George, L. (2014). Housing in rural America. In C. Bailey, L. Jensen, & E. Ransom (Eds.), *Rural America in a globalizing world* (pp. 677–692). Morgantown, VA: West Virginia Press.

Marcouiller, D., Lapping, M., & Furuseth, O. (Eds.) (2011). *Rural housing, exurbanization, and amenity-driven development: Contrasting the 'haves' and the 'have nots'.* Burlington, VT: Ashgate.

McGranahan, D., Cromartie, J., & Wojan, T. (2010). *Non-metropolitan outmigration counties: Some are poor, many are prosperous.* Economic Research Report No. ERR-107. Washington, DC: United States Department of Agriculture Economic Research Service.

National Council of State Housing Agencies. (2015). *State HFA factbook: 2013 NCSHA annual survey results.* Washington, DC: Author.

Nelson, P., & Cromartie, J. (2014). Subprime lending and its impacts on rural housing markets. *Housing and Society, 41(2),* 145–176.

Partnership for Sustainable Communities. (2012). *Federal resources for sustainable rural communities*. Washington, DC: Partnership for Sustainable Communities and U.S. Department of Agriculture.

Peck, S. (1999). Many harvest of shame: Housing for farmworkers. In J. N. Belden & R. J. Wiener (Eds.), *Housing in rural America: Building affordable and inclusive communities* (pp. 83–90). Thousand Oaks, CA: Sage Publications.

Scally, C. P., & Lipsetz, D. (2017). New public data available on USDA Rural Housing Service's single-family and multifamily portfolio. *Cityscape, 19*(1).

Schwartz, A. (2014). *Housing policy in the United States* (3rd ed.). New York, NY: Routledge.

Tighe, J. R. (2013). Responding to the foreclosure crisis in Appalachia: A policy review and survey of housing counselors. *Housing Policy Debate, 23*(1), 111–143.

U.S. Department of Agriculture Economic Research Service. (2015a). *Rural America at a glance: 2015 edition: Economic Information Bulletin 145.* Washington, DC: Author.

U.S. Department of Agriculture Economic Research Service. (2015b). Geography of poverty. Retrieved January 17, 2016 from www.ers.usda.gov/topics/rural-economy-population/rural-poverty-well-being/geography-of-poverty.aspx

U.S. Department of Agriculture Rural Development. (2016). *2015 progress report.* Washington, DC: Author.

U.S. Department of Agriculture Rural Housing Service. (2016). *2015 Annual fair housing occupancy report.* Washington, DC: Author.

U.S. Department of Housing and Urban Development. (2013). Low-Income Housing Tax Credit Database. Retrieved from http://lihtc.huduser.gov/

7 Sustainable housing development

The Hopi way

Carlos V. Licón and Ignacio San Martín

A village in need of assistance

In the summer of 2000, a group of Hopis from the Village of Moenkopi traveled south to Tempe, Arizona, in search of assistance with ideas to resolve housing needs. During recent years, the number of young couples in their community had been growing, but new homes were not available for these new families, forcing them to live with relatives or in mobile homes in nearby towns. The original request by this group, the Moenkopi Housing Commission, who met with Arizona State University's design and planning faculty, was presented in very simple terms. The village needed a housing design project to resolve the immediate need for additional homes. The number or type of units was not clear, but the need was evident to them.

Through the years, government agencies have provided assistance to the Native American population and built homes in different communities. The Hopis are no exception. In different parts of the Hopi Nation, one can find examples of homes built to alleviate needs, but they show little resemblance to local spatial patterns and construction materials traditionally used by the Hopis (LaMantia 2014). The request by the Moenkopi Hopis quickly made clear that there were issues of viability and affordability at stake. Moenkopi is not only a village with a limited suitable area, but growth is a highly restricted concept in for the Hopis (McIntire 1971). As the project evolved, different experts, faculty, and students from Architecture, Landscape Architecture, Bioclimatic Science, Planning and Engineering joined the team to contribute their ideas, which resulted in many discussions, revisions and proposal changes.

Rural housing in the Hopi land

What started as a rural housing project for a group of young Hopi families transformed into a learning journey into a special culture and place. The complexities of the project challenged professional approaches and methods, directing efforts to sustainability, not as an afterthought or an addition to enhance the environmental quality of the project, but as a coherent response to the Hopi cultural traditions and the community's needs. Together, we created an ambitious vision of the future, hoping that our plans could trigger a meaningful action plan for the Hopi people.

It is not uncommon for rural housing initiatives to have relief assistance con-notations. Rural housing efforts may suggest policies and actions conducive to alleviating inequities, including communities in economic distress, or supporting community efforts to reach development levels similar to nearby urban places. Policy efforts may be directed to address evident or perceived imbalances in tech-nical and economic capacities and, in some cases, as a response to political pressures and policies. Even though housing projects in rural communities can be based on a combination of these factors, it is important to acknowledge the impact these interventions make on a small local community and the opportunity they represent to materialize values and aspirations that are strongly rooted in these communities, very often through generations of sacrifice and hard work.

Since the 1960s, Federal Housing programs have provided housing assistance through projects and built units for different Native Americans, including the Hopis, but, according to Ahmed (1993), with no attention to cultural or spiritual uses of space, resulting in "single-family detached units built on western stand-ards of ranch style homes with multiple rooms" (Ahmed 1993, p. 59). The Hopis currently delegate housing issues to the Hopi Housing Authority, which operates under the Hopi Tribal Government and follows a public hearing process to advance and consider housing initiatives (Ahmed 1993). Other attempts to explore alterna-tive design approaches to Hopi housing have focused from energy efficiency and bioclimatic design (Cook 2000; Friederici 2004; La Mantia 2014), archaeological studies on Hopi settlements (Cameron 1991; McIntire 1971) and traditional spatial configurations of Hopi homes (Ahmed 1993; Houk and Nutlouis 2004).

This chapter describes a project with long-term aspirational goals, initially by a small village, but potentially by a whole Native American community. It is a plan-ning and design project responding to specific practical needs with limited finan-cial and material resources, but it is also a project focused on how to understand and incorporate community values, cultural identity, to support a long-term vision beyond the immediate relief produced by a typical housing scope. How can a pro-ject support visionary leadership and the emergence of a new identity? And how can this new identity blend a contemporary understanding of sustainability with core traditional stewardship values?

An emerging housing paradigm

Shortly after the Moenkopi Housing Commission had explained their needs and concerns about community, identity, legacy and tradition, the university team real-ized the need to approach the housing problem in an integrated and holistic way. The lack of infrastructure to support a conventional development and the vulner-ability of the landscape, which requires careful interventions to maintain a healthy place, offered the opportunity to explore alternative approaches to development. A new way to organize and design could support easily viable ways to establish sustainable development patterns, to create a long-term plan and to introduce new technology systems, not very often accessible to small communities with limited resources.

The trust that both groups, Hopis and scholars, had in each other created a productive and creative work environment, which resulted in fewer barriers to advance alternative planning and design proposals. Work on this project ranged from regional climate analysis to biophysical site studies to housing, neighborhood and village design. The project also developed initial studies of building typologies and energy needs.

Building a case for Hopi sustainability

Cultural sustainability is intrinsically linked to economic and environmental sustainability. Not only the measurable quality of life matters in sustainable development. Especially evident among the Hopi people is the fact that values of community, belonging, legacy and stewardship shape their identity and bind them together in time and space. While defining tourism strategies for the Hopi Tribe, Swanson and DeVereaux found that "cultural sustainability focuses on the preservation of cultural heritage and identity. In most interactions with Hopi, conversations and actions routinely focus on the importance of the Hopi Way, and the preservation of heritage and identity above all else" (2014, p. 491). Understanding and incorporating the Hopi Way and operationalizing these aspirations can help build new generations of Native Americans where the contemporary and the traditional are combined in new expressions of cultural meaning and environmental stewardship.

The Hopi people

Among the oldest Native American communities, the Hopi Reservation was created by executive order in 1882 (Hopi Tribe 2014b) on the same land they have occupied for centuries. According to Oliff (2012), the Hopi people have two of the oldest continuously inhabited villages in the United States. Walpi and Oraibi villages date back at least 1,000 years. The Hopi Nation occupies 1.6 million acres (2,500 square miles) in the northeastern portion of the state of Arizona. The Hopi tribal lands also include the Moenkopi District with 61,000 acres restored to the Hopis in 1996 (Hopi Tribe 2014a). Figure 7.1 shows the location map of the Hopi Nation.

Some demographic aspects of the Hopis

According to the Hopi Tribe (2014b), there is a tribal enrollment of 14,000 members from 12 villages as of September 2014, with half of them living inside the reservation and the off-reservation trust lands. The median age in 2010 was 32 years, a younger community compared to the state of Arizona, with a median age of 36. Among the Hopis, one-third of the population is younger than 18 and 11 percent older than 65 years (MAG 2014).

Families in the Hopi Nation have a particular configuration. Census data show 24 percent of Hopi households are occupied with members of the extended family, more than triple the 7 percent occupation rate for the state of Arizona. Hopi

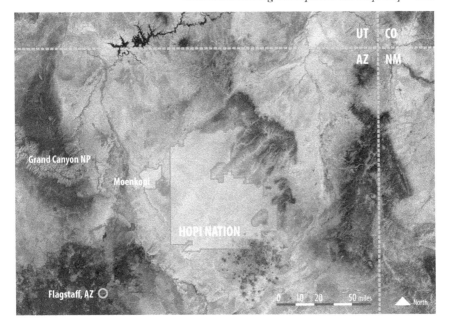

Figure 7.1 Location Map of the Hopi Nation (ESRI 2013; Hopi Tribe 2014a)

2014 Hopi Tribal Land Base (Hopi Tribe, 2014a).

Hopi Main Reservation 1,625,686 acres (District Six & Hopi Partitioned Lands restored in 1974).

Moenkopi District Reservation 61,604 acres (Restored to Hopi Tribe in 1996).

Hopi Three Canyon Ranch Lands 175,441 acres (Hopi Indian Trust Lands 2010, managed by DNR).

communities have strong family ties with a high percentage of women household leadership, resulting from a combination of tradition and necessity. This presents challenges for the Hopi families as, according to the 2010 census, 43 percent of households are headed by a female with no husband present.

Box 7.1   Demographic Profile (MAG 2014)

Hopi membership	14,000
Hopis living on the reservation	7,000
Hopis in Moenkopi	960
Unemployment on Hopi Reservation	18 %
Hopis below the poverty line	35 %
AZ residents below poverty line	15 %
Young Hopis below the poverty line	48 %
Young AZ residents below the poverty line	22 %

The 2010 census shows that 35 percent of the Hopi population is living below the poverty line. This is more than double of the 15 percent for the State of Arizona. This rate increases for the young population, with 48 percent of the Hopis 18 or younger living in poverty, compared to 22 percent for the same group at the state level. Current reports prepared for the Arizona Commission of Indian Affairs by the Maricopa Association of Governments (MAG 2014) show an unemployment rate of 18 percent.

Hopi governance and land ownership

Hopi villages are considered autonomous under Hopi rule. It was not until the 1930s that the Hopi villages established joint leadership and created a tribal government (Richland 2007). The internal governance structure of clans is described by Sekaquaptewa (1999) as a group of Hopi families with a matriarchal structure. The clan is derived through the mother's line. The autonomous Hopi system of governance has challenges for the consistent planning and the coordinated development and administration of tribal resources among the different villages. Consequently, different views emerge with respect to commercial development in relation to preservation of culture (MDC 2015).

The "Hopi Way," according to Swanson and Devereaux (2014), embodies cultural sustainability as it captures the interest of the Hopi people to maintain their cultural identity and heritage. These traditional ways are "deeply rooted [in] religion and spirituality" (Oliff 2012). This strong sense of community guides multiple aspects of their lifestyle, including land allocation. Inside the Hopi tribal lands, land is passed down through matrilineal clans (MDC 2015). "Though the men own the livestock and the fruit trees, the women own all the land, even that under the fruit trees" (Smith 1998). Once assigned, land can be passed on to other female relatives but not sold or rented (Forde 1931).

The village of Moenkopi

The Village of Moenkopi (see Figure 7.2), adjacent to the Navajo community of Tuba City, lies west of the main tribal territory and is physically separated from the main Hopi Mesas. In 2010, the village of Moenkopi had a population of 969 living in 361 homes, with 13 percent of its residents living under the poverty line and an unemployment rate of 17 percent for adults 25 and older (U.S. Census Bureau 2015). The Moenkopi district represents 14 percent of the total tribal lands with 4 percent of the Hopi population living in the tribal lands.

Moenkopi climate considerations

The Moenkopi region is characterized by large monthly temperature range variations during each month of the year. Winter months can reach freezing temperatures for at least three months with wind chill factors reaching below 20 degrees. Summer average temperatures are moderate with June and July reaching 90 degrees.

Figure 7.2 The Village of Moenkopi

Photo by Carlos Licón.

With the exception of a few summer months, Moenkopi housing needs to account for heating, a condition that can be in large part achieved by using passive solar heating. This is a critical factor influencing the siting of architectural buildings. To benefit from solar heat during winter months, building orientation should be facing ten to 15 degrees east of south. Average wind speed in the Moenkopi Plateau is eight miles per hour, with a dominant east and southeast directions. North and northeastern winds do occur in winter. The Moenkopi Plateau is subject to seasonal storms of high velocity and long duration winds with peak gusts of 50 miles per hour.

A first typology in response to bioclimatic analysis

Early in the planning process, the team captured initial bioclimatic findings in a conceptual house typology for the Moenkopi area. Courtyard-type housing arrangements can help achieve a higher level of bioclimatic comfort. During the peak summer months, excess heat can be controlled by shading devices, natural ventilation and the utilization of evaporative cooling systems. Summer dominant winds come from the West and Southwest. Sand dune activity, evident in Figure 7.5, shows clear evidence of prevalent southwestern winds. Selecting appropriate plant materials for dune stabilization and reducing wind speeds are necessary for comfortable outdoor activities.

Figure 7.3 shows a prototype home design with a courtyard configuration that creates a wind shelter and a comfortable microclimate. This prototype home can expand as the family grows and later can be easily subdivided into two homes maintaining a shared outdoor space. From this housing type, variations in size allow for a diverse arrangement while responding to climate and family size needs.

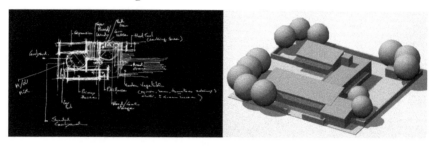

Figure 7.3 Hopi house typology concept from bioclimatic analysis. This concept represents a courtyard arrangement of the houses with shading elements on the southern part of the house and protected from wind with large-canopy trees. Wind-shaded areas toward the east side of the house (right side) offer possibilities of comfortable outdoor activities. This home is also capable of growing by addition as it can be subdivided when new families are formed from the core resident family.

Establishing a planning process

From the early stages of the project to the final revisions of proposals, the role of the Hopi community was an important driving force. For a period of two years, multiple meetings and working sessions resulted in joint decisions and considerations between all the project participants. The project provided a valuable learning opportunity for everybody involved. As participants became more familiar with the contributions and views of the other participants, the process became a more open dialogue and focused in relevant issues.

Establishing a decision-making process through the project was based in building trust. Multiple site visits, meetings at the village and trips to visit other projects, were important to open communication and learn from each other. Using graphic media to present ideas helped clarify concepts and discuss ideas. Expectations sometimes combined conflicting issues, such as individual preferences and sense of community, identity and diversity or traditional ways and new technologies. In many ways, this project described many of the current Native American dilemmas about their roots and contemporary American visions. All these issues have implications about how they see their future and how this project helps them build a place for the next generation.

It became obvious during preliminary conversations and first site visits that the project needed to start almost from nothing. There was no land specifically allocated for future village growth, no alternative sites had been explored, and no supporting infrastructure existed to connect a new settlement. Energy, water or waste management systems were not in place to support a new expansion. If a new village, or any other form of permanent settlement, was going to occupy this place, it needed to provide its own supporting infrastructure for energy, water, waste disposal etc. Distance to other Hopi communities is also a significant challenge for Moenkopi, which makes the supply of goods and services complicated and expensive.

With no existing support systems for a new development, any housing expansion requires the construction of new dedicated infrastructure. This cost of additional energy, water and transportation systems has to be factored in the new project. Both choices, a conventional expansion of remote energy network or a locally generated energy supply system, had a significant financial impact on the project. The Moenkopi Plateau is a vulnerable environment, and the consideration of potential impacts have a significant role in the decision of building more permanent human settlements. Exploring infrastructure and development alternatives with potential lower environmental costs became a foundational approach toward a sustainable development.

Recent infrastructure studies done by the Village of Moenkopi show their interest in alternative energy generation under the advice of local power companies and the National Renewable Energy Lab (Nahsonhoya 2015). Securing a water source has also been a problem, as wells are expensive or not productive enough (Nahsonhoya 2015).

The lack of infrastructure, suppliers, or existing development was perfect to try innovative ways of allocating resources for a future Hopi village. Construction materials would need to rely heavily on locally available sources. Energy could be generated from wind and sun, both in great abundance in the region. The lack of easy water availability was a considerably limiting factor and would have to be carefully managed and treated for multiple uses. Environmental sustainability in a housing project for the Moenkopi District would depend on the smart application and management of these critical resources.

The site analysis process was guided by four basic aspects. These considerations embody planning and design principles for sustainable development efforts. Figure 7.4 shows the specific elements of each component considered to determine the site location for the new village:

- Biophysical features. Include natural resources and land form characteristics capable of supporting a housing development.
- Bioclimate. This category emphasizes passive and low-energy strategies by considering local conditions relevant to the design of outdoor and indoor spaces that can provide comfortable environments.
- Transportation network. The connectivity of the new community is an important consideration for its viability. Finding the right point of access from the existing road provides safety and convenience for the new development.
- Cultural landscape. Hopi expressions and attitudes toward the land are important determinants of the location of the village and its elements. Any effort in understanding how the land and the culture are connected increases the chances of a more culturally appropriated design.

Selecting a site for the new village

The Hopis at Moenkopi pointed out that in recent years, the Hopi Tribe reassigned more than 60,000 acres of ancestral grazing land to the Moenkopi District. From multiple site visits and a study based on the core factors described earlier (see Figure 7.4), three sites were identified as potential places for the new community

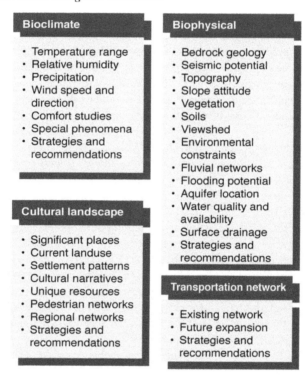

Figure 7.4 Core Factors Considered for a Hopi Housing Planning and Design Project

(see Figure 7.5). These sites are located in the Moenkopi Plateau south of the Moenkopi Wash and east of the Little Colorado valley. The Plateau is at 5,500 feet of elevation, with a topographic relief of 800 feet above the Little Colorado valley.

- Site 1 is located on the south side of the Moenkopi Wash, immediately west of State Road 264, the only paved road crossing the district.
- Site 2 is located two miles southeast of the original Moenkopi Village. This site is east of a land formation that shields the site from southwestern winds. The site is also accessible through SR264. Sites 1 and 2 have significant panoramic vies of the Moenkopi valley. In addition, Site 2 is adjacent to several natural springs and has access to farming fields in the Moenkopi Wash floodplain.
- The location of Site 3 is five miles away from the village. It is a large, open and flatter location, but more distant from the original village and less sheltered from local winds. Access through SR264 is also possible for this site.

A suitability analysis weighs and combines all the different site features to determine the most viable land use and identifies potential land improvements needed. This suitability study shows Site 2, with a score of 59 percent of the available points, as the best place for the new housing settlement. Site 2 is protected from strong

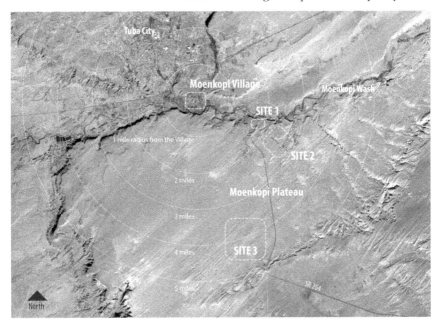

Figure 7.5 Landsat Image of the Moenkopi Plateau
Adapted from Image Service 2015.

winds, safe from potential flooding, and has adequate slopes for passive solar hous-ing. Even though the other two sites scored slightly lower than Site 2, they have characteristics of wind or solar access that made them ideal places for energy gener-ation, an important goal of this project. Currently there is no electricity available at this site, which makes it easier to suggest alternative, more environmentally friendly options. Site 1, at the edge of the Moenkopi Wash, has the right solar exposure for photovoltaic arrays. Five miles to the south, Site 3 is exposed to the constant wind that characterizes the area, making it the ideal place for wind turbines for power generation. The suitability and fitness of these three sites are summarized in Table 7.1 and mapped in Figure 7.7.

Overall, if these three sites are developed as suggested, they can configure a powerful and mutually complementary image of a sustainable community, with energy-efficient bioclimatic housing design, supported by locally generated alter-native energy with minimum environmental impact. Together, these three sites can configure a community that functions, looks and advocates sustainability (see Figure 7.6).

Water has been and will continue to be a severely limiting factor for human set-tlements in the area. Any development in the area must guarantee an efficient use of water and the safe release of treated wastewater for long-term goals of high quality and sufficient quantity of water for the future residents of the new village.

Table 7.1 Evaluation of Environmental Factors for Site Selection

Bioclimatic	Observations	Max score	Site 1	Site 2	Site 3
Temperature range	Peak winter months' temperature below 30F; however, yearly average temperature increasing over the last ten years with reduction in precipitation. Presence of drought conditions.	5	3	3	3
Wind speed and direction	Mean wind speed about 8 mph. Peak gust winds 50 to 60 mph.	5	3	3	2
Comfort studies	Building orientation critical. Favorable for passive solar energy design.	5	3	3	2
Special phenomena	Subject to seasonal storms with high-velocity winds and capable of moving large amounts of sand.	5	3	3	2
Biophysical					
Bedrock geology	Depth to bedrock unknown.	5	2	2	2
Seismic potential	Seismic hazard potential. Earthquakes recorded at Cameron and vicinity. Need to evaluate seismic zone classification.	5	2	3	3
Slope attitude	South- and Southeast-facing slopes optimum with a 2% to 5% slope preferred.	5	2	3	2
Vegetation	Typical Great Basin Desertscrub. Current drought conditions are affecting vegetation coverage reestablishing sand dune activity.	5	2	2	2
Soils	Poor soil conditions exist as the result of long periods of sand dune accumulation.	5	2	2	2
Viewshed	Panoramic views of regional landscape.	5	3	5	2
Aquifer location	Depth and yield of N-Aquifer unknown.	5	2	2	3
Surface drainage	2% to 5% slope for adequate surface water drainage.	5	3	4	3
Cultural landscape					
Significant places	Proximity to Lower Moenkopi Village is important.	5	3	4	2
Unique resources	Proximity to and access to agricultural fields. Panoramic views of the countryside.	5	4	4	2
Transportation network					
Existing network	Proximity to existing road network.	5	4	4	4
Access to infrastructure	Proposed sites are absent of infrastructure.	5	0	0	0
Total sum		**80**	**41**	**47**	**36**
Degree of compliance from ideal			51%	59%	45%
Site 2 score is 15% better than Site 1					
Site 2 score is 30% better than Site 3					

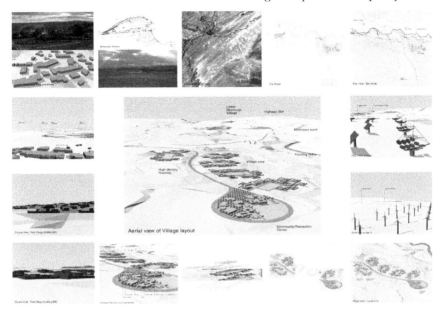

Figure 7.6 The New Moenkopi Landscape is Shaped by a Sustainable Community with Power-Generating Solar Panels and Wind Turbine Systems

Conceptual planning model

The planning and design process focused on three main components: the housing unit, the housing cluster and the new community. These three scales of the project were developed under a series of guiding principles shown in Figure 7.4. These principles supported alternative approaches for sustainable housing with a smaller ecological footprint, increased efficiency and arrangements in an organic and flexible pattern to allow for a long process of configuration and growth for the new settlement. In the interest of making the process simple to understand and clear in its delivery to the Hopis of how these principles can guide a planning and design process, the team grouped them under the well-known marketing frame of the three R's – recycle, reuse and reduce – as detailed in Figure 7.8. Every principle adopted in the project was to achieve at least one of these three larger "goals," or it could be described as having an effect of reducing, reusing or recycling materials, energy or space in the village, the home or the larger environment. This approach proved to be a successful way to introduce purpose to the project in a non-technical way.

Under this assumption, a sustainable community would be a place that explicitly reduces energy and water consumption through energy-efficient buildings and low-water-usage practices. Sustainable housing will reduce thermal loss through the right use of materials and the adequate placement of buildings. Reduction in the use of toxic substances and a reduction of waste is important to prevent negative environmental impacts to the place and its inhabitants. Similarly, reuse is important to achieve efficiencies in this new community. Innovative design and planning

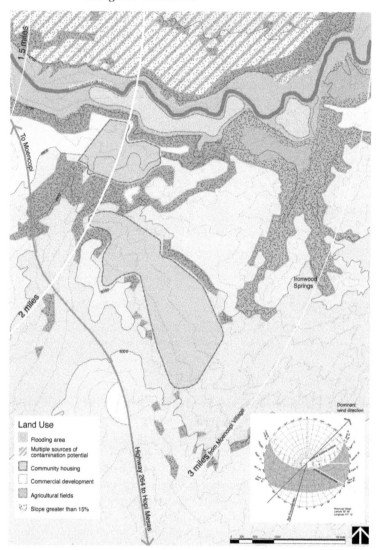

Figure 7.7 Land Suitability Analysis Map

practices will favor the creation of multifunctional spaces. The reuse of water in a place like Moenkopi is paramount in the sustainability of the place. The recycling of materials, water and waste is important to achieve efficiency goals and to reduce the external sourcing of goods and energy.

Making a program of project requirements

Several meetings with the Moenkopi residents resulted in a basic program of needs and spatial concepts. The Hopi, whose name means "the peaceful people," were certainly kind and welcoming, as well as private and quiet. Multiple planning meetings with many questions about the "Hopi way" of living helped understand spatial needs and create adequate dwelling typologies. Some of the unique programmatic pieces of information include the following:

- Homes need separate outdoor gathering spaces for women and men.
- Families want to live near their relatives.
- Hopi celebrations are closed to non-Hopi visitors. During these ceremonies, people gather in open plazas created by the arrangement of homes.
- Ceremonial spaces need designated areas.
- A new community needed to be in close proximity to the existing village as access to the existing kiva is imperative.
- Traditional homes are small, with thick walls that prevent heat loss.
- Homes are built close to each other, creating a characteristic appearance for Hopi settlements. In form and method of construction, traditional Hopi dwellings are similar to other Pueblo groups of the American Southwest and, according to McIntire (1971), are a clear continuation of the building tradition of the Anasazi culture (p. 511).

Guiding principles	Village program
REDUCE • Energy • Water • Thermal loss • Window glazing • Electricity consumption • Toxic detergents **REUSE** • Roof as garden • Roof as solar collector • Water from wetlands into irrigation **RECYCLE** • Water • Construction materials • Waste recycling • Composting • Other products: paper, plastic, glass	• Land requirements • Expansion potential • Housing • Public spaces, private spaces, religious • Meeting halls • Arts and crafts • Plaza • Agricultural land, organic farming • Water recharge, wetlands • Cooling towers • Water recharge • Irrigation via water harvested from rain runoff

Figure 7.8 Guiding Planning and Design Principles Adopted for the Project Together with the Program Elements for the New Village

Project description

From large to small scale, from public to private or from community to individual systems, this project can be divided into three distinctive parts. Each one of these parts is approached through the same guiding principles while solving problems of a different nature and integrating solutions of a different scope. These three parts configure and organize solutions at the village or community level, addressing public space needs, a neighborhood "pod" at the family and clan clusters of homes, and the housing unit, which proposes solutions at the individual family scale.

Each one of these dimensions – the family, the clan and the village – demands a particular spatial configuration in response not only to functional aspects, but also to landscape characteristics and cultural considerations. A holistic approach to a sustainable housing development requires settlement patterns with an understanding of a multigenerational community, supporting a high quality of life through a productive and protected environment. This is not an unfamiliar concept to the Hopi traditional ways and therefore establishes a powerful aspirational goal for them.

A new village layout

The community layout allows for flexible growth by proposing multiple pods of housing that are built as new homes are needed. With this layout, organic growth can be accommodated while maintaining a compact and connected community. The distribution of these clusters of homes responds to careful studies of vistas and to the allocation of common open space. Clusters are separated by the distance that is needed for the creation of cultivated fields, which then serve as community gardens.

Housing density was an important consideration, especially in trying to achieve walkable distances between homes and a visual image that resembles traditional Hopi villages. Clusters of homes are defined by common public plazas and community gardens. Next to the housing clusters, the village includes a community center, as illustrated in Figure 7.9, which provides space for supporting necessary services and amenities.

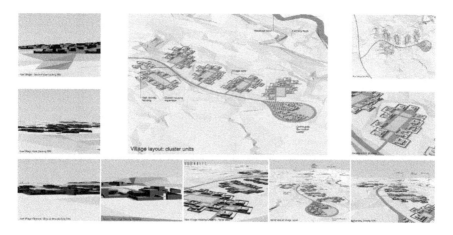

Figure 7.9 Village Layout

Housing pods

The village is organized and defined by a sequence of pods of homes along a collector road. Each pod is a cluster of ten to fifteen homes and resembles traditional Hopi settlements with the large communal open plaza in the middle (see Figure 7.10). By creating multiple clusters, different public spaces are available for various ceremonies and public activities. According to the Hopi tradition, each cluster can represent a specific group of families or clans. Pods are distributed along a central access street, minimizing the building and upkeep of roads and maintaining a clear identity for each cluster within the larger community. This type of arrangement of clustered units allows the community to appear complete at every stage of growth. The simple addition of new pods increases the number of homes without affecting the existing ones. Building densities and house types can vary depending on needs and family sizes. Additionally, the use of low, solid walls surrounding properties reinforces the volume effect typical of ancestral Hopi settlements. A fully configured community will have about five to eight pods with a total of 60 to 120 units, allowing an increase of 30 percent of the current homes in the Moenkopi Village.

The space between the pods, allocated for community gardens, helps to create a visual separation in the neighborhood while at the same time bringing neighbors together as they share responsibilities in growing food. It can also be a place to continue the planting of corn, which, as observed by Ahmed (1993), has special spiritual meaning for the Hopis. In addition, the community gardens contribute to enhancing comfortable microclimates and offering productive uses for treated wastewater and harvested rain water.

Housing units

> The [Hopi] house as a unit, embodies all the environmental cues needed to sustain societal continuity.
>
> (Ahmed, 1993, p. 24)

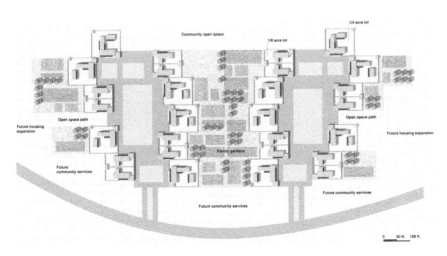

Figure 7.10 Housing Pods

Working sessions with the Moenkopi residents and guest planning and architecture academics resulted in a design approach that had the following principles at heart: Homes should be designed and built with special considerations to high environmental performance standards and adequate functional needs and with sensitivity to cultural understandings of dwellings and lifestyles. The house design needed to respond to a very unique spatial typology, as Hopis prefer undifferentiated or personalized homes because that would be seen as a threat to their sense of community (Ahmed 1993). For Hopis, the outdoor areas require a male space, a female space and an additional ceremonial space in which the piki house is erected. In it, the Hopis prepare the piki bread, a ceremonial bread, on a stone over an open fire (Cameron 1991). Common practice in traditional villages is the use of roofs and terraces as sitting places for community ceremonies and gatherings. Access to public space is of utmost importance. Every traditional Hopi settlement analyzed, current and archaeological, had a very characteristic layout. Homes are arranged around notably long plazas, and the community surrounds this sequence of public spaces distributed and aligned throughout the town. The compact clustered homes and the multiple plazas account for the two most recognizable characteristics of any traditional Hopi settlement, as shown in Figure 7.11.

The design team partnered with architecture faculty and students to produce alternative home designs. Students produced multiple variations from a basic typology. They did not always include a courtyard, but explored other approaches to create outdoor and indoor connections, accommodate internal growth and transformation as families change composition, size and needs over time and to incorporate passive bioclimatic designs with the right shape and orientation to produce comfortable indoor and outdoor spaces with the right solar exposure, the necessary

Figure 7.11 Ground-level view of housing units. The dominant volumes of walls and buildings surrounding long plazas define the overall image of the new village.

wind protection and the appropriate insulation to deal with temperature variations through the seasons and the typical diurnal variations of a desert climate.

Some of the aspects considering in the proposed architectural housing typologies include:

- Solar and wind considerations for thermal comfort.
- Visual connection from inside the homes to the outdoor landscape.
- Walled terraces with different solar orientation alternatively offer sun and shade.
- Thick walls with storage capacity.
- Modular units to adapt to specific family needs.
- Indoor and outdoor cooking and eating options.
- Large common space capable of providing space for large, extended-family gatherings.
- Capacity of rooms and spatial configuration to change as family needs change with time.

Energy and water systems

In order to understand the technical feasibility of alternative energy systems (solar and wind), an Arizona power company provided support through engineering calculations for electricity loads as a way to determine energy needs and the size of solar and wind-generating facilities. Figure 7.12 shows simulated energy needs scenarios for a typical housing unit.

Water is a critical component to the viability of this new village, including wastewater, which needs to be treated before put back in the land. Multiple strategies are needed to capture and to process water in order to maximize its use, reduce its waste and create an adequate supply in quantity and quality. Even though the project has been approved by the Hopis, to this day, one of the biggest challenges to advance the realization of the project has been securing a water supply. After reviewing different options, the Village of Moenkopi has identified a nearby well capable of providing enough water for the new development at an affordable cost (Nahsonhoya 2015). As this project confronts multiple reality checks, critical issues emerge to define the realization of the project under a sustainable vision. The long-term availability of water and an efficient and clean energy source, in combination with adequate responses to harsh climate conditions test the sustainability of the place and create difficult boundaries for its construction. Good planning and design can contribute to establish a viable framework for the implementation and operation of a sustainable Hopi village.

Public space in the Hopi village

The village concept includes three different types of open and public space. Homes in each pod face a long plaza similar to those community spaces found in traditional

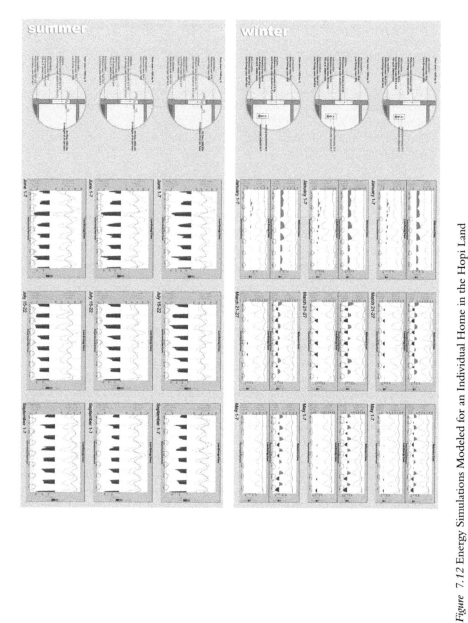

Figure 7.12 Energy Simulations Modeled for an Individual Home in the Hopi Land

villages. Even though Hopis do not consider plazas as social centers and do not occupy them in that manner (Ahmed 1993), they are important places for ceremonial activities and community gatherings during religious events throughout the year.

A second form of open space is the larger landscape surrounding the village. The visual aspects of the surrounding landscape constitute an important element in contextualizing the village and in connecting residents with the larger ecosystem that provides for their settlement. Connections are primarily visual and symbolic but also practical, making clear the land determines the livability of the Hopis in this region, and, therefore, it must be carefully protected. And finally, there is a third community space to consider, one that provides community services (see Figure 7.13). At one end of the village, a cluster of facilities provides a possible place for a small school, or a clinic or a senior center. This community services space can also include opportunities for outdoor activities. The concept presented in the first round of designs for this particular village included a community orchard and a baseball field.

Because this new village is considered an extension of the Moenkopi Village, the siting or construction of a ceremonial center, a kiva, is not considered. This ceremonial areas condition patterns of growth and locations of new constructions (Cameron 1991). This restriction intensified the need to establish the new village within walking distance of the existing kiva.

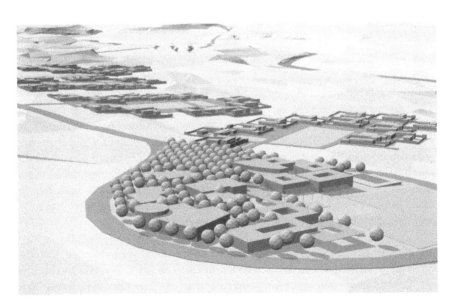

Figure 7.13 Community Center with Supporting Services for the New Village

Toward a sustainable native American identity

After several years of deliberations, presentations and the gathering of political and financial resources and support, during the last two years, planning efforts were conducted by a professional firm. Finally, this project is undergoing the approval process for a possible ground-breaking ceremony that will culminate in the efforts of this visionary and patient group of Hopis (Nahsonhoya 2015). This culmination is only the beginning of a new journey in sustainability led by those who have understood for centuries what a true holistic development needs to look like.

Final thoughts

The problem expressed by the Moenkopi Housing Commission who visited Arizona State University 15 years ago was very specific and focused, and their expectations were simple and direct. Young families did not have a good place to live and were often forced by necessity to live with family members or in mobile homes away from their community. It was also very clear that unemployment was high and income, if available, was low, so the affordability of housing for these young families was very limited. Embedded in this short-term request by the housing commission, there were long-term concerns. What will the future of these young generations of Hopis be? How can the Hopi communities stay together? Can the Hopis keep their traditions alive and relevant?

The journey for the Moenkopi residents has not been without challenges. Securing financial support and untangling the complexities of federal, state and tribal regulations and procedures has taken significant time and effort. Their interest in pursuing these approvals is driven by their explicit conviction that this project represents them well. Their aspirations, their cultural ways and their current needs were captured and transformed into a meaningful vision of a modern Hopi settlement.

Even a modest housing project for young families, when approached with a well-grounded vision and the confidence to trust that a well-framed solution will help resolve great difficulties, teaches important lessons not only for the Hopis, but for the professions and the institutions that manage the development process. The creativity and the ingenuity expressed in this project through the collaboration between Hopis and scholars are important steps to advance meaningful efforts toward sustainability. Adopting, implementing and later branding and exporting sustainability can be a path for improved quality of life for future generations of Hopis while reinforcing cultural foundations and embracing a thoughtful incorporation of technological advancements into their lifestyles. Traditions from the old world can be carried over to the modern world, and enhance the sustainability of development, making it more grounded and meaningful.

> [Hopis] have lived in Hopitutskwa and have maintained our sacred covenant with Maasaw, the ancient caretaker of the earth, to live as peaceful and humble farmers respectful of the land and its resources. Over the centuries we have survived as a tribe, and to this day have managed to retain our culture, language and religion despite influences from the outside world.
>
> (Hopi Tribe 2014b)

References

Ahmed, R. (1993). *Housing from a cultural perspective: The Hopi way of dwelling.* (March Master's Thesis), University of Arizona, Tucson, AZ. Retrieved from http://hdl.handle.net/10150/291835

Cameron, C.M. (1991). *Architectural change at a Southern Pueblo.* (Ph.D. Dissertation), University of Arizona, Tucson, AZ.

Cook, J. (2000). *New Hopi village: Housing for community sustainability.* Tempe, AZ: Herberger Center for Design Excellence, College of Architecture and Environmental Design, Arizona State University.

ESRI (Cartographer). (2013). *Tribal Lands, 4 Corners States.*

Forde, C. D. (1931). Hopi agriculture and land ownership. *The Journal of the Royal Anthropological Institute of Great Britain and Ireland, 61,* 357–405.

Friederici, P. (2004). Something new – and old – Under the sun: Hopi's native sun. In P. Friederici, R. Houk, & T. Marinella (Eds.), *A New Plateau: Sustaining the Lands and Peoples of Canyon Country* (pp. 118–120). Minneapolis, MN: Renewing the Countryside.

Hopi Tribe. (2014a). Department of natural resources. Retrieved October 5, 2015 from www.hopi-nsn.gov/tribal-services/department-natural-resources-2/

Hopi Tribe. (2014b). The Hopi tribe: The official website. Retrieved October 5, 2015 from www.hopi-nsn.gov

Houk, R., & Nutlouis, R. (2004). Moving forward in dignity: Lilian Hill's Sustainable housing for indigenous people project. In P. Friederici, R. Houk, & T. Marinella (Eds.), *A New Plateau: Sustaining the Lands and Peoples of Canyon Country* (pp. 99–101). Minneapolis, MN: Renewing the Countryside.

Image Service (Cartographer). (2015). *Landsat 8 Oli, 15m Pansharpened Natural Color Image.* Retrieved from http://landsat2.arcgis.com/arcgis/rest/services/Landsat8_PanSharpened/ImageServer

LaMantia, R. (2014). *Housing for the Hopi community: Designing sustainable, affordable and energy efficient housing in the Hopi community, linking to cultural patterns of sustainability.* (Sustainable Built Environments Senior Capstone), University of Arizona, Tucson, AZ. Retrieved from http://hdl.handle.net/10150/337371

MAG, Maricopa Association of Governments. (2014). *Demographic profiles for Arizona Indian reservations: 2010 Decennial U.S. Census and 2011 American Community survey 5-year estimates.* Phoenix, AZ: Maricopa Association of Governments for the Arizona Commission of Indian Affairs.

McIntire, E. G. (1971). Changing patterns of Hopi Indian settlement. *Annals of the Association of American Geographers, 61*(3), 510–521.

MDC. (2015). Experience Hopi. Retrieved December 2015 from www.experiencehopi.com

Nahsonhoya, L. (2015). Village of lower Moenkopi Moves forward with the development of a new community "Poosiwlelena", local news. *Hopi Tutuveni.* Retrieved from www.hopi-nsn.gov/news/hopi-tutuveni/

Oliff, H. (2012). Reservation Series: Hopi. *Partnership with Native Americans.* Retrieved November 15, 2015 from http://blog.nativepartnership.org/reservation-series-hopi/

Richland, J. B. (2007). Pragmatic paradoxes and ironies of indigeneity at the "edge" of Hopi sovereignty. *American Ethnologist, 34*(3), 540–557.

Sekaquaptewa, P. (1999). Evolving the Hopi common law. *Kansas Journal of Law & Public Policy, 9*(4), 761–791.

Smith, L. M. (1998). Hopi: The real thing. Retrieved October 2015 from www.ausbcomp.com/redman/hopi.htm

Swanson, K. K., & DeVereaux, C. (2014). Culturally sustainable entrepreneurship: A case study from Hopi tourism. In K. F. Hyde, C. Ryan, & A. G. Woodside (Eds.), *Field Guide to Case Study Research in Tourism, Hospitality and Leisure* (Vol. 6, pp. 479–494). Bingley, UK: Emerald.

U.S. Census Bureau. (2015). Community Facts from U.S. Department of Commerce. Retrieved from www.factfinder.census.gov

8 Examining the housing dilemma in the rural South's Alabama Black Belt and Mississippi Delta regions

Stephanie A. Pink-Harper

Most Americans envision or define the "American Dream" as owning their own home. Interestingly, according to the United States Department of Housing and Urban Development (HUD) (2008), America is the best-housed nation in the world. Millions of American families however struggle to find homes and apartments within their budgets. There are many barriers that limit access to achieving that dream. According to the Housing Assistance Council (HAC) (2005) the root of some communities' housing issues are tied to persistent spatial segregation or racial inequalities. For others, it may be a financial barrier, while others may allude to socioeconomic factors. As a result, many Americans are often forced to live in sub-standard housing or in over-crowded conditions due to factors that drive up costs for some families.

Whatever those barriers may be, it is vital to understand the impact that access to adequate housing and excessive housing cost can have on a community's overall quality of life and their potential for economic prosperity. This examination is particularly necessary considering the changes in today's economy. The expansion of international trade and the trend of globalization have resulted in significant challenges for communities competing in today's economy. These economic changes have resulted in a myriad of development challenges particularly for America's rural and impoverished communities, which have traditionally fallen behind other regions (Bellamy and Parks 1994). Communities in the rural South such as the Mississippi Delta and the Alabama Black Belt have suffered the hardest as a result of these global market expansion trends (Bellamy and Parks 1994). Additionally, many of these rapid changes in the economy have results in the rural South struggling to sustain their economy and adapt to these challenges (Sumners and Lee 2004).

Why examine the Alabama Black Belt and Mississippi Delta regions?

References to the term "Black Belt" are typically attributed to Booker T. Washington (1901) and W.E.B. DuBois (1903). Washington (1901) and DuBois (1903) used the term to describe the rich dark soil and agricultural advantages of the Southern region. The Alabama "Black Belt" region specifically refers to the rich agriculture and dark soil found in counties located in the central portion of the state

(Gibbs 2003). The term has also been used to refer the geographic region comprised of Southern counties with disproportionately persistent patterns of poverty and high populations of African-Americans (Wimberley 2010). The entire Black Belt region expands beyond Alabama, including counties as far east as Virginia to Florida and portions of Alabama, Mississippi and eastern Texas (Wimberley 2010).

The Lower Mississippi Delta was originally defined by the U.S. Congressional Lower Mississippi Delta Commission in 1988 (Poston Jr. et al., 2010). According to the Delta Regional Authority (DRA), the Lower Mississippi Delta region includes select counties along the Mississippi River of Arkansas, Illinois, Kentucky, Missouri, Mississippi and Tennessee. Today, the Delta Regional Authority (DRA) is the task force responsible for addressing the economic perils and challenges of the communities in this region (DRA 2016).

The southern Black Belt and Lower Mississippi Delta regions have both been extensively explored by sociologists, political scientists, economists and many other social scientist researchers (Bellamy and Parks 1994; Wimberley 2010; see Bukenya 2004; McDaniel and Casanova 2003). However, empirical statistical analysis exploring the factors that impact the economic growth and development trends of these regions are sparse. To test this relationship, this study seeks to identify the factors that impact a community's ability to attract businesses and jobs in these regions.

The purpose of this research is to explore the impact that adequate housing and excessive housing cost have on a community's economic sustainability. The aim of this research is to provide insight for rural communities to revitalize their economy. Due to the small number of counties in these regions, all Alabama and Mississippi counties are included in this study to generate a reasonable population size to empirically test the research question guiding this study. The focus of this analysis however is counties in the rural South's Mississippi Delta and Alabama Black Belt regions. Regional variables were also created to statistically analyze the impact of the research question in each of the defined geographic locations. The central question guiding this research is stated below.

> *Research question:* What impact does adequate housing have on county economic growth and development trends?

The Mississippi Delta status of counties was determined by inclusion in the DRA's definition of service counties in Mississippi (DRA 2016). Due to the lack of consistency in the defined Alabama Black Belt counties, the DRA, the Encyclopedia of Alabama and the University of Alabama's Center for Economic and Business Research's list of Alabama Black Belt counties were consulted. Maps highlighting the counties included in each region are presented below in Figure 8.1.

Exploring the research question previously mentioned, this study is organized as follows. First, this research examines previous literature on the impact that housing and other factors have on a region's economic growth and development trends. A discussion of the methodology used and the source of the data are then provided. Next, the results and findings of the analysis conducted are presented. Specifically, the results from the Ordinary Least Square (OLS) regression are provided to

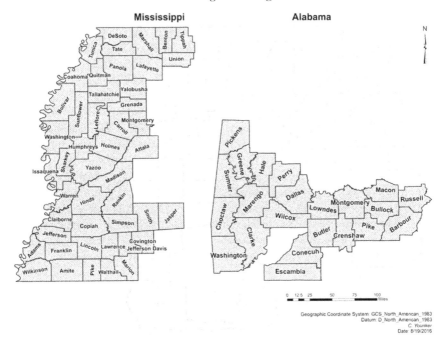

Figure 8.1 Alabama Black Belt & Mississippi Delta Counties Selected

determine the impact that the proposed hypothesis has on the economic growth and development trends of the Alabama Black Belt and Mississippi Delta regions. Following the results section is a discussion of the limitations and suggestions for future research. This research concludes by first offering policy implications regarding ways to improve the quality of housing in rural counties. Lastly, policy implications for enhancing the quality of life and potential for attracting businesses and jobs for residents in Alabama and Mississippi are provided.

Literature review

Housing and economic development

According to the Housing Assistance Council (2000), adequate housing is one of the biggest challenges facing rural America. U.S. Representative Bennie Thompson (Mississippi) suggested that for rural communities to gain economic advantages, adequate housing stock are a necessity. This is an important factor because the communities in these regions have been known for attracting only low-wage and low-skill jobs (Gibbs 2003).

What impacts do adequate housing and excessive housing cost have on the economic growth and development trends of residents of these rural communities? Empirical testing using regression to analyze the impact that adequate housing and excessive housing cost has on a community's economic stability is sparse. The existing research on this topic is dated and lacks conclusive recommendations for local government officials and researchers' seeking to identify the factors that influence this relationship. Allen-Smith (1994) posits that researchers' lack of interest in rural minority populations is possibly due to their small populations compared to larger metropolitan areas. Jensen (1991) argues that residents of rural communities where high concentrations of poverty and minorities exist tend to be substantially disadvantaged in comparison to large urban communities. One of the challenges these communities face is their remote locations, which results in decreased opportunities for increased economic growth and quality of life standards.

Dating back to the 1970s, researchers examining the factors that impact economic growth and development trends in the rural South have found that the rural poor face harsh economic conditions (Colclough 1988). Problematic, residents of these communities in rural Southern counties gain employment opportunities, but typically from low-wage jobs. Additionally, Till (1986) found that in these regions, the number of jobs grew, but typically from low-skill manufacturing jobs.

Bellamy and Parks's (1994) analysis of rural development explores the factors that impact economic growth across Southern counties. In their analysis, economic growth is defined as manufacturing plant establishments, and the number of manufacturing jobs. The results from the demographic characteristics and plant establishments models reveals that urban counties with less poverty and more educated populations were more likely to experience increases in the number of manufacturing plant establishments. Their regression results for manufacturing jobs showed that counties with less educated populations and less poverty were more likely to have more jobs. In Black Belt counties, they found that higher percentages of educational attainment and higher poverty resulted in lower manufacturing jobs trends. They also explore the factors that impact county per capita income growth. The findings from the analysis reveal that counties with a less educated population lead to growth in per capita income. Bellamy and Parks (1994) posit that these perplexing results may be due to the low-wage types of jobs attracted into these counties.

The South's economic development strategies towards business attraction over the past three decades have resulted in increased employment growth opportunities for these communities. Interestingly, the types of jobs and businesses gained as a result of these strategies were low-skill manufacturing jobs. Bellamy and Parks (1994) credit this success to offering tax breaks and other economic incentives to lure businesses into their jurisdiction. Problematically, despite these trends, the economic status of communities in the rural south have continued to fall behind others (Bellamy and Parks 1994).

In 1975 the Home Mortgage Disclosure Act was established to monitor minority access to the mortgage market (Munnell et al., 1996). The data collected as a result of this act include applicant's race, gender, income and whether their home loan application was accepted or denied. Lin and White (2001) examine several factors that impact the market for mortgage loans. In their analysis using Home Mortgage Disclosure Act data, they find that housing loan applicants from small metropolitan areas and rural areas had a higher probability of being turned down for home loan purchases than applicants from large metropolitan areas. Thus, we can conclude that rural counties are more likely to have higher percentages of loan denials. Megbolugbe and Cho (1993) also examine housing and mortgage markets trends. The findings of their research indicate that low-income and minority households experience extremely lower patterns of mortgage loan lending guarantees. Similarly, Newman and Struyk (1983) examine the relationship between persistent poverty and housing deficiency in communities. They find that 80 percent of families considered poor have excessive housing expenditures. In other words, more than 30 percent of income of these families is spent on housing expenses. They also find that 11 percent of families living in poverty also live in overcrowded housing conditions. Furthermore, their findings indicated that a large percentage of the families living in permanent poverty resided in rural areas.

As previously stated, research collectively examining the relationship between adequate housing (or excessive housing cost) and economic development are sparse. This research seeks to bridge this gap in this literature by analyzing the relationships between these two bodies of research. Thus, it is hypothesized that if a county has adequate housing then they are more likely to have higher economic growth and development trends. In comparison, counties with inadequate housing are expected to have lower economic growth and development trends. Specifically, counties that have lower percentages of household crowding, lower housing cost-burden percentages and lower percentages of loan denials are more likely to have higher economic growth and development trends.

> *Hypothesis:* Counties with adequate housing are more likely to have higher economic growth and development trends than counties with inadequate housing.

Methodology and data

Data are collected from multiple sources to create a robust dataset to identify the predictors of economic growth and development trends in Alabama and Mississippi. More specifically, data are collected from 2000 and 2010 from the Census Bureau and the Department of Agriculture's Atlas of Small and Rural Town America, the Bureau of Labor Statistics and the Bureau of Economic Analysis.

Independent variables

To examine the impact that housing factors have on rural community's economic growth and development trends, the three main independent variables included in this analysis are household crowding, housing cost-burden and mortgage loan denials. These three factors have been included in research conducted by the Housing Assistance Council (2005) as measurements of housing and housing finance indicators. These factors are used as proxies to illustrate the impact that adequate housing and excessive housing cost can have on a communities' economic growth and development trends. Household crowding, a measurement of adequate housing, is defined as households with occupied units of 1.01 or more occupants per room (Housing Assistance Council 2016). The household crowding data were obtained from the 2000 U.S. Census Bureau, Decennial Census. Housing cost-burden, an excessive housing finance indicator, is measured as housing costs that are 30 percent or more of the household's income as defined by the HUD (Housing Assistance Council 2016). It includes both owner and renter household income costs at 30 percent or more. Housing loan denials are also an excessive housing finance indicator that is calculated as the number of denied housing mortgage loans divided by the total number of mortgage applications per county (Housing Assistance Council 2016). The housing loan denials percentage data was unavailable for 2000, so it was obtained from the Consumer Financial Protection Bureau for the earliest available date, 2007.

Controls

To determine the impact that housing factors have on predicting economic growth and development trends, the impact that household crowding, housing cost-burden and loan denials are examined. In particular, the economic growth and development trends of counties are examined while controlling for population, poverty, non-metropolitan status, per capita market income, unemployment rate, educational attainment and race. A summary of the variables, their measurement and the descriptive statistics are presented below in Table 8.1. These variables have similarly been employed in other economic development research, yet not collectively in housing and economic development research (see Feldman and Desrochers (2003); Donegan et al. (2008); Goldstein and Drucker (2006); Betz et al. (2012); and Pink-Harper (2015).

The remaining control variables are measured as follows. Population is measured as the county population size/count in 2000 according to the U.S. Census, Decennial Census. Persistent poverty is defined by the U.S. Department of Agriculture, Economic Research Service, Atlas of Rural and Small-Town America for 2000. The variable is defined as the classification of counties by poverty level in 2000. Definitions of rural vary dramatically. Thus, for this study, the non-metropolitan status of counties as determined by the Office of Management and Budget 2003 classification of counties metro or non-metropolitan definitions is employed. Per capita market income is a distress measurement indicator defined by the Appalachian Regional Commission (2016). The Commission uses per capita market income to "identify and monitor the economic status of Appalachian counties." They calculate per capita market income as the county total personal income minus any government transfer payments divided by the county population. Generally, these data are used to determine if a community meets requirements for grants based upon income. These data were collected from Stats America's five-year calculations. The unemployment rate for counties was collected from the Local Area Unemployment Statistics from the U.S. Bureau of Labor Statistics for 2000. Unemployment rate indicates a county's economic status and revels the necessity for more economic opportunities, i.e. jobs in a community. Human capital is measured as the percent of

Table 8.1 Variable Descriptions and Source

Variable	Measurement	Source	Year	Mean	Std. Dev.	Min.	Max.
		Independent Variables					
% Household Crowding	% occupied units crowded	U.S. Census Bureau	2000	4.401	2.141	1.3	11.7
% Housing Cost-burden	% of occupied units with 30% or more housing cost	U.S. Census Bureau	2000	18.049	4.790	10.419	31.111
% Loan Denial	% mortgage loan denials	Consumer Financial Protection Bureau	2007	28.445	28.760	2.850	361.905
		Control Variables					
Black Belt/Delta	Black Belt/Delta = 1 Otherwise = 0	Delta Regional Authority University of Alabama Encyclopedia of Alabama	–	0.4631	0.5003	0	1
Non Metropolitan Status	Non Metropolitan Status =1 Otherwise =0	U.S. Department of Agriculture, Economic Research Service, Rural and Small-Town Atlas	2003				
Persistent Poverty	County Persistent Poverty = 1 Otherwise = 0	U.S. Department of Agriculture, Economic Research Service, Rural and Small-Town Atlas	2000	0.490	0.502	0.490	1
Unemployment	Unemployment rate	Bureau of Labor Statistics	2000	5.942	1.746	5.942	13.1
Educational Attainment (High School Degree)	% with a high school diploma	U.S. Census Bureau	2000	31.729	4.240	31.729	43.6
				0.490	0.502	0.490	
Per Capita Market Income	ACS five-year per capita market income	Stats America	2000	5.942	1.746	5.942	34334
Population	County population	U.S. Census Bureau	2000	48937.97	73592.69	2274	662047
% Black	% county Black	U.S. Census Bureau	2000	34.531	21.782	.4	86.5
		Dependent Variables					
% Change Business Establishments	% change in business establishments from 2010–2000	Bureau of Labor Statistics	–	-.845	12.907	-24.699	55.1358
% Change Number of Jobs	% change in the number of jobs from 2010–2000	Bureau of Economic Analysis	–	-.778	15.101	-29.993	63.512

adults over the age of 25 with a high school diploma. This educational attainment data were collected from the 2000 U.S. Census. Race is measured as the county percentage that is African-American (Black). These data were obtained from the 2000 U.S. Census.

Dependent variables (economic growth and development measurements)

In this study, the dependent variable consists of a group of variables, including business establishments, number of jobs and average annual pay. To access the impact that housing factors have on county economic growth and development trends, this research builds upon the work of Pink-Harper (2015); Hoyman and Faricy (2009); Donegan et al.'s (2008) definitions of these variables. Specifically, in this research, economic development is defined as job gains and percent in business establishment.

Each dependent variable is measured as the percent from 2000 to 2010 for business establishments, job growth, and average annual pay. The percent data for each variable include the start number of each indicator in 2000 and the end number in 2010 due to the availability of data collected from the following sources. The business establishments and average annual pay data were collected from the Bureau of Labor Statistics (www.bls.gov). The job growth data were collected from the Bureau of Economic Analysis (www.bea.gov). A summary table including the measurements of the variables, the data sources and descriptive statistics are presented in Table 8.1.

Summary descriptive analysis results

In this section, summary descriptive analysis statistics are presented. These illustrations provide visualizations of the adequate housing options in the Black Belt and Delta counties in comparison to non-Black Belt and Delta counties in Alabama and Mississippi. The summary statistics are presented below in Figures 8.2–8.4.

The chart in Figure 8.2 shows that the mean for household crowding in the Black Belt and Delta counties is higher than non-Black Belt and Delta counties. Specifically, the average household crowding percentages in the Black Belt and Delta counties is 5.64 percent, in comparison to 3.3 percent in the non-Black Belt and Delta counties in 2000. These illustrations show that residents in the Black Belt and Delta are more likely to reside in crowded housing. In other words, residents in the Black Belt and Delta are more likely to reside in households with 1.01 occupants per room or more.

The housing cost-burden mean statistics are presented below in Figure 8.3. The chart in Figure 8.3 reveals that the average housing cost-burden was 19.60 percent in Black Belt and Delta counties in comparison to 16.70 percent in non-Black Belt and Delta. These statistics include both owner and renter occupied housing where housing cost is 30 percent or more of their selected monthly income. The Black Belt and Delta counties are 2.9 percent more likely to have housing cost-burden.

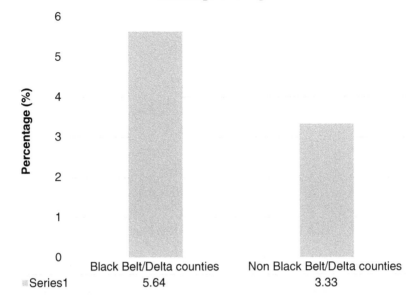

Figure 8.2 % Household Crowding

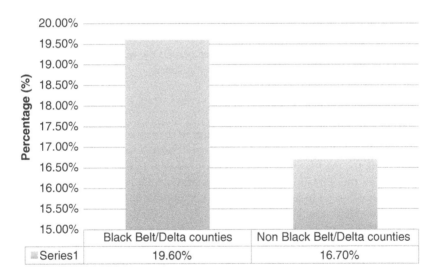

Figure 8.3 Percent Housing Cost-Burden

The housing mortgage loan statistics are presented in Figure 8.4 and reveal that the rate of loan denials in Black Belt and Delta counties is higher than non–Black Belt and Delta counties. The mean housing loan denial rate is 29.80 percent in Black Belt and Delta compared to the non–Black Belt and Delta housing loan

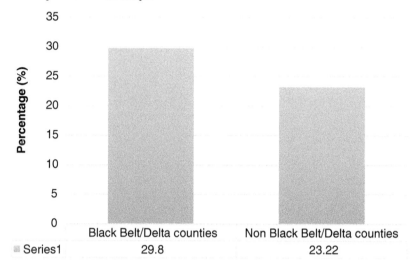

Figure 8.4 Percent Housing Loan Denials

denial rate of 23.22 percent. In the Black Belt counties, there is a 6.58 percent increase in housing loan denials in comparison to the non-Black Belt and Delta counties, the largest percentage difference in the adequate housing measures. In sum, collectively, the mean statistics presented in Figures 8.2–8.4 show that the Black Belt and Delta counties continue to lag behind the non-Black Belt and Delta counties across various measures of adequate housing.

Regression analysis results

The OLS regresssion results are presented here in the regression results section. The models were checked for outliers using Fox's (1991) recommendations for the test. After testing the models for outliers, those identified were removed because of their influence on the substantive findings in the analysis. Multicollinearity diagnostics were also run, but no indication of its presence was found since the variance inflation factors' values were below 10.

The OLS regression analysis is employed to determine the statistical impact and the relationship between the adequate housing measures and county economic growth and development trends. The regression models presented are vital to further understand the impact adequate housing has on economic growth and development trends of a community, particularly since an OLS regression analysis to date has not been conducted of these communities collectively. In Tables 8.2–8.4, the direction of the relationships found in each model are presented. The positive (+) sign refers to a statistically significant relationship found between the independent variables included in the model as predictors of the dependent variable (i.e. business establishments and number of jobs). The negative sign indicates that there is a negative statistical relationship between the independent and dependent variables.

Table 8.2 Summary of the Household Crowding Regression Results

Independent Variables	Model 1: Business Establishments	Model 2: Business Establishments (Black Belt & Delta)	Model 3: Number of Jobs	Model 4: Number of Jobs (Black Belt & Delta)
% Household Crowding	+	No Effect	No Effect	No Effect
Black Belt/Delta	No Effect	−	No Effect	−
Population	−	−	−	−
Persistent Poverty	+	No Effect	+	+
Non-metropolitan	−	−	−	−
Per Capita Market Income	+	+	+	+
Unemployment Rate	No Effect	No Effect	+	+
Educational Attainment	−	−	−	−
% Black	−	−	−	−

Key:

No Effect = No statistical relationship.

+ (Positive) = For every 1 percent increase in the independent variable, there is an increase in the dependent variable.

− (Negative) = For every 1 percent decrease in the independent variable, there is a decrease in the dependent variable.

Table 8.3 Summary of the Housing Cost-Burden Regression Results

Independent Variables	Model 1: Business Establishments	Model 2: Business Establishments (Black Belt & Delta)	Model 3: Number of Jobs	Model 4: Number of Jobs (Black Belt & Delta)
Housing Cost-burden	No Effect	+	−	No Effect
Black Belt/Delta	No Effect	−	+	−
Population	−	No Effect	No Effect	No Effect
Persistent Poverty	+	No Effect	+	+
Non-metropolitan	−	−	−	−
Per Capita Market Income	+	No Effect	+	+
Unemployment Rate	No Effect	No Effect	+	+
Educational Attainment	−	No Effect	−	−
% Black	−	−	−	−

Key:

No Effect = No statistical relationship.

+ (Positive) = For every 1 percent increase in the independent variable, there is an increase in the dependent variable.

− (Negative) = For every 1 percent decrease in the independent variable, there is a decrease in the dependent variable.

Table 8.4 Summary of the Housing Loan Denial Results

Independent Variables	Model 1: Business Establishments	Model 2: Business Establishments (Black Belt & Delta)	Model 3: Number of Jobs	Model 4: Number of Jobs (Black Belt & Delta)
Housing Loan Denials	–	–	No Effect	No Effect
Black Belt/Delta	No Effect	–	No Effect	–
Population	–	No Effect	+	No Effect
Persistent Poverty	–	No Effect	+	+
Non-metropolitan	–	No Effect	+	+
Per Capita Market Income	+	No Effect	+	+
Unemployment Rate	No Effect	No Effect	+	+
Educational Attainment	–	+	+	+
% Black	–	+	+	+

Key:

No Effect = No statistical relationship.

+ (Positive) = For every 1 percent increase in the independent variable, there is an increase in the dependent variable.

– (Negative) = For every 1 percent decrease in the independent variable, there is a decrease in the dependent variable.

The variables with no effects listed indicates that there was no statistically significant relationship identified between the independent and dependent variables. In addition to the Summary Tables 8.2–8.4 presented here, the actual OLS regression results are included in the appendix.

The results for Household Crowding, an indicator of adequate housing in a community, are presented in Table 8.2. The household crowding and business establishment results presented in Model 1 include all counties from both states. The results presented in Model 2 examine counties in the Black Belt and Delta only. In sum, the results in Model 2 are consistent with the full business establishment result presented in Model 1. However, given declines in manufacturing in rural communities, these results are likely due to small businesses.

The variables statistically significant in Model 2 are population, non-metropolitan, per capita market income, educational attainment and percent Black. These results show that for each one percent increase in population, there is a .0000681 percent decline in business establishments. In other words, in the Black Belt and Delta counties larger counties are more likely to have decreases in business establishment from 2000–2010. Non-metropolitan in comparison to metropolitan counties are also more likely to have decreases in business establishments. In non-metropolitan counties in comparison to metropolitan counties, there is a – 9.55 percent decline in business establishments. These trends could be explained by the remote locations of some counties and illustrating the challenges of isolated communities to gain new business opportunities in their jurisdiction. Counties with higher levels of per capita market income are more likely to have higher percent increases in business establishments. The results for per capital market income show that for each one percent increase in per capita market income there is a .0017975 percent increase in business establishments. Counties with lower educational attainment levels are more likely to have higher percent increases in business establishments trends. For the educational attainment variable, the results show that for each one percent increase in the number of individuals in a county with a college degree or more, there is a −.704956 decline in the business establishment percent change. Additionally, counties with higher percentages of Blacks are more likely to have higher percent increases in business establishments. The results for the percent Black variable show that for each one percent increase in the percent Black in county there is a −.2991584 percent decline in the business establishments from 2000–2010.

Presented in Models 3 and 4 are the number of jobs and household crowding trend results. The results for the full number of jobs and Black Belt and Delta counties are consistent in regards to the variables significant and the direction of the relationships across both models. The findings from Model 4 for Black Belt and Delta counties reveal that there is a positive statistical relationship between persistent poverty, per capita market income and unemployment rate and number of jobs. There is a negative statistical relationship between population, non-metropolitan status, educational attainment and percent Black as predictors of the number of jobs in Black Belt and Delta counties in the number of jobs model. Most interesting in the number of jobs models is that the percent household crowding does not statistically influence the number of jobs trends in Black Belt and Delta counties. Also, interestingly the unemployment rate variable is now significant in Model 3 and Model 4 but was not in Model 1 and Model 2. The results for the unemployment rate variable in the Black Belt and Delta counties model that for each 1 percent increase in the unemployment rate, there is a 4.34 percent increase in business establishments. This finding shows that counties with high demands for jobs are more likely to receive increases in the number of jobs in their county. However, these perplexing result in comparison to the other results show that although counties in demand gain jobs, it does not mean that the jobs are high-quality, high-wage jobs. Last, in Model 3 for Black Belt and Delta counties classified in persistent poverty there is a 6.934 percent increase in the number of jobs, this variable was not statistically significant in Model 2.

The results for housing cost-burden are presented below in Table 8.3. The results for Black Belt and Delta counties presented in Model 2 show that counties with higher housing cost-burden are more likely to have higher percent change increases in business establishments. The remaining statistically significant factors influencing business establishments in the Black Belt and Delta counties are non-metropolitan status and percent Black. Both of these factors had a negative impact on business establishments.

In Table 8.3, the number of jobs results for housing cost-burden are presented in Models 3 and 4. The results in Model 4 for the Black Belt and Delta counties show that the positive and statistically significant predictors of number of jobs are persistent poverty, per capita market income and unemployment rate. The remaining statistically significant predictors of number of jobs trends are negative and include housing cost-burden, non-metropolitan status, educational attainment and percent Black. Most interesting in the number of jobs full model is the results for housing cost-burden. In this model, this shows that for each 1 percent increase in housing cost-burden, there is a −.5994507 percent increase in the number of jobs percent change from 2000 to 2010.

The housing loan denials summary regression results are presented below Table 8.4. The findings for these models reveal that housing loan denial is only a statistically significant predictor of business establishment trends in the full model and for Black Belt and Delta counties. In Model 2, the Black Belt and Delta only results show that the additional statistically significant predictors of business establishments are negative and include educational attainment, and percent Black. In the number of jobs Model 4 for Black Belt and Delta counties only, the housing loan denials is not a statistically significant predictor of this measure of economic growth and development. The positive statistically significant predictors are persistent poverty, per capita market income and unemployment rate. These results revel that for each 1 percent increase in each variable (per capita market income and unemployment rate and counties that are persistently in poverty) there was an increase in the number of jobs trends from 2000–2010 in the Black Belt and Delta counties. The negative statistically significant predictors of number of jobs trends are non-metropolitan status, educational attainment and percent Black. Although not always statistically significant, the per capita market income was always positive across Models 1–4 for housing loan denials.

Overall, the results of these analysis reveal that counties in these rural southern counties continue to lack and are underdeveloped. In sum, collectively, the results of this study ultimately highlight the necessity of examining both the types of business establishments (i.e. small vs. larger) and the types of jobs (i.e. low-wage vs. high-wage).

The results reported in the OLS regression analysis fail to support the hypothesis that counties with adequate housing are more likely to have higher economic growth and development trends than counties with inadequate housing. However, they do support the works of Bellamy and Parks (1994). Thus, continued extensive research is needed to further explore the impact adequate housing has on economic growth and development trends. To date, most of the housing and economic development research focuses on case studies of rural communities yet lack statistical analysis of the relationship between these factors. Thus, additional research is needed in defining the indicators of adequate housing. As shown in this study, homeownership might not be the best measurement of adequate housing. For example, ample adequate rentals or public assistance housing may exist for families that cannot afford to purchase.

The results of these analysis show that although counties in need of more economic growth and development opportunities received them does not mean that the quality of these opportunities adequately meets the needs of these economically depressed communities. In other words, the types of jobs and businesses that are in these communities remains unclear given the data employed in this study. For example, it is unclear given the data used in this study if the figures include new business startups from within a community or expansions of existing businesses. Future studies should seek to explore these vital distinctions to better understand the impact adequate housing can have on a community.

Consistent with previous works (see Bellamy and Parks 1994), the control variables, county demographic characteristics, remained the significant predictors of economic growth and development trends.

The results of this analysis should, however, caution conclusions that these counties' overall economic stability is improving. In other words, although the results of this analysis show that these counties did have more economic growth and development trends, they do not provide insight into the types of opportunities provided. For example, according to McLaughlin (2002), rural economies tend to lack diversity in regards to businesses and job opportunities for residents. Similarly, Bellamy and Parks (1994) posit that although these counties may appear to have gained economic growth and development opportunities, the quality of the jobs and businesses gained must be further explored. They argue that these increases in growth may be a reflection of the labor-intensive, low-wage jobs gained. Additionally, further research is needed to understand the types of jobs and the types of businesses locating in these communities. For example, are the types of jobs locating to these communities one-person startups or small businesses. In other words, future research should explore the size of the jobs and businesses included in the analysis.

Future research should examine counties in the rural south in comparison to other rural geographic regions. Future research should also examine the types of business establishments and jobs created during the periods of examination. For example, are the job and business attractions in the rural South low-skill or creative class classification jobs? This is particularly important, since the results of this study unexpectedly revealed that counties in the rural South with inadequate housing are more likely to experience increased economic growth and development trends. Although unexpected, these results may reveal that in these counties, businesses and jobs and opportunities are actually being provided for in these communities. However, the jobs provided and the businesses established may not adequately provide the pay and wages needed to address issues of poverty in these areas; in other words, the quality of these jobs may be lacking despite other gains.

Further research is also needed to examine the impact adequate housing factors have on the economic growth (i.e. increases income in these communities). In other words, future research is needed to further explore the impact that adequate housing has on the pay trends in rural communities. The average annual pay trends explored in this analysis are not statistically significant, thus warrants further examination of the factors that influence it in future studies. For example, do the increases in the number of jobs in rural communities result in higher pay and wages for these residents? Do increases in business establishments in rural communities result in higher pay and wages for residents in these communities?

Nearly 15 percent of the U.S. population resides in non-metropolitan communities (USDA, ERS). Thus, rural communities are a vital component to America's economy. If America is going to remain a competitive player in the globalized economy, the challenges that are unique to these communities must be further addressed. That means, new job opportunities for creative, knowledge- and technology-based work are essential. Furthermore, similar to Bellamy and Parks's (1994) recommendation, increased attention to educational attainment must remain a priority. If local communities desire to attract different job opportunities for their residents, they must ensure their workforce has the knowledge and skills to attract higher-wage jobs and businesses into their jurisdiction.

Appendix

OLS regression results (Tables A8.1–8.3)

Table A8.1 Household Crowding Regression Analysis

	Model 1: Business Establishments	Model 2: Business Establishments (Black Belt & Delta Only)	Model 3: Number of Jobs	Model 4: Number of Jobs (Black Belt & Delta Only)
Constant	−6.921803 (.038)	18.66421 (1.00)	−15.35814 (−0.89)	−5.375271 (−0.25)
% Household Crowding	2.023867 (3.97)***	1.090641 (1.51)	.7978194 (1.10)	−.7683173 (−0.91)
Black Belt/Delta	6795036 (0.38)	—	2.84227 (1.13)	—
Population	−.0000281 (−2.59)**	−.0000681 (−2.06)**	−.0000338 (−2.18)**	−.0001046 (−2.59)**
Persistent Poverty	5.549261 (2.78)**	5.409073 (1.60)	7.129069 (2.54)**	6.934447 (1.77)*
Non-metropolitan	−3.354548 (−1.99)**	−9.550166 (−2.77)**	−10.83562 (−4.46)***	−16.88549 (−4.03)***
Per Capita Market Income	.0017975 (5.86)***	.0015308 (3.44)***	.0021094 (4.75)***	.0023295 (4.28)***
Unemployment Rate	−.8707795 (−1.41)	.5388865 (0.52)	1.713242 (1.92)*	4.336148 (3.49)***
Educational Attainment	−.704956 (−3.72)***	−1.036873 (−3.57)***	−.9278442 (−3.55)***	−1.265101 (−3.98)***
% Black	−.2991584 (−4.57)***	−.4466228 (−4.13)***	−.2006454 (−2.19)**	−.2425719 (−1.93)*
Adjusted R Square	0.5670	0.5624	0.4076	0.4578
F Statistic	21.81*	11.28*	12.08*	7.86*
N	144	65	146	66

Unstandardized coefficients with t-scores in parentheses reported.

*Significant at the <.05 level, two-tailed test; ** Significant at the <.05 level, two-tailed test; *** Significant at the <.001 level, two-tailed test.

Table A8.2 Housing Cost-Burden Regression Analysis

	Model 1: Business Establishments	Model 2: Business Establishments (Black Belt & Delta Only)	Model 3: Number of Jobs	Model 4: Number of Jobs (Black Belt & Delta Only)
Constant	6.496392 (0.37)	14.02223 (0.57)	22.32845 (1.10)	20.22607 (0.71)
Housing Cost-burden	.1943733 (0.77)	.6269501 (1.79)*	-.6456643 (-2.14)**	-.5994507 (-1.48)
Black Belt/Delta	2.117328 (1.04)	—	4.560294 (1.89)*	—
Population	-.0000349 (-2.54)**	-.0000467 (-1.11)	-.0000129 (-0.79)	-.0000101 (-0.21)
Persistent Poverty	6.316684 (2.72)**	4.425304 (1.20)	7.71321 (2.83)**	7.927073 (1.87)*
Non-metropolitan	-5.590126 (-2.85)**	-12.03845 (-3.18)**	-11.92699 (-5.15)***	-14.03703 (-3.20)**
Per Capita Market Income	.0015213 (3.87)***	.0007258 (1.07)	.0014302 (2.97)**	.001314 (1.68)*
Unemployment Rate	-.4997736 (-0.71)	1.148425 (1.07)	2.113854 (2.49)**	3.708464 (2.94)**
Educational Attainment	-.8680335 (-3.24)**	-.5540535 (-1.52)	-1.29833 (-4.02)***	-1.155383 (-2.73)**
% Black	-.2551537 (-3.49)***	-.5229013 (-4.40)***	-.2338114 (-2.66)**	-.3496243 (-2.53)**
Adjusted R Square	0.4740	0.4265	0.3151	0.2209
F Statistic	15.62*	7.23*	8.31*	3.34*
N	147	68	144	67

Unstandardized coefficients with t-scores in parentheses reported.

*Significant at the <.10, two-tailed test; ** Significant at the <.05 level, two-tailed test; *** Significant at the <.001 level, two-tailed test.

Table A8.3 Housing Loan Denials Regression Analysis

	Model 1: Business Establishments	Model 2: Business Establishments (Black Belt & Delta Only)	Model 3: Number of Jobs	Model 4: Number of Jobs (Black Belt & Delta Only)
Constant	18.72777 (1.53)	52.78015 (3.03)	-.1913892 (-0.01)	3.944583 (0.18)
Housing Loan Denials	-.3658146 (-2.88)**	-.766931 (-4.03)***	.0263636 (0.22)	-.0079008 (-0.06)
Black Belt/Delta	1.583496 (0.86)	—	3.012829 (1.25)	—
Population	-.0000232 (-2.00)**	-.0000463 (-1.36)	-.0000259 (-1.71)*	-.0000591 (-1.40)
Persistent Poverty	4.635798 (2.21)**	.4177686 (0.12)	8.00826 (2.96)**	7.245604 (1.75)*
Non-metropolitan	-3.152375 (-1.79)*	-4.68792 (-1.38)	-12.27812 (-5.28)***	-14.46425 (-3.49)***
Per Capita Market Income	.0012067 (3.50)***	.0001837 (0.32)	.0014443 (3.15)**	.0011931 (1.69)*
Unemployment Rate	.0137875 (0.02)	.9206902 (1.04)	2.14548 (2.52)**	3.192022 (2.81)**
Educational Attainment	-.8906444 (-4.82)***	-.8614039 (-3.42)***	-.9410088 (-3.90)***	-.840075 (-2.73)**
% Black	-.1738761 (-2.64)**	-.2562155 (-2.39)**	-.2469958 (-2.84)**	-.2938514 (-2.35)**
Adjusted R Square	0.4803	0.5032	0.3431	0.1853
F Statistic	15.68	9.48*	9.24*	2.82
N	144	68	143	65

Unstandardized coefficients with t-scores in parentheses reported.

*Significant at the <.10, two-tailed test; **Significant at the <.05 level, two-tailed test; ***Significant at the <.001 level, two-tailed test.

References

Allen-Smith, J. E. (1994). Blacks in rural America: Socioeconomic status and policies to enhance economic well-being. *The Review of Black Political Economy*, *22*(4), 7–24.

Allen-Smith, J. E., Wimberley, R. C., and Morris, L.V. (2000). America's forgotten people and places: Ending the legacy of poverty in the rural south. *Journal of Agricultural and Applied Economics*, *32*(2), 319–329.

Appalachian Regional Commission. (2016). County economic status and distress areas in Appalachia. Retrieved from www.arc.gov/appalachian_region/CountyEconomicStatus andDistressedAreasinAppalachia.asp

Bellamy, D. L., and Parks, A. L. (1994). Economic development in southern black belt counties: How does it measure up? *The Review of Black Political Economy*, 22(4), 85–108.

Betz, M. R., Partridge, M. D., Kraybill, D. S., & Lobao, L. (2012). Why do localities provide economic development incentives? Geographic competition, political constituencies, and government capacity. *Growth and Change*, 43(3), 361–391.

Bukenya, J. O. (2004). Socioeconomic perspectives on infant morality in Alabama. *Southern Rural Sociology*, *20*(1), 39–63.

Colclough, G. (1988). Uneven development and racial composition in the deep south: 1970-1980. *Rural Sociology*, *53*(1), 73–85.

Consumer Financial Protection Bureau. (n.d.) Home mortgage disclosure act data: Loan denial data. Retrieved January 3, 2016 from www.consumerfinance.gov/hmda/explore#!/as_of_year=2014&section=filters

Delta Regional Authority (DRA). (2016). DRA States. Retrieved December 15, 2015 from http://dra.gov/about-dra/dra-states/

Donegan, M., Drucker, J., Goldstein, H., Lowe, N., & Malizia, E. (2008). Which indicators explain metropolitan economic performance best? Traditional or creative class. *Journal of the American Planning Association*, *4*(2), 180–195.

Du Bois, W. E. B. (1903). *The souls of black folk*. Chicago: A.C. McClurg.

Encyclopedia of Alabama. Black Belt region in Alabama. Retrieved January 3, 2016 from www.encyclopediaofalabama.org/article/h-2458

Feldman, M., & Desrochers, P. (2003). Research universities and local economic development: Lessons from the history of the Johns Hopkins University. *Industry and Innovation*, *10*(1), 5–24.

Fox, J. (1991). *Regression diagnostics: Qualitative applications in the social sciences*. Newbury Park, CA: Sage Publications.

Gibbs, R. M. (2003). Reconsidering the southern black belt. *The Review of Regional Studies*, *33*(3), 254–263.

Goldstein, H., & Drucker, J. (2006). The economic development impacts of universities on regions: do size and distance matter? *Economic Development Quarterly*, *20*(1), 22–43.

Housing Assistance Council. (2000). Initiatives in the Mississippi Delta. *Rural Voices*, *57*(2).

Housing Assistance Council. (2005). Housing in the Lower Mississippi Delta. Retrieved from http://216.92.48.246/manager/uploads/missdelta.pdf

Housing Assistance Council. (2016). Household crowding, housing cost-burden, loan denials. *Data*. Retrieved December 4, 2015 from www.ruraldataportal.org/definitions.aspx

Hoyman, M., & Faricy, C. (2009). It takes a village a test of the creative class, social capital, and human capital theories. *Urban Affairs Review*, *44*(3), 311–333.

Jensen, L. (1991). The double jeopardized: Non-metroplotian blacks and mexicans. In C. B. Flora & J. A. Christenson (Eds.), *Rural Policies for the 1990s: Rural Studies Series of the Rural Sociological Society* (181–193). Boulder, CO: Westview Press.

Lin, E. Y., & White, M. J. (2001). Bankruptcy and the market for mortgage and home improvement loans. *Journal of Urban Economic, 50*(1), 138–162.

McDaniel, J., & Casanova, V. (2003). Pines in lines: Tree planting, H2B guest workers, and rural poverty in Alabama. *Southern Rural Sociology, 19*(1), 73–96.

McLaughlin, D. K. (2002). Income inequality in America: Non-metro income levels lower than metro, but income inequality did not increase as fast. *Rural America, 17*(2), 14–20.

Megbolugbe, I. F., & Cho, M. (1993). An Empirical analysis of metropolitan housing and mortgage markets. *Journal of Housing Research, 4*(2), 191–224.

Munnell, A. H., Tootell, G. M. B., Browne, L. E., & McEneaney, J. (1996). Mortgage lending in Boston: Interpreting HMDA data. *The American Economic Review, 86*(1), 25–53.

Newman, S. J., & Struyk, R. J. (1983). Housing and poverty. *The Review of Economics and Statistics, 65*(2), 243–253.

Pink-Harper, S. A. (2015). Educational attainment: An examination of its impact on regional economic growth. *Economic Development Quarterly, 29*(2), 167–179.

Poston Jr., D. L., Singlemann, J., Siordia, C., Slack, T., Robertson, B. A., Saenz, R., & Fontenot, K. (2010). Spatial context and poverty: Area-level effects and micro-level effects on household poverty in the Texas borderland & lower Mississippi delta: United States, 2006. *Applied Spatial Analysis, 3*(2), 139–162.

Stats America. (n.d.). Measuring distress. A tool for economic development. Retrieved December 18, 2015 from www.statsamerica.org/distress/distress.aspx

Sumners, J. A., & Lee, L. (2004). *Crossroads and connections: Strategies for rural Alabama*. Auburn University.

Till, T. E. (1986). The share of southeastern black counties in the southern rural renaissance. *Growth and Change, 17*(2), 44–54.

United States Department of Commerce. Bureau of Economic Analysis. Regional Economic Account. (n.d.). *Regional data, local area personal income, GDP & Personal income: Total full-time and part-time employment (Number of Jobs 2000 and 2010)*. Retrieved January 3, 2016 from www.bea.gov/iTable/iTable.cfm?reqid=70&step=1&isuri=1&acrdn=5#reqid=70&step=1&isuri=1

United States Department of Commerce, Census Bureau. American FactFinder. *Educational Attainment, Race, and Population*. Retrieved January 3, 2016 from http://factfinder.census.gov/faces/nav/jsf/pages/searchresults.xhtml?refresh=t

U.S. Department of Housing and Urban Development. (2008). The Federal Housing administration. Retrieved from www.hud.gov/offices/hsg/fhahistory.cfm

United States Department of Labor. Bureau of Labor Statistics. (n.d.). Local area unemployment statistics: Unemployment Rate. Retrieved June 4, 2015 from www.bls.gov/lau

United States Department of Labor. Bureau of Labor Statistics. (n.d.). Quarterly census of employment and wages, state and county wages: (Business establishments 2000 and 2010). Retrieved June 4, 2015 from www.bls.gov/cew/home.htm#databases

U.S. Department of Agriculture: Economic Research Service. (n.d.). Atlas of rural and small town America. *Persistent Poverty*. Retrieved January 3, 2016 from www.ers.usda.gov/data-products/atlas-of-rural-and-small-town-america/download-the-data.aspx

Washington, B. T. (1901). *Up from slavery: An autobiography*. New York: Doubleday, Page.

Wimberley, D. W. (2010). Quality of life trends in the southern black belt, 1980–2005: A Research Note. *Journal of Rural Social Science, 25*(1), 103–118.

9 The people left behind

A look at rural housing policy implications at the half-century mark

*Leslie T. Grover, Tiffany W. Franklin
and Eric Horent*

In 1966, President Lyndon B. Johnson created the National Advisory Commission (NAC) on Rural Poverty as part of his War on Poverty Campaign. At the time, poverty was affecting the lives of millions of Americans everywhere, and particularly those in rural areas. However, decades before the War on Poverty, poor rural populations and their living conditions were addressed during the Roosevelt Administration. There were four major government actions regarding poverty in rural populations important to housing. First came the Homestead Act of 1862 which initially allowed any American who had never fought against the U.S., including freed slaves and other minorities to put in a claim for up to 160 acres of federally-owned land. The Country Life Commission was the second major piece, set up in 1908 under the Roosevelt administration to investigate why rural residents were leaving for opportunities in urban areas. Third, the Resettlement Administration was formed in 1935 under the auspices of the Department of Agriculture in order to move impoverished rural and urban residents to federally planned communities. Finally, there was the Farm Security Administration, which was set up in 1937 to address rural poverty issues. Both administrations were created as part of the New Deal package of programs meant to fight poverty and encourage agricultural activities.

Though these federal actions were not sufficient enough or targeted enough to address the needs of the rural poor, housing needs included, they did set the groundwork for addressing poverty in rural areas. The NAC used the implications of these policies as a backdrop for their own research with a goal of eradicating rural poverty completely.

In September 1967, the NAC produced a 160-page report, *The People Left Behind*, just months before President Johnson signed the Fair Housing Act of 1968 into law on the heels of the assassination of Martin Luther King, Jr. The report found those in rural America experienced vastly different well-being outcomes than their non-rural counterparts. This was particularly true in chronically poor areas of concentrated poverty. From access to socioeconomic opportunities to education, populations in high poverty counties often experienced poverty based on distinct regional racial concentrations. Chief among all the policy recommendations in the report was to address racial discrimination against Blacks, migrant farm-workers and Native Americans. It warned against concentrating poor minorities in communities, and it suggested racial isolation was at the crux of deeply entrenched rural poverty. For housing in particular, the NAC named both the lack of quality and racially equitable rural housing as major reasons for severe rural poverty. The report recommended more resources be put into improving housing quality and lessening discrimination based on race and ethnicity.

Study rationale

This paper examines current trends in poor rural counties in the southern part of the Mississippi Delta region, with particular attention to housing, and it seeks to explore the implications of racial contexts for rural housing and rural development policy. This region, which partly consists of the poorest counties in Mississippi, Arkansas and Louisiana, was one of the poorest regions in the nation during the time of *The People Left Behind*, and it continues to be so even at the half-century mark. In this study, we differentiate between the overall region that spans from the mouth of the Mississippi River in Louisiana into southern Illinois, which we refer to as the Delta Region, and the actual southern portion of the region from which our sampling of counties is taken, which we refer to as the Lower Mississippi Valley Delta, or LMVD. In other words, the Delta region is the entire region including the area into southern Illinois, and the LMVD is that part of the region specifically in the southern portion of the Delta region – Louisiana, Mississippi and Arkansas.

The Economic Research Service (ERS), under the guidance of the U.S. Department of Agriculture (USDA), has chronicled the characteristics of concentrated populations of impoverished Whites, Blacks, Hispanics and Native Americans in high-poverty rural areas at the county level. The majority of high-poverty counties and their poor residents are located in specific geographic areas with histories of distressed economies, dependency on natural resources amenities or the presence of a prodigious low-skill population. In these counties, race serves as a proxy for the nature of economic isolation and lack of access to employment, health and educational resources. The way in which each of these populations experience poverty is paramount in governance and problems with the provision of public services that tax the already limited resources that rural state and local governments can use to address the poverty in these areas. Each county has its own set of characteristics specific to its racial makeup and to the rural development context in which poverty occurs.

Generally, a county's geographic context has significant implications for its economic opportunities. These opportunities accrue to a place by virtue of both its size and its access and proximity to larger economies. Centers of information, communication, trade and finance enable a smaller economy to connect to national and international marketplaces (Economic Research Service 2005). Because so much of today's economic activity is based on interactions of communication, technology and trade, the allocation of economic resources throughout rural areas may differ by access to such marketplace activities (Barkley 1995).

We use county level data from the American Community Survey (ACS) and the ERS to examine access to plumbing, working kitchens, crowding and housing burden across racially concentrated high-poverty counties. Our focus is the poorest, most rural counties, which are predominantly Black and located in the Southern U.S. These are acutely rural places the original report acknowledged.

Now, as we near the 50-year anniversary mark of the publication of *The People Left Behind*, there is still a significant paucity in public policy discussions regarding how rural areas of racially concentrated poverty inform housing and rural development beyond notions of access. Further, the number the rural poor living in racial isolation has barely declined since the creation of report and the signing of the Fair Housing Act.

Though rural poverty was as chronic and deep-rooted as poverty in urban areas in the 1960s, the urban focus of the Civil Rights Movement focused many policies on urban areas almost exclusively. By the time the *People Left Behind* report was released in 1967 rural poverty affected just shy of one in ten Americans. However, this number is likely higher than reported in terms of individual families who experienced rural poverty during this time, as many rural poor migrated to urban areas. The point here is that though they moved to urban areas, their poverty experiences were acutely more rural than their urban counterparts. The report put forth a menu of policy recommendations meant to eradicate rural poverty, most dealing with equal access and equal opportunity; implementation of previous policy goals focusing on full employment; income support for all residents of rural communities; improvements in rural education and in health; improvements in housing; and greater public administration controls to administer more rurally targeted economic development programs (Belden and George 2015). The report further called for more representation in decision-making from rural residents themselves, along with more effective governance and partnerships between all levels of government and rural communities. In essence, *The People Left Behind* painted in broad strokes the foundation for examining the policy implications for being poor and rural in the U.S.

Rural housing policy implications of *The People Left Behind*

An examination of *The People Left Behind* illustrates well families and individuals living in rural areas were not experiencing safe, stable housing, regardless of race. In fact, rural populations were experiencing overall poverty at more than twice the rate of their counterparts in both suburban and urban areas. While one in 15 residents experienced poverty in the suburbs, and one in eight experienced poverty in urban areas, one in four residents experienced poverty in rural areas (Breathitt 1967). This statistic is particularly important for the purposes of this study, as part of the description of poverty included "dilapidated housing in need of repair" (Breathitt 1967). During the time of the report, nearly half of all dilapidated housing was located in a rural area; almost 30 percent of rural housing was deteriorating or dilapidated within rural areas, which was twice the percentage of urban areas; more than one million of those homes were considered not fit for human habitation and beyond repair that might make them so; and less than a quarter of farms even had running water (Breathitt 1967). This means during the *People Left Behind* era, people in rural areas were experiencing a lack of basic structural housing elements: sound structures, running water and otherwise technically basic housing components, such as electric wiring and full plumbing systems.

Race was another important factor affecting the lives of rural residents. By far, people of color, and particularly Black people, occupied the worst of the worst housing structures. The only other minority group experiencing worse living conditions were Native Americans on reservations, who were living in almost complete destitution. At the time of this report, 98 percent of the people of color in rural housing were Black, and nearly one of every three Black households was classified as substandard or dilapidated (Breathitt 1967). Nearly one half-million Black-owned houses throughout the rural U.S. were deteriorating, and less than one in ten Black homes in rural areas had central heating (Breathitt 1967). Race was also a proxy for wealth in terms of homeownership. Blacks were only about 3/5 as likely as their White counterparts to own their own homes and were twice as likely to be renters. The report points out:

> The deplorable condition of rural housing is a matter of neglect and discrimination. The rural poor simply cannot provide adequate housing for themselves out of their meager earnings; nor have they shared equitably in Federal housing programs. Not until 1961 were funds appropriated for public housing for the rural poor. If the problem is to b solved, a multifaceted program must be instituted. New programs must be developed to increase the supply of housing for renter and owner-occupied housing.
>
> (p. 94)

Regarding the issues of race, housing and development, the report called for more investment in rural communities from not only government, but also from private and non-profit sectors.

The original *The People Left Behind* report initially made policy recommendations regarding rural households, many of which seemed to have contributed to improvements among the rural poor and particularly poor Black households. First is the recommendation rental supplements be targeted toward those who were not benefitting from housing ownership programs, financing programs with low interest rates or those who were under employed. The USDA still administers the Section 521 Rental Assistance program, which is a project-based program, that provides an additional subsidy for tenants in Section 515- or 514/516-financed rental housing with incomes too low to pay the subsidized rent from their own resources. This program pays the owner the difference between the tenant's contribution (30 percent of adjusted income) and the monthly rental rate, which is calculated based on the owner's project costs. The tenants who qualify under Sections 515 or 514/516 are either renting from owners who have gotten loans to build or improve rental properties for low income rural families (515) or for housing for farmworkers (514/516).

Next is the recommendation a public housing system be placed in rural areas in order to remedy the dilapidated and deteriorated housing conditions, as well as set up a housing authority to administer programs to rural populations. According to a 2015 study by the Center on Budget and Policy Priorities the federal government's three largest rental assistance programs – Section 8 Housing Choice Vouchers, Public Housing and Multifamily units – provided over 4.5 million units of assisted housing. Thirteen percent of those units were located outside of metropolitan areas, including nearly 10 percent of voucher households in 2014 and 18 percent of public housing units and 13 percent of multifamily units in 2013 (Center for Budget and Policy Priorities 2015). In addition to these programs administered by the HUD, the USDA's Rural Housing Service provided rental assistance to an additional 268,020 households in 2014 (Center for Budget and Policy Priorities 2015).

The third recommendation had to do with self-help housing. This model meant that individuals and communities in rural areas would provide the labor and "do-it-yourself" skills for building and improving housing with funding, grants, loans and technical assistance coming from the government. These programs, too, are still in place under Section 502 with rural housing. The Section 502 Mutual Self-Help Housing Loan program is used primarily to help very low- and low-income households construct their own homes. The program is targeted to families who are unable to buy decent, safe and sanitary housing through conventional methods. Under this program, participating families in a mutual self-help project perform about 65 percent of the construction labor on their own and each other's homes under qualified supervision. The savings from the reduction in labor costs allow otherwise ineligible families to own their homes. This addresses not only housing structures themselves but also affordability among impoverish rural residents.

The final recommendation deals with equal access meant to combat racial discrimination inherent in the overall housing policy schema in the U.S. The Housing Act of 1934 was the first federal attempt to address housing challenges. The Act created the Federal Housing Administration (FHA), which was set up to insure home mortgages. However, for families of color. the FHA solidified racial segregation in communities that still exists today and in part has contributed to the spatially concentrated levels of poverty. As Greer (2014) points out:

> The FHA's strict lending standards, contained in the FHA *Underwriting Handbook*, determined which kinds of properties it would approve mortgages for. In addition to physical quality standards, the FHA based its decisions on the location, and racial and ethnic composition of the neighborhood where the property existed. For example, in 1934 the FHA *Underwriting Handbook* incorporated "residential security maps" into their standards to determine where to mortgages could or could not be issued . . .
>
> These maps which separated neighborhoods primarily by race paved the way for segregation and discrimination in lending. Many argue that it was these maps that set the original precedent for racial discrimination and allowed for it to be an institutional practice.

While the immediate effects of this practice were felt in urban and suburban areas, rural areas were also eventually impacted, as it was more difficult for Black people and other people of color to secure loans for home mortgages and construction. Added to the layer of race, too, was the economic vitality of the local communities and potential for economic growth. In combination, these forces played a major role in relegating many Blacks and other minorities to the role of renter instead of homeowner. By the time the *People Left Behind* was released these patterns of inequality, underscored by institutional race based practices were part of the lending landscape.

Taken together, these recommendations form a basis for the discussion on race, rural housing quality and disparity. *The People Left Behind* mentioned the Delta and the hill country of Mississippi as noticeable areas with high concentrations of poverty. Half a century later, the Mississippi Delta is one of the three remaining regions of the United States with poverty rate of more than 30 percent. The others being Indian reservations in the Southwest and the upper Great Plains (ERS 2015).

Housing is the centerpiece for well-being, particularly in rural areas. When residents have safe stable housing, well-being tends to improve as well. Housing is a matter of public health. When the housing component of a community is strong, there are less incidences of communicable diseases and improvements in mental health outcomes for adults and cognitive outcomes for children (Shaw 2004).

Note in particular the relationship between housing and education. Housing creates opportunities for improved educational outcomes, particularly among lower-achieving children and their families. As housing improves, so does overall academic success (Cunningham and MacDonald 2012). Housing is even tied to labor market performance, as improved rates of housing and housing prices appears to play a critical role in determining the overall health and viability of the labor market (Rogers and Winkler 2013). Bratt et al. (2006) capture the importance of housing in particular, when it comes to race, in that "where one lives, particularly if one is a person of color, plays a critical role in fixing one in society, and in the local community. Living in substandard housing in a 'bad' neighborhood may limit people's ability to secure an adequate education for their children, reduce chances of finding a decent job, and deprive them of decent public services and facilities" (p. 2). Further, housing is directly tied to education by the proximity of schools to neighborhoods and the property taxes paid to education. Poor housing is tied to poor schools, and poor schools more often than not, translate to poor academic outcomes.

It is through the lens of housing and education that the basis for the implications for rural development are unpacked. Gjelten's (1982) rural school typology demonstrates this relationship between housing, education and the overall development of an area. He contends rural schools have special economic ties and social ties to rural communities and that they are different from their urban counterparts. Based on these relationships, he recognizes five types of relationships: high growth, reborn, stable, depressed and isolated. High-growth schools are rural schools greatly influenced by the social and economic dynamics occurring in cities due to their close geographic location to urban areas. Reborn rural communities are those saturated by city residents seeking to escape congestion, crime, polluted environments and other perceived negative aspects of city life. Stable rural communities are still influenced by urban areas, but maintain their "ruralness" while keeping up with national trends. The stability of their economies allows them a symbiotic relationship between rural amenities, such as hiking trails, and urban economic benefits, such as diverse market activities. Depressed rural areas have underdeveloped local economies, and residents often leave these areas in search of economic opportunities in less rural places. Lastly, isolated rural communities are those far removed from transportation and commerce centers. High proportions of their populations live below federal poverty standards, and these communities are the most likely to suffer from population and economic decline.

The Lower Mississippi Valley Delta today

In rural areas, being located in the LMVD has implications for economic outcomes based on aspects of place for which housing serves as a proxy, capturing educational and poverty outcomes, such as income, the types of employment and the ability to own a home. Incomes in the LMVD are well below those of both their states and the nation, and because income plays such a large role in determining federal poverty definitions, the poverty rate is as well. Further, the percentage of college degree holders shows an inverse trend with the unemployment rate and homeownership, which may contribute to chronic intergenerational poverty (Harkness and Newman 2003).

Rural states and communities traditionally tend to have higher homeownership rates overall than the nation, and racial differences in homeownership have actually declined overall for rural areas since the publication of *The People Left Behind* (Allen 2002). However, for those who live in the LMVD with lower educational rates, this is overall not the case. This is particularly true in Louisiana, where the racial and educational trends have changed over the past decade, likely due to changes in those who returned to affected rural counties after rebuilding efforts from Hurricane Katrina (Groen and Polivka 2010). The difference between the composition of evacuees who returned and the composition of evacuees who did not return is the primary force behind changes in the composition of the affected areas in the first two years after the storm (Groen and Polivka 2010). Katrina is associated with a decrease in the percentage of residents who are Black and an increasing presence of the percentage of older residents, a decrease in the percentage of residents with low income/education and an increase in the percentage of residents with high incomes and education (Groen and Polivka 2010). These changes in totem may explain why homeownership rates are higher in this region of the LMVD, but not significantly so much higher that the trends indicate extreme disadvantages for lower educational attainment or lower incomes should be ignored.

In part because of the persistence of dismal poverty, and in part because of the international scrutiny brought about by the Civil Rights Movement, poverty in the LMVD continues to attract nationwide media attention and even worldwide attention. In an article for the *Los Angeles Times*, Horsey (2015) refers to the region as "the Mississippi of Mississippi" and a "neglected corner of America." In another article from the *Economist*, a high-ranking official from of the Delta Regional

Authority is quoted as saying, "You can't out-poor the Delta" (Scratching a living 2013) In 1994, *Time Magazine* named Lake Providence, a parish[1] in northeast Louisiana, "The Poorest Place in America," and published an extensive article about the parish in which it is stated, "If there is a poorer place in America, the Census Bureau cannot find it" (White 1994). Sutter (2013) found East Carroll Parish, a neighboring parish of Lake Providence, to be the "most unequal place in America" based on census data from 2010.

Much of the narrative about the Delta region focuses on the challenges it faces and the consequences of these challenges. If acknowledged, progresses in the region are presented as slow and limited. In this context, it is not surprising housing in the region is presented in a negative light. For instance, Horsey (2015) notes houses in Greenwood, MS, "are just a small step above shacks, needy of paint and repairs." In an article from 2012, the *BBC Magazine* states about Belzoni, a town in Humphreys County, MS, "Third Street is still lined with ramshackle, draughty wooden shacks. Though they now have running water and toilets, the dilapidated houses look just the way they did 44 years ago" (Poverty and progress in the Mississippi Delta 2012).

Methodology: sample

Narrowly defined, the Mississippi Delta refers to the area between the Mississippi River and the Yazoo River south of the Arkansas border and includes 19 counties. The Arkansas Delta includes 14 to 23 counties in the southeast part of the state, depending on the definition used, and some parishes in Northeast Louisiana are also considered to be part of the Mississippi Delta region by official authorities (DRA) and others. Although divided by state lines, the Mississippi Delta, Arkansas Delta and Louisiana Delta share a unique history marked by cotton production, slavery, sharecropping and Jim Crow. They also present similar geographic and socioeconomic characteristics, and in turn, face the same challenges. As a region, they are part of the LMVD. We use this reference to refer to the cluster of counties collectively across the three states, which form the southern part of the vast Mississippi Delta region. Figure 9.1 contains a map of this region.

While anecdotes about poor housing conditions in the Delta region are plentiful, empirical evidence is lacking in the literature. Data that could be used to assess past and present policies or orient future policies are being collected by the U.S. Census Bureau through the annual ACS. This study uses these data to assess some key characteristics of housing units in Delta region. It is a simple descriptive analysis of the characteristics examined in *The People Left Behind*.

The ACS provides data about basic physical characteristics, occupancy characteristics, and financial characteristics of housing units at the county level (Table DP 04: Selected Housing Characteristics). Because of potential issues of reliability related to small samples at the county level, the data are averaged over a five-year period. We use 2010–2014 ACS 5-year estimates for this study.

In addition to evidence for the Delta region as a whole, we present data for the Mississippi Delta, Arkansas Delta and Louisiana Delta to identify potential variations in housing conditions across states. We also present data for the United States and the states in which each county is located for the sake of comparison.

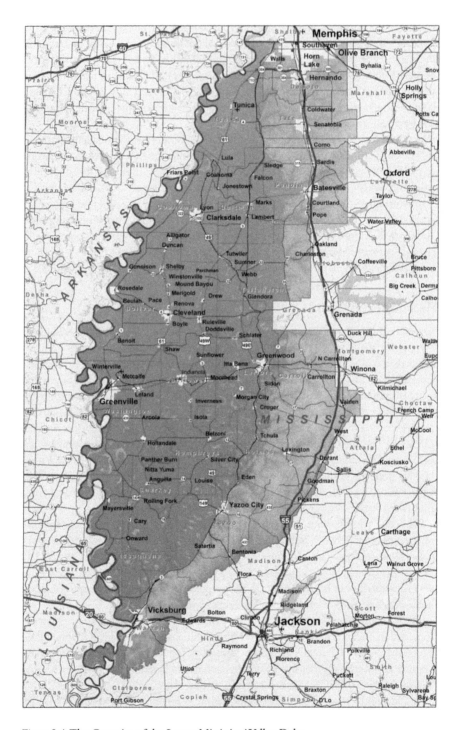

Figure 9.1 The Counties of the Lower Mississippi Valley Delta

Overall, our sample of counties (and parishes in Louisiana) for the LMVD includes 41 counties. Sixteen of the 19 counties making up the Mississippi Delta are included. The counties of DeSoto, Tate and Tunica are not because they are part of a metropolitan area (Memphis).[2] For the same reason, Crittenden County is also excluded from our sample of the Arkansas Delta, which includes the other 13 counties most commonly included in the various definitions of the Arkansas Delta.[3] Twelve of the 13 parishes that make up the Louisiana Delta are included in our sample. Ouachita Parish is excluded because it is part of a metropolitan area (Monroe).[4]

Findings

Before assessing the characteristics of housing units, to provide some context to housing related issues, we first present in Table 9.1 some evidence about basic socioeconomic characteristics of the region, specifically income, poverty, unemployment and educational attainments. These data are also 2010–2014 ACS five-year estimates. The median household income, poverty rate and unemployment rate are included in Table DP 03 (Selected Economic Characteristics). College attainment, which is defined as the percentage of the population 25 years or older with a bachelor's degree or more, is from Table S1501 (Educational Attainment).

Table 9.1 shows the mean of the median household income for the 41 counties of the Delta region in our sample is barely above $31,000, or less than 60 percent of the national average. There is little variation in median household income between the Mississippi Delta, Arkansas Delta and Louisiana Delta, where the median household income is between 70 and 78 percent of the state average.

Unsurprisingly, the region experiences poverty at a rate almost twice as high as the United States as a whole, with close to 30 percent of the total population living in poverty. When the poverty rate is computed for children (under the age of 18)

Table 9.1 Socioeconomic Characteristics

Geography	Household Income (Median)	Poverty Rate	Unemployment Rate	College Degree Holders	Homeownership
United States	$53,482	15.6%	9.2%	29.3%	64.4%
Delta Region	$31,043	29.8%	14.5%	13.5%	63.8%
Mississippi Delta	$29,542	33.2%	17.8%	15.4%	63.9%
Mississippi	$39,464	22.6%	10.9%	20.4%	68.9%
Louisiana Delta	$31,591	28.9%	11.9%	11.4%	66.4%
Louisiana	$44,991	19.6%	8.7%	22.1%	66.3%
Arkansas Delta	$32,385	26.5%	12.8%	13.0%	61.3%
Arkansas	$41,264	19%	8.4%	20.6%	66.5%

and adults separately, it reveals an extremely high rate of poverty among children in the region, with over 40 percent of the children living in poverty. Almost half the children in the Mississippi Delta – 48.3 percent – live in poverty.

The unemployment rate in the Delta region overall is more than 50 percent higher than nationwide. When comparing sub-regions of the Delta, in the LMVD, the unemployment rate exhibits the same pattern as poverty. It is higher in the Mississippi Delta, where almost 18 percent of the labor force is unemployed, than it is in the Arkansas Delta or the Louisiana Delta. The development of oil and gas production that took place since the 1990s in the Arkansas Delta or the Louisiana Delta appears to explain at least in part this pattern. Indeed, ACS estimates suggest a significantly larger number of workers are employed in natural resources related activities in the Arkansas Delta and the Louisiana Delta compared to the Mississippi Delta.

The flight of better-educated individuals and families out of the LMVD, created by the lack of employment opportunities and other factors, is nowhere more visible than in the percentage of college or graduate degree holders within the adult population 25 and older. It is very low throughout the region compared to the United States as a whole, but it is particularly low in the Louisiana Delta, where barely 10 percent of the adult population holds at least a college degree.

Poverty and unemployment do not necessarily translate in lower rate of home-ownership in the LMVD, however. The region has a rate of homeownership essentially equal to the national average. The portion of homeowners is even higher in the Mississippi Delta and Arkansas Delta than statewide. It is nearly identical in the Louisiana Delta and the state of Louisiana. High rates of homeownership may be the results of high incomes and/or lower housing costs. Table 9.1 clearly indicates the average income in the Delta region is anything but high. Table 9.2 shows that indeed, the average value of housing units in the region is exceptionally low.

Table 9.2 Basic Characteristics of Housing Units

Geography	Value	Recent Housing Units	Number of Rooms (Median)	Crowded Housing Units
United States	$175,700	15.9%	5.5	3.3%
Delta Region	$70,846	11.2%	5.4	3%
Mississippi Delta	$70,150	10.8%	5.4	3.4%
Mississippi	$100,800	19.6%	5.4	2.9%
Louisiana Delta	$68,273	11.7%	5.5	3.0%
Louisiana	$140,400	17.9%	5.4	2.6%
Arkansas Delta	$74,077	11.2%	5.3	2.4%
Arkansas	$108,700	18.7%	5.4	2.5%

Table 9.2 first presents the median value of owner-occupied housing units. The percentage of housing units built since 1990 is presented next to assess the age of the housing stock in the Delta region. Table 9.2 also shows the median number of rooms per housing unit, which serves as a proxy for the average size of housing units. The last column of the table shows the percentage of households who live in an overcrowded home. Following the U.S. Census Bureau, an overcrowded home is defined as a unit in which more than one occupant per room reside.

The median value of owner occupied units is slightly more than $70,000 in the overall Delta region, less than half the national median. It is also consistently low across throughout the region. The relatively low percentage of recent housing units may in part explains this fact. Table 9.2 indeed shows that, while there have been more new constructions in Mississippi, Louisiana and Arkansas than nationally over the last 25 years (some of which may be explained by reconstruction following Katrina, Rita and Gustav hurricanes during that time period), the percentage of recent housing units has remained low in the LMVD region. It barely represents 11 percent of the stock of housing units, compared to 18–20 percent for the states.

The data on the median number of rooms indicate the average size of housing units in the LMVD is essentially the same as nationwide and statewide. Obviously, the average square footage of rooms may differ between the LMVD region and the rest of the country, even though the number of rooms is the same, especially because housing units tend to be older in the region. The ACS and other surveys from the Census Bureau we examined do not provide data on square footage of housing at the county level.

Although we recognize the housing units in the LMVD may be somewhat smaller in terms of square footage than suggested by the median number of rooms, we believe the consistency of the results for the median number of rooms across geographies indicates it is an adequate proxy for housing size. Furthermore, it has long been used as a proxy for housing size in the real estate literature (Oates 1969; Wassmer 1993).

While overcrowding was a predominant issue in the LMVD region at the time of the publication of *The People Left Behind*, the region currently experiences a lower rate of overcrowding than the nation as a whole. Only 3 percent of homes are over-crowded in the region. The departures of families, especially young families with children, from the region certainly contributed to the drastic reduction in over-crowding in the region. Estimates from the Table DP 04 of the ACS not presented here indicate that indeed the average household size for both owner-occupied and renter-occupied units in the Delta is smaller than nationwide and statewide.

Table 9.3 shows the percentage of occupied housing units that lack complete plumbing facilities, complete kitchen facilities and telephone service. The extremely low percentages of house units without complete plumbing and kitchen facilities in the LMVD suggests substandard housing is no longer the issue it used to be. In fact, the percentage of units with complete kitchen facilities is even lower, though not significantly, in the region than the United States.

Table 9.4 provides some evidence about the financial burden housing represents for home owners and renters. The Selected Monthly Owner Costs (SMOC) and

Table 9.3 Selected Characteristics of Occupied Housing Units

Geography	Lacking Complete Plumbing Facilities	Lacking Complete Kitchen Facilities
United States	0.5%	0.9%
Delta Region	0.6%	0.7%
Mississippi Delta	0.7%	0.9%
Mississippi	0.6%	0.8%
Louisiana Delta	0.6%	0.7%
Louisiana	0.5%	0.8%
Arkansas Delta	0.4%	0.7%
Arkansas	0.5%	0.9%

Table 9.4 Financial Characteristics of Occupied Housing Units

Geography	SMOC	SMOCAPI	Gross Rent	GRAPI
United States	$1,522	34.2%	$920	43.2%
Delta Region	$913	31.3%	$555	48.5%
Mississippi Delta	$959	37.6%	$552	42.7%
Mississippi	$1,090	32.3%	$714	44.7%
Louisiana Delta	$865	28.0%	$533	49.6%
Louisiana	$1,207	28.7%	$786	53.4%
Arkansas Delta	$899	26.5%	$579	54.6%
Arkansas	$1,027	26.0%	$675	49.2%

Note. SMOC: Selected Monthly Owner Costs. SMOCAPI: Selected Monthly Owner Costs As Percentage of Income. GRAPI: Gross Rent As Percentage of Income.

gross rent provide an indication of the nominal cost of owning and renting a home, respectively. The SMOCAPI and GRAPI show the cost of owning and renting a home as a percentage of a household income.

In line with the discrepancy in the value of housing units between the Delta region and the nation as a whole, both the mean SMOC and mean gross rent in the Delta region are 40 percent lower than they are nationwide. Because the average income in the Delta region is low though, housing costs for home owners as a percentage of income are only lower in the Louisiana Delta and Arkansas Delta than nationwide. They are even higher in the Mississippi Delta. The costs of renting as a percentage of income in the Delta are slightly higher than nationwide, but they are similar to the ones reported for the states. As a possible sign of economic disparity within the Delta region, we note that, while the costs of housing represent almost half the income of renters, they represent less than a third of the income of homeowners.

Broadly speaking, the data trends show strides in the overall housing quality of residential structures in rural areas compared to the 1960s. Overall, in the poorest of rural counties, the houses tend to have a similar number of rooms to other houses in the areas (though likely much smaller) and have basic kitchen and bathroom necessities. However, the houses are less modern, less valuable and occupied by fewer people here at the half-century mark.

The findings in this study suggest that there has been success in the set of recommendations made a half century ago regarding housing structures and property. Access, too, has improved for Blacks and other minorities. However, the chronic poverty that exists there entrenched in the geographic isolation of some of these counties still exists, and it expresses itself in the nature of less modern, less valuable and smaller occupation rates in housing compared to state and national counterparts. The housing reflects lower populations, lower education levels and less wealth than their state- and national-level counterparts.

Implications for current and future rural housing policy

While *The People Left Behind* shed light upon the conditions in the overall Delta region, and certainly in the LMVD, by no means are policymakers unaware of the challenges faced in the region today. Many efforts have been made to address the economic and community development needs of the Mississippi Delta region. In 1988, Congress authorized the creation of the Lower Mississippi Delta Commission to investigate the social, political and economic conditions of this region and propose recommendations to bring about change and improve conditions in the region. The commission ultimately recommended a series of actions around human capital, social, economic, and community development. Further, in 2000, the DRA was authorized, under the Delta Regional Authority Act of 2000, to provide a "unified, regional approach to economic and community development" in the region. The DRA has crafted a Regional Development Plan that proposes an investment strategy to help the region grow and prosper (Taking Stock Report 2010).

However, as *Taking Stock* points out, and as the data we presented show, there have been both progress and stalled results at the same time in terms of rural development. Major manufacturing plants have opened in communities across the region and renewed interest in the region's history and culture have led to increased tourism to plantations, battlefields and museums, yet one-fifth of the region's population still experiences "some of the most pressing social, economic, and community development needs in the country" (Taking Stock 2010). Added to the ongoing economic and social struggles that have plagued the region, the region further has been hard hit by a number of natural and manmade disasters. From hurricanes Katrina, Rita and Gustav in the mid-2000s to the numerous tornados and storms that touched down in the region, these natural disasters have devastated communities in the region. The 2010 Gulf oil spill, and the resulting moratorium on drilling, have had untold environmental and economic impacts (Taking Stock 2010).

The vast racial inequality that exists in the Delta Region and the LMVD must be addressed. While progress in racial outcomes has been made in terms of public policy, there are still effects from the historical slave and sharecropping systems present in the region today. As Horsey (2015) points out, while describing a site in Greenwood, MS, where pivotal civil rights and economic awareness of inequality based on race took place, the region still bears out the contrasts between the quality of life experienced by Blacks versus that of their White counterparts:

> There is not much black power in Greenwood today. The roadside sign marking the site of Carmichael's speech is in the black section of town. The surrounding houses are just a small step above shacks, needy of paint and repairs. Old storefronts stand empty ... At a railroad crossing, we wait for the train they call the City of New Orleans to pass by, then cross to Greenwood's modest business district. Over a bridge beyond, we enter the town's white neighborhood and find large, well-kept houses with antebellum columns and vast lawns. The economic contrast and the racial divide is stark.

To address racial inequality is to address one of the most critical keys to the chronic, deeply entrenched poverty in the region.

Current housing policies must be developed or revised to combat the disparities in impoverished communities. The following policy recommendations are made to assist with issues in the LMVD.

Issue

Affordable housing for low-income families and eradicating pockets of rural poverty, particularly in terms of race and location.

Policy recommendation

Provide supplemental housing vouchers and support services that will increase skillsets that lead to employability for low-income families.

Although race is a sensitive issue in the Nation, specifically in the LMVD, the fact remains there are significant inequalities for Blacks in this area regarding the allocation of resources. Race has historically been a central issue in the Delta overall and the LMVD specifically. From slavery to sharecropping to civil rights to the 21st century, the Delta region is inextricably tied to issues of race and the legacy of economic exploitation and racial segregation. These ties have put in place structural inequalities that are captured by race and location. As such, the socioeconomic problems plaguing the region are serious and more pronounced in the rural areas of the region and among the region's African-American population (Housing Assistance Council 2013).

To improve the quality of life in the LMVD, families need adequate access to resources. When families spend over half of their income on rent or mortgages, finances to manage other household necessities are insufficient. High poverty rates are symptomatic of local economies that have, for the most part, not been able to create jobs that would enable residents to earn higher wages (Housing Assistance Council 2013). According to the National Low Income Housing Coalition (2016), Louisiana Ranks thirtieth and Mississippi ranks forty-sixth, which means that housing is "out of reach," as residents in Louisiana must make $15.81/hr. and residents in Mississippi must make $14.07/hr. to afford a two-bedroom rental unit. Therefore, to provide shelter, individuals in Louisiana and Mississippi must have two household incomes and work at least 71 hours per week to pay rent. These statistics are overwhelming and may continue to cycle of poverty in both states. Homelessness becomes another factor when families are not able to meet their housing obligations.

Issue

Providing vouchers will increase affordability for those whose incomes make homes out of reach due to structural inequalities based on race, location or lack of income.

Policy recommendation

Establish economic incubators in isolated rural areas in order to encourage growth, particularly among microbusinesses

Today's rural public policy is often national policy that has been created with little or no thought for its implications for rural communities (Stauber 2002). Along with the aforementioned policy recommendations, incubators are provided through government program opportunities in low income communities. The economic incubators will provide skills training to individuals in underserved communities in the Delta region. Leveraging resources through Title I and Title II funding streams will provide resources to people in low-income areas. Title I funds include occupational skills training programs that lead to postsecondary credentials and are aligned with in-demand industry sectors or occupations in a local area. Title II funds focus on adult education, literacy and English language services to include transition to postsecondary education and employment (Bird et al. 2014). With the changing trends in employment industries, it is imperative to prepare citizens to meet the demands and needs of the nation's workforce.

Issue

Homelessness.

Policy recommendation

To provide shelter for individuals who do not have access to affordable housing.

In large part, homelessness stemmed from paying steep rent or mortgages that forced individuals onto the streets, as they were unable to financially maintain their dwellings. Highly effective urban solutions aimed at homelessness too often falter in rural America, where nonprofits – not governments – often provide services and where those who are homeless are often less conspicuous, but no less in need of assistance. Homelessness is a global issue which is heavily impacted by affordability problems.

Although there are some policies in place that provide subsidies, states and localities have more say in deciding what kinds of housing should be subsidized, the kinds of households who should receive priority, where the housing should be built, the extent to which nonprofit or for-profit developers should be involved and even over the type of subsidy provided (Buckley and Schwartz 2011). Over time, the absence of sufficient income has forced many out of their homes. As noted in much of the existing literature, homelessness in areas like the LMVD is not as visible compared to more urban areas. As the old cliché goes, "out of sight, out of mind." Does this make rural less needy than urban areas? The answer is NO.

To assist with providing shelters in rural areas, providing resources to collect and analyze data in low-income areas would be beneficial to better assess the needs. The invisibility of homelessness in rural areas sends mixed messages to policymakers, indicating that services are not necessary in impoverished areas. The fact that rural areas have relatively less investment in shelters and other temporizing measures can, in some places, allow more flexibility to spend available funds to help people escape homelessness immediately. Funds could be used to more directly house people who become homeless (Housing Assistance Council (HAC) 2016).

Issue

Reinstate technical assistance to low-income communities.

Policy recommendation

Provide more resources to strengthen the DRA to develop a coalition of experienced and rural citizens who will serve as a referral source or center for resources to provide programs for individuals to raise awareness of opportunities and policies that supports their rural housing needs.

Programs must be developed and brought directly to impoverished areas in the Delta Region that address housing and related support services that lead to stable and affordable housing. These programs must also encourage a sense of ownership among rural citizens. According to (Honadle 2001), rural advocacy groups work on two fronts simultaneously: (1) help Federal policymakers understand the rural context and consequently their programs will better meet the needs in the rural environment and (2) show the interdependent relationship of the rural and urban problems and issues in order to change the inaccurate perception of a zero-sum game. This work can be accomplished using a task force of passionate community people and experts who are seeking positive changes in their communities in conjunction with the DRA.

The task force coalition should consist of citizens and professional individuals who are knowledgeable of the field of public administration and housing policies. The group must have an understanding of the specific needs of people in impoverished communities with severe racial disparities.

The sole purpose of the coalition is to develop strategies that will provide citizens with the tools they need to find stable, affordable housing. In addition, the coalition will make sure that equality exists among those who need services. The task force should also seek additional funding, educational and research opportunities to allocate adequate resources that meet the needs of citizens in the community.

Conclusion

Though a half-century has passed since the publication of *The People Left Behind* report, the nature of the poverty in the Delta region and particularly the LMVD counties remains unlike poverty anywhere else. The insidious and stubborn nature of the poverty there expresses itself in housing, but because housing is so closely tied to educational outcomes, access to health services, employment and other indicators of well-being, these avenues should be addressed with an eye towards housing policy.

Understanding and effectively addressing the poverty in the region is a complex, politically charged and resource-heavy investment the states in the region and the federal government, too, will eventually have to make in order to turn around its housing systems to address the overall effects of poverty housing outcomes. The region, then, must be willing to make drastic changes in the way it approaches social mores dealing with race, housing and investments in rural development overall in in order to fully participate and avoid falling behind the rest of the U.S. even further.

Notes

1 Louisiana parishes are equivalent to counties in other states.
2 The counties from the Mississippi Delta included in the study are: Bolivar, Carroll, Coahoma, Grenada, Holmes, Humphreys, Issaquena, Leflore, Panola, Quitman, Sharkey, Sunflower, Tallahatchie, Warren, Washington and Yazoo counties.
3 The counties from the Arkansas Delta included in the study are: Chicot, Clay, Craighead, Cross, Desha, Drew, Greene, Lee, Mississippi, Monroe, Phillips, Poinsett and St. Francis counties.
4 The parishes from the Louisiana Delta included in the study are Caldwell, Catahoula, Concordia, East Carroll, Franklin, LaSalle, Madison, Morehouse, Richland, Tensas and West Carroll parishes.

References

Allen, B. L. (2002). Race and gender inequality in homeownership: Does place make a difference? *Rural Sociology*, 67(4), 603–621.

Barkley, D. L. (1995, December). The Economics of Change in Rural America. *American Journal of Agricultural Economics*, 77(5), Proceedings Issue, 1252–1258.

Belden, J., & George, L. (2015). "'The People Left Behind' are Today the People Still Behind". Retrieved from www.ruralhome.org/sct-information/rural-voices/rv-digital/156-rvpoverty2014/1055-rvpoverty2014-left-behind

Bird, K., Foster, M., & Ganzglass, E. (2014). *New Opportunities to Improve Economic and Career Success for Low-Income Youth and Adults: Key Provisions of the Workforce Innovation and Opportunity Act (WIOA).* Center for Postsecondary and Economic Success at CLASP.

Bratt, R. G., Stone, M. E., & Hartman, C. W. (2006). *A right to housing: Foundation for a new social agenda.* Temple University Press.

Breathitt, E. T. (1967). *The people left behind, a report by The President's National Advisory Commission on Rural Poverty.* Washington DC.

Buckley, R. M., & Schwartz, A. F. (2011). Housing policy in the U.S.: The evolving subnational role. *International Affairs at The New School.* The New School, New York: Graduate Program in International Affairs.

Center on Budget and Policy Priorities. (2015). Rental Assistance in Rural and Urban Areas. Retrieved January 2, 2016 from www.cbpp.org//sites/default/files/atoms/files/RentalAssistance-RuralFactsheetandMethodology.pdf

Cunningham, M. K., & MacDonald, G. (2012). Housing as a Platform for Improving Education Outcomes among Low-Income Children. Retrieved January 20, 2016 from www.urban.org/research/publication/housing-platform-improving-education-outcomes-among-low-income-children

Economic Research Service. (2005). Areas with Lower Educational Attainment Face Additional Challenges. Retrieved December 16, 2015 from www.ers.usda.gov

Economic Research Service. (2015). Geography of Poverty. Retrieved January 31, 2016 from www.ers.usda.gov/topics/rural-economy-population/rural-poverty-well-being/geography-of-poverty.aspx

Gjelten, T. (1982). *A typology of rural school settings.* Clearinghouse on Rural Education and Small Schools, Charleston, WV. (ERIC Document No. ED 215 858).

Greer, J. L. (2014). Historic home mortgage redlining in Chicago. *Journal of the Illinois State Historical Society (1998-), 107*(2), 204–233.

Groen, J. A., & Polivka, A. E. (2010). Going home after Hurricane Katrina: Determinants of return migration and changes in affected areas. *Demography, 47*(4), 821–844.

Harkness, J., & Newman, S. (2003). Differential effects of homeownership on children from higher-and lower-income families. *Journal of Housing Research, 14*(1), 1.

Honadle, B. W. (2001). Rural Development Policy in the United States: Beyong the Cargo Cult Mentality. *The Journal of Regional Analysis and Policy,* 93–108.

Horsey, D. (2015, March 5). Mississippi Delta locked in the poverty of the past. *Los Angeles Times.* Retrieved January 31, 2016 from www.latimes.com/opinion/topoftheticket/la-na-tt-mississippi-delta-20150304-story.html

Housing Assistance Council. (2013). *Housing in the Lower Mississippi Delta.* Washington, DC: Housing Assistance Council.

Housing Assistance Council (HAC). (2016). *Rural voices: Rural homelessness.* Washington, DC: Housing Assistance Council (HAC).

National Low Income Housing Coalition. (2016). *Out of Reach 2016.* Washington, DC: National Low Income Housing Coalition.

Oates, W. E. (1969). The effects of property taxes and local public spending on property values: An empirical study of tax capitalization and the Tiebout hypothesis. *Journal of Political Economy, 77*(6), 957–971.

Poverty and progress in the Mississippi Delta. (2012, January 4). *BBC Magazine.* Retrieved January 31, 2016 from www.bbc.com/news/magazine-16385337

Rogers, W. H., & Winkler, A. E. (2013). The relationship between the housing and labor market crises and doubling up: an MSA-level analysis, 2005–2011. Retrieved January 31,

2016 from www.bls.gov/opub/mlr/2013/article/the-relationship-between-the-housing-and-labor-market-crises-and-doubling-up.htm

RuralHome.org. (2010). *Taking stock: Lower Mississippi Delta*. Retrived February 3, 2016 from www.ruralhome.org/storage/documents/ts2010/ts-report/ts10_ms_delta.pdf

Scratching a living: A shocking rate of depopulation in the rural South. (2013, June 8). *The Economist*. Retrieved January 31, 2016 from www.economist.com/news/united-states/21579025-shocking-rate-depopulation-rural-south-scratching-living

Shaw, M. (2004). Housing and public health. *Annual Review of Public Health, 25*, 397–418.

Stauber, K. N. (2002). Why invest in rural America – -and how? A critical public policy question for the 21st century. *Economic Review*, 33–63.

Sutter, J. D. (2013). The most unequal place in America. Retrieved January 31, 2016 from www.cnn.com/2013/10/29/opinion/sutter-lake-providence-income-inequality/

Wassmer, R.W. (1993). Property taxation, property base, and property value: an empirical test of the new view. *National Tax Journal, 46*, 135–160.

White, J. E. (1994). The poorest place in America: Lake Providence's poverty is extreme and, despite civil rights progress, too familiar in the South. *Time Magazine*. Retrieved January 31, 2016 from http://content.time.com/time/magazine/article/0,9171,981266,00.html

10 Manufactured home living across rural America

William Dyar, Jungmin Lim and Mark Skidmore

Introduction

The proportion of households in rural counties across America living in manufactured homes increased from 1 percent in 1950 to nearly 8 percent by 2010. In 5 percent of rural counties, more than a third of households live in manufactured homes. Though there can be stigma attached to this type of housing arrangement, manufactured home living has become an essential component of affordable housing across America.

Manufactured homes have been increasingly the preferred housing option in the growing southern portions of rural America. New housing is not needed in many rural places in the Upper Midwest where population is in decline; thus, manufactured home growth has been more subdued in this region. Contrary to the notion that manufactured homes are typically located in parks where manufactured home owners pay rent for use of land and public services, in fact about 70 percent of manufactured homes are placed on owners' property. Importantly, manufactured homes save households as much as 50 percent in costs over other housing types of similar size, quality and age. Thus, manufactured home living offers an affordable housing option with a measure of privacy not available with other types of affordable housing.

Though the terms "mobile home" and "manufactured home" are often used interchangeably, there is a distinction. "Mobile home" refers to factory-built housing constructed prior to the establishment of federal standards implemented in 1976; "manufactured home" refers to factory-built housing constructed in the years following the establishment of the federal standards. (Apgar et al. 2002). Manufactured homes can be placed on a permanent or temporary foundation, although manufactured homes are rarely relocated once placed. Given that in this chapter consider data on manufactured home living from 1980 through 2010, we use the term "manufactured home" throughout the chapter.[1]

To date, the research on the increase in manufactured home living in America is limited. While some research is available on manufactured home quality, satisfaction (Aman and Yarnal 2010) and affordability (Gentz 2001; Boehm and Schlottmann 2008), to our knowledge, there is little research on the growing demand for manufactured home living in rural areas. This chapter is meant to fill this gap by offering a formal assessment of manufactured home living in rural America.

The remainder of this chapter is organized as follows. The next section offers a discussion of housing choices faced by households, emphasizing the role of economic and demographic forces that may influence housing choice. We then summarize information on the costs of manufactured home living relative to other housing options as well as discuss changes in manufactured home quality over time. The sections on housing choice, affordability and quality lead to a statistical analysis of the socioeconomic forces that have led to the growth of manufactured home living in rural America. Specifically, we use county-level panel data in ten-year intervals from 1980–2010 to estimate the determinants of manufactured home living. As a prelude, we find that several economic and demographic factors are significant drivers of the increase in manufactured home living over time; increasing rental costs and the increase in the proportion of households headed by females are the two most important factors.

Housing options

To frame the discussion regarding the increasing attractiveness and importance of manufactured home living in rural areas, we present a brief discussion of housing options available to households; housing choice depends on factors such as marital status, household size, income, personal preferences as well as the relative costs of alternative living arrangements. While there are many possible housing options, consider the following housing tree, which provides a basic overview of the available living arrangements. Note that all the housing types in Figure 10.1 are available to either rent or own.

The first branch of the housing tree illustrates the choice between multifamily and single-family residences. The multifamily branch has several options, which include apartments, condos and duplexes, whereas the single-family branch has two options: a traditional home or manufactured home. Under the manufactured home branch, one can either live in a manufactured home park, on one's own land or some other type of rented land. As noted above, one's housing choice depends on needs, preferences, income and the relative costs of alternatives. The manufactured home option could offer more privacy and living area than a typical multifamily dwelling; however, a manufactured home park may not provide as much privacy as the other land options. As discussed next, the quality of manufactured homes has

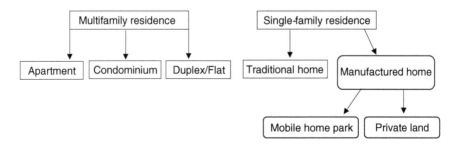

Figure 10.1 Housing Tree

increased substantially over time; quality improvement is largely attributed to the establishment of the Manufactured Housing Program by the U.S. Department of Housing and Urban Development (HUD) in 1976.

Housing and Urban Development Manufactured Housing Program overview

This section provides an outline of the federal program that set national industry-wide manufactured home building and construction standards that led to an increase in manufactured home quality and availability. We present a detailed overview of the program to show that the quality improvements have played an important role in the increase in manufactured home living.

The Manufactured Housing Program (MHP) was established to regulate manufactured homes in order to "protect the health and safety of the owners of manufactured (mobile) homes through the enforcement of the federal manufactured home construction and safety standards and administration of dispute resolution" (U.S. Department of Housing and Urban Development, Office of Manufactured Housing Programs). Prior to this program, manufactured home builders set their own standards, leading to significant heterogeneity in home quality across the industry. As previously noted, manufactured homes are factory built homes constructed after June 15, 1976 in accordance with the new federal codes. Under the new guidelines, a manufactured home is a prefabricated dwelling unit of at least 320 square feet, built on a permanent chassis that is transported to a site and allows for continued transportability (U.S. Department of Housing and Urban Development, "Homeowner's Fact Sheet").

A primary objective of the MHP was to establish the Manufactured Home Construction and Safety Standards (1975) for "all equipment and installations in the design, construction, transportation, fire safety, plumbing, heat-producing and electrical systems of manufactured homes designed to be used as dwelling units."[2] In effect, the MHP introduced federal regulations that defined standards that apply to all manufactured homes without consideration of the jurisdiction in which the home is built, transported or located;[3] this differs from site-built residential and commercial buildings that must adhere to national, state and local governments' building codes that often vary depending on the jurisdiction in which construction occurs. A second objective of the program was to administer dispute resolution via periodic checks of manufactured home plant records and establish a process to address consumer complaints (U.S. Department of Housing and Urban Development, "Homeowner's Fact Sheet").

A manufactured home that satisfies the complete list of regulations contained in the standards receives a dated certification label on each transportable section of the home. Because manufactured homes are built on a permanent transportable chassis, it is practical for the federal government to impose regulations that allow the manufactured home to be built, moved and placed in different state and local jurisdictions with uniform safety standards. The HUD codes also include a program to administer dispute resolution between the consumer and manufactured home builders. According to HUD, 37 states participate in a partnership with the federal government to regulate and enforce the MHP, while the citizens in the remaining 13 states are assisted directly by HUD[4] (2016). However, it is important to note that HUD only resolves complaints related to the manufacturing process of the home; states are given the authority to oversee the installation of the home within their jurisdictions and are responsible for handling complaints related to the installation process (Manufactured Home Construction and Safety Standards 1975).

Manufactured home costs: purchase, financing, taxes and insurance

Site-built homes and condominium prices, as well as the cost of rental units, are determined by many factors including the amenities and location. Purchasing a home typically means the owner is financing the home with a mortgage, which requires a down payment and monthly installments. Recurring costs also include homeowner's insurance, property taxes, utilities, such as electricity and gas, and maintenance. For the renter, one pays monthly rent, where these costs are often included within the monthly payment (other than utilities that are often paid directly by the renter), and possibly renter's insurance. Manufactured homes possess similar cost attributes. However, as these are not site-built homes, state and local governments, lending institutions and insurance companies treat them differently than traditional housing structures. Below, we discuss the purchase and recurring payment price differences between traditional and manufactured homes.

Figure 10.2 shows the average sales price of manufactured homes and site-built, single-family homes from 1980 through 2010 in 2009 inflation adjusted dollars. Note that the figure includes cost data for the two primary types of manufactured homes: single-wide units, which are 18 feet or less in width and 90 feet or less in length, and double-wide units, which are 20 feet or more in width and 90 feet or less in length (Manufactured Home Construction and Safety Standards 1975).

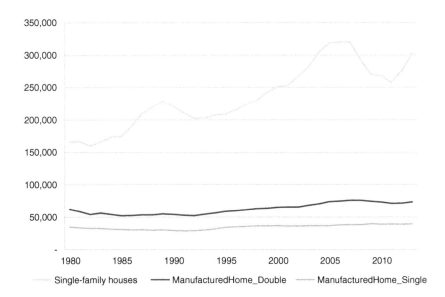

Figure 10.2 Average Sales Price of New Manufactured Homes and Single-Family Homes

Source: United States Census Bureau (2014a). *Manufactured Housing Survey Annual Data*, United States Census Bureau (2014b). *New Residential Sales Historical Data*.

The average sales price for traditional single-family homes generally increased throughout the period, with average prices starting around $170,000 in 1980 and increasing to $300,000 in 2010. Note that traditional home sales prices fluctuated throughout the period. In particular, traditional home prices dropped substantially during the Great Recession. On the other hand, the average sales price for double-wide and single-wide manufactured home units experienced relatively constant and small increases in price over the period. Manufactured homes did experience slight drops in prices during the recession periods, but were much more stable than traditional homes. In 1980, double-wide units cost approximately $105,000 less than traditional family homes; by 2010, the price gap had widened to approximately $225,000, on average. Double-wide units generally cost $25,000 to $30,000 more than single-wide units and the price gap between them throughout the period was stable. Clearly, manufactured homes are a less expensive alternative to traditional site-built homes. However, on average, manufactured homes have not appreciated as much as traditional homes over time. Note that traditional family homes are sold with land, whereas the manufactured home prices in Figure 10.2 do not include land or lot rental fees, which is an additional expense.

For a better comparison, Table 10.1 presents the average cost per square footage from 2007–2013 for each type of home, excluding land. In 2013, the average cost per square footage of a new manufactured home was $38.36 for a single-wide unit and $45.70 for a double-wide unit; a new single-family site-built home, excluding land cost, was $93.70. During this period, new site-built homes are 2.4 times costlier than single-unit manufactured homes and two times costlier than double-unit manufactured homes. We can conclude that manufactured homes are, by all measures, a lower-cost alternative to traditional housing.

A consumer generally purchases a manufactured home with cash assets or through financing.[5] Manufactured homes are available for financing through Federal Housing Administration (FHA)-approved lenders. However, differences exist between manufactured home loans and site-built home loans. While site-built home loans often allow for a maximum 30-year loan term, manufactured home loan terms are limited to 20 years for a manufactured home, 25 years for a manufactured home and

Table 10.1 New Manufactured Homes and New Single-Family Site-Built Homes Per Square Foot Cost Comparison (2007–2013)

| | *Average Cost per Sq. Ft.* | | | | | | |
	2007	*2008*	*2009*	*2010*	*2011*	*2012*	*2013*
New Manufactured Homes: Single	$ 33.91	$ 34.55	$ 35.35	$ 35.59	$ 36.41	$ 37.36	$ 38.36
New Manufactured Homes: Double	$ 41.80	$ 42.95	$ 42.94	$ 43.06	$ 43.34	$ 43.88	$ 45.70
New Site-Built Homes	$ 92.51	$ 88.31	$ 83.89	$ 84.07	$ 83.38	$ 86.30	$ 93.70

Source: These data are collected from United States Census Bureau (2015), *Manufactured Housing Survey Annual Data*, produced by the U.S. Commerce Department's Census Bureau from a survey sponsored by the U.S. Department of Housing and Urban Development.

lot loan and 15 years for a manufactured home lot only loan (U.S. Department of Housing and Urban Development, "Financing Manufactured (Mobile) Homes"). Additionally, MHP allows borrowers to receive loans whether they purchase or lease a site lot – if a lot is leased, the lease term must be of a minimum of three years. As of 2015, maximum loan amounts are also limited to $69,678 for a manufactured home, $92,904 for a manufactured home and lot and $23,226 for a lot (U.S. Department of Housing and Urban Development, "Financing Manufactured (Mobile) Homes"). Further, like site-built homes, eligible borrowers must be able to pay the minimum required down payment and demonstrate adequate income for making the monthly payment. The home must also be a principle residence (manufactured homes used as vacation homes would not be able to be financed through FHA-approved lenders).[6] In addition, a suitable lot, either in a manufactured home park via a lot lease or borrower-owned land, must be available to site the home. HUD recommends using a lending institution that specializes in financing manufactured homes.

The purchaser of a manufactured home must also pay for transportation costs associated with moving the manufactured home from the retailer to its destination (or moving from one destination to another); transportation cost estimates vary from $3,000 to $10,000, depending on the size of the manufactured home and the transportation distance. Transporting manufactured homes involves risks factors such as possible damage to the manufactured home. Installation expenses include: grading the ground for placement and hooking the unit up to water, sewer and power services; these expenses vary by location. These additional costs explain why manufactured homes are rarely moved once placed at a site.

As previously mentioned, the three main options for locating a manufactured home are on land owned by the purchaser of the manufactured home, on rented land, or on a manufactured home park. Note that rented land could be one of many options, including the purchaser of a manufactured home placing the home on family land, which could be attractive in rural areas to decrease costs. If a manufactured homeowner would like to purchase their own property, they must pay for the land and the costs to hook up basic utility services such as sewerage and electricity. If manufactured homeowners opt to place a home on leased land in a manufactured home park, they would be required to pay park fees for the land, service connections, and any possible amenities located within the park. The costs associated with the location of a manufactured home vary considerably.

While state and local governments do not oversee the construction and safety standards, these jurisdictions do possess the power to create laws and regulations that tax manufactured homes, just as they can tax personal property (i.e. vehicles) and real property (i.e. site-built homes). Manufactured home tax rates and their assessment categories vary considerably by state; The Ohio Department of Taxation (2009) includes a comparison of other states' manufactured home tax rates; we have selected a few states to illustrate the variation. California assesses and taxes manufactured homes as real property if the structure is fixed to a permanent foundation (i.e., unable to be moved), but as personal property if not fixed to a permanent foundation; the maximum amount of the tax cannot exceed 1 percent of full cash value. Kentucky classifies all manufactured homes as real property, and they are assessed at full cash value; therefore, manufactured homes are taxed at the same rate as traditional homes. In contrast, Michigan assesses manufactured homes as real property at the local levy mill rate if located on land that is assessable as real property, or at $3 per month if located in a manufactured home park. West Virginia assesses manufactured housing as residential real property if affixed to land owned by the homeowner, or as personal property if not situated on one's own land. Clearly, property assessment and tax practices vary significantly across the states.

Manufactured home quality

Prior to 1976, mobile home quality varied considerably as manufacturers could adopt their own construction standards. However, manufactured home quality improved with the imposition of the federal HUD code in 1976 that defined minimum safety and construction standards; if consumers were aware of the standards, the increased assurance of quality could have factored in to the significant increase in manufactured home living over the last 30 years. The Manufactured Home Construction and Safety Standards (1975) includes regulations for light and ventilation, minimum room size dimensions, bathroom requirements as well as body and frame materials, element resistance, and structural design. In addition, the standards set fire safety requirements, structural load limits, formaldehyde emission levels, and testing of windows and doors. Air filtration, cooling and heating, plumbing, and electrical system standards were also specified. Additional safety requirements protect against shock and vibration during transportation. These federal regulations increased the safety homogeneity of manufactured homes and provided a signal of quality assurance to consumers.

With the establishment of federal standards, manufactured homes can now be built in a factory and shipped to any location regardless of local building codes. The HUD code is considered to be at least as stringent as local building codes (Manufactured Housing Institute, 2016). As construction and safety improved, so have the features of manufactured homes. The feature and amenity improvements have caused manufactured homes to have a similar feel and style to traditional site-built homes compared to the manufactured homes of the past. Manufactured homes vary in size, ranging from 320 square feet for a single-wide unit and up to 2,000 square feet for a double-wide unit.[7] Manufactured homes allow for customization options that rival traditional homes, including custom floor plans, vaulted ceilings, modern full kitchens, and porches.

Empirical analysis of rural manufactured home living

To investigate the increased popularity of manufactured homes in rural areas, we use statistical analysis to better understand the determinants of the growth in manufactured home living. We use county level panel data in ten year intervals from 1980–2010, which consists of major socioeconomic and housing data from the U.S. Decennial Census of Population and Housing and the ACS for 1,949 rural counties.[8] Table 10.2 presents summary statistics for the variables used in the empirical analysis; variable names, definitions and data sources are provided in the appendix.

The dependent variable is the number of manufactured homes divided by the total number of housing units; the variable provides the total percent of manufactured

Table 10.2 County Summary Statistics

	Rural County by Year				Rural	Urban
	1980	*1990*	*2000*	*2010*	*Avg.*	*Avg.*
Dependent Variable:						
Pct Manufactured Homes	9.97%	14.42%	15.92%	14.83%	13.79%	10.47%
	(5.48)	(7.71)	(9.31)	(8.94)	(8.32)	(8.55)
Independent Variables:						
Population	20,889	21,108	22,838	23,669	22,127	192,414
	(18,960)	(19,734)	(21,413)	(22,823)	(20,817)	(478,849)
Pct Under 18	29.53%	27.13%	25.41%	23.11%	26.29%	26.38%
	(3.62)	(3.60)	(3.37)	(3.42)	(4.22)	(3.85)
Pct Over 65	13.33%	15.13%	15.04%	16.05%	14.89%	11.75%
	(3.87)	(4.11)	(3.90)	(3.88)	(4.06)	(3.51)
Pct Rural Population	72.36%	72.78%	70.49%	70.06%	71.42%	44.49%
	(24.52)	(24.32)	(25.40)	(25.58)	(24.98)	(31.60)
Poverty Rate	17.45%	18.61%	15.58%	17.46%	17.27%	13.17%
	(7.53)	(8.14)	(6.73)	(6.61)	(7.34)	(5.94)
Pct Female-Headed Household	7.83%	9.27%	10.07%	10.85%	9.51%	10.70%
	(3.22)	(4.12)	(4.35)	(4.59)	(4.25)	(3.43)
Pct Bachelor's Degree	10.28%	11.79%	14.36%	16.84%	13.32%	18.53%
	(4.28)	(4.78)	(5.73)	(6.47)	(5.94)	(9.47)
Real Median Housing Value	$67,360	$64,629	$85,707	$105,196	$80,734	$124,856
	(24,946)	(31,011)	(45,061)	(64,510)	(47,007)	(75,694)
Real Median Contract Rent	$262	$298	$363	$431	$339	$488
	(92)	(101)	(110)	(131)	(127)	(198)
Real Median Income	$28,618	$31,755	$38,712	$39,353	$34,616	$44,093
	(6,232)	(7,001)	(7,490)	(8,260)	(8,595)	(12,357)
Real Top 10% Income	$67,518	$79,276	$100,140	$ 133,729	$95,189	$113,553
	(10,772)	(12,729)	(17,965)	(17,427.)	(29,293)	(32,575)

Standard deviations in parenthesis. Based on 1,949 non-metropolitan counties and 1,157 metropolitan counties. All monetary terms are deflated to 2009 dollars.

homes in rural county jurisdictions. The percent of manufactured homes in rural counties grew significantly from 1980 to 2000 but decreased slightly between 2000 and 2010. Notably, the largest increase in manufactured home living occurred between 1980 and 1990; during this decade, there was a 4.4 percentage point increase in the overall percent of households living in manufactured homes. By 2010, a quarter of rural counties throughout the United States had more than one manufactured home per five total housing units. Also, reflecting the popularity of manufactured homes in rural areas, the percent of manufactured homes in rural counties are greater than that of the urban counties throughout each decade. While manufactured homes can be either owned or rented, they are predominately owner-occupied; the average manufactured homeownership rate is 77 percent throughout the period.

Figures 10.3 and 10.4 provide maps to illustrate the percent of household living in manufactured homes in 1980 and 2010, respectively. The counties are divided into quartiles in 1980 and the same ranges are used for the 2010 map. General themes are evident: The Western and Southern regions possess the highest rates of manufactured home living. The Southern region experienced the highest growth in manufactured home living between the periods, whereas the Midwest and Northeast have the lowest percent of manufactured home living. Note that a few areas have especially low rates of manufactured living: Southern California, the center of the United States, and along the coast of the Northeast.

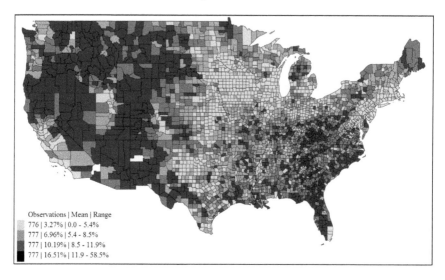

Observations | Mean | Range
776 | 3.27% | 0.0 - 5.4%
777 | 6.96% | 5.4 - 8.5%
777 | 10.19% | 8.5 - 11.9%
777 | 16.51% | 11.9 - 58.5%

Figure 10.3 Percent of Households Living in Manufactured Homes, 1980

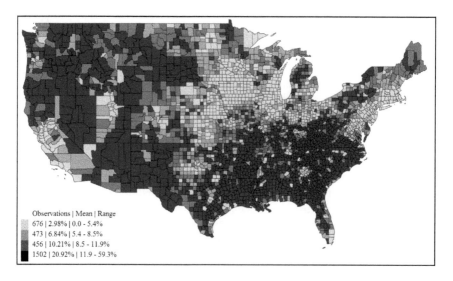

Observations | Mean | Range
676 | 2.98% | 0.0 - 5.4%
473 | 6.84% | 5.4 - 8.5%
456 | 10.21% | 8.5 - 11.9%
1502 | 20.92% | 11.9 - 59.3%

Figure 10.4 Percent of Households Living in Manufactured Homes, 2010

Figure 10.5 shows the percent change in manufactured home living from 1980–2010 for rural counties only. The Southern region experienced the highest percent change in manufactured living in rural counties (and, although not shown on the map, for urban counties also). Many of the counties that possessed a low rate of manufactured home living in the previous two maps are urban counties. The Western region experienced moderate growth in manufactured home living, although these rates were already high in 1980 relative to the rest of the United States.

Turning to the statistical analysis, the explanatory variables capture a wide range of socioeconomic conditions that may play a role in housing choice: demographics, economic factors, such as median household income and the poverty rate, and local housing market conditions. On average, the total rural population has increased over the period while the percent of people under 18 years of age steadily declined, whereas the elderly population (over 65 years of age) increased.

We also examine the effect of household characteristics and education level on manufactured home demand by including the percent of female-headed households, poverty rate and the proportion of county residents aged 25 or older that possess at least a bachelor's degree. According to the 2012 Census, families headed by a single adult are more likely to be headed by women, and these female-headed families are at a greater risk of poverty; 34.2 percent of households where no husband was present were below the poverty line, and 16.9 percent of these households were living in deep poverty (defined as households with income under 50 percent of the poverty line). In this regard, female-headed households are among the most vulnerable group of people and have limited economic and social resources; therefore, a manufactured home could be an attractive affordable housing alternative. The percent of female-headed households and the percent of people aged 25 or older with bachelor's degree in rural counties have steadily increased over time. As shown in Table 10.2, both rates are relatively small compared to metropolitan counties, which

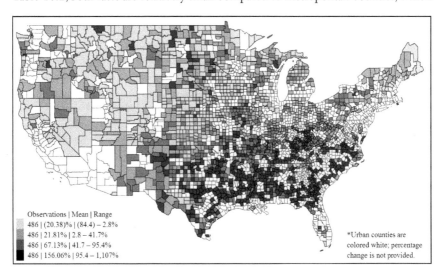

Figure 10.5 Percent Change of Rural County Households Living in Manufactured Homes, 1980–2010

were reported to be 10.7 percent and 18.5 percent on average during 1980–2010, respectively. On the other hand, the average poverty rate of people in rural counties are greater than nationwide poverty rates. The poverty rate dropped to 15.58 percent in 2000, but increased between 2000 and 2010 because of the Great Recession.

To investigate how the economic status and housing market conditions affect one's home choices, we include county-level median household income, top tenth percentile income level,[9] median housing value,[10] and median contract rent.[11] Monetary values are inflation adjusted to 2009 dollars.

The economic status of a household is one of the most critical determinants of housing choice. During the 1980–2010 period, both median household income and the top ten percentile income level grew considerably in both rural and urban areas. In rural counties, median household income increased from $28,618 to $39,353 – 38 percent growth over the period. During the same period, metropolitan counties' median household income rose from $35,263 to $49,488, or 40 percent growth. The top tenth percentile income level of households in rural counties almost doubled, up from $67,518 to $133,729, or 98 percent growth; it has risen much more so than median income. In our regression analysis, we expect the two income variables and the poverty rate to play a role in housing choice patterns across the country.

Further, including median housing value and median contract rent allows us to examine the relationship between local housing market conditions and manufactured home demand. Since the median housing value variable does not include manufactured home values, it provides information on the median sales price of conventional site-built homes in counties. As shown in Table 10.2, these values increased significantly over time. The median housing value in rural counties is 56 percent higher in 2010 than it was in 1980, and the median contract rent also increased 65 percent during the period. Note that metropolitan areas experienced a greater increase in housing values, experiencing a median housing value increase of 86 percent over the period. Also, variability in housing values, measured by the standard deviation of median housing value, increased substantially in both rural and urban counties. In contrast, manufactured home prices were relatively stable over the period. With rising site-built housing prices, rental costs, and the widening affordability gap, manufactured homes seem to be an attractive affordable housing option that can compete with lower cost site-built housing, rental homes and apartments in local housing markets.

Table 10.3 reports the regression using socioeconomic variables to explain the growth of manufactured home living in rural counties – urban counties are excluded from the analysis. The analysis allows us to examine how changing socio-economic conditions such as growing income disparity, changing demographics and changing household composition affect the proportion of households living in manufactured homes. We use a two-way fixed-effects regression technique to control for the time-invariant unobserved heterogeneity (county fixed effects) and nationwide trends (time indicator variables). Finally, we also use robust standard errors to address possible differences in error variance across observations.

As shown in Table 10.3, nearly all the socioeconomic and housing factors attain statistical significance at the 1 percent level. First, we discuss the impact of economic conditions on the choice of manufactured home living. As expected, lower median income level is associated with a larger demand for manufactured homes as these

Table 10.3 Manufactured Home Demand in Rural Counties

Dependent Variable: Percent Manufactured Homes	
Log(Population)	3.242***
	(5.567)
Pct Under18	−0.309***
	(−6.303)
Pct Over65	−0.410***
	(−8.907)
Pct Rural Population	0.0485***
	(5.912)
Poverty Rate	−0.101***
	(−4.275)
Pct Female-Headed Households	0.396***
	(5.395)
Pct Bachelor's Degree among adults	−0.369***
	(−11.95)
Log(Real Median Housing Value)	−1.620***
	(−3.399)
Log(Real Median Contract Rent)	9.247***
	(13.81)
Log(Real Median Income)	−3.355***
	(−3.406)
Log(Real Top 10% Income)	−0.366
	(−0.456)
Time Dummy: Year 1990	3.675***
	(11.03)
Time Dummy: Year 2000	4.192***
	(7.679)
Time Dummy: Year 2010	2.448***
	(2.934)
Constant	−2.067
	(−0.184)
Observations	7,793
Number of Units	1,949
Within R-squared	0.557

Robust t-statistics in parentheses. *** $p<0.01$, ** $p<0.05$, * $p<0.1$.

types of homes are more affordable for households with lower than average income. Also, when the top tenth percentile income level of a county is higher, less people in the county choose to live in manufactured homes, holding all other conditions constant. However, the top ten percent income variable is not statistically significant. The impact of a one standard deviation increase in the median household income level ($8,595) is associated with a 0.83 percentage point decrease in the manufactured home living rate, meaning that counties with lower income levels have higher demand for manufactured homes. A greater poverty rate is found to decrease manufactured home demand, holding other factors constant. Consider two counties with the same median income: If one county has a higher poverty rate than the other, the other must have a greater proportion of high income households (i.e. a larger income inequality). Thus, the negative sign for the coefficient on the poverty rate variable suggests that increases on both ends of the income distribution (the very poor and the very rich) reduce the demand for manufactured homes. In other words, our findings imply an inverse-U shape relationship between income level and manufactured home demand. Those in lowest income group cannot afford to buy or access financing to purchase a manufactured home, whereas those in the highest income group prefer to live in a higher-quality conventional site-built home.

We also examine the relationship between housing market conditions and manufactured home demand. The negative relationship between the median value of conventional site-built homes and the percent of manufactured homes reveals a pattern of housing choices in rural areas. Contrary to expectations, a one standard deviation increase in the median housing value ($47,007) leads to a 0.94 percentage point reduction in the percent of manufactured homes. This finding suggests that households living in a community with growing property values tend to prefer a traditional site-built home over a manufactured home.

In addition, the rental price is found to be one of the most important drivers of growing manufactured home demand. The regression results suggest that when the rental price is higher, more people choose to live in manufactured homes. A one standard deviation increase in median contract rent ($127) increases the percent of manufactured homes by 3.46 percent age point. These estimates suggest that rising rental costs are driving households to consider manufactured home living.

We now turn to the effects of changing demographics and household makeup on the choice of manufactured home living. First, the regression results show that a shrinking rural population is associated with a lower demand for manufactured homes, as well as other types of housing, whereas rural counties with a shrinking proportion of young and/or elderly have a higher demand for manufactured homes. A one standard deviation decrease in the population leads to a 3.05 percent age point drop in manufactured homes living.

Household type and education attainment are estimated to be important factors that affect manufactured home living. Our findings show that a higher concentration of female-headed households in rural counties is associated with more manufactured homes in those areas, holding all other conditions constant. A one standard deviation increase in the percent of female-headed households is found to increase the percent of manufactured homes by 1.68 percent age point. However, we are cautious in our interpretation: It is possible that single men (who have for some reason split from their families) tend to live in affordable manufactured homes. The correlation between female-headed households with no husband present and male-headed households with no wife present is 0.97. On the other hand, higher education attainment is negatively associated with manufactured home living. The findings imply that, in general, manufactured homes appear to be attractive for households with low to moderate socioeconomic status, but may not be an appropriate choice for those living significantly below the poverty line. As discussed earlier, since manufactured homes are less costly than a comparable site-built home and manufactured homes may provide more desirable housing services than multi-family rental units, low to moderate income households who have some choice among housing alternatives may find it desirable to live in manufactured homes.

Our regression analysis provides statistical evidence that certain household demographic and economic characteristics, along with housing market conditions, are important drivers in the rising demand for manufactured home living in rural America. Local rental costs appear to be the primary driver that induces people to turn to manufactured homes that can meet their housing needs. Findings also shed light on the fact that households with a lower socioeconomic status, such as female-headed households and low- to moderate-income households, find manufactured homes an attractive housing option. Our findings emphasize the growing role of manufactured homes as an affordable housing alternative in the context of changing housing costs, household needs and resources. Though stigma is sometimes attached to manufactured homes, they may in fact offer a quality affordable housing opportunity to those of low to moderate means; we expect manufactured homes to continue to fill an important housing niche in rural America in the coming years.

In the appendix, we also present regressions for owner-occupied and renter-occupied manufactured homes. However, apart from larger or smaller magnitudes of the coefficients on population, median income, and female-headed household variables in the additional regressions – specifications (2) and (3) in Table A10.2 – the results were similar to the pooled regression in Table 10.3 and are therefore not discussed in any further detail.

Conclusions

Most of the growth in manufactured home living has occurred in rural places, and about 30 percent of new housing stock in recent years is in the manufactured home category; these homes are now an essential component of the affordable housing stock across America, especially in rural places. Importantly, manufactured homes are an important source of unsubsidized, low-cost housing. With the adoption of federal standards, the quality of such housing is now much improved and more uniform. Our analysis suggests that manufactured home living is within reach of low to moderate income families, but not households living in poverty. A key constraint for those living in poverty may be access to credit. From a policy perspective, federal policymakers have a trade-off to consider. Currently, a high proportion of those living in poverty receive federal housing subsidies. If policymakers wanted to reduce reliance on federally subsidized housing, they might consider ways to extend low-income loans for manufactured homes so that more of these households would have this housing option available to them; however, this policy shift could be risky, as poor households are less stable and more likely to default on loans. Nevertheless, such policies might reduce reliance on federal subsidies and engender increased personal responsibility.

Changing demographics and household makeup have also played a role in the growing demand for manufactured homes. In particular, the increasing number of female-headed households (or single male-headed households) has played a role in generating demand for manufactured homes; it is unclear, however, whether it is the mother with children or the single men that tend to live in manufactured housing. More generally, a range of demographic and economic factors are shown to be important determinants of the increasing demand for manufactured homes. While manufactured homes are more affordable, a higher proportion of manufactured homes within a community may serve to reduce the property tax base; relative to traditional homes, manufactured homes add less to the tax base and yet require a similar level of public services. As manufactured home living increases, the impact on the property tax base is an important consideration to local government fiscal health.

While negative stigma is sometimes associated with manufactured home living, it is an adequate housing option that meets the needs of low- to moderate-income households. Importantly, manufactured housing is unsubsidized and thus reduces costs to the federal government as many manufactured home residents might otherwise qualify for federally subsidized housing. Though local governments must consider a mix of high- and low-income housing to meet housing needs in a way that results in fiscal balance (increased property tax revenues should cover increased public expenditures associated with development), manufactured housing offers communities an important component of a balanced housing stock.

Notes

1 Manufactured and mobile homes are distinctly different than modular homes. Modular homes are built in sections at a factory, then assembled on a permanent foundation at the location; these are not included in the analysis.
2 Detailed information regarding these standards can be found in 24 CFR Part 3280 by accessing the U.S. Government Electronic Code of Federal Regulations.
3 There are some exceptions (i.e. manufactured homes located in wind zones – see 24 CFR Part 3280).
4 The 13 states assisted directly by HUD include: Alaska, Connecticut, Delaware, Hawaii, Indiana, Kansas, Maine, Montana, New Hampshire, Ohio, Oklahoma, Vermont and Wyoming (and the District of Columbia).
5 Note that manufactured homes can also be rented; however, the rental process would work similarly to the rental of a house or home, so the discussion is excluded from the section.
6 Unfortunately, our data do not allow us to distinguish between homestead and vacation mobile home properties.
7 Triple-wide (and even bigger) units are available but are less common.
8 We define "rural counties" based on the "non-metropolitan" classification used by the Office of Management and Budget in 2013: "The Office of Management and Budget designates counties as Metropolitan, Micropolitan, or Neither. A Metro area contains a core urban area of 50,000 or more population, and a Micro area contains an urban core of at least 10,000 (but less than 50,000) population. All counties that are not part of a Metropolitan Statistical Area are considered rural. Micropolitan counties are considered non-Metropolitan or rural along with all the counties that are not classified as either Metro or Micro."
9 Since the U.S Census does not provide county-level data for the top 10th percentile (or 90th percentile) income level, we restore an (approximate) income distribution using the reported number of households in each of the available ten income categories. By assuming households are distributed uniformly in each income category, we created an estimate of the top 10th percentile income level for each county.
10 Per the U.S. Census, the median housing value represents the median value of the respondent's estimate for how much the property (house and lot) would sell for if it were on the market. The housing value data includes only specified owner-occupied housing units and excludes manufactured homes, houses with a business or medical office, houses on ten or more acres and housing units in multiunit structures. Ideally, median housing value of the same size (or cost per square footage) would be a better measure for the analysis. However, to our knowledge this information is unavailable at the county level. Therefore, the county-level median housing value data provided by the U.S. Census are used alternatively in our analysis.
11 Per the U.S. Census, the contract rent is the monthly rent agreed upon regardless of any furnishings, utilities or services that may be included.

Appendix

Table A10.1 Definitions and Sources of Variables

Variable	Definition	Source
Pct Manufactured Homes	Percent of mobile homes or trailers in total housing units	Census
Population	Population	Census
Pct Under 18	Percent of people under age 18	Census
Pct Over 65	Percent of people aged 65 and over	Census
Pct Rural Population	Percent of people living in rural territories	Census
Poverty Rate	The percentage of people who are below poverty	Census
Pct Female-Headed Household	Percent of female-headed households in total family households	Census
Pct Bachelor's Degree	Percent of people 25 and over with bachelor's or higher degree	Census
Median Housing Value	The median value of the respondent's estimate of how much the property (house and lot) would sell for if it were for sale (specified owner-occupied housing units only).	Census
Median Contract Rent	The median value of the monthly rent agreed to or contracted for, regardless of any furnishings, utilities, fees, meals or services that may be included	Census
Median Income	The median income divides the income distribution into two equal groups, one having incomes above the median, and other having incomes below the median.	Census
Top 10% Income	The top tenth percentile (or 90th percentile) income level of U.S. households	Census

Table A10.2 Owner-Occupied and Renter-Occupied Manufactured Home Regressions

Variables	(1)	(2)	(3)
	All	*Owner-occupied*	*Renter-occupied*
	Pct Manuf. Homes	*Pct Manuf. Homes*	*Pct Manuf. Homes*
Log(Population)	3.242***	1.573**	6.917***
	(5.567)	(2.456)	(9.225)
Pct Under18	−0.309***	−0.304***	−0.317***
	(−6.303)	(−5.366)	(−5.649)
Pct Over65	−0.410***	−0.517***	−0.231***
	(−8.907)	(−9.811)	(−3.908)
Pct Rural Population	0.0485***	0.0496***	0.0499***
	(5.912)	(5.771)	(5.052)
Poverty Rate	−0.101***	−0.150***	−0.190***
	(−4.275)	(−5.601)	(−5.722)
Pct Female-Headed Households	0.396***	0.613***	0.126
	(5.395)	(7.722)	(1.591)
Pct Bachelor's Degree Among Adults	−0.369***	−0.347***	−0.363***
	(−11.95)	(−9.724)	(−8.541)
Log(Real Median Housing Value)	−1.620***	−1.168**	−1.762***
	(−3.399)	(−2.149)	(−3.008)
Log(Real Median Contract Rent)	9.247***	9.040***	11.59***
	(13.81)	(11.71)	(13.00)
Log(Real Median Income)	−3.355***	−3.760***	−11.01***
	(−3.406)	(−3.393)	(−7.396)
Log(Real Top 10% Income)	−0.366	−0.889	0.921
	(−0.456)	(−0.877)	(0.905)
Time Dummy: Year 1990	3.675***	3.821***	4.013***
	(11.03)	(10.17)	(11.55)
Time Dummy: Year 2000	4.192***	4.005***	5.542***
	(7.679)	(6.578)	(9.746)
Time Dummy: Year 2010	2.448***	0.961	4.174***
	(2.934)	(1.017)	(4.936)
Constant	−2.067	20.91	14.71
	(−0.184)	(1.639)	(1.004)
Observations	7,793	7,793	7,793
Number of Units	1,949	1,949	1,949
Within R-squared	0.556	0.522	0.460

Robust t-statistics in parentheses. *** p<0.01, ** p<0.05, * p<0.1.

References

Aman, D., & Yarnal, B. (2010). Home sweet mobile home? Benefits and challenges of mobile home ownership in rural Pennsylvania. *Applied Geography, 30*, 84–95

Apgar, W., Calder, A., Collins, M., & Duda, M. (2002). An Examination of Manufactured Housing as a Community- and Asset-Building Strategy. *Neighborhood Reinvestment Corporation* (report to the Ford Foundation.)

Boehm, T., & Schlottmann, A. (2008). Is Manufactured home housing a good alternative for low-income families? Evidence from the American Housing Survey. *Cityscape, 10*(2), 159–224. Retrieved from http://www.jstor.org/stable/20868658

Gentz, R. (2001). Why advocates need to rethink manufactured housing. *Housing Policy Debate, 12*(2), 393–414

Manufactured Home Construction and Safety Standards, 24 CFR Part 3280 (1975).

Manufactured Home Tax. (2009). Ohio Department of Taxation. Retrieved from www.tax. ohio.gov/portals/0/communications/publications/brief_summaries/2009_brief_summary/manufactured_home_tax.pdf

Manufactured Housing Institute. (2016). Understanding today's manufactured housing. Retrieved from www.manufacturedhousing.org/wp-content/uploads/2016/11/1837temp.pdf

Office of Management and Budget. (2013). Revised delineations of metropolitan statistical areas, metropolitan statistical areas, and combined statistical areas, and guidance on uses of the delineations of these areas. OMB Bulletin No, 13–01. *Executive Office of the President, Office of Management and Budget.*

United States Census Bureau. (2015). Cost and size comparison for manufactured and site built homes, 2007–2013. *Manufactured Housing Survey Annual Data.* Retrieved from www.census.gov/data/tables/2014/econ/mhs/2014-annual-data.html

United States Census Bureau. (2014a). Historic annual average sales price by State, 1980–2013. *Manufactured Housing Survey Annual Data.* Retrieved from www.census.gov/data/tables/time-series/econ/mhs/historical-annual-average-sales.html

United States Census Bureau. (2014b). Median and average sales price of houses sold by region, 1980–2013. *New Residential Sales Historical Data.* Retrieved from www.census.gov/construction/nrs/pdf/pricerega.pdf

U.S. Department of Housing and Urban Development. (2016). Manufactured Housing Standards Program. Retrieved from https://portal.hud.gov/hudportal/documents/huddoc?id=31-FY16CJ-MHSProgram.pdf

U.S. Department of Housing and Urban Development. Financing Manufactured (Mobile) Homes. Retrieved from http://portal.hud.gov/hudportal/HUD?src=/program_offices/housing/sfh/title/repair

U.S. Department of Housing and Urban Development. Homeowner's Fact Sheet. Retrieved from http://portal.hud.gov/hudportal/HUD?src=/program_offices/housing/rmra/mhs/factsheet

U.S. Department of Housing and Urban Development. Office of Manufactured Housing Programs. Retrieved from https://portal.hud.gov/hudportal/HUD?src=/program_offices/housing/rmra/mhs/mhshome

11 Housing challenges and policy implications of shale oil development in rural communities

Felix Fernando, Anne Junod, Jeffrey Jacquet, Robert Hearne and Lynette Flage

Introduction

Rural communities experiencing rapid shale oil development and accompanying population and economic growth face significant and perhaps unique housing challenges atypical to those of their rural counterparts in non-energy development communities. During the past decade, many communities across western North Dakota saw a dramatic increase in hydraulic fracturing and horizontal drilling as a result of shale oil development in the Bakken region. Further, the increase in oil industry activity, in conjunction with growing levels of in-migration and accompanying socioeconomic changes, generated ripple effects across Bakken periphery communities, particularly those in northwestern South Dakota.[1] This chapter discusses housing challenges in five communities in western North Dakota (Williston, Dickinson, Belfield, Ray and Watford City) and three communities in northwestern South Dakota (Belle Fourche, Lemmon and Buffalo) as they relate to population and economic growth accompanying rapid shale oil development.

Like many rural communities across the American Midwest and the Great Plains regions, much of western North and South Dakota incurred population losses in recent decades, denoted by the corresponding phenomena of out-migrating youth, increasingly elderly populations and declining community economic vitality. Since the early 2000s, energy development in the Bakken region attracted thousands of new residents from across the United States to western North Dakota, a region previously typified as agrarian and predominantly rural. Between 2005 and 2013, concomitant with the dramatic increase in shale oil development, the five North Dakota communities experienced significant population increases, particularly in comparison to the South Dakota periphery communities, which experienced either modest population growth or population stagnation (see Figure 11.1).

Prior to dramatic increases in Bakken shale oil development in the early 2000s, all eight communities in North and South Dakota exhibited limited housing stocks as net population losses over previous decades led to a reduction in demand for new home construction, further compounding housing challenges. Accordingly, a central issue across all the communities is the quality of much of the existing housing stock due to advanced age, in addition to concerns related to both availability and affordability. None of the eight communities experienced considerable housing

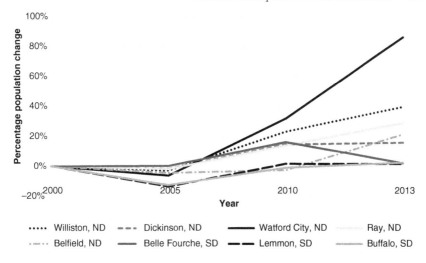

Figure 11.1 Percentage Population Change from 2000–2013 in the Eight Communities

stock growth from 2000 to 2010; in fact, during this period, the housing stock stagnated or declined in three of the communities (Belfield, North Dakota, Lemmon, South Dakota, and Buffalo, South Dakota).

In communities experiencing rapid population growth due to energy and related industrial development, housing challenges are often tied to the demands of the industrial workforce. Drilling and fracking a well that is expected to produce for decades takes only a few weeks, but the accompanying labor demands during this period are significant. During the drilling and development phase, workers construct and install well pads, access roads, pipelines, other supporting infrastructure as well as facilitate drilling and fracking completion operations to make a well production ready. Further, workers are needed for direct support activities such as hauling water, chemicals and other resource inputs necessary for drilling and fracking. However, once a well advances to the production phase and pipelines are in place to transport the produced oil and gas, the number of workers required to maintain a well declines dramatically, usually to not more than two to four workers per well. As a result, workforce demand for housing drastically decreases when the industry transitions from the drilling and development phase to the production phase. Accordingly, understanding the dynamics associated with the social and economic aspects of industrial housing demand is critical to informing responsive and appropriate housing initiatives and interventions in energy impacted communities.

In this chapter, a timeline of housing development in oil impacted communities across the Bakken region is outlined along with a discussion of the social, economic and structural factors affecting housing availability and affordability. In addition, an assessment of rental and home mortgage options for public service employees in North and South Dakota is provided. Further, the economic pressures public service employees face in securing housing against the cyclical backdrop of the new mini-boom, mini-bust energy development landscape are described. Finally, an array of potential housing interventions at the local, state and federal levels that may be employed across energy-impacted communities working to stabilize and improve their housing stocks in the new mini-boom, mini-bust era of shale oil development is discussed.

Housing phases in the Bakken region

Oil and gas development in rural areas can precipitate varying levels of housing needs that manifest across multiple time horizons, causing impacted communities to experience distinct phases of housing needs. Three phases of housing development have been identified in the Bakken region so far, each requiring distinct principal housing responses and implementations. These phases have transpired concurrently rather than sequentially due to the rapid pace of shale oil development in the region. With time and based on how the industry evolves, other distinct housing phases may emerge.

Phase One

During the first phase, the dramatic workforce influx – comprised primarily of males seeking employment – generates immediate demand for housing that cannot be satisfied by the quality and quantity of available housing stock in affected communities. This phase coincides with relatively labor intensive drilling/fracking operations and related support industries pursuing housing solutions that can satisfy the high demand within a short period of time. Since many Bakken oil companies hold leases that would expire if drilling operations are not executed by a specified date, companies quickly expand their drilling operations and corresponding workforce. In response, housing suppliers and developers focus on providing immediate, temporary workforce housing, such as "man camps." Other temporary housing options, including trailers, campers and hotel rooms, are also used to satisfy demand. At the same time, most or all available single- or multi-family housing units in impacted communities are secured by oil development and related support industries for workforce housing. Industry drives to secure housing increases rents across all housing types, which provides a significant financial incentive and opportunity for investors and builders to construct permanent housing. Land values rapidly increase in accordance with the demand; however, a portion of the workforce – particularly those involved in drilling and fracking operations – remain transient, and as a result, demand for workforce housing does not cease until the industry transitions from drilling phases into the less labor-intensive production phases.

Phase Two

During the second phase, housing developers and investors focus on providing multifamily housing units to capitalize on higher rents and provide better-quality housing options to the growing, increasingly place-based workforce. As apartments and multifamily units become available, much of the workforce transitions from temporary housing to more permanent housing. During this phase, hotel rates and those of other temporary housing and rental units begin to decline and housing ownership transitions from company-owned/leased to owner-occupied. The industry focuses on stabilizing the workforce and encourages new and existing workers to move their families to the area. As more families move into the impacted communities, the demand for single-family homes increases; however, housing affordability remains a significant challenge. As such, housing suppliers focus on manufactured, trailer and modular homes as cost- and time-effective housing solutions, in addition to twin homes, town homes and duplexes that can be built at comparatively lower costs than stick-built, single-family homes.

Phase Three

During the third phase, the workforce stabilizes and the demand for better-quality single-family homes continues to increase. Housing suppliers and developers largely focus on providing conventional stick-built single-family housing. Employees and families with sufficient financial assets and those who plan to become permanent community residents transition into higher-quality or more conventional single-family homes, whereas those who remain undecided about how long they will be living in the area, or those who do not have financial resources to purchase a single family home, continue to live in multifamily, trailer or manufactured homes. None of the communities in the Bakken have yet fully transitioned into Phase Three.

Factors and conditions affecting housing affordability

As outlined in the first housing phase, the oil industry drive to secure all available housing in conjunction with their willingness to pay, what can have often become inflated sums to secure housing, in rural communities with limited housing stocks, has led to a rapid and dramatic increase in both area rents and home values.

Challenges to provision of adequate and affordable housing in energy impacted communities must be considered and analyzed with the interrelatedness of developing appropriate and responsive interventions. In communities already experiencing steady or rising levels of outmigration and stagnant or declining business and industry climates, rapid population influxes such as those experienced by many Bakken-area communities can precipitate significant scarcity in not only affordable quality housing options, but community public services and resources across market, state and civil society sectors. Figure 11.2 reflects a framework illustrating the interrelatedness of these and joint conditions contributing to inadequate affordable housing in the Bakken region. As Figure 11.2 indicates, lack of adequate and affordable housing leads to several barriers to economic and community development and growth, which are discussed in detail in the following section.

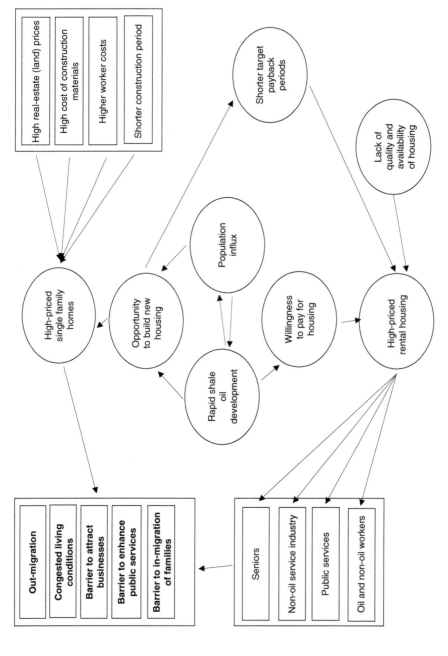

Figure 11.2 Conditions and Factors that Contribute to Lack of Affordable Housing and Implications on Communities

Landlord and developer constraints

Rapid increases in rent present opportunities for housing developers and investors to buy and build different forms of housing. During peak drilling activity in 2008 and 2009, many housing and rental properties in the central and periphery Bakken region were purchased at premiums by outside investor groups, which prompted new and existing landlords to increase rents to cover their investments and increase profits. At the same time, the uncertainty associated with the boom-bust cycle of oil development prompted many real estate investors to target shorter than expected payback periods of approximately three to eight years, compared to more conventional payback periods of ten to 20 years across the real estate industry. This reduced time period meant new owners must yield much higher returns on their investments compared to more typical markets where time constraints are not as pressing.

Today, prices of most newly constructed single-family homes in the central Bakken region are over $250,000 and not readily affordable for many people working in non-oil-industry jobs. For new and existing residents across the region, purchasing a home in present housing market conditions can be a considerable challenge, especially if they are not working in oil or related support industries. Several factors, such as supply and demand mechanisms precipitating a rapid increase in real estate and land prices, high cost of construction materials and higher worker costs[2] contribute to high prices of new single-family homes in the Bakken region. In addition, the climate conditions in western North and South Dakota prompt a shorter construction period, which further limits developers' ability to satisfy growing housing demands.

Impact disparity and outmigration

Lack of affordable housing is a central challenge affecting many senior citizens, retired residents and disabled residents, in addition to non-oil-industry workers living in rental housing in particular. Most residents living on fixed incomes cannot afford the two-to-three-fold rent increases sustained across many Bakken-area communities as a result of shale oil development activities in the region.[3] There is also a considerable wage disparity between the oil industry and non-oil industry employees, creating a new lower class comprised primarily of retail and food service industry and public service employees.[4] The median wages of non-oil-industry workers, such as retail and food industry workers, as well as public service employees, such as education, health and law enforcement professionals, are not sufficient to meet what has become the typical $2,000 per month rent in many central Bakken communities. Even if these populations were able to afford these or comparable rates, the budget strain would place them in housing-induced poverty (Stone 2006) and make it difficult for them to purchase other necessities.

Further, lack of affordable housing is a central factor forcing out-migration. When faced with unaffordable rental rates, residents, including seniors and young families with local roots,[5] generally face four housing options: move in with parents or other family; live in shared tenant housing with other renters; move into a temporary home such as a trailer; or move out of the community. These availability challenges are magnified by escalating property prices or home values, which in turn present opportunities for property owners to sell or for those residents wishing to move out of the community.

In energy-impacted communities in the Bakken region, several factors have prompted residents to move away from their communities. First, the populations of many communities prior to shale oil development were older, with many residents nearing or past retirement age. As a result of the out-migration of many younger populations, some parents no longer have family or children in the area and wish to move to the areas where their children are. Some elderly residents also require special amenities and services, such as specialized healthcare, and move to areas where it is more easily accessible. Second, some residents simply do not like the changes in the community, real and perceived, resulting from increased energy development activities.

Lack of affordable housing affects the service industry in several ways. When service industry workers cannot find affordable housing, they move away, creating both a worker and service industry shortage. As a result, many service industries, ranging from gas stations to fast food establishments, have increased wages and benefits to retain and attract workers. This increase in wages causes an inflationary increase in prices of area goods and services, in turn contributing to the increasing cost of living across the region.

Escalation of rent also hinders provision of public services because many employees are unable to find affordable housing. With too few public service workers and significantly higher housing demand than before shale oil development began, public services that are available, such as law enforcement and education, are often overwhelmed. Law enforcement personnel shortages and overcrowded classrooms are typical across many Bakken-area communities. As a result, many non-oil-service-industry businesses and public services have entered the real estate market as landlords and begun offering housing to their employees at subsidized rates. The inability of public services to meet the needs of growing populations affects feelings of safety and security of community members and poses considerable challenges to community development.

Due to resultant pressure on public services, precipitating influence on out-migration and disproportionate impact on elderly, disabled and retired populations, lack of affordable housing has become the central challenge to community development activities across energy-impacted communities in western North Dakota. The rapid influx of new residents within a relatively short period of time led to a dramatic increase in demand for essential public services, including education, law enforcement, health care and municipal and county services. These services are essential and critical for maintaining a satisfactory community quality of life. As a result, the affordability and availability of rental and single-family homes for essential service workers is a central concern associated with rapid shale oil development. The following analysis of housing affordability is focused on essential service workers, including teachers, social workers, law enforcement professionals and civil engineers and city planners.

Housing affordability analysis

Housing affordability is an issue of both income and housing cost. Many adminis-trative or supervisory-level staff in the Bakken communities stated that a high per-centage of new hires in essential service positions are recent graduates or younger employees that were initially hired for entry-level positions. As a result, housing affordability for entry-level workers is a critical issue the oil-impacted communities.

Table 11.1 summarizes the monthly incomes for several essential service worker categories in North and South Dakota.[6] Table 11.2 shows the rental housing costs of different communities with rental properties organized by number of bedrooms. Comparison of the income data presented in Table 11.1 and the rental data in Table 11.2 shows that based on the 30 percent income limit guidelines commonly used to determine housing affordability (Stone 2006), all essential service worker categories in North Dakota experience financial constraints in securing rental housing.

For example, the 30 percent income limit of an entry-level secondary school teacher in North Dakota is $921 for rent or a mortgage payment per month, whereas the lowest average rental for a one bedroom housing/trailer in the North Dakota communities is $1,133.[7] Of all essential service personnel, only an entry-level civil

Table 11.1 Analysis of Monthly Income in West Non-Metro Region of North and South Dakota

	North Dakota		South Dakota	North Dakota 30% income limits		South Dakota 30% income limits
	Entry Level	Average	Average	Entry Level	Average	Average
Elementary School Teachers	$2,953	$3,805	. . .	$886	$1,142	. . .
Secondary School Teachers	$3,070	$4,115	. . .	$921	$1,235	. . .
Preschool Teachers	$1,938	$3,378	$2,184	$581	$1,013	$655
Child, Family and School Social Workers	$3,408	$3,866	$2,746	$1,023	$1,160	$824
Police Detectives	$3,745	$4,768	$4,060	$1,124	$1,431	$1,218
Police Patrol Officers	$3,397	$4,223	$2,795	$1,019	$1,267	$839
Civil Engineers	$4,309	$5,393	$5,444	$1,293	$1,618	$1,633
City and Regional Planning Aides	$1,958	$2,862	. . .	$587	$859	. . .
Civil Drafters	$3,317	$4,233	. . .	$995	$1,270	. . .
Construction and Building Inspectors	$3,158	$5,316	$2,875	$947	$1,595	$863
Nursing Assistants	$2,204	$2,635	$1,800	$661	$791	$540
Registered Nurses	$3,744	$5,003	$4,392	$1,123	$1,501	$1,318

Table 11.2 Monthly Rental Costs in the North and South Dakota Communities

	Primary Rental Data[8]	Secondary Rental Data[9]	Primary Rental Data	Secondary Rental Data	Primary Rental Data	Secondary Rental Data
	1 Bedroom		2 Bedroom		3 Bedroom	
Williston	$2,080	$2,134	$2,462	$2,670	$3,258	$3,461
Dickinson	$1,454	$1,681	$2,024	$2,038	$2,456	$2,669
Watford City	$2,112	$2,020	$2,696	$2,395	$3,256	$3,362
Ray	...	$1,133	...	$1,952	...	$2,528
Belfield	...	$1,239	...	$1,740	...	$2,191
Belle Fourche	$500	$451	$587	$610	$750	$818
Lemmon	...	$1,037	...	$1,324	...	$1,890
Buffalo	...	$516	...	$635	...	$881

engineer would meet the 30 percent housing affordability criteria for a single-bedroom dwelling based on average area rents. Due to these inflated housing costs, essential service institutions in western North Dakota, ranging from law enforcement agencies to school districts, have had to offer subsidized rental housing to attract and retain essential service workers.

Across the South Dakota communities, housing affordability, availability and quality are central and interrelated challenges that, like the North Dakota communities, existed prior to shale oil development and escalated with its growth in recent years. To a lesser extent than the North Dakota communities, housing affordability in the South Dakota communities is a growing concern. As many oil industry families look to settle in the periphery of the Bakken region – close enough to commute, but far away enough to avoid perceived negative aspects of oil development – the South Dakota communities experienced an induced demand for quality single-family housing and quality rental housing.

In Belle Fourche, Buffalo and to a lesser extent in Lemmon, this induced demand further increased the strain on the communities' already limited housing market. Similarly, challenges associated with the quality and availability of housing in the South Dakota communities have been magnified by North Dakota's oil development. For example, prior to shale oil development, the majority of the South Dakota communities' housing stocks had been built before the 1960s and many exhibited considerable need for improvements, while at the same time little to no new housing development took place. During and after shale oil development, increased regional demand for construction and related labor, drove contractor prices up and availability down as many contractors focused their business activities to the North, where they could command higher premiums for their services. As a result, across the South Dakota communities, lack of affordable home contractors – both to refurbish existing homes and build new ones – remains a significant challenge to improving the quality and availability of housing stocks.

Existing housing subsidy options

Public service and non-oil-industry sectors in North and South Dakota have used a variety of financing arrangements to supply housing to workers. These include the use of mobile/trailer homes, the purchasing of homes when they become available and construction of new multifamily homes. For example, Watford City, North Dakota, built a 42-unit multifamily rental home complex and Ray and Belfield, North Dakota, built duplexes and trailer homes to house essential service workers such as teachers and police officers.[10] The rents of these subsidized housing units depend on the financing funds that are used to construct the units such as Housing Incentive Fund (HIF) or LEPP (Law Enforcement Pilot Program). For example, the maximum rent limits under LEPP in Williams County (where Williston and Ray are located) are: 1bedroom (br) – $762, 2br – $915, 3br – $1,056, 4br – $1,179.

In South Dakota, three oil-related contract firms in Buffalo purchased mobile and trailer homes as well as single-family homes in recent years to house their employees, who would otherwise have no housing options due to extremely limited availability. Further, the school district of Harding County, where Buffalo is located, faces significant challenges in housing new teachers, and is presently considering constructing several Governor's Homes on district-owned property to satisfy growing demand and limited availability. The Governor's Homes program is a South Dakota housing program in conjunction with South Dakota prison system, which provides the labor, in offering modest, affordable housing options to income-qualifying homebuyers. Unlike the comparatively fewer options available in South Dakota, the subsidized rental housing options in North Dakota are designed and intended for use as transitional housing so that with time, employees transition into homes or apartments elsewhere in the community. Figure 11.3 and Figure 11.4 illustrate these and other housing stock examples in North and South Dakota.

Affordability of single-family homes

Employees' transition into homes depends on the affordability of available options. Table 11.3 shows the estimated monthly housing costs for 15- and 30-year fixed-rate mortgages (FRM) based on median home prices[11] of available homes for sale built after 2005 in the eight communities. Based on the 30 percent affordability income limits outlined in Table 11.1, a one- to two-bedroom home on a 30-year FRM would not meet the affordability criteria of any entry-level, single, essential service worker (e.g., a single city engineer or a single police detective) in North Dakota. Even for an experienced, single, secondary school teacher or a police patrol officer, a 30-year FRM for a one- to two-bedroom home would not meet the 30 percent limit of income affordability criteria, based on average income data. For a family of two entry-level essential service workers, such as two teachers (with the exception of a family with two pre-school teacher wage earners), or two police officers, or a pre-school teacher and a police patrol officer, a one- to two-bedroom home or a three-bedroom home may fall within the 30 percent affordability criteria; however, another concern may be whether they would have the financial

Contractor housing trailer in Buffalo

Mobile home, trailer, and modular housing in Buffalo

New housing development in Belle Fourche

Dilapidated housing in Lemmon

Figure 11.3 South Dakota Housing Stock Examples

Watford City rental housing complex

A trailer used as teacher housing in Belfield

A duplex built for teachers in Belfield

A conventional home used as teacher housing in Ray

Figure 11.4 North Dakota Housing Stock Examples

Table 11.3 Estimated Monthly Single-Family Housing Costs in North Dakota Communities Based on Median Home Price during May–June 2015

	15-Year Fixed-Rate Mortgage					*30-Year Fixed-Rate Mortgage*			
	Down[1] *Payment*	*Principle and Interest*[2]	*Property Tax*	*Home Insurance*	*Monthly Total*	*Principle and Interest*	*Property Tax*	*Home Insurance*	*Monthly Total*
				North Dakota					
1–2 Bedrooms	$54,360	$1,532	$180	$113	$1,825	$1,059	$180	$113	$1,352
3 Bedrooms	$62,000	$1,747	$205	$129	$2,081	$1,208	$205	$129	$1,542
4 Bedrooms	$56,190	$1,583	$185	$117	$1,885	$1,095	$185	$117	$1,397
5+ Bedrooms	$84,520	$2,381	$279	$175	$2,835	$1,646	$279	$175	$2,100
				South Dakota					
1–2 Bedrooms	......					......			
3 Bedrooms	$55,990	$1,578	$26	$116	$1,720	$1,091	$26	$116	$1,233
4 Bedrooms	$56,000	$1,578	$26	$116	$1,720	$1,091	$26	$116	$1,233
5+ Bedrooms	$94,950	$2,675	$44	$197	$2,916	$1,850	$44	$197	$2,091

1 Down payment was calculated at 20 percent. If it is less than 20 percent, financiers would require mortgage insurance, further increasing monthly housing costs.

2 Interest rate used for a 15-year FRM is 3.285 percent and for a 30-year FRM is 4.165 percent.

capacity to pay the 20 percent down payment, generally required by lending institutions, because of high home prices. Many recent graduates with student loans and other financial commitments might not have the financial capacity to pay the down payment needed. In addition, if down payments are less than 20 percent, most lending institutions require mortgage insurance, further increasing monthly housing payments and reducing home affordability.

In addition to affordability concerns, most new housing options available in small communities such as Ray and Belfield, North Dakota, and Buffalo, South Dakota, are trailer, modular and manufactured homes, with limited availability of adequate quality homes a common concern. In South Dakota, all three communities are experiencing challenges associated with poor quality or dilapidated housing, particularly in relation to obtaining contractors, but also in relation to the market rate values of many homes being less than the necessary costs to bring the homes into compliance or up to date. Despite increasing need for improved quality and availability of housing stocks, particularly since shale oil development in North Dakota accelerated in recent years, this discrepancy poses a significant barrier to both homeowner and developer investment in improving existing homes.

Conventional single-family housing assistance programs

Many conventional single-family housing assistance programs, such as USDA, FHA and state-level Housing Finance Agency programs are directed towards low- or moderate-income earners. Table 11.4 shows the income limits[12] used for the USDA

Table 11.4 2014 USDA Income Limits for Loans in the North Dakota Communities

	Direct Loan- Moderate Income Limit					Guaranteed Loan- Income Limit		
	1 Person	2 Person	3 Person	4 Person	5 Person	1 Person	2 Person	3 Person
McKenzie County (Watford City)	$44,900	$50,550	$56,150	$61,800	$66,300	$83,500	$83,500	$83,500
Williams County (Ray)	$45,650	$51,400	$57,100	$62,850	$67,450	$83,500	$83,500	$83,500
Stark County (Belfield)	$46,850	$52,800	$58,700	$64,600	$69,350	$84,950	$84,950	$84,950
Butte County (Belle Fourche)	$40,150	$45,100	$50,050	$55,000	$58,950	$75,650	$75,650	$75,650
Perkins County (Lemmon)	$40,150	$45,100	$50,050	$55,000	$58,950	$75,650	$75,650	$75,650
Harding County (Buffalo)	$40,150	$45,100	$50,050	$55,000	$58,950	$75,650	$75,650	$75,650

Section 502 Direct Loan Program[13] and the Guaranteed Loan Program.[14] Based on the income levels in Table 11.1, an entry-level essential service worker family of two interested in purchasing a single-family home would qualify for a Direct Loan only if they (a teacher or police officer etc.) are the major or the only income earner in a household. Only a family of two entry-level preschool teachers, who have the lowest combined income as a family of all essential worker categories considered, would qualify for a direct loan.

Most housing finance assistance programs designed for low (50 percent of area median income) or moderate (80 percent of area median income) income earners would be of little benefit in addressing housing issues of essential service workers in western North Dakota. The income limits of guaranteed housing loan programs of FHA and USDA are capped at 115% of the area median income. Entry-level essential service worker families such as two teachers, or a police detective and a teacher or a teacher and a registered nurse would qualify for a guaranteed loan. As a result, guaranteed loans are the only single-family housing assistance option available for qualifying entry-level essential service workers in western North Dakota. Based on the average wages for each worker type, experienced essential service worker households would qualify for a guaranteed loan only if they are the major or the only income earner in a household, with the exception of a family of two preschool teachers.

Shale oil development has prompted growth in demand for virtually every type of industry and public service, creating an opportunity to spur community development by attracting new businesses services, and residents. Figure 11.2 shows that the combination of inflated rents and expensive single-family homes inhibit multiple growth and development opportunities that spread across numerous sectors of the community. Exacerbating the situation is North Dakota Century Code,

Chapter 47–16–02.1, which expressly prohibits rent control. In addition, rent control might discourage investors and hinder growth. However, neither impacted communities nor the oil industry can function without the support of the service industry and public services, as both the private and public service sectors require employees and, accordingly, places for them to live.

Community options to assist with affordable housing

Community land trust model

A community land trust (CLT) is a nonprofit organization created to hold land for the benefit of the community and of individuals within the community (Peck 1993). The CLT model is designed to provide perpetually affordable home ownership to low- and moderate-income households, whereby homebuyers retain ownership of the housing structure but not the land. Accordingly, the initial purchase price of a land trust home generally excludes the cost of the land on which the home sits and may also reflect other subsidies (Bourassa 2007).

Belle Fourche is the only community out of the eight North and South Dakota communities employing the CLT model. In partnership with the city's economic development board and NeighborWorks Dakota Home Resources, Dakota Land Trust has made available land trust options for three recently built Governor's Homes in the community. In Belle Fourche's land trust program, the land value of home purchases may be enrolled in the trust program and leased back to the homeowner on a 99-year lease for $1. The homeowner retains all development rights to the land and may build on it and otherwise use it as they wish, and the land value is deducted from the homebuyer's total mortgage. If the homeowner chooses to sell their home at a later date, 75 percent of the property's equity resulting from market fluctuation increases (and not the homeowner's improvement efforts) is retained by Dakota Land Trust with the homeowner receiving the remaining 25 percent. The retained 75 percent is rolled into the continuation of the program. Although not required, Dakota Land Trust attempts to retain land trust properties and prefers that if an enrolled property is sold, the new homebuyer will elect to purchase it on land trust as well. When this occurs, the new homebuyer initiates a new 99-lease. If the home's market value decreases and an enrolled property sells at a loss, Dakota Land Trust retains nothing.

In Belle Fourche, land trusts are available to income-qualifying homebuyers for the new Governor's Homes, as well as a number of upcoming city-initiated development projects planned in the coming years. However, due to both the land trust's relative newness and a lack of community awareness about and understanding of the program, only one Belle Fourche home is currently enrolled in the land trust program.

The cost of one ready-to-build parcel of land in North Dakota communities range from $50,000 to over $95,000 based on contractor and home builder estimates. A similar lot would cost between $10,000 and over $50,000 in the South Dakota communities. Based on a conservative estimate of $50,000 for a typical lot in North Dakota communities, a CLT model would reduce monthly estimated housing costs by about $340 or 17 percent across all bedroom types on a 15-year FRM and by about $250 or 17 percent across all bedroom types on a 30-year FRM.

In the South Dakota communities, based on a conservative estimate of $10,000 for a typical lot, a CLT model would reduce the monthly estimated housing costs by approximately $65 or 3 percent across all bedroom types on a 15-year FRM and by about $45 or 3 percent across all bedroom types on a 30-year FRM. Both savings amounts and percentages in North Dakota and South Dakota would be higher if considered land prices are higher.

Substantial benefits to homeowners begin to materialize with lower initial mortgage valuations, when property taxes are assessed on home values alone, and with lower down payment amounts. In addition, a CLT would be eligible for a number of HUD financing programs, including Community Development Block Grants (CDBG) and various HOME Investment Partnership Programs. In many cases, it is also possible to combine FHA-insured loans under a CLT model to further reduce down payment burdens.

Low interest and down payment requirement model

Although some public service employees in the communities may be able to afford the inflated regional monthly mortgage costs, an associated challenge is having the financial capacity to meet initial down payment requirements. As discussed in the single-family home affordability section, the most significant challenge facing non-oil-industry or public service worker families that may be able to afford the monthly mortgage costs within the 30 percent income limit criteria is lack of financial capacity to meet down payment requirements. If homebuyers qualify for USDA/FHA-guaranteed loans, down payment requirements may be as low as 3.5 percent. However, not all worker categories meet the FHA/USDA income limits, and even if income limits are met, mortgage insurance premiums likely still increase monthly housing costs. Accordingly, a down payment assistance program coupled with a low-interest loan model – implemented at the state level through housing financing agencies – would improve the feasibility of affordable homeownership for service workers in these and similar communities impacted by energy development. For example, if interest rates are reduced by 1 percent,[15] monthly housing costs would decrease by 5.5 percent in North Dakota and 6.2 percent in South Dakota communities on a 15-year FRM across all bedroom types. On a 30-year FRM, monthly housing costs would decrease by 9 percent in North Dakota and 10 percent in South Dakota across all bedroom types.

Simplification of community zoning

Another potential housing intervention is the simplification of community zoning, which is already underway in Belle Fourche, South Dakota. Simplified zoning lessens pressures on potential future housing intervention initiatives as communities work to establish sustainable and adequate housing mixes that will prove resilient during ongoing mini-boom, mini-bust cycles. In the South Dakota communities, from which many home and commercial developers exited during peak Bakken drilling activity, convoluted, inadequate or outdated zoning regulations are but one deterrent for potential home developers and further limit potential housing assistance programs that may otherwise be implemented in the future. In Belle Fourche, community civic leaders described concerns that zoning regulations left unresponsive to the community's growing population may deter potential home developers from building in their community, which prompted the recent updating of the community's planning and zoning regulations from two to five different types of housing zones to support increasingly diverse housing needs. Prior to this recent intervention, zoning regulations in Belle Fourche had not been substantively updated since the 1960s.

Expanding existing housing support programs

Designated development funds supported through North Dakota severance taxes provide some support to infrastructure and housing projects in the Bakken region, but additional resources are needed to meet ongoing housing demands. Currently three funds, the Energy Impacts Fund, the Housing Incentive Fund (HIF) and the Law Enforcement Pilot Program (LEPP) all receive state oil revenue to support housing development. Increased financial resources for these initiatives would yield much-needed additional grants and low-interest home mortgage loans. In addition, tax-supported housing incentive suggestions may be able to utilize Renaissance Zone funds[16] in downtown business districts for residential multifamily projects.

Proactive state and municipal policy initiatives

Proactive state-and-municipal-level policy initiatives supporting diverse economic development and revitalization initiatives in the long run will serve to mitigate single-industry saturation and future potential shocks as mini-boom, mini-bust energy development cycles continue across the region. For example, to improve housing stock in periphery communities across western South Dakota, practical local and regional policy approaches may include: tax abatements or related liability-reduction incentives for home developers; technical training or tuition assistance for individuals entering the contractor/development field; and/or increased vocational training opportunities at the secondary education level. Further, diversified economic and industry development initiatives, such as, for example, investment in wind and other renewable energies or downtown revitalization/ housing projects that meet existing or ongoing needs of oil-impacted communities ensure a more stable employment base through mini-boom, bust cycles as well as improve housing and industry quality and mix over the long term.

Long term perspective

Bangsund and Hodur (2013) project that by 2036 there will be 32,500–46,200 producing wells in North Dakota.[17] The monthly rig count in North Dakota, which is an important indicator of activity, averaged approximately 200 at the time of these projections; since then, oil prices have fallen by more than 50% and the average monthly rig count in North Dakota in May 2015 was 83. This reduction in drilling activity demonstrates the sensitivity to and dependence of oil production on oil prices. As of April 2015, there were 12,500 producing wells in North Dakota. Under current technology recovery rates, more than two-thirds of Bangsund and Hodur's projected producing wells remain to be drilled and completed. With the decline in oil prices, it is anticipated that this activity will be prolonged over a longer period of time than initially estimated.

Jacquet and Kay (2014) posit that the established, singular boom-bust model is incompatible with modern shale oil development. More realistically, communities experiencing energy development today are likely to sustain repeated waves of mini-booms and mini-busts over the course of multiple decades. This more protracted, cycling boom-bust pattern has already been described by many community members and can be expected to continue in western North Dakota in the coming decades. Accordingly, volatile and cyclical oil prices will produce concomitant patterns of oil development over time.

For example, break-even prices in the four highest oil producing counties in the Bakken (Williams, Dunn, Mountrail, and McKenzie counties) range between $29-$41 per barrel, whereas break-even prices remain higher in many Bakken threshold counties such as Divide and McLean counties where prices remain at $73 and $77 per barrel, respectively (Helms 2015). Due to higher break-even prices in periphery counties, drilling activity in recent years has concentrated primarily in the four central Bakken counties. However, if and when oil prices increase and drilling technologies improve, drilling in periphery counties may prove profitable. Given the historical volatility and cyclical nature of oil prices, it can be expected that future oil development in the Bakken will be more prolonged than initially anticipated, with cyclical prices mirroring mini-boom and mini-bust patterns.

These cyclical patterns in turn can be expected to reflect in supply-and-demand dynamics of housing across the Bakken region. Further, as more producing wells are completed and additional oil-support infrastructure is developed, the number of permanent oil industry production-or-maintenance-related jobs will increase. Accordingly, housing concerns associated with more conventional, singular, boom-bust energy development patterns, such as a surplus of abandoned houses following a climactic, punctuated bust, may not be a concern in the emerging mini-boom, mini-bust energy development context.

Recent reduction in oil prices and associated reduction in the pace of oil development has led to a reduced demand for oil and related support industry employee housing across the Bakken region. This decreased demand, in combination with the preponderance of new multifamily, trailer and manufactured housing units that have been developed in recent years, has forced the cost of rental housing down by approximately $200–$300 across all bedroom types in the western North Dakota communities. This reduction has generated some concern among investors and housing suppliers regarding further development of multifamily housing units, especially in southwestern North Dakota communities like Belfield. With further and prolonged decreases in oil prices, the rental prices can be expected to decline. As oil development takes on a more protracted, cyclical patterning that mirrors fluctuating oil prices, determining the appropriate housing mix to avoid overbuilding has become a central goal of housing suppliers and community policymakers in both Bakken communities in North Dakota and periphery communities in South Dakota.

The supply composition of multifamily and single-family housing will change according to cyclical increases and decreases in oil industry activity in response to oil price fluctuation. Periods of high activity will prompt provision of multifamily housing (e.g., apartments, duplexes etc.), and rents will likely increase in accordance with workforce demands. In contrast, periods of low activity may prompt development of single-family housing (e.g., manufactured, modular and stick-built homes) as workers with permanent employment in the region seek to transition into conventional housing.

Housing developers experienced a growing number of available construction workers with the slowing of oil development in North Dakota, while South Dakota communities still indicate the opposite, suggesting that many contractors from their areas had moved north to capitalize on Bakken oil development. Despite the slowdown, much of northwestern South Dakota contractor business activity is still concentrated in the Bakken region of North Dakota. At the same time, the reduction in drilling activity has also provided an opportunity for housing suppliers in North Dakota to focus more on the provision of conventional, single-family housing options, while in South Dakota, new housing development of any kind remains limited, particularly in Buffalo and Lemmon.

Across all the eight communities, land prices still remain high, which is a central barrier to affordable housing in North Dakota and although to a lesser extent, a growing concern in the South Dakota communities. Land prices can be expected to remain high as demand continues and industry activity becomes temporally elongated and more cyclical in nature, in accordance with the mini-boom, mini-bust model. In such contexts, the CLT model may have an important role in improving the affordability of single-family homes for essential service workers over time. As only one community in North and South Dakota oil impacted communities recently began incorporating the CLT model, the further development of this intervention seems an area for potential growth in these and other oil impacted communities.

Conclusion

As oil prices continue on a downward trend, energy impacted communities in North and South Dakota may be well-positioned to address some of the ongoing housing challenges they face as a result of shale oil development activities in the Bakken region. Many of the short-term housing options previously employed during times of rapid oil development can now be re-evaluated, and additional and alternative options, including many of those described in this chapter, may be considered and implemented. A combination of bottom-up community interventions, such as CLTs and local financial and educational incentives to attract and retain housing developers and related professionals, in addition to top-down state and federal interventions, such as tax subsidies and down payment assistance programs – as just a few examples – may be tailored to the specific needs of these and similar energy impacted communities to both satisfy existing housing demands and better position such communities to sustain resilient and responsive housing stocks in the future.

Notes

1 For the purposes of this study, periphery communities were defined as those located either along the outermost limits of the Bakken shale formation.
2 Cost of workers are higher in western North Dakota compared to other areas for several reasons. The shortage of workers in the area prompts builders to bring in worker crews from their home communities. These workers have to be provided with housing, lodging and transportation back and forth. In addition, the competition from the oil industry for workers with similar skills has led to escalation in wages.
3 Some seniors have benefitted from mineral rights and other lease rights. But the seniors who do not own minerals or leases are mostly on fixed incomes.
4 As an example of the wage disparity, according to North Dakota Job Service data, the 2013 average weekly wage in the oil and gas industry in Williams County was $1,946. The average weekly wage in the same County for educational services, health services and public administration were $713, $895 and $873, respectively.
5 Even those who moved back into the community.
6 The data for North Dakota are based on wage data for the Far West Non-Metro Region and Non-Metro South Dakota region.
7 Although no primary data were available in Ray and Belfield on cost of rental housing, according to interviewed residents rent in the community averaged about $1,000 per bedroom. In Ray, where the average rent was lowest for rentals among all North Dakota communities, almost all new housing options comprised of trailer homes or modular homes.
8 Data were collected by surveying rental listings available in each community. Dickinson and Williston rental data were gathered during 2014 and the rental data of rest of the communities were gathered during 2015.
9 Data were gathered from www.rentbits.com a real-estate market research company
10 North Dakota Housing Incentive Fund (HIF II), LEPP Fund and Energy Impact Funding are state-level funding mechanisms devised to facilitate housing that is affordable. All three funds have been used to construct the complexes.
11 A survey of prices of single-family homes available for sale in all the communities (except in Williston and Dickinson) was done during May and June 2015. Median home price was calculated based on all the homes available for sale of a particular bedroom type within the communities in North or South Dakota. For example, there was a total of 32 three-bedroom homes built after 2005 available for sale in the North Dakota communities, and the median price was calculated based on those 32 properties.
12 Other housing programs use similar income limits.
13 Provide payment assistance to low-income borrowers.
14 Guarantees a loan for a borrower from an approved private lender.
15 Compared to the rates used in the original monthly housing cost calculation, which are 3.285 percent for a 15-year FRM and 4.165 percent for a 30-year FRM.
16 Renaissance Zone fund under Act N.D.C.C. 40–63 make it possible for North Dakota cities to create a Renaissance Zone within their jurisdiction and provide financial assistance for residential and commercial properties that need to be revitalized and redeveloped in the zone to attract businesses and residents.
17 This projection was based on the activity level and energy prices in early 2012.

References

Bangsund, D. A., & Hodur, N. M. (2013). *Williston Basin 2012: Projections of future employment and population, North Dakota summary.* North Dakota State University. Agribusiness and Applied Economics Report No. 704, Fargo, ND.

Bourassa, S. C. (2007). Community land trusts and housing affordability. In G. K. Ingram & H. Yu-Hung (Eds.), *Land Policies and Their Outcomes* (pp. 333–366). Cambridge, MA: Lincoln Institute of Land Policy.

Helms, L. D. (2015). North Dakota Department of Mineral Resources. Presentation for the House Appropriations Committee. August 1st 2015, Bismarck ND.

Jacquet, J. B., & Kay, D. L. (2014). The unconventional boomtown: Updating the impact model to fit new spatial and temporal scales. *Journal of Rural and Community Development, 9*(1), 1–23.

Peck, S. (1993). *Community land trusts and rural housing.* Washington DC: Housing Assistance Council (HAC).

Stone, M. E. (2006). Housing affordability: One third of a nation shelter poor. In R. Bratt, M. E. Stone, & C. Hartman (Eds.), *A right to housing: Foundation for a new social agenda* (pp. 38–60). Philadelphia: Temple University Press.

12 Growth, development and housing stock quality in the administrative U.S. Appalachian region

Russell Weaver

Introduction

Each year, the federal Appalachian Regional Commission (ARC) in the United States computes a composite index based on three economic performance indicators – unemployment rate, per capita market income and poverty rate – to measure the degree of economic "distress" in the counties within its jurisdictional boundaries (ARC n.d.[a]). The index provides an annual snapshot of a county's economic status, relative both to other counties in the ARC region and to the nation as a whole. Past empirical and anecdotal evidence suggests that improvements in the index tend to coincide with a county's location in a "growth-prone" metropolitan region (Moore 2005: 56). In other words, a perception seems to exist that *development*, as operationalized by a reduction in economic distress, might accompany *growth* in ARC counties.

On that backdrop, this chapter investigates the prospect that the perceived inverse relationship between growth and economic distress in the ARC region is moderated by the quality of a county's housing stock. As Glossop (2008, p. 1) observes:

> housing matters to economic development. It can enhance economic performance and place competitiveness, but it can also lead to segregation and spatial concentrations of poverty.

Stated another way, the purported link between growth and development in ARC counties is expected to take on different directions and magnitudes for qualitatively different housing situations.

While the general notion that growth can lead to various combinations of development and/or distress depending on context is far from novel (e.g., United Nations 1990; Sen 1999; Daly and Farley 2004), the more specific extent [if any] to which housing quality substantively alters the interrelationships among these phenomena has received comparably less attention in research and policy discourses. Less still is known about the possibility that the anticipated interactions between housing quality and growth might correlate with different socioeconomic developmental outcomes in rural versus non-rural settings. This chapter takes incremental steps toward bridging these gaps. Most pertinently, change in the ARC economic distress index is analyzed as a function of population and business growth, change in housing stock distress, rurality, interactions between these variables and a handful of controls. The results demonstrate that while business growth does, on average, appear to correlate with decreased economic distress in ARC counties, changes in housing stock quality can either negate or amplify this association depending on whether they are positive or negative in nature. Further, rural counties experience these interaction effects with much different intensity than counties in metropolitan regions. The findings therefore suggest that housing stock quality and upkeep might be critical leverage points at which to intervene in (especially rural) social systems to meaningfully enhance quality of life in the administrative Appalachian region.

Theoretical foundations

Prior to carrying out the applied empirical project, this section situates the research on appropriate theoretical foundations. Two streams of literature are especially useful toward that end. First, social scientists from numerous disciplines argue that most public planning and policy systems in North America, at least in recent history, and at least implicitly, possess a mental model in which *growth* is tantamount to *success* (e.g., Leo and Anderson 2006; Kantor 2010). In contemporary, globalized societies, households and firms enjoy greater overall geographical mobility than ever before (Sassen 1999). As a result, state and local decision-makers who operate within market-based systems are said to behave like entrepreneurs that compete with one another for these mobile assets (i.e. residents and businesses) (Peck et al. 2009). In this manner, a "growth-first" approach to economic and social development has become the norm in North America (Peck and Tickell 2002). There is a belief that "winning" competitions for more people or businesses or jobs raises aggregate wealth in a given place, which makes it possible for standards of living to increase throughout that place (see the discussions by Leo and Anderson (2006) and Kelly and McKinley (2015).

The problems with this mental model become clear when *growth* is distinguished from *development*. The former is defined as an upward quantitative adjustment to the size (scale) of a given entity, such as a population or economy (Weaver et al. 2016). The latter constitutes an upward qualitative adjustment to the goods, services and/or opportunities available to the people of a place. Development, then, manifests as increased human well-being *for a given-sized population or economy*, where growth is evidenced by *an expanding population or economy*, regardless of whether expansion is accompanied by positive, negative or no changes to human well-being (Daly and Farley 2004). Thus, there is no guarantee that growth leads to development. And, furthermore, there is a non-trivial risk that some types of growth will significantly lower human standards of living (e.g., Tiemstra 2008).

Whereas the distinction between growth and development is now a staple in the scholarly literature (e.g., Sen 1999; Todaro and Smith 2006), in practice, North American planning and policy institutions still largely pursue the idea that, by increasing the size of the aggregate economic pie, growth inexorably brings development (see Kelly and McKinley 2015). Among the reasons for the durability of this belief is the fact that some persistently shrinking or declining places become characterized by internal senses of powerlessness and low self-worth (Martinez-Fernandez et al. 2012). Accordingly, public decision-makers feel pressure to inject new life into these areas, frequently through attempts to attract new residents (e.g., members of the "creative class") and businesses (Sager 2011). Consider, for example, that for decades the Appalachian region in the United States (see the next section) has lagged behind the rest of the nation in terms of per capita income, educational attainment, employment rates, and several other metrics of social and economic well-being (e.g., Eller 2008). In response, large-scale policy programs in the region have "focused on creating an infrastructure for conventional economic [growth] . . . to hypothetically attract industry." Yet, this growth-first approach "has not managed to significantly change the relative degree of poverty in the region" (Keefe 2009: 6).

The outwardly weak or lacking connection between growth-oriented economic strategies and increased human well-being (e.g., reduction in poverty) in Appalachia and elsewhere is a function of countless interacting political, social, economic, cultural and environmental factors (e.g., Agyeman 2013; Flora et al. 2015; Green and Haines 2016). While it is not feasible to enumerate and study all of these factors and their complex interrelationships, the second stream of literature relevant to this investigation provides a valuable and arguably underemployed lens through which to evaluate variation in intra-regional experiences with growth and development. Namely, the seminal work of William Grigsby (1963; Grigsby et al. 1987; Galster 1996; Megbolugbe et al. 1996), and researchers who built on his contributions to the analysis of neighborhood dynamics (e.g., Rothenberg et al. 1991), implies that *housing* plays a pivotal role in the extent to which quantitative forces of growth in fact correlate with qualitative adjustments to the overall socioeconomic profile of a place. To understand how such a relationship arises, observe first that Grigsby conceptualized "neighborhood change" as a shift in the socioeconomic composition of a spatial neighborhood (Grigsby et al. 1987). As the average income level of a neighborhood's constituents changes, eventually so too will the "social and political institutions and services" present therein. These latter, and all attendant, changes in turn send the affected neighborhood into a qualitatively different regime (Megbolugbe et al. 1996, p. 1789).

Among the factors that Grigsby and his collaborators identified as determinants of this precise conceptualization of neighborhood change are: changes in population, changes in business investment patterns, physical deterioration in the built environment, housing abandonment and property owner disinvestment (Megbolugbe et al. 1996, pp. 1790–1). The first two of these factors, population and business (de)growth, are exogenous. The remaining factors, including physical deterioration, abandonment and property disinvestment, are endogenous to the geographic area under investigation. Crucially, within Grigsby's framework, these endogenous factors are assumed to have balancing or reinforcing effects on the directions of change that are "generated by the operation of [the] exogenous forces . . . on existing neighborhoods" (Megbolugbe et al. 1996, p. 1790). In other words, as suggested above, one should expect that internal changes to housing stocks (e.g., deterioration, disinvestment and abandonment) will moderate the degree to which external forces of population and business (de)growth contribute to overall patterns of *quali-tative change* within a geographic territory.

Although this framework is conventionally used to describe and explain qualitative change at the neighborhood level (Grigsby et al. 1987), this chapter applies it to a coarser-grained unit of analysis. In particular, counties feature as one of the most decisive geographies for policy and planning initiatives of the U.S. ARC. Among those initiatives, ARC counties which are deemed to be "distressed" are eligible to receive allocations from specially earmarked sums of federal funding (ARC, n.d.[b]). Monitoring and attempting to explain change in ARC county-level distress is therefore an important domain of applied social science research (e.g., Moore 2005) that weighs heavily on regional policy discourses (e.g., Wood 2005; Partridge et al. 2009; Ezzell et al. 2012). Vitally, the ARC currently measures distress as a function of three socioeconomic well-being indicators (ARC, n.d.[a]), which are essentially compositional characteristics (Thrift 1983). That is, they describe socioeconomic attributes of the people who make up ARC counties. Thus, drawing on Grigsby's conceptualization of neighborhood change as a shift in neighborhood socioeconomic *composition* (Megbolugbe et al. 1996), change in the ARC's distress index is plausibly a broader indicator of structural adjustments (i.e., qualitative change) taking place at the county level. Reductions in distress reasonably signify *development*, or increases to overall human well-being in ARC counties, whereas rising levels of distress suggest that a given county is *declining*, or tending toward a lower qualitative regime (Weaver et al. 2016).

Viewed through this conceptual lens, change in the ARC economic distress index is a function of much more than externally driven growth. Above all – at least for the remainder of this chapter – internal changes in housing stock quality are expected to materially affect the ability of *growth* to bring *development* in the administrative Appalachian region.

Research context

Media coverage of a presidential campaign stop by John F. Kennedy in the early 1960s exposed the majority of the U.S. to the plight of some families in rural "Appalachia" (Strickland 1999). Subsequently, improving standards of living for people in the Appalachian region became a national policy priority. As part of his War on Poverty, President Lyndon B. Johnson recommended in 1964 that Congress formally establish the ARC (which was proposed earlier by Kennedy). Since that time, the ARC has operated as a multijurisdictional regional economic development agency charged with meeting "the physical and social needs" of Appalachia, primarily through "federally funded projects such as highways" (Gatrell and Fintor 1998, pp. 886–7). The spatial definition of Appalachia currently used by the ARC is shown in Figure 12.1.

It is worth noting that the administrative ARC borders pictured in Figure 12.1 do not coincide with many observers' and stakeholders' perceptions of "Appalachia" as a cultural region. Consequently, Appalachian researchers tend to challenge these borders and suggest that they might not be fit for a variety of social science

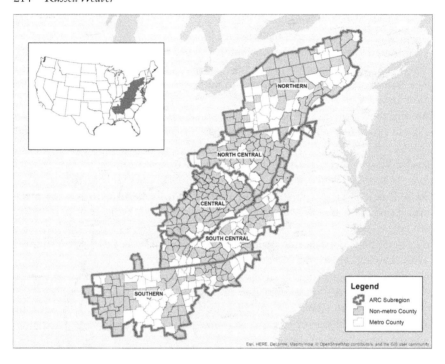

Figure 12.1 The ARC Region and Subregions, by County Classification as (Non-)Metropolitan

inquiries (for a recent review, see Weaver 2016)). Nevertheless, the boundaries are integral, and therefore appropriate, for this study, insofar as they represent the set of counties that are eligible to participate in federal ARC programs and funding initiatives (ARC n.d.[b]). It follows that these counties are also the ones whose distress levels are regularly monitored for signs of *development* or *decline* (e.g., Wood 2005). Thus, efforts to augment extant understandings of patterns of qualitative change and change processes in the administrative ARC region have the potential to substantively influence public policy in the near term – given that an established regional development institution (i.e., the ARC) is already available to marshal its resources toward quality-of-life-enhancing ends (e.g., Ezzell et al. 2012).

With those caveats in mind, the study area pictured in Figure 12.1 includes 428 counties or equivalents (independent cities in Virginia), which the ARC groups into five subregions. The five subregions represent spatially contiguous areas within the ARC administrative boundaries that are said to exhibit "relatively homogenous . . . topography, demographics, and economics" (ARC n.d.[c]). According to the 2015 edition of the United States Department of Agriculture (USDA) Economic Research Service (ERS) county typology dataset (USDA ERS n.d.[a]), 274 (64 percent) of these counties are classified as non-metropolitan – a commonly adopted proxy for "rural" in American policy and social science studies (USDA ERS n.d.[b]).[1] Collectively, then, the study area for this research contains a unique mix of rural and non-rural counties that are distributed between the so-called American "Sun" (e.g., the subregions labeled Southern and South Central in Figure. 12.1) and "Rust" belts (e.g., the subregions labeled Northern and North Central in Figure. 12.1). Accordingly, there ought to be sufficient variation in intra-regional patterns of (de)growth, development and decline to facilitate the empirical analyses described above (see, for example, Mencken et al. [2006]).

Variable descriptions and data

Dependent variable: economic distress index

Indicators that enter into comprehensive measures (indices) of a geographic area's "overall well-being . . . must be standardized or put on a common scale" prior to being combined (Kingsley et al. 2014, p. 293). The ARC satisfies this requirement for its economic distress index by transforming the index's three constituent parts – poverty rate, unemployment rate and per capita market income – into percentages of their respective national averages for all U.S. counties (ARC n.d.[a]). In other words, the poverty rate of a given county is divided by the mean poverty rate for all U.S. counties, and, *mutatis mutandis* for unemployment rate and per capita market income. With respect to the latter, per capita market income (PCMI) is defined as the aggregate income (less public assistance payments) measured for a county, divided by the county's total population (ARC n.d.[a]). Because greater PCMI is considered to be a positive indicator of well-being – while poverty and unemployment are negative indicators – after a county's PCMI is transformed into a percentage of the national average, it is multiplicatively inverted. In other words, if the PCMI in County X is 80 percent of the national average, then the inverted PCMI for that county is $1 \div 0.8 = 1.25$. By inverting the PCMI variable, all three indicators contribute positively to the ARC's conceptualization of *economic distress* (i.e. the higher the indicator, the higher the level of distress). As such, the three commonly scaled indicators (see Kingsley et al. 2014) are then combined via straightforward arithmetic averaging to form a composite economic distress index (ARC n.d.[a]).

Inasmuch as the indicator variables are measured at regular temporal intervals, the ARC economic distress index is updated frequently (ARC n.d.[d]). Hence, it is possible to analyze change in the index over time, as a function of relevant covariates. This chapter computes the index for a starting period of 2000 – which is approximately the year that the ARC began using the distress index – and an ending period of 2013 – which is the most recent year of data used by the ARC to compute county index values for its current fiscal year (ARC n.d.[a]). Data collection procedures for each of the three indicators that combine to form the economic distress index are sketched out in the appendix to this chapter. For now, Table 12.1 summarizes the economic distress data for all counties and county-equivalents in (1) the U.S. and (2) the ARC region. Consistent with received wisdom (e.g., Eller 2008), average poverty and unemployment rates are higher in the administrative Appalachian region relative to the nation, and average PCMI is lower than the national average. Table 12.1 also reports the average economic distress index for ARC counties. If ARC counties were characterized by poverty, unemployment and

Table 12.1 National and ARC County Averages for the Three Economic Distress Indicators

Variable	National Average		ARC Region Average	
	2000	*2013*	*2000*	*2013*
Poverty Rate	0.142	0.167	0.164	0.195
Unemployment Rate	0.048	0.080	0.057	0.093
Per Capita Market Income (2013$)	24,350	22,847	22,532	20,156
Average Economic Distress Index	n/a	n/a	1.15	1.17
n	3,142[a]	3,142[a]	428[a]	428[a]

a   All census data for 2000 were collected and compiled from the Longitudinal Tract Data Base (LTDB) available through Brown University (Logan et al. 2014). The LTDB provides crosswalk files for fitting year-2000 (and prior) census data into current census geographies. Because political boundaries can change over time – indeed, one independent Virginia city merged with its adjacent county between 2000 and 2010 – this step was necessary to measure the time-varying data used in this chapter for consistent geographic boundaries.

PCMI measures that exactly matched national averages in the given time periods, then their economic distress indices would take on values of 1. Values greater than 1 indicate that a county is more economically distressed than the typical U.S. county, which appears to be the case for ARC counties (on average).

Population and business growth

Recall from the framework explicated above that change in economic distress is an indicator of broader, place-level qualitative change. Increases in the economic distress index represent *decline*. Contrastingly, reductions in the index signal *development* or increases in human well-being. Now recall that exogenous processes of (de) growth were theorized to be important drivers of place-based change (Megbolugbe et al. 1996, p. 1791). Accordingly, patterns of (de)growth should vary systematically with changing patterns of development and decline, where the latter are operationalized as changes in the economic distress index. Here, patterns of (de)growth are measured in two dimensions. First, because places with growing populations are seen as "winners" of competitions for mobile residents (e.g., Leo and Anderson 2006), *population growth* is measured as the percentage change in a county's population from the 2000 SF3 Census Bureau dataset to the 2009–2013 ACS dataset. Second, and for analogous reasons, *business growth* is measured as the percentage change in the number of incorporated establishments reported for a county in the 2000 U.S. Census *County Business Patterns* (CBP) dataset, relative to the county's corresponding entry in the 2013 CBP (U.S. Census Bureau n.d.).

Housing distress index

Whereas population and business growth are external drivers of place-based development or decline, changes to a county's housing stock quality are conceptualized as internal drivers (Megbolugbe et al. 1996, p. 1791). According to Grigsby's integrated framework of neighborhood change (Grigsby et al. 1987), internal changes to housing stock quality will moderate the ways in which external factors (*viz.*, population and business growth) covary with patterns of development and decline (see above). Attempting to detect and understand the nature of this moderated relationship is one of the core objectives and intended contributions of this chapter. Toward that end, it is necessary to operationalize housing stock quality. To do so, a composite index of *housing distress* that draws inspiration from the ARC's economic distress index is developed on the backs of Census Bureau data indicators. Like the ARC economic distress index, the housing distress index is made up of three constituent indicators that are all "standardized or put on a common scale" (Kingsley et al. 2014, p. 293) by transforming them into percentages of their respective national averages.

Average owner-occupied home value

Per Grigsby's framework, decisive internal determinants of neighborhood change include physical deterioration, property disinvestment and abandoned housing (Megbolugbe et al. 1996: 1791). Conventional wisdom and academic research suggest that housing value conveys information about local property quality (e.g., Rothenberg et al. 1991). All else being equal, higher average property values tend to imply lower levels of physical deterioration and disinvestment (e.g., Weaver and Bagchi-Sen 2014). Therefore, one component of the adopted housing distress index is mean owner-occupied property value, as a percentage of the national average. Data for this indicator were obtained through the U.S. Census Summary File 3 (SF3) for the year 2000, and American Community Survey (ACS) for the period 2009–2013. The precise figures come from a table called "Aggregate Value (Dollars) By Mortgage Status", which reports the total value of all owner-occupied units in a given geographic unit [for which value was recorded]. The quantity of interest is then obtained by dividing a given county's aggregate housing value by the number of owner-occupied units for which value was recorded. The county-level national and ARC averages for this variable are listed in Table 12.2.

Average gross rent

Following the reasoning from the previous paragraph, the average price paid for rental housing ought to convey at least some information about the quality of the non-owner-occupied housing stock in a given location. As such, the second component of the housing distress index is mean gross rent, as a percentage of the national average. The data again come from the U.S. Census SF3 (for 2000) and ACS (for 2009–2013), by way of a table called "Aggregate Gross Rent (Dollars)". As before, the quantity of interest is derived by dividing the reported aggregate gross rent by the number of renter-occupied units for which gross rent was reported.

Table 12.2 National and ARC County Averages for the Three Housing Distress Indicators

Variable	National Average		ARC Region Average	
	2000	2013	2000	2013
Owner-Occupied Housing Value (2013$)	137,644	164,475	117,611	136,315
Gross Rent (2013$)	620	625	541	533
Fraction of "Other Vacant" Housing Units	0.106	0.145	0.104	0.145
Average Housing Distress Index	n/a	n/a	1.13	1.19
N	3,142[a]	3,142[a]	428[a]	428[a]

a   Refer to the footnote on Table 1.

Fraction of "Other Vacant" units

Whereas changes in home values and rents are expected to communicate at least some information regarding the [lack of] deterioration and disinvestment in local housing stocks, these variables do not adequately capture the issues of housing abandonment that also feature prominently in Grigsby's framework (Grigsby et al. 1987). Usefully, though, the U.S. Census SF3 and ACS both report the total number of housing units by county, along with the number of those units classified as "vacant." Vacancy refers to non-occupancy, such that a vacant housing unit is not occupied by a full-time householder. Within census datasets, such units are broken down by type (e.g., vacant for rent, vacant for sale, seasonal and other). In discussing the classification scheme used by the Census Bureau to assign a type to a vacant housing unit, Schilling and Logan (2008) argue that the category "Other Vacant" is a suitable surrogate measure of property abandonment. Abandonment occurs when an owner stops performing at least one essential responsibility of property ownership, where ownership responsibilities include, among others, maintenance, taxpaying and occupancy (Mallach 2005). Compared to simple non-occupancy (i.e. vacancy), abandonment is more likely to result in visual blight and neighborhood decay (Schilling and Logan 2008). Thus, the third component of the adopted housing distress index is the fraction of a county's housing units classified as "Other Vacant," as a percentage of the national average.

Combining the indicators

Table 12.2 summarizes the housing distress data for all counties and county-equivalents in (1) the U.S. and (2) the ARC region. To mirror the ARC's concern with *distress*, after mean housing value and mean gross rent are transformed into percentages of their respective national averages (Table 12.2), these variables are multiplicatively inverted. Hence, below [national] average home values or rents, which may signal lower quality housing stocks (e.g., Rothenberg et al. 1991), are made to increase the composite distress index. Because the abandoned housing

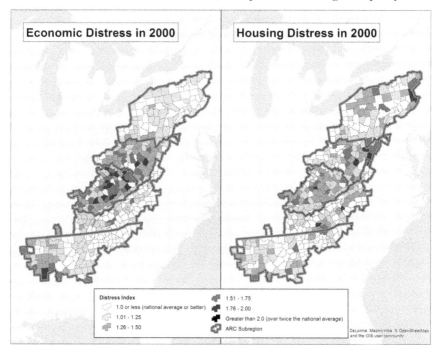

Figure 12.2 Economic (Left) and Housing (Right) Distress in ARC Counties, 2000

proxy variable is already assumed to contribute positively to housing stock distress, it does not require inversion. That being said, the two inverted variables and the remaining abandonment variable are then combined via arithmetic averaging to produce the composite housing distress index. As with the earlier economic distress index, if ARC counties mimic the national averages in mean home value, mean gross rent and fraction of "Other Vacant" housing, then their composite housing distress index scores will be 1. Values greater than 1 indicate greater housing distress relative to the national average. In Table 12.2, the mean values of the housing distress index for the two time periods under investigation suggest that, on average, housing stocks are more distressed in the ARC region than in the nation as a whole. Figure 12.2 maps the distributions of the economic and housing distress indices for 2000, and Figure 12.3 maps the equivalent distributions for 2013.

Control variables

Together, the (1) economic distress index, (2) measures of growth and (3) housing distress index constitute the necessary components for testing the assertion that the relationship between *growth* and *development* in the administrative ARC region changes for different levels of housing stock quality. However, in evaluating such a hypothesis, it is important to control for other factors that might influence the

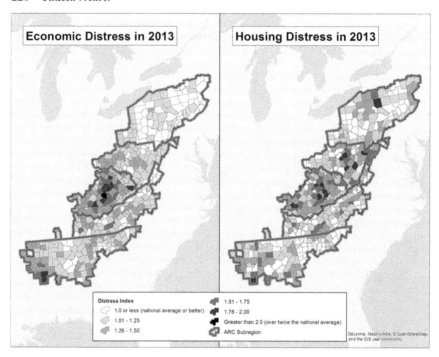

Figure 12.3 Economic (Left) and Housing (Right) Distress in ARC Counties, 2013

outcome variable (which, again, is change in economic distress). In this case, because economic distress is a composite measure of poverty, unemployment and income, reasonable control variables include changes in labor force education and housing tenure. First, it is often assumed that, relative to a less educated workforce, a better educated adult population correlates with lower poverty and unemployment, and higher average income (e.g., Wagner et al. 2003). Relatedly, due to the high costs of homeownership (e.g., Galster 1996), one might expect decreases in economic distress to accompany increases in the fraction of owner-occupied housing units in a given county. Data for both of these variables are available in the Census SF3 (for 2000) and ACS (for 2009–2013) datasets. The labor force education variable is measured as the fraction of persons 25 years or older – the base population for the Census Bureau's educational attainment variable – with a college degree. The housing tenure variable is measured as the fraction of all occupied housing units that are owner-occupied. Finally, subregional dummy variables are used to capture unobserved fixed effects due to location in one of the five [relatively internally homogeneous] ARC subregions (ARC n.d.[c]).

Table 12.3 presents descriptive statistics for all of the variables that are used below to analyze change in economic distress in the administrative Appalachian region. With the exception of the *Rural* dummy variable, which indicates whether or not a county is classified by the federal government as "non-metropolitan," all of the

Table 12.3 Descriptive Statistics

Variable	Mean	Std. Dev.	Minimum	Maximum
Δ Economic Distress Index	0.023	0.207	−0.746	0.555
Δ Housing Distress Index	0.059	0.135	−0.543	0.411
Population Growth	0.050	0.119	−0.208	0.859
Business Growth	−0.047	0.149	−0.357	1.328
Rural[a]	0.635	n/a	n/a	n/a
Δ Owner Occupants	−0.026	0.029	−0.273	0.047
Δ College Graduates	0.031	0.019	−0.031	0.092

n = 419[b]

a   Dichotomous variable (mean = proportion).

b   Nine counties are missing data for one or more of the key variables used in the chapter's regression analysis, and are accordingly excluded.

variables represent changes over time. The Greek letter Δ denotes "change in," and where it appears in Table 12.3, it describes an arithmetic difference. In other words, Δ *Economic Distress* is equal to the value of the economic distress index measured for the ending time period minus the value of the economic distress index measured for 2,000. Likewise, Δ *Owner Occupants* is the ending fraction of occupied units that are owner-occupied minus the corresponding fraction for 2,000. Population and business growth are measured as percent changes – i.e.: [(ending value − 2,000 value) / 2,000 value].

Hypotheses and method

The central hypothesis of this study, grounded in Grigsby's integrated framework of neighborhood change (Grigsby et al. 1987), is that internal adjustments to housing stock quality reinforce or balance the broader qualitative adjustments that occur in ARC counties as external changes (population and business growth) operate on them (Megbolugbe et al. 1996, p. 1790). With the data described above, this general statement can be partitioned into two pieces:

- Hypothesis 1 (H1): Change in the housing distress index will moderate the effect that population growth has on change in the economic distress index.
- Hypothesis 2 (H2): Change in the housing distress index will moderate the effect that business growth has on change in the economic distress index.

Formally, a moderated relationship exists when the strength or direction of the effect that one independent variable has on a dependent variable changes as a function of a second independent variable (Jaccard and Jacoby 2010, p. 150). Such relationships are detectable in regression models with multiplicative interactions – that is, by including both independent variables (e.g., for H1, change in housing distress and population growth), as well as their product, in a regression of the dependent variable (Jaccard and Turrisi 2003). In this type of model, housing distress is allowed to have its own independent partial effects on economic distress. And it may also affect economic distress via its moderating influences on the effects of the growth variables. While the *ex ante* position of this chapter regarding the perceived relationship between growth and development is agnostic; if growth does in fact contribute to a reduction in economic distress (i.e., development) in the ARC region (e.g., Moore 2005, p. 56), then the expectations are that this relationship will be (1) reinforced in counties that experienced decreases in housing stock distress and (2) counteracted in counties that endured increases in housing distress.

Recall now from the outset of this chapter that a secondary hypothesis also motivates this research. Namely, if changes in housing stock quality do in fact moderate the association between growth and development in the ARC region, then *this moderated relationship might manifest differently in rural and non-rural counties.* This statement is tantamount to saying that rurality acts as a "second order moderator" in the proposed conceptual model (Jaccard and Jacoby 2010, p. 133). The operational hypotheses involved in such circumstances are:

- Hypothesis 3 (H3): Location in a rural (non-metropolitan) county will moderate the way in which housing stock distress alters the relationship between population growth and economic distress.
- Hypothesis 4 (H3): Location in a rural (non-metropolitan) county will moderate the way in which housing stock distress alters the relationship between business growth and economic distress.

Much like the process of incorporating a single moderator into a regression model, second order moderators are accommodated via three-way multiplicative interactions between all of the explanatory variables involved in the "moderated-moderated" relationship (Jaccard and Turrisi 2003). Figure 12.4 illustrates all of the paths consistent with the moderated, and moderated-moderated, relationships that are described in H1-H4. Also pictured in Figure 12.4 are the paths from the proposed control variables to the dependent economic distress index variable.

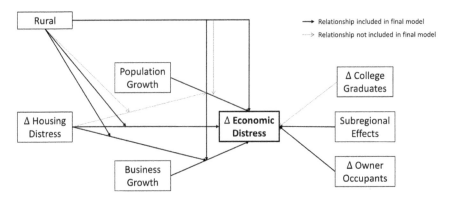

Figure 12.4 Designing and Estimating the Empirical Model

Notice that Figure 12.4 uses two distinct path symbols. Based on the continuous nature of the dependent variable (Δ *Economic Distress*) and the ARC's grouping of counties into relatively "homogeneous" subregions (ARC n.d.[c]), the empirical model adopted for the analysis was a least squares regression with subregional dummy variables (e.g., Bourassa et al. 2007). An initial run of the saturated model – in which all 14 possible paths from Figure 12.4 were included in the regression – revealed that not all paths added explanatory power to the statistical model. Accordingly, a stepwise model selection procedure was used to incrementally remove paths from the saturated model that did not significantly improve the model's Akaike Information Criterion (Venables and Ripley 2013). The final, stepwise-selected model featured only the bold paths pictured in Figure 12.4. The paths represented with dashed gray lines were dropped from the analysis. Thus, prior to even presenting the results, it is possible to conclude that H1 and H3, which posited a moderated relationship between population growth and economic distress, are not supported by the analysis.

Results

The results from estimating the stepwise-selected model shown in Figure 12.4 are presented in Table 12.4. Beginning with the control variable, increases in the fraction of owner-occupied housing units from 2000 to 2013[2] correlate negatively with change in economic distress. Put differently, as anticipated, when the relative share of owner-occupants in a county increases, economic distress tends to decrease. Next, both of the growth variables are statistically significantly linked to changes in economic distress. Interestingly, however, holding all else constant only *business growth* appears to correlate with *development* in the model. That is, the partial (independent) effect of positive business growth on the economic distress index is estimated to be negative. On the other hand, the independent effect of population growth on economic distress is positive – suggesting that population growth in the ARC region since 2000 may have, on average, coincided with qualitative decline. Notably, the bivariate Pearson correlation between *Population Growth* and Δ *Economic Distress* is 0.42 and highly significant ($p<0.001$), which supports this conclusion. Furthermore, generalized variance inflation factors do not point to multicollinearity issues, meaning that the opposite (independent) influences of the two growth variables on economic distress are not likely to be an artifact of the statistical model.

Although these findings support the earlier claim that growth does not inexorably lead to development in the ARC region, they are secondary to the core research questions of this chapter. More important are the estimated relationships between the hypothesized interaction effects and economic distress. Recall that, because of their omission from the stepwise-selected model, neither of the relationships described in hypotheses H1 and H3 were supported by the analysis. Observe now that the interaction effect between *Business Growth* and Δ *Housing Distress Index*, which was posited in H2, is not statistically significant in the estimated model (see Figure 12.2). Thus, the empirical analysis does not support H1, H2 or H3.

Table 12.4 Regression Results (Dependent Variable: Δ Economic Distress Index)

Variable[a]	Coef.	Std. Err.[b]	t-Value	Sig.
Population Growth	0.669	0.093	7.21	***
Business Growth	−0.244	0.085	−2.86	***
Δ Housing Distress Index	0.212	0.109	1.94	*
Rural	0.010	0.015	0.67	
Δ Owner Occupants	−0.860	0.290	−2.96	***
Business Growth * Rural	0.104	0.109	0.96	
Δ Housing Distress Index * Rural	−0.019	0.133	−0.14	
Business Growth ★ Δ Housing Distress Index	−0.414	0.453	−0.91	
Business Growth * Rural * Δ Housing Distress Index	2.588	0.834	3.10	***
Subregional Dummies	✓			
Intercept	−0.142	0.028	−5.11	***
N	419			
R²	0.482			
Adjusted R²	0.465			
AIC	−377.9			

*p<0.10 ***p<0.01.

[a] The continuous explanatory variables involved in the interactions take on negative and positive values (Table 3), where values of zero indicate no change (e.g., no business growth). For that reason, the variables are not mean-centered – which a common practice in regressions with interaction effects – because zero is a meaningful value (see Jaccard and Turrisi 2003).

[b] White's standard errors.

However, the three-way interaction between rurality, business growth and housing stock distress is highly statistically significant and large in magnitude. In plainer terms, the model is strongly supportive of H4: Housing quality substantively affects the association between business growth and socioeconomic development in ARC counties, and the nature of this moderated relationship is significantly different in rural (non-metropolitan) and metropolitan counties.

   Because multiway interaction effect regression coefficients are difficult to interpret, the *Zelig* software package for R developed by Owen and colleagues (2013) was used to take simulation draws from the estimated model for various scenarios. Such techniques allow researchers to derive expected values for the dependent variable in a regression model, given pre-specified values of the model's independent variables (Owen et al. 2013). In this case, for each ARC subregion, *Business Growth* was set to two values of interest: (1) high growth, or one standard deviation above the mean; and (2) mean (de)growth, or the average value of the variable, which was negative for the time period of interest (see Table 12.3). The Δ *Housing Distress Index* variable was allowed to range from -0.50 to +0.50 in increments of 0.01 (Table 12.3). All other variables were set to their mean values. Finally, 1,000 simulation draws were taken from the model for all possible combinations of the variable values just described, for both rural and non-rural counties. The results from these simulations were four separate distributions of dependent variable values for each ARC subregion. For parsimony, the results for one selected subregion, *Northern* (see Figure 12.1), are unpacked here as an illustration. Analogous results for the remaining four subregions are shown in the appendix.

Panel (a) of Figure 12.5 plots the expected value of Δ *Economic Distress* across the set range of Δ *Housing Distress* for the case of high business growth in ARC counties. The panel contains two separate functions. The dark line shows the expected values for rural counties, and the lighter line shows the same information for metropolitan (non-rural) counties. Although neither line passes directly through the origin of the graph, the qualitative result is that increases in housing distress (i.e., Δ *Housing Distress* > 0) increase economic distress (i.e., Δ *Economic Distress* > 0) in both rural and non-rural counties. Similarly, reductions in housing distress coincide with decreased economic distress. Critically, though, these effects are much more intense in rural counties. Where business *growth* is high, improvements to housing

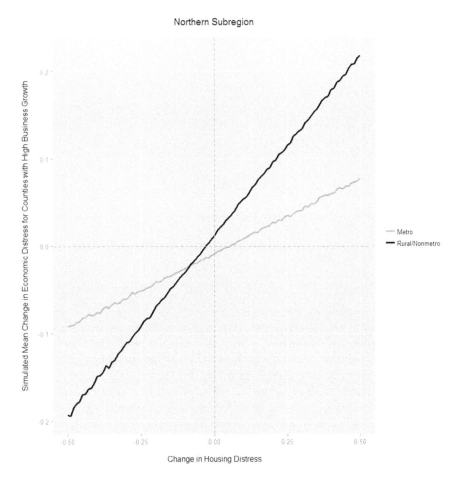

Figure 12.5a Expected Change in Economic Distress for Counties with High Business Growth

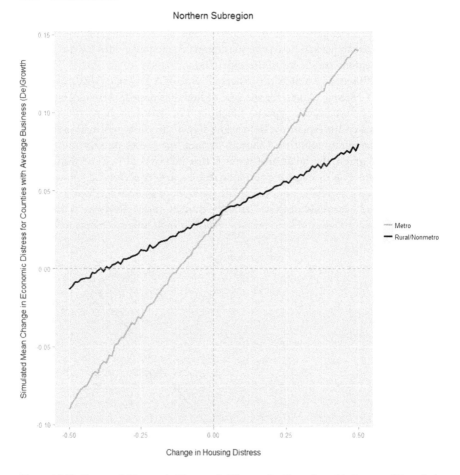

Figure 12.5b Expected Change in Economic Distress for Counties with Average (Negative) Business Growth

stock quality seemingly correlate with significantly greater *development* (less economic distress) in rural counties compared to metropolitan counties. Alternatively, as housing stock quality declines, economic distress becomes significantly more severe in growing rural counties relative to non-rural counties. The opposite outcomes occur when business growth is negative (see Figure 12.5b).

While the intercepts of the graphs for the remaining four subregions vary from subregion to subregion (see the appendix), the overall patterns are identical to those pictured in Figure 12.5. In short, when ARC counties experience high business growth, improvements in housing stock quality sharply decrease economic distress and contribute to qualitative development. Thus, the positive independent effects of business *growth* on socioeconomic *development* in the ARC region are amplified by housing stock improvements. At the same time, those positive effects are counteracted, and can even be completely reversed, as housing stocks become more distressed. In the case of business growth, these effects are much more pronounced in rural counties compared to metropolitan counties (see Figure 12.5a). On the other hand, when ARC counties experience business *de*-growth, these patterns of intensity are switched (though the same general, positive relationship between housing stock distress and economic distress holds). An immediate takeaway, therefore, is that strategic housing stock investments may be capable of (1) accelerating socioeconomic improvements in rural counties that are undergoing economic expansion and (2) mitigating socioeconomic decline in metropolitan counties that are undergoing economic contraction.

Discussion and policy implications

The empirical results provide acute examples of "spiraling" or feedback effects that can take place in geographic territories. More explicitly, Flora and colleagues (2015) suggest that place-based communities possess varying degrees of seven interrelated forms of "capital": natural, built, financial, human, social, cultural and political. Precise definitions of these seven concepts go beyond the scope of this chapter and can be accessed elsewhere (Flora et al. 2015; Green and Haines 2016). What is most important here is the idea that the seven forms of capital are interlinked and characterized by feedbacks. In other words, when a particular change affects one of these capital "stocks" at a given point in space and time, the interconnectivity of that one stock with all of the others can bring about a cascade of effects that is many orders of magnitude greater than the initial change. Both positive and negative qualitative changes are subject to reinforcement/spiraling in this manner (e.g., Flora et al. 2015).

By applying Grigsby's integrated framework of neighborhood change (Megbolugbe et al. 1996) to an investigation of growth, development and housing quality in the administrative Appalachian region, this chapter sought to demonstrate that at least two changes to county-level capital "stocks" – a quantitative change the number of businesses and a qualitative change to the nature of residential housing – do interact in complex ways (consistent with feedback effects) that have not been adequately explored in the literature. Specifically, contrary to comparatively linear perceptions that economic growth tends to spur socioeconomic development (see the discussion by Leo and Anderson (2006)), the statistical analyses carried out in this chapter imply that the capacity for growth to meaningfully reduce economic distress in ARC counties is contingent on at least one other form of community capital: built/residential housing.

One interpretation of this finding is that housing stocks and business investments are *interdependent leverage points* for public policy in the ARC region. Yet, arguably, the tradition in the Appalachian region has been to decouple the latter from the former. For instance, decades of well-intentioned, but perhaps underachieving, policy interventions in ARC counties have prioritized investments into infrastructure and technology aimed at attracting new businesses over alternative courses of action (Keefe 2009). A key weakness with this piecemeal approach is that – even where and when business growth does contribute positively to socioeconomic development – the growth-induced socially beneficial qualitative changes can be undermined, and even more than offset, by parallel reductions in housing stock quality (see Table 12.4; Figure 12.5). Contemporary scholars and practitioners have thus pointed to the need for new, appreciative, participatory development strategies that make simultaneous investments into multiple forms of community capital (e.g., Flora et al. 2015; Green and Haines 2016), especially in the Appalachian region (Keefe 2009). The ARC has responded to these calls by embarking on a shift toward more "asset-based" approaches to economic development – in which local community capital resources are identified and built on within ARC counties – as opposed to traditional approaches in which challenges are framed and addressed by outside experts (ARC n.d.[f]). Nevertheless, a deeper commitment to participatory decision-making and people-focused development are clearly needed (Keefe 2009, pp. 6–9). As such, the next section offers several brief, concluding thoughts on this topic as a starting point for future policy-oriented research. Limitations of the study are also addressed. In reading these remarks, keep in mind that policies are never one-size-fits-all, and their successful implementation hinges on contextual circumstances.

Concluding remarks and limitations

First, the empirically detected positive association between business growth and socioeconomic development fails to obtain in ARC counties that endure concurrent (significant) declines in their housing stock qualities. Accordingly, future growth-oriented infrastructure projects – e.g., roadways, broadband networks etc. – in the ARC region must be undertaken as part of broader community visioning and strategic planning efforts that expose decision-makers to potentially unforeseen negative spillover effects on residential home values from the proposed infrastructure investments. These participatory processes should bring together the people of the places targeted for development, key decision-makers and geospatial technology specialists and analysts, so that community input can be incorporated directly into spatial decision support models (e.g., Steinitz 2012). Collaborative efforts are presumably essential for maintaining housing stock quality in the face of growth-related pressures (e.g., Flora et al. 2015).

Second, existing efforts to promote entrepreneurship and increase the number of locally-owned businesses in Appalachia (e.g., Ezzell et al. 2012) might be usefully coupled with ARC funding or technical assistance to facilitate participatory municipal or regional land use planning and zoning code updates. For instance, if it is difficult for would-be entrepreneurs to open and operate businesses from their (say) residentially-zoned homes, then comparably flexible regulations that are more amenable to certain types of home-based enterprises might reduce barriers to entrepreneurship. To wit, such flexibility can lower business startup costs by removing the immediate need for separate office space – at the same time, then, it frees up entrepreneurs' resources for reinvestment into home maintenance and upkeep.

Third, a variety of shared-equity homeownership programs – such as community land trusts – have been established to concurrently maintain housing affordability under growth pressures (through deed and resale restrictions), while enforcing property upkeep standards through stewardship agreements and monitoring organizations (Davis 2012). Because economic growth is sometimes linked to escalating home values and rising property maintenance standards (e.g., Weaver et al. 2016), institutions aimed at protecting the cost and quality of housing for existing residents is an important policy priority. Once again, the aim is to acknowledge and appreciate the *interdependence* of economic growth and housing stock quality in pursuits of development (see Table 12.4).

These three brief thoughts intentionally align with contemporary positions that (1) collaborative and inclusive democratic decision-making, combined with (2) efforts to enhance local ownership of businesses and housing, are preconditions of socioeconomic *development* in geographic areas (Kelly and McKinley 2015). Piecemeal and growth-oriented economic strategies of the past have not brought sufficient wealth to the people and places of the administrative Appalachian region (Keefe 2009). The interconnections between the many stocks of "community capital" (Flora et al. 2015), such as the interaction between business growth and housing stock quality uncovered in this chapter (Megbolugbe et al. 1996; see Table 12.4), offer a more holistic framework in which to design and test policy interventions and programs for catalyzing development in Appalachia (Keefe 2009). Nevertheless, it is necessary to temper the findings and implications from above by pointing out that linkages between external and internal forces of place-based qualitative change (Grigsby et al. 1987) are complex and multidirectional. Along those lines, the statistical models estimated in this chapter reveal associational relationships, not causal relationships.

Arguably, these associations still provide meaningful starting points for conceptualizing a relationship between growth and development that is moderated by housing stock quality. However, future studies are needed to introduce additional control variables into the analysis, and to engage directly with the possibility of endogeneity (see Mencken et al. 2006). In addition, other forms of community capital must be incorporated into the analyses. In an ongoing project, using the same data described above, the author is examining the relationships between economic growth, changes to housing stock quality and changes to various indicators of social (in)justice, such as income inequality and residential segregation, in the ARC region. Inchoate results from that project are suggesting that housing stock improvements may be more important to social justice than to economic growth, particularly in rural ARC counties. On that same note, additional research is needed to investigate the reasons why rural housing stock improvements appear to have a premium over metropolitan housing stock improvements during periods of business growth – and why the converse applies in periods of business contraction (see Table 12.4; Figure 12.5). All told, then, the framework developed in this chapter, and the findings and implications produced from the chapter's analysis, generate many more questions than answers. Certainly this situation reflects the limitations of the study, but it also opens many doors and possibilities for future research on the role of housing quality in rural planning, policymaking, growth and, ultimately, socio-economic *development* in the Appalachian region.

Notes

1 Note well that federal designations of "non-metropolitan" and "rural" are useful for facilitating empirical inquiries and policy analyses. As a consequence, they are employed throughout this chapter. Nevertheless, observe that such designations are highly imperfect and problematic proxies that mask the substantial heterogeneity that characterizes actually existing "rural" communities and environments. Indeed, many scholars observe that rural may be nothing more than a social construction (e.g., Reimer and Bollman 2010).
2 Note that the ACS data used in the analysis are five-year period estimates for 2009–2013.

References

Agyeman, J. (2013). *Introducing just sustainabilities: Policy, planning, and practice.* Zed books.

ARC (n.d.[a]). *Source and methodology: Distressed designation and county economic status classification system, FY 2007-FY 2016.* Retrieved from www.arc.gov/research/Sourceand MethodologyCountyEconomicStatusFY2007FY2016.asp

ARC (n.d.[b]). Distressed counties program. Retrieved from www.arc.gov/distressedcounties

ARC (n.d.[c]). Subregions in Appalachia. Retrieved from www.arc.gov/research/Mapsof Appalachia.asp?MAP_ID=31

ARC (n.d.[d]). Maps of Appalachia. Retrieved from www.arc.gov/maps

ARC (n.d.[e]). ARC Code. Retrieved from www.arc.gov/publications/ARCCode.asp

ARC (n.d.[f]). Asset-based development. Retrieved from www.arc.gov/abd

Bourassa, S. C., Cantoni, E., & Hoesli, M. (2007). Spatial dependence, housing submarkets, and house price prediction. *The Journal of Real Estate Finance and Economics, 35*(2), 143–160.

Daly, H. E., & Farley, J. (2004). *Ecological economics: Principles and applications.* Island Press.

Davis, J. E. (2012). Shared-equity homeownership. In *Encyclopedia of Housing* (Second Edition), Andrew T. Carswell, ed. Los Angeles, CA: Sage Publications, Inc.

Eller, R. (2008). *Uneven ground: Appalachia since 1945.* University Press of Kentucky.

ESRI. (2014). *Business Analyst 2014.* Redlands, CA: Environmental Systems Research Institute.

Ezzell, T., Lambert, D., & Ogle, E. (2012). *Strategies for economic improvement in Appalachia's distressed rural counties. An analysis of ten distressed and formerly distressed Appalachian counties* (Prepared for the Appalachian Regional Commission). Knoxville: The University of Tennessee Community Partnership Center.

Flora, C. B., Flora, J. L., & Gasteyer, S. (2015). *Rural communities: Legacy+ change.* Westview Press.

Galster, G. (1996). William Grigsby and the analysis of housing sub-markets and filtering. *Urban Studies, 33*(10), 1797–1805.

Gatrell, J. D., & Fintor, L. (1998). Spatial niches, policy subsystems, and agenda setting: The case of the ARC. *Political Geography, 17*(7), 883–897.

Glossop, C. (2008). *Housing and economic development: Moving forward together.* Housing Corporation.

Green, G. P., & Haines, A. (2016). *Asset building & community development.* Sage Publications.

Grigsby, W. (1963). *Housing markets and public policy.* Philadelphia: University of Pennsylvania Press.

Grigsby, W., Baratz, M., Galster, G. & Maclennan, D. (1987). *The dynamics of neighbourhood change and decline.* Oxford: Pergamon.

Jaccard, J., & Jacoby, J. (2010). *Theory construction and model-building skills: A practical guide for social scientists*. Guilford Press.

Jaccard, J., & Turrisi, R. (2003). *Interaction effects in multiple regression* (No. 72). Sage.

Kantor, P. (2010). City futures: politics, economic crisis, and the American model of urban development. *Urban Research & Practice, 3*(1), 1–11.

Keefe, S. E. (2009). *Participatory development in Appalachia: Cultural identity, community, and sustainability*. University of Tennessee Press.

Kelly, M., & McKinley, S. (2015). *Cities building community wealth*. Democracy Collaborative.

Kingsley, G.T., Coulton, C.J., & Pettit, K. L. (2014). *Strengthening communities with neighborhood data*. Washington, DC: Urban Institute.

Leo, C., & Anderson, K. (2006). Being realistic about urban growth. *Journal of Urban Affairs, 28*(2), 169–189.

Logan, J. R., Xu, Z., & Stults, B. J. (2014). Interpolating US decennial census tract data from as early as 1970 to 2010: A longitudinal tract database. *The Professional Geographer, 66*(3), 412–420.

Mallach, A. (2005). *Bringing buildings back: From abandoned properties to community assets: A guidebook for policymakers and practitioners*. Rutgers University Press.

Martin, L. L., & Schiff, J. H. (2011). City – County consolidations: Promise versus Performance. *State and Local Government Review*, 0160323X11403938.

Martinez-Fernandez, C., Audirac, I., Fol, S., & Cunningham-Sabot, E. (2012). Shrinking cities: urban challenges of globalization. *International Journal of Urban and Regional Research, 36*(2), 213–225.

Megbolugbe, I. F., Hoek-Smit, M. C., & Linneman, P. D. (1996). Understanding neighbourhood dynamics: A review of the contributions of William G. Grigsby. *Urban Studies, 33*(10), 1779–1795.

Mencken, F. C., Bader, H., & Polson, E. C. (2006). Integrating civil society and economic growth in Appalachia. *Growth and Change, 37*(1), 107–127.

Moore, T. G. (2005). Defining Appalachia: Public policy and regional dynamics in Appalachia's low-income counties, 1965–2000. *Journal of Geography, 104*(2), 49–58.

Owen, M., Imai, K., King, G., & Lau, O. Zelig. (2013). Everyone's Statistical Software, 2013. R package version, 4–2.

Partridge, M., Lobao, L., Enver, A., Jeanty, W., Beaulieu, B., Gallardo, R., & Goetz, S. (2009). *Developing and assessing potential forward-looking distress indicators for the Appalachian region*. Washington, DC: Appalachian Regional Commission.

Peck, J., Theodore, N., & Brenner, N. (2009). Neoliberal urbanism: Models, moments, mutations. *SAIS Review of International Affairs, 29*(1), 49–66.

Peck, J., & Tickell, A. (2002). Neoliberalizing space. *Antipode, 34*(3), 380–404.

Reimer, B., & Bollman, R. D. (2010). Understanding rural Canada: Implications for rural development policy and rural planning policy. In *Rural planning and development in Canada* (pp. 10–52), David J. A. Douglas, ed. Toronto: Nelson Education Ltd.

Rothenberg, J., Galster, G.C., Butler, R.V., & Pitkin, J.R. (1991). *The maze of urban housing markets: Theory, evidence, and policy*. University of Chicago Press.

Sager, T. (2011). Neo-liberal urban planning policies: A literature survey 1990–2010. *Progress in Planning, 76*(4), 147–199.

Sassen, S. (1999). *Globalization and its discontents: Essays on the new mobility of people and money* (Vol. 9). New York: New Press.

Schilling, J., & Logan, J. (2008). Greening the rust belt: A green infrastructure model for right sizing America's shrinking cities. *Journal of the American Planning Association, 74*(4), 451–466.

Sen, A. (1999). *Development as freedom*. Oxford University Press.

Steinitz, C. (2012). *A framework for geodesign: Changing geography by design*. Redlands, CA: Esri.

Strickland, J. L. (1999). The Appalachian regional commission in Kentucky: A question of boundaries. *Southeastern Geographer, 39*(1), 86–98.

Thrift, N. J. (1983). On the determination of social action in space and time. *Environment and Planning D: Society and Space, 1*(1), 23–57.

Tiemstra, J. P. (2008). Rethinking the Costs of Economic Growth. Association for Social Economics Presidential Address, 2008. *Review of Social Economy, 66*(4), 423–435.

Todaro, M. P., & Smith, S. C. (2006). *Economic development* (9th ed). Addison Wesley.

United Nations (1990). *Human development report 1990*. Oxford University Press.

US Census Bureau. (n.d.). County business patterns. Retrieved from www.census.gov/econ/cbp/

USDA ERS. (n.d.[a]). County typology codes. Retrieved from www.ers.usda.gov/data-products/county-typology-codes.aspx

USDA ERS. (n.d.[b]). Rural classifications. Retrieved from www.ers.usda.gov/topics/rural-economy-population/rural-classifications.aspx

Venables, W. N., & Ripley, B. D. (2013). *Modern applied statistics with S-PLUS*. Springer.

Wagner, F., Joder, T., & Mumphrey Jr, A. (Eds.). (2003). *Human Capital investment for central city revitalization*. Routledge.

Weaver, R. (2016). Appalachia, USA: An empirical note and agenda for future research. *Journal of Rural Social Sciences, 31*(1), 1–23.

Weaver, R., & Bagchi-Sen, S. (2014). Evolutionary analysis of neighborhood decline using multilevel selection theory. *Annals of the Association of American Geographers, 104*(4), 765–783.

Weaver, R., Bagchi-Sen, S., Knight, J., & Frazier, A. (2016). *Shrinking cities: Understanding urban decline in the United States*. New York: Routledge.

Wood, L. E. (2005). *Trends in national and regional economic distress, 1960–2000*. Washington, DC: Appalachian Regional Commission.

Appendix

Derivation of the ARC economic distress index

Poverty rate

Poverty rates for the starting period of the analysis were derived from the 2000 decennial census Summary File 3 (SF3) (ARC n.d.[a]). The SF3 summarizes responses obtained from a long-form survey that was distributed to samples of households during decennial censuses prior to 2010. One of the variables included in the SF3 is the percentage of persons, for whom poverty status is determined, that live below the applicable federal annual income threshold to be classified as impoverished. To obtain comparable data for the desired ending period, the same variable was extracted from the 2009–2013 five-year vintage of the U.S. Census American Community Survey (ACS). The ACS replaced the SF3 subsequent to the 2000 census. ACS data are now collected on a rolling basis and pooled together to create large, reliable [period] samples. For small population (e.g., rural) areas, the number of households surveyed in any one year is relatively low. Therefore, given the preponderantly rural nature of ARC counties (Figure 12.1), the ARC relies on ACS poverty data collected over five-year intervals (ARC n.d.[a]) to maximize the reliability of the estimated poverty rates.

Unemployment rate

In an effort to measure "long-term structural unemployment," every year, the ARC averages the three most recent years of civilian labor force unemployment rate data from the U.S. Bureau of Labor Statistics (ARC n.d.[a]). Thus, to compute county-level long-term structural unemployment rates for 2000, the author downloaded and averaged BLS county unemployment rate data for 1998, 1999 and 2000. Following the same procedure, the BLS county unemployment rate data for 2011, 2012 and 2013 were downloaded and averaged to measure long-term structural unemployment for the ending period of the analysis.

Per capita market income (PCMI)

The U.S. Bureau of Economic Analysis (BEA) publishes an annual "Local Area Personal Income & Employment" dataset from which the ARC extracts measures of PCMI for most of the county-level jurisdictions within its administrative borders (ARC n.d.[a]). Somewhat problematically, however, the BEA does not provide PCMI data for "independent cities," which exist outside of, and are separate from, counties (Martin and Schiff 2011). Such cities, which in the U.S. are found mostly within the state of Virginia, are considered county equivalents by the Census Bureau. Put differently, they perform all essential city and county local government functions (Martin and Schiff 2011). While independent cities are therefore their own counties for all practical purposes, the BEA combines them with adjacent counties to produce its PCMI dataset. Thus, the ARC is left to make these same aggregations in its index calculations for the eight independent Virginia cities that lie within its boundaries (ARC n.d.[a]; Figure 12.1).

One issue with this procedure is that, because independent cities and adjacent counties each have their own elected local governments, they presumably define their own needs and priorities – and those needs and priorities are likely to be quite dissimilar. For instance, in 2014 the eight independent Virginia cities within the ARC region had an average population density of approximately 1,329 persons per square mile. Their adjacent counties, by contrast, had an average population density of 96 persons per square mile (Esri 2014). In other words, the independent cities are much denser, and are likely to have more of an urban character, than their surrounding low density (rural) counties. These differences in population densities will almost certainly translate into differences in local policy objectives (e.g., Reimer and Bollman 2010). Furthermore, the levels of economic distress in independent cities and surrounding counties have the potential to differ markedly. For all of these reasons, this chapter eschews the ARC's reliance on the BEA dataset, and instead draws on U.S. Census SF3 and ACS data to estimate PCMI (i.e., the same data sources that are used for poverty rate). Within these latter datasets, the Census Bureau reports values for "Aggregate Household Income" and "Aggregate Public Assistance Income." Following the ARC's definition of PCMI as total income, less transfer payments, divided by population (ARC n.d.[a]) for each time period in the analysis, aggregate public assistance income was subtracted from aggregate household income in a county and divided by the county's corresponding (with respect to time) total population. The upshot is that the economic distress index adopted in this chapter is not an exact replica of the ARC index. But it will paint similar – and potentially clearer – pictures of distress for *all* counties and equivalents in the administrative Appalachian region. Indeed, the analytical treatment of independent cities as counties better captures the real world relationships that govern ARC project funding protocols – wherein funds are distributed to states, and states, in turn, allocate monies to county and equivalent local governments (ARC n.d.[e]).

Simulation results for remaining ARC subregions

Figure A12.1 Simulated Expected Value of the Dependent Variable, by Subregion, for the Case of High Business Growth

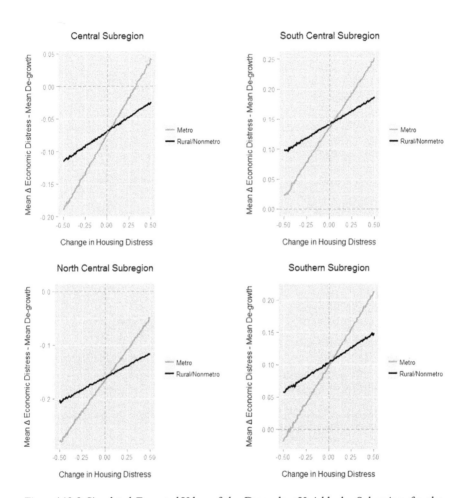

Figure A12.2 Simulated Expected Value of the Dependent Variable, by Subregion, for the Case of Average Business (De)Growth

13 Meeting rural housing needs through local community development[1]

*Kim Skobba, Ebunoluwa Odeyemi
and Karen Tinsley*

Providing housing that matches residents' needs presents a challenge for most communities, regardless of location. These challenges are exacerbated for rural communities, which face inadequate infrastructure, lack of technical capacity and limited financial resources (Virgil 2010). The smaller populations and geographic isolation that define rural places also make it difficult to address housing issues, which are fundamentally a market-based activity (Virgil 2010). Rural communities have unique characteristics and wide differences in economic bases and social structures (Flora and Arnold 2012). The housing market implications for communities differ, as does their capacity respond to problems of housing quality, availability and affordability (Morton et al. 2004; Ziebarth et al. 1997). These differences, as well as the relatively limited research on rural housing when compared to urban housing, mean that rural communities lack the template of programs and practices used to meet community housing needs often available in urban places.

Meeting local housing needs necessarily involves the complementary processes of housing policy and community development. Housing policies provide the framework for access to a healthy, stable supply of housing, often with a focus on those with the greatest housing needs. At the federal level, housing policy is carried out through a variety of programs that promote homeownership, foster access to affordable rental housing for low-income households and combat residential discrimination through enforcement of the Fair Housing Act (Landis and McClure 2010). Local-level housing policies tend to focus on supply-side production of housing, particularly the expansion of the owner-occupied housing stock through land use and other regulatory tools. Community development complements federal and local housing policies by providing a local plan of action. Defined as "a participatory effort to mobilize community assets that increases the capacity of residents to improve their quality of life," community development is essential in addressing the multiple challenges of providing an ample supply of appropriate, decent, and affordable housing in rural communities. (Green and Haines 2016, p. 13). The community development process includes locally-based strategies implemented by skilled, committed leaders. Local leaders who foster community networks to mobilize internal and external resources are crucial to creating change in the housing stock and are the core of local community development activities (Cook et al. 2009).

The remainder of this chapter will draw upon a review of literature on rural housing and neighborhood issues and will explore how local leadership serves as the hub in meeting local housing needs by leveraging social capital through community development efforts. The chapter will close with a case study of a program designed to increase local capacity to address housing issues in rural and small towns in Georgia. This case study will examine how communities of varying sizes, economic and demographic characteristics use community social capital to provide affordable, safe and stable housing. Policy implications will be identified and addressed.

Housing and neighborhood revitalization in rural communities

Local housing markets are diverse and are influenced by a combination of economic, physical and locational factors. For small and rural towns in non-metropolitan areas, this diversity includes chronically poor rural communities, which have high poverty rates and are physically isolated, and resource-dependent rural communities facing economic and population decline. It also includes ex-urban and amenity-rich small towns with accessible locations that experience growth as they attract affluent professionals, retirees, and newcomer residents and businesses. (Hamilton et al. 2008). In between are communities with weakened economies but also the potential for amenity-based growth. The shift in economic activities, demographic characteristics, and the influence of globalization on rural communities shape the type of housing communities have and need (Tremblay 1988). Whether urban or rural, high poverty communities show evidence of disinvestment through a prevalence of dilapidated homes, high levels of vacancies, lower home values and levels of homeownership and high housing cost-burdens. In more affluent, amenity rich communities, the influx of high-income groups, a shift that can happen in a drastic manner, brings a demand for newer, larger homes and increased property values to rural communities (Hamilton et al. 2008). These growing, non-isolated small towns tend to have lower rental vacancy rates and fewer affordable housing options, making it difficult for long-term, less-affluent residents to find and keep a place to live (Ziebarth et al. 1997).

Communities across the rural-urban continuum experience problems with housing quality, availability, adequacy and affordability (Ziebarth et al. 2000). Using housing age and adequacy as key measures, a significant portion of the housing in rural and small towns in the U.S. is old and in need of repair. Over one-third of the housing in rural and small towns is at least 50 years old. Nearly 30 percent of occupied homes in rural and small towns in the U.S. are considered to be of inadequate quality (Housing Assistance Council 2013). While the portion of homes lacking in plumbing or a complete kitchen is relatively small, rural houses are more likely to lack complete plumbing than homes in urban and suburban communities (Housing Assistance Council 2013). About 10 percent of the non-seasonal homes in rural and small towns in the U.S. are vacant (Housing Assistance Council 2013). Vacant and substandard housing contributes to neighborhood blight, which is often thought of as an urban problem. However, problems with vacant, abandoned and substandard housing due to disinvestment affect small cities and towns, resulting in declining property values and increased costs for local governments (Vacant Property Research Network 2015).

Increasing housing choice is needed to improve rural housing opportunities available to the rural residents. In their study of rural housing in nine Midwestern states, Yust et al. (2006) found that regardless of size, very few communities offered a range of rental and ownership options. Participants in the study cited the need for more moderate cost single family housing, more rental housing overall, multi-family housing for low-income households and more housing options for seniors. Reflecting the tenure preference for ownership of single-family detached homes, the vast majority of rural and small town housing in the U.S. is owner-occupied and is either single-family detached housing (71.7) or mobile homes (14.4) (Housing Assistance Council 2013). The lack of multifamily housing combined with the large portion of owner-occupied homes in rural and small town communities may make it difficult for residents who either need to or prefer to rent and those who need or desire the features often provided in multifamily housing (single-level living, accessibility, lower maintenance) to find housing that meets their needs.

Rural and small towns are often perceived as more affordable places to live relative to urban areas. Yet housing costs relative to household income suggest that many rural and small town households struggle to pay for housing. Cost-burden arises when households spend 30% of their income or more on housing costs. Households experiencing cost-burden often have difficulties meeting other basic needs such as food, medical care, day care and other necessities. The Housing Assistance Council's tabulations of ACS Housing Data from 2009–2013 found that 30 percent of rural and small-town households were cost-burdened and 13.1 percent experienced extreme cost-burden by paying 50 percent or more in their income on housing costs. The problem is particularly acute for renters in the U.S., with just over half of all renter households experiencing cost-burden. Renters in rural communities are no exception. Slightly less than half of rural and small town renter households are experiencing cost-burden. Cost-burden among homeowners was also common, with slightly less than one-quarter of rural and small-town households experiencing cost-burden (Housing Assistance Council 2013).

Housing, local leadership and community social capital

Strong leadership in rural communities is essential to developing a plan and securing the funding needed for housing. Cook et al. (2009) identified a sequence of housing activities, which includes housing planning, finance, and inventory changes, that contribute to increased community vitality. Embedded within this sequence of housing activities are local leaders who foster community networks to mobilize internal and external resources. Mobilizing resources is an inherent component of leadership abilities for any locality (Brown and Nylander 1998). Community leaders serve as catalysts, facilitators and coaches that work with clients (i.e. communities) to solve problems (Wilson 1997). Strong leadership and the active involvement of stakeholders with a passion for housing issues, including local lenders, business owners, contractors and home builders, social-service professionals, local housing activists and citizens, can help to support the sequence of activities that lead to inventory changes that contribute to increased community vitality (Cook et al. 2009). This sequence of housing activities includes the articulation of community values, conducting a needs assessment, formulating goals and identify and securing funds and resources needed and available to meet community housing needs. Ziebarth (2000) describes the convening of a steering group or housing coalition, who represent local stakeholders and actively seek input from a broad range of residents and community groups, as the first step in initiating new housing projects. Morton et al. (2004) hypothesized that based on ways groups work together, norms in the community and the flow of information affect local land use decisions, building codes, enforcement of some regulations and incentives/disincentives that maintain housing conditions. They also posit that democratic laws in most rural communities provide for citizen involvement in public decision-making, noting that the significance of social relations in rural communities is a community structure that can limit or expand the capacity of rural places to deal with housing issues.

The gathering of the necessary resources by local leaders can be likened to resource mobilization. Agnitsch et al. (2006) pinpointed community social capital as a means to mobilize local and extra-local resources to act effectively. Social capital creates a collective sense of responsibility that ensures broad-based participation in problem-solving. It is embedded in the day-to-day relationships of people that strengthens neighborhoods and increases the quality of life. (Agnitsch et al. 2006; Hamdan et al. 2014; Lang and Hornburg 1998; Putnam 1995). The characteristics of social capital, including networks, norms and trust are the part of social organizations that encourage coordination and cooperation for mutual benefit enabling people to act together (Putnam, 1995). Norms that emphasize community benefit, inclusive public dialogue and a high degree of communication are associated with increased capacity of rural towns to address housing issues (Morton et al. 2004). To address social problems, individuals and communities must possess *bonding* social capital characterized by dense and multifunctional ties with strong but localized trust; *bridging* social capital that facilitates access to resources and opportunities; *linking* social capital that provides the capacity to leverage resources, ideas and information from formal institutions beyond the community; and *vertical* social capital that facilitates connections to people in positions of power and influence (Ling and Dale 2014; Woolcock and Narayan 2000). Local community development efforts can address local housing needs by leveraging these various forms of local social capital to build human, financial, physical and political capital required for community development (Green & Haines, 2016).

Social capital is also a means for community building that promotes business networking and faster flow of information (Wilson 1997). Green and Haines (2016) identified social relations and networks as a form of social capital due to the time and energy required as well as the productive results it yields to individuals or group of people. The formation of networks of individuals and groups within a community accommodates interaction, providing a structure for solving community problems such as housing (Morton et al. 2004). These social networks, which provide a medium for residents and leaders to communicate, interact and convey necessary information about the community, can be a resource to address housing needs.

The following is a case study of the Georgia Initiative for Community Housing, a program that provides technical assistance and leverages local leadership and community social capital through the formation of a local housing team and structured housing planning activities to meet local housing needs. The case study provides a description of the program model and summaries of three communities that participated in the program.

A model for addressing rural housing needs

The Georgia Initiative for Community Housing is a three-year capacity-building program that supports local municipalities in the formation of a housing team and the creation and launching of a housing plan to address local needs. The program was created with the recognition that small cities, towns and rural communities must build social, human and political capital to create a multifaceted and sustained housing and community development program (Tinsley and Massey 2009). The program, which is administratively housed at the University of Georgia, was created through a collaborative partnership between University of Georgia's (UGA) Housing and Demographics Research Center, the Georgia Department of Community Affairs (DCA) and the Georgia Municipal Association. During its 11-year history, the program has served 55 communities across Georgia, with a focus on smaller, non-metropolitan communities. Several partners provide funding and program support, including Georgia Power Company, USDA Rural Development as well as several UGA Public Service and Outreach units and Extension. This program has generated $745,000 in federal grants and leveraged these funds for an additional $440,000 over the life of the program. The partnership has afforded additional teaching, research and outreach opportunities. For example, a service-learning course has been developed, with Georgia Initiative for Community Housing cities collaborating as community partners and the students completing a housing needs assessment. These projects have assisted the Georgia Initiative for Community Housing program in helping communities improve their quality of life and economic vitality, as well as prepared civic-minded students with hands-on, real world applications of course content. Furthermore, a five-year grant from USDA was received to study how communities use social capital to address housing and community development needs. The findings will be used to enhance the program and local teams as well as provide outreach materials and trainings for communities in the Southeast region of the United States.

Program model

The Georgia Initiative for Community Housing program model is consistent with the conceptual model of influences on rural community vitality by Cook et al.

(2009), which links local leadership to the housing decision chain, or sequence of activities needed for community success. This sequence includes the formation of a group that conducts housing planning activities (identification of goals and needs assessments), securing funding to meet local housing needs and improved housing inventories.

The program admits five new communities per year through a competitive, two-step application process. First, communities submit a written application detailing their housing team membership, local housing needs and current activities, as well as the desired outcomes from participation. Next, site visits to ten finalists are conducted, where the selection committee meets with the housing team to determine the communities' readiness to participate. Each community forms a housing team comprised of six to 20 members who represent various local stakeholder groups and who harness the human, political and social capital needed to bring about change. While the composition of the housing teams may evolve as gaps are identified, they include a diverse group of individuals from local government, non-profit housing and social service organizations, faith-based organizations, private business, real estate and finance, intermediary organizations and university extension and public service and outreach staff.

During the first year of the program, each housing team develops and launches a local housing plan with the support of the program. The centerpiece of the program is a series of retreats where 200 housing team members from 15 communities develop new ideas and learn about approaches and available resources to meet local housing needs. Georgia Initiative for Community Housing program partners design the agendas with input from the participating communities and tailor it to their specific needs. Arrangements for speakers, team facilitators and resource representatives are made by the program, but planning and implementation take place at the local level. Housing team members from all participating communities attend biannual retreats to learn about different approaches and available resources to meet housing and neighborhood needs. Through expert speakers, resource representatives and networking opportunities, the program seeks to increase housing-related human capital as well as build social capital at the local level. This education and technical assistance is what enables the community to produce and begin implementing the housing plan. Communities give progress reports designed to facilitate sharing, collaboration and accountability, and alumni team representatives serve as retreat speakers and mentors for new communities. The Georgia Initiative for Community Housing waives all registration fees, but each community is responsible for travel costs.

Housing challenges and community development tools

The housing challenges faced by communities participating in the Georgia Initiative for Community Housing program are consistent with the literature on rural and small towns. Lack of funds, substandard and dilapidated housing, the lack of a range of housing types and prices to meet the needs of residents and significant infrastructure shortcomings are problems for most communities participating in the program, regardless of size or location. The program is designed to provide community housing teams with the capacity to address these issues. The program provides team members with knowledge of community development tools needed to implement the housing decision chain identified by Cook et al. (2009). Communities receive training on how to conduct housing needs assessments, considered one of the first steps needed to secure funds to address housing and neighborhood issues in rural communities. Developing knowledge of federal and state financing tools is also emphasized in the program. A recent program evaluation survey suggests that most Georgia Initiative for Community Housing participants begin the program with little or no knowledge of USDA housing programs, Community Development Block Grant (CDBG), state HOME Funds and tax credit housing development, which are essential for neighborhood revitalization, housing construction and rehabilitation and the support of low- and moderate-income home-ownership. Participating in the program appears to result in knowledge gains in these key financing tools; over 60 percent of participants in the third year of the program identified themselves as having at least some or detailed knowledge of the state HOME funds program and CDBG funding, and a little less than half identified having at least detailed knowledge of USDA housing programs and tax credit housing development.

While the communities taking part in the Georgia Initiative for Community Housing vary by size, location, local resources and economic activity, their housing goals are often similar – addressing problems with neighborhood blight and increasing the inventory of affordable rental and owner-occupied housing. The following section highlights the housing goals and steps to achieve these goals for three non-metropolitan cities that have completed the Georgia Initiative for Community Housing. These communities (names have been changed) were chosen because they represent three common types of small and rural towns – Graytown, a small city that serves as the economic center of a non-metropolitan region; Smithtown, a small coastal community that is adjacent to a tourist destination community; and Millville, a small agricultural community in a rural county. A summary of community characteristics is found in Table 13.1.

Graytown

Graytown is a small city, with a population of about 35,000, which covers nearly 32 square miles of land and serves as the economic hub for a non-metropolitan MSA region. Located less than 100 miles from Atlanta, the city is located outside of the Atlanta commuter shed but close to the outer suburbs of the metropolitan area. The median household income in Graytown is $39,791. About 25 percent of the families living in Graytown have incomes that fall below the federal poverty level. The vast majority of households are renters. The median gross rent is $816. Slightly more than one-third of the housing units owner-occupied. The median value for all owner-occupied units is $150,700.

The Graytown GICH housing team developed a housing plan that achieved the team's goal of strengthening the quality of life through coordinated and sustained

Table 13.1 Characteristics of Case Study Communities

	Graytown	Smithtown	Millville
Total population	34,938	15,648	3,880
Area (land, sq. mile)	31.93	17.07	5.47
Median household income ($)	39,791	26,775	27,250
Family poverty rate %	24.7	34.3	29.9
Population 25 years and over with at least a bachelor's degree (%)	23.7	11.5	9.1
Total housing units	13,016	7,161	1,776
Single family housing units as percentage of housing stock	49.7	69.8	52.7
Mobile homes as percentage of housing stock	.7	1.3	28.7
Owner-occupied housing units (%)	36.0	36.2	54.3
Median owner-occupied house value ($)	150,700	87,900	58,300
Median gross rent ($)	816	711	528

Note: Summary demographic and housing data obtained from Social Explorer, (2014).

efforts to improve housing conditions, create housing opportunities and connect people to housing resources. To improve housing conditions, Graytown's housing team started a housing inventory and assessment and began the process of creating a Land Bank Authority in partnership with county. Through their participation in the GICH program, the housing team was able to begin identifying and addressing issues in and securing funding for projects in targeted neighborhoods. The city repaired sidewalks on 15 streets and demolished two dilapidated homes. In addition, they worked with 11 homeowners, who voluntarily demolished, reconstructed or substantially rehabilitated their homes. To foster connections between local organizations, Graytown's GICH hosted the City's first-ever Housing Summit, which connected more than 20 housing-focused agencies. Following this event, the City hosted a half-day Housing Festival to connect agencies with 100 residents in need of assistance.

Smithtown

Smithtown is a coastal city with a total population of 15,648 that is located within a small metropolitan area with a population of fewer than 250,000. As a coastal community, Smithtown is located in an area with many natural amenities and has some tourism and recreation activity. However, the community has not experienced the same influx of higher-income residents as its neighboring community, which serves as a tourist destination in the state. The city's median household income is $26,755, which is significantly lower than the state median of $49,342. There are more renters than homeowners, with only 36 percent of the households owning their home. Smithtown has a median home value of $87,900. The population has a relatively small portion of college-educated residents, with about 11 percent holding a bachelor's degree or higher. Nearly a quarter of the population over the age of 25 has less than a high school education.

The Smithtown housing team developed a housing plan to address emergency and transitional housing needs and neighborhood redevelopment and restoration in the community. After identifying gaps in emergency and transitional housing services, the team created a housing pathway, established a local support system and developed a community service web portal to increase access to services for homeless families and households facing housing insecurity. This service delivery system included a local partner who provided housing and credit counseling to residents in the community. To reach their neighborhood redevelopment goals, the community applied for and received federal Neighborhood Stabilization Program, Community Development Block Grant and state HOME funds, as well as city housing rehabilitation funds to renovate and rebuild housing in the community. This funding resulted in the new construction of ten homes and 85 homes that were rehabilitated for low-income families and seniors in the community. The community established a community land trust to preserve affordability and increase homeownership opportunities and proactively address rising land costs brought on by increasing higher cost infill housing. While taking part in the GICH program, Smithtown was particularly effective in bringing together a diverse team of local partners. Their community housing team included city and county staff, representatives from faith-based organizations, the school system, a health system, real estate companies, the local housing authority, NeighborWorks America and several non-profit and for-profit organizations. Near the end of their participation in the program, the housing team developed a database of existing partners and invited new partners and extended a renewed invitation to previous members/partners. This work resulted in a greater integration of the city's commission, downtown development authority, planning department and private and non-profit partners.

Millville

Millville is a small town located in southern Georgia in an area known for cotton and peanut production. Located an hour from the nearest economic hub, Millville is a relatively small and isolated rural community, with a population of about 3,900 and a total area of 5.5 sq. mi. The median household income in the city is $27,250. The family poverty rate of the city is about 30 percent. There are more homeowners (54 percent) in Millville than renters. Also, the city has a relatively low median rent of $528 and median owner-occupied housing values of $58,300.

While participating in the Georgia Initiative for Community Housing, the Millville community housing team worked to improve the City's low-income housing stock, to rid all neighborhoods of blighted properties and improve infrastructure and to educate the public about homeownership issues and opportunities. To address the community's housing stock and neighborhood conditions, Millville executed a three-point approach that included 1) aggressive steps against blighted neighborhoods by revisiting the city's code and making necessary changes; 2) determining the condition of existing housing stock; and 3) looking for ways to assist owners of substandard and near-substandard properties in making improvements to their homes. As a result of this work, Millville has demolished 16 dilapidated homes, removed or demolished 21 substandard mobile homes and had 36 junked vehicles removed. The approach has resulted in providing property that is now available for infill construction and in residents taking an active role in keeping their community clean. The city received nearly $300,000 in CDBG funds, and an additional 27 homes have been or are on the schedule to be reconstructed or rehabilitated using Community HOME Investment Program (CHIP) Grant funds.

Conclusion and policy implications

The Georgia Initiative for Community Housing program model highlights the importance of three key elements necessary for addressing local housing needs. The first is the formation of an organized group of individuals who focus on local housing needs. The ways in which organized housing teams engage local leadership and generate stakeholder participation is consistent with previous research on community social capital. Community social capital operates by individuals and communities possessing the bridging social capital to facilitate access to resources and opportunities. The ability of small towns to mobilize external and internal resources for rural development activities depends in large part on the social networks of their community leaders and other residents (Brown and Nylander 1998). Due to the complexity of housing as a product and process, addressing community housing needs must involve the collaborative efforts of government officials, housing intermediaries and the general public.

The use of a housing plan is the second key element. Planning is an integral part of the decision-making about housing in most communities. Comprehensive plans, the most common form of planning, take into account existing conditions, future trends and goals and offer a long-term view of the physical design and land use patterns (Conglose n.d.). Strategic plans are another way in which communities plan to meet community housing needs. While these forms of planning may offer important documentation of existing conditions, goals and strategies, they often lack a short-term, targeted action plan to address pressing housing needs. That more vital communities form groups to identify housing goals and conduct housing needs assessments is supported by research by Cook et al. (2009) and is documented by Ziebarth (2000) as the process for meeting community housing needs. Included within this process are shorter-term work plans that frame and serve as a guide to achieving objectives. The Georgia Initiative for Community Housing uses the concept of stake-holder-driven, local housing plan to set goals and create and an actionable work plan. Each community begins the three-year program developing a locally based housing plan developed by their housing team. This process of moving from the formation of team, to goal setting to the development of an action plan is evident in the three case summaries presented earlier. Millville, for example, focused on eliminating blighted properties and improving infrastructure in all neighborhoods. Within a relatively short period of time, the community was able to address specific items on its housing plan that resulted in a reduction of blight and new opportunities for infill housing.

The third element is increasing local knowledge of housing finance mechanisms. While most housing team participants begin the program with a lack of knowledge about the primary funding programs for housing and neighborhood revitalization, the majority of participants have obtained this knowledge by the final year of the program. Awareness and understanding of these funding programs is crucial for rural and small-town communities to submit competitive grant applications and secure funding for targeted projects. This ability to secure federal funding to address housing and neighborhood issues was present in all three case study communities.

The Georgia Initiative for Community Housing provides a replicable community development model that supports rural communities of varying size, local assets and locations. The use of local housing teams comprised of local stakeholders who are committed to housing issues with capacity-building technical assistance on community development tools is effective in helping rural communities develop and implement a plan of action to address local housing and neighborhood challenges. The program achieves a large reach and impact at relatively low cost. Staffed by a program director housed within a large state university, the direct program budget of $75,000 is supported by the university, corporate partners and federal grant funding. Most of the technical assistance training is provided by volunteers. While the program is a competitive program and the participating communities may possess different levels of community capital than those not participating in the program, it appears that the Georgia Initiative for Community Housing offers a viable program and practices that can serve as a template to meet rural housing needs in rural regions and states across the United States. More research is needed to understand these differing levels of community capital as well as the processes through which communities prepare to address housing issues.

Note

1 This research was funded through an Agriculture and Food Research Initiative (AFRI) grant titled *Utilization of Social Capital to Address Community Housing Needs*, from National Institute of Food and Agriculture (NIFA).

References

Agnitsch, K., Flora, J., & Ryan, V. (2006). Bonding and bridging social capital: The interactive effects on community action. *Community Development*, *37*, 36–51.

Brown, R. B., & Nylander III, A. B. (1998). Community leadership structure: Differences between rural community leaders' and residents' informational networks. *Community Development*, *29*, 71–89.

Conglose, J. B. (n.d.). Comprehensive planning. Retrieved from http://extension.illinois.edu/lcr/comprehensiveplanning.cfm

Cook, C. C., Crull, S. R., Bruin, M. J., Yust, B. L., Shelley, M. C., Laux, S., & White, B. J. (2009). Evidence of a housing decision chain in rural community vitality. *Rural Sociology*, *74*, 113–137.

Flora, C., & Arnold, N. (2012). *Community development.* University of Montana Scholar Works. Rural Institute for Inclusive Communities. Retrieved from http://scholarworks. umt.edu/ruralinst_independent_living_community_participation/37/

Green, P., & Haines, A. (2016). *Asset building and community development* (4th Ed). Thousand Oaks, CA: SAGE Publications.

Hamdan, H., Yusof, F., & Marzukhi, M. A. (2014). Social Capital and Quality of Life in Urban Neighborhoods High Density Housing. Procedia – *Social and Behavioral Sciences,* *153,* 169–179.

Hamilton, L. C., Hamilton, L. R., Duncan, C. M., & Colocousis, C. R. (2008). Place matters: Challenges and opportunities in four rural Americas. *Carsey Institute Reports on Rural America, 1*(4). Durham, New Hampshire: University of New Hampshire. Retrieved from http://scholars.unh.edu/carsey/41/

Housing Assistance Council. (2013). *Rural data portal.* Washington: DC: Author. Retrieved from www.ruraldataportal.org/index.aspx

Landis, J. D., & McClure, K. (2010). Rethinking federal housing policy. *Journal of the American Planning Association, 76*(3), 319–348.

Lang, R. E., & Hornburg, S. P. (1998). What is social capital and why is it important to public policy? *Housing Policy Debate, 9,* 1–16.

Ling, C., & Dale, A. (2014). Agency and social capital: Characteristics and dynamics. *Community Development Journal, 49*(1) 4–20.

Morton, L. W., Allen, B. L., & Li, T. (2004). Rural housing adequacy and civic structure. *Sociological Inquiry, 74*(4), 464–491.

Putnam, R. D. (1995). Bowling alone: America's declining social capital. *Journal of Democracy, 6,* 65–78.

Social Explorer Tables: ACS 2014 (5-Year Estimates)(SE), ACS 2014 (5-Year Estimates), Social Explorer; U.S. Census Bureau.

Tinsley, K., & Massey, J. (2009). The Georgia initiative for community housing: A program note. *Housing and Society, 36*(2), 5–26.

Tremblay Jr, K. R. (1988). *Meeting housing needs in rural America.* Paper presented at the Annual Institute on Social Work and Human Services in Rural Areas (13th, Fort Collins, CO, July 24–27, 1988).

Vacant Property Research Network. (2015). *Charting the multiple meanings of blight: A national literature review on addressing the community impacts of blighted properties.* Alexandria, VA: Metropolitan Institute of Virginia Tech. Retrieved from www.kab.org/sites/default/files/ Charting_the_Multiple_Meanings_of_Blight_FINAL_REPORT.pdf

Virgil, S. M. (2010). Community economic development and rural America: Strategies for community-based collaborative development. *Journal of Affordable Housing & Community Development Law, 20*(1), 9–33.

Wilson, P. A. (1997). Building social capital: A learning agenda for the twenty-first century. *Urban Studies, 34,* 745–760.

Woolcock, M., & Narayan, D. (2000). Social capital: Implications for development theory, research and policy. *World Bank Research Observer, 15*(2).

Yust, B. L., Laux, S. C., Bruin, M. J., Crull, S. R., & Memken, J. A. (2006). Housing needs in rural communities. *Journal of Family and Consumer Sciences, 98*(4), 15–19.

Ziebarth, A., Brown, K., & Elgatian, P. (2000). *Community housing development: Building a brighter future.* Circular 1367. University of Illinois Extension.

Ziebarth, A., Prochaska-Cue, K., & Shrewsbury, B. (1997). Growth and locational impacts for housing in small communities. *Rural Sociology, 62*(1), 111–125.

14 Home improvement investment in rural America

Spatial pattern and determinants

Haoying Wang

Introduction

Housing affordability and quality have been recognized as two major issues of rural living conditions, especially among the rural poor. The housing quality issue, in particular, has not gained much insight from the literature other than observational facts. The literature on rural housing is limited, compared to research on urban housing. Most of the existing studies focus on documenting fragmented facts and lack explorative analysis. This gap of knowledge has largely hindered our understanding of rural socioeconomic status and led to ineffective policy interventions. Among many factors, spatial heterogeneity could be a reason that many universal housing policies have failed. In rural areas, the persistency of spatial heterogeneity is much stronger than those observed across metropolitan urban regions, due to both slow population dynamics and socioeconomic inertia. To provide implications for relevant policy and program design that could potentially assist rural communities in improving housing conditions, it is necessary to obtain deep insights through quantitative analysis with increasingly rich housing data.

The key task of the analysis is to understand the spatial heterogeneity in rural housing market, and how it affects both the supply and the demand of rural housing. For example, research has shown that rural households on average spend a higher proportion of income on housing compared to their urban counterparts (Dolbeare 1999). To learn the implication of such a spending trend for rural housing policies, it is important to obtain unbiased estimates on income elasticity (responsiveness) of housing demand, which requires careful handling of spatial heterogeneity. However, it is too ambitious to cover all aspects of rural housing demand and supply in one chapter. In this chapter, we focus on an important topic related directly to rural housing quality – rural home improvement investment. Here we treat the term home improvement in a generic sense that it includes both qualitative and quantitative improvements of a housing unit.

Home improvement contributes substantially to overall housing supply (Dipasquale 1999; Wang 2016), and it can be an effective adjustment to existing housing stocks in both the short run and the long run. Home improvement/maintenance costs are often ignored from housing cost equation, mainly because these costs are not upfront and binding. It is inevitable that, however, inadequate home improvement/maintenance investment will worsen housing condition both finan-cially and physically in the long run (Knight and Sirmans 1996). From a policy perspective, if assistance or financial aid towards new development squeezes out a significant amount of home improvement investment on existing housing stock, then the policy may fail at the goal of improving overall welfare. In an analyti-cal simulation framework, assuming stable population growth, Wang (2016) shows that with neighborhood level spillover effects, home improvement investment can reduce the need for new land development through potentially longer duration of residence. Park (2008) also shows that good home improvers can have positive spillover effects to the neighborhood.

The objective of this chapter is to explore the spatial variation of rural home improvement investment using the American Housing Survey (AHS) data. While controlling for spatial heterogeneity, regression models are used to learn about the income elasticity of home improvement demand and identify other important determinants of home improvement investment. Given the restricted spatial refer-ence information in the data, the spatial pattern is difficult to infer at local scale. Still, by comparing between urban and rural households, useful information can be revealed at the metropolitan scale. The next section discusses some background on rural home improvement. The following sections focus on empirical evidence and policy implications of the results. The last section briefly concludes the chapter.

Rural home improvement

The definition of a "rural area" varies across the literature and policy documents. According to Cromartie and Bucholtz (2008), the boundary between rural and urban can be drawn based on three different concepts: administrative, land-use, and economic. The three definitions represent progressively expansive urban bounda-ries (hence smaller rural area) that differ considerably from one to another. The administrative definition is used by many USDA rural development programs, and the land-use definition is more often used by the Census Bureau and the Housing and Urban Development (HUD) agency (Cromartie and Bucholtz 2008). In this chapter, we use the term rural housing/home following the definition of AHS and define rural housing as all housing not included in the urban categories, which reflects more of a land-use and demographic concept.

Homeownership, in general, is a critical asset for households to stabilize fam-ily finance and hedge against economic uncertainty. Rural households, relative to urban households, are usually found more vulnerable to income shocks, and likely having higher asset-income ratio (Wang 1995). From an asset management perspec-tive, periodic (planned or unplanned) home improvement can help to maintain the property value, which further assists households in smoothing economic fluctuations and other exogenous shocks. From a public health perspective, studies have shown that poor housing conditions are associated with different types of health conditions, such as respiratory infections, asthma, injuries and even mental conditions (e.g., Krieger and Higgins 2002). Home improvement can help preventing such condi-tions through a better living environment. As Dillman and Tremblay (1977) point out, housing provides more than just shelter. As the base of one's community living experience, it shapes and reflects one's well-being in all dimensions of life.

With both the economic role and the public health role that rural housing plays, concerns about rural housing conditions have been raised frequently (Lazere et al. 1989; Arnold 1990; Dolbeare 1999; Vallejos et al. 2009). According to Dolbeare (1999), 6.4 million households in the U.S. had inadequate housing in 1995, with about 7 percent of rural households live in substandard housing units. Among the rural households with inadequate housing, a third of them had income below poverty line. Therefore, a foremost factor that limits potential home improvement investment is the income level. Also, rural households tend to suffer from more severe income fluctuations. One reason is the seasonality in rural employment opportunities, and many jobs are either temporary positions or subject to seasonal business cycles. Another reason is that, revenue from the agricultural sector is more vulnerable to exogenous shocks (e.g., climate, international trade, and commodity markets).

According to the most recent AHS data in 2013, average home improvement expenditure of rural households is about $2,000 per year. For rural households with farm-related income ($1,000 or more as defined in AHS questionnaire), however, the average expenditure is more than $5,000 per year. Of course, the significant difference may reflect the fact that many on-farm housing units have larger square footage and more rooms. On the other hand, it also indicates that rural households facing more risks tend to make extra investments to secure their assets and hedge against future uncertainty. These aspects will be further explored in the following empirical evidence section.

Empirical evidence

Spatial pattern

The spatial pattern of home improvement investment can be examined from three different scales: regional, metropolitan and local. The regional pattern can be revealed through looking at inter-metro differences either aggregately or in a particular demographic category. However, since the AHS public use file restricts the number of MSAs published in the data, we can only draw limited inference through examining the inter-metro differences.

At the metropolitan scale, we can examine the intra-metro differences of home improvement investments based on the urban spatial structure. Given a monocentrically structured metro area, for example, different rings around the metro center represent different land uses and socioeconomic classes, which usually goes from urban to suburban, then to rural, with some transitory areas in between. The AHS public use data are suitable for studying the differences among intra-metro areas, which will be one of the focuses of the analysis in this chapter. The following regression and graphical analysis sections discuss the details.

Perhaps the most policy relevant scale is the local scale – home improvement differences between heterogeneous communities or across local jurisdictional boundaries. Due to the enormous spatial heterogeneity in housing markets, any effective housing policies need to take into consideration both the geographical heterogeneity and the socioeconomic heterogeneity. Because of confidentiality restrictions, the AHS public use data is not spatially referenced. Each housing unit observation in the data can only be identified down to the Primary Metropolitan Statistical Areas (PMSA) level.[1] Therefore, we are not able to learn insights directly at the local scale. However, using regression analysis and through controlling for PMSA level time-invariant effects, we can learn the determinants of home improvement investment in an average sense across metropolitan areas.

Empirical framework

Economic theory suggests that income and the interest rate are the primary determinants of home improvement investment, both of which affect the affordability of home improvement projects directly (e.g. Seek 1983; Lazere et al. 1989; Potepan 1989; Wang 2016). The spatial heterogeneities can influence how home improvement investment gets determined by income and interest rates at different levels. Household characteristics, housing characteristics and neighborhood characteristics usually are important determinants to consider. Beyond these factors, natural/built environment and the policy environment are also influential dimensions to take into account.

In this chapter, specifically, a fixed-effects regression model is used to identify factors from different categories that may affect home improvement expenditures of individual households. The model allows each location (e.g., PMSA) to have a different baseline level of home improvement expenditure. The goal of using regression models is to diagnose different determinant variables, rather than getting precise numerical estimates for statistical inference. The factors that are found being significantly associated with home improvement expenditure are further explored through graphical analysis. The slope (of the fitted line) estimated from the regression models represents the marginal effect of the given factor on home improvement expenditure. To eliminate impacts of outliers and noise due to random shocks, log-transformed home improvement expenditure is used as the dependent variable in the regression models. The transformation affects the quantitative interpretation of the slope, but not the qualitative interpretation. Note that, if a particular determinant variable is log-transformed as well, then the corresponding slope estimate can be interpreted as the economic elasticity of home improvement demand with respect to that determinant variable. The fixed effects in the regression models are used as a control for unobservable PMSA level time-invariant heterogeneities. We first look at the impact of income level and the interest rate and then other potential determinants. The next two sections discuss descriptive statistics for the data and graphical analysis. The definitions of all variables used in the regression analysis are listed in the appendix, which can also be found in the Codebook for the AHS Public Use File (1997 and later).

Descriptive statistics

The data used for analysis in this chapter come from the AHS 2013 National Public Use File. The data cover all nine divisions of the U.S. Census, including 145 PMSAs. Based on their urban/suburban/rural status, households are classified into: central city of MSA (1), inside MSA, but not in central city – urban (2), inside MSA, but not in central city – rural (3), outside MSA, urban (4), outside MSA, rural (5). In this chapter, 1, 2 and 4 are defined as urban, and 3 and 5 are defined as rural. About 23 percent of the observations are rural households, 77 percent are urban households. Among a total of 84,355 households in the data, 17,890 of them have non-zero home improvement expenditures incurred. Therefore, the effective estimation sample size is 17,890, 27.14 percent of which are rural households. On average, an urban household spent $9,063 on home improvement in 2013, and its rural counterpart spent $7,677 during the same time period.

Regression and graphical analysis

Household income

The first set of analyses looks at the income effect of home improvement demand. It is intuitive that higher-income households tend to spend more on home improvement projects, due to potentially larger square footage. In policy contexts, income elasticity is a more meaningful measure. Because it tells the likely proportional change of home improvement expenditure relative to a 1 percent income change, instead of the statistical association between income and the expenditure only. Figure 14.1 shows the income elasticity estimates of home improvement spending for different types of households. Here the income variable is log-transformed as well, so the estimated slope of the fitted regression line can be interpreted as income elasticity measure directly.

As shown in Figure 14.1, the overall income elasticity of home improvement expenditure is around 0.34 across the country. That is, every 1 percent increase in household income leads to an average of 0.34 percent increase in home improvement expenditure. The estimate is comparable to similar estimates on the income elasticity of housing demand in the literature. Zabel (2004) finds that the (permanent) income elasticity for housing services is between 0.35 and 0.40, using 1993 and 2001 AHS data. Earlier estimates tend to be larger, ranging from around 0.50 to 1.00 (e.g., Carliner 1973; Mulford 1979; Harmon 1988; Hansen et al. 1998). The top-right and bottom-left panels show the income elasticity estimates for urban households and rural households, respectively. There is a clear difference between two groups. The rural households have a substantially higher income elasticity of home improvement expenditure, which is around 0.37. This difference could be due to the fact that on average rural households have lower income, or due to certain characteristics related to rural housing units. For example, there may be diminishing income effect on home improvement expenditure. This contradicts

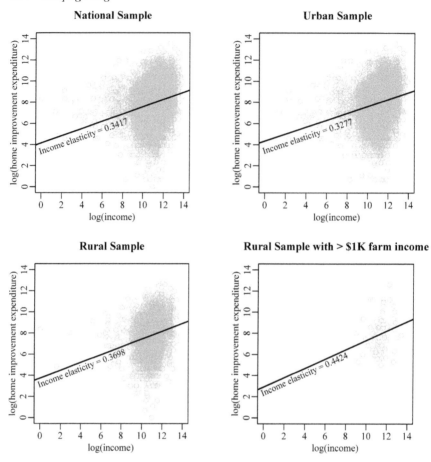

Figure 14.1 Income and Home Improvement Expenditure

with the findings in the urban economics literature, where it finds that the elasticity of housing demand increases as income level goes up (Hansen et al. 1996 and 1998). Therefore, it is more likely that the difference is attributed to differences in housing characteristics.

Among all rural households, there is still a considerable amount of heterogeneity which may drive variation of the income elasticity. To investigate this, the bottom-right panel shows results with only rural households that have farm-related income of $1,000 or more in 2013 (a very small portion of the rural sample). The even larger slope indicates that if a rural household has farm related annual income of $1,000 or more, the income elasticity of home improvement expenditure is higher than other rural households. This could be explained by the low income level of households living on farm income. Another contributing factor may be the relatively large housing square footage occupied by the rural households, as mentioned before.

Interest rate, access to credit, financial burden

Highly related to household income level, interest (mortgage) rate and access to credit may also affect household home improvement investment from a cost perspective. The mortgage rate itself is an indicator of household's access to credit and financial burden, among other measures. In this section, we examine the effects of annual real estate tax payment as a percentage of housing value (*p_amtx*), down payment percentage (*downpct*), mortgage rate (*intr*), monthly payment for mortgage as a percentage of housing value (*p_pmt*), while controlling for current value of housing unit (value). Figure 14.2 plots the results of three statistically significant factors (for both all households and rural households) revealed from the regression analysis: down payment percentage, mortgage rate and current housing value.

The significant relationship between housing value and home improvement expenditure is directly confounded through the size of living space as one would expect, holding other factors same. A higher mortgage rate means higher housing financial burden to a household, which reduces potential spending on home improvement. The significant negative slope estimate is consistent with the intuition. Such a budget constraint effect is about the same for both urban and rural households as indicated by the magnitude of the slope estimates.

The interpretation of down payment percentage is difficult, due to the fact that the variable itself measures potentially two things. A higher down payment percentage, on the one hand, may imply that the household has enough liquidity or savings to pay off a higher percentage of the principal upfront. On the other hand, it could also indicate that the household does not have a good credit or stable enough income, and the lending agent requires a higher percentage of down payment for the mortgage. The significant positive estimate on the variable cannot structurally distinguish these two effects. What we can infer from the results is that the liquidity effect dominates, but it is weaker for rural households. This is consistent with economic intuition, given that rural households often suffer more from liquidity constraints.

Household characteristics

Household characteristics can affect home improvement investment through both the demographic and economic channels. For example, householders with more education may prefer spending more on their homes, due to either income effect or neighborhood selection effect. In this section we examine the following factors: householder age (*age*), if any household members 65 years or older (*elder*), householder ever owned home before (*frstho*), householder education level (*grad*), number of children under 18 years (*kidu18*), marital status of householder (*married*), if householder moved in last year (*movedly*), number of persons in the household (*per*) and household income as percent of poverty line (*poor*). Among these, *elder*, *frstho*, *married* and *movedly* are {1, 0} indicator variables. Figure 14.3 and Figure 14.4 plot the estimation results.

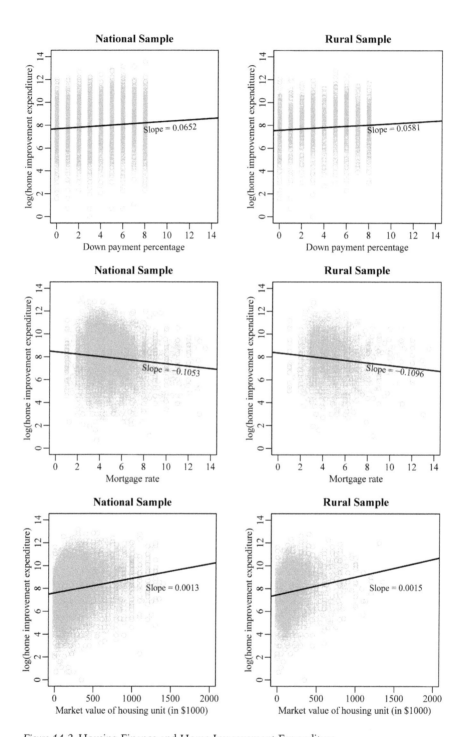

Figure 14.2 Housing Finance and Home Improvement Expenditure

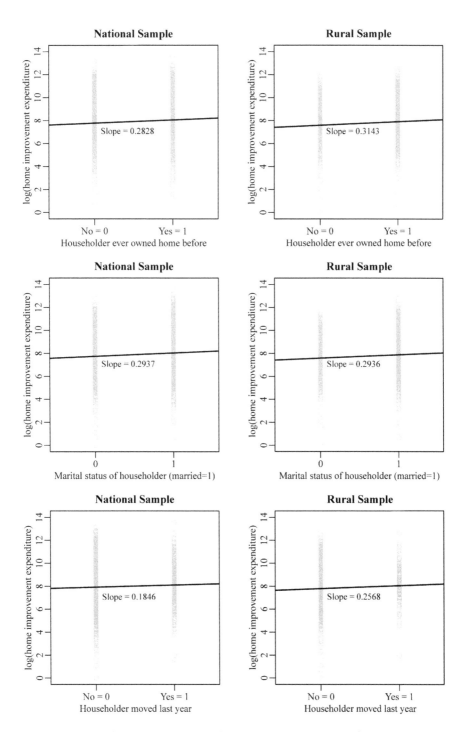

Figure 14.3 Household Characteristics and Home Improvement Expenditure

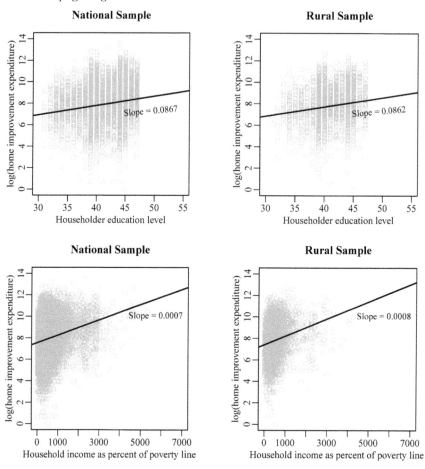

Figure 14.4 Household Characteristics and Home Improvement Expenditure (Continued)

Overall, it appears that homeownership experiences in the past (*frstho*=1), householder education level, being married (*married*=1), recent moving experience (*movedly*=1) and household income relative to local poverty standard are important determinants. Between urban and rural households, there is no large difference detected among these factors. In terms of magnitude, recent moving experience is the only factor that shows some significant difference. The larger slope for the rural sample indicates that a recently moved rural household tends to spend more on home improvement compared to its urban counterpart. One possible explanation for the difference is that, rural households usually expect to have longer duration of residence once settled, which gives more incentive for home improvement investment after moving to a new place. Or, it is possible that longer tenure from the former occupant translates into need for more updates.

In the previous section, we explored the effect of absolute income level on home improvement investment. The second row of Figure 14.4 shows the effect of relative income (adjusted to local poverty line). Again, it suggests a positive income elasticity as expected. Another interesting question regarding the above results is whether the effects of these determinants vary across racial groups. A further regression analysis with householder race included as fixed effects gives slope estimates of no significant differences from those without race fixed effects. In other words, the household characteristics related determinants of home improvement expenditure are consistent across racial groups. However, this does not exclude the fact that different racial groups have different baseline level of home improvement expenditure or housing spending in general, as suggested in the literature. Such a difference across racial groups is absorbed into the time-invariant fixed effects here.

Housing characteristics

Household characteristics capture the demographic aspects of factors driving home improvement investment. Housing characteristics, on the other hand, reflect the physical aspects of driving factors at household level. The hedonic valuation literature has shown that many housing characteristics are significantly valued by the housing markets (e.g., see Sirmans et al. 2005). Subject to data availability of AHS, this section explores the following characteristics: number of bathrooms (*baths*), age of housing unit as of 2013 (*unit_age*), having basement (*cellar*), number of floors (*floors*), having garage (*garage*), subjective rating of unit as a place to live (*howh*), had inside water leaks in last 12 months (*ileak*), square footage of lot (*lot*), purchase price of unit and land (*lprice*), new construction in last four years (*newc*), number of rooms in the unit (*rooms*) and square footage of the unit (*unitsf*). Among these, significant factors are plotted in Figure 14.5, Figure 14.6 and Figure 14.7.

From the graphical results we can see that, as expected, characteristics that are positively correlated with structure or property size (*baths, cellar, floors, garage, lot, lprice, rooms, unitsf*) have positive effects on home improvement expenditure. Age of unit has a positive effect, but insignificant for rural households. Household rating of unit as a place to live (from 1 to 10, 10 being the highest) appears to be an important determinant. However, there may be simultaneity issue between home improvement expenditure and the rating. Hence the interpretation of the estimate magnitude conditional on the rating scale should take caution. An indicator of water leaks (*ileak*) is used to control for housing maintenance condition. Leaks are usually a signal of inadequate maintenance on the unit. An indicator of new construction is used to control for new units which naturally require less improvement. The model with all households shows an expected negative sign. However, it is insignificant in all models, possibly because new construction often requires items such as landscaping.

Neighborhood characteristics

The recent literature has shown that neighborhood spillover effects and social interactions are important in shaping housing markets at local scale (Ioannides 2011; Topa and Zenou 2015; Wang 2016). Neighborhood characteristics can be measured

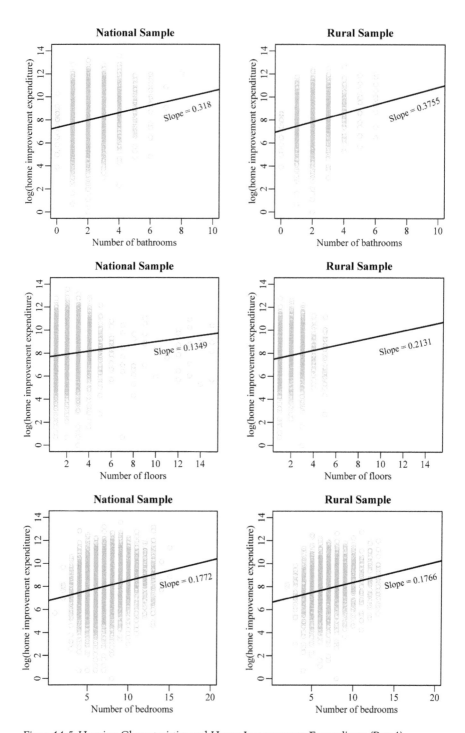

Figure 14.5 Housing Characteristics and Home Improvement Expenditure (Part 1)

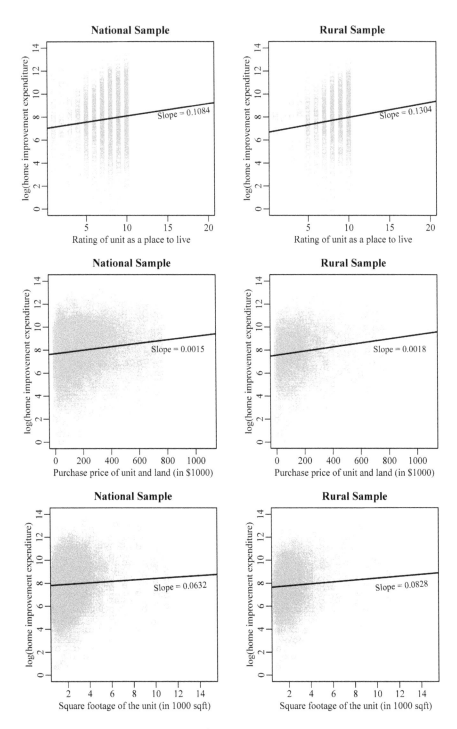

Figure 14.6 Housing Characteristics and Home Improvement Expenditure (Part 2)

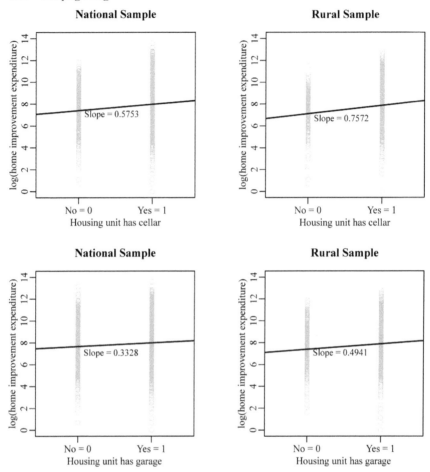

Figure 14.7 Housing Characteristics and Home Improvement Expenditure (Part 3)

both objectively and subjectively. In this section we examine neighborhood value sharing (*sharvals*), having abandoned/vandalized buildings within 1/2 block (*eaban*), subjective rating of neighborhood as place to live (*hown*), log-transformed area average median income (lmed) and neighborhood police protection satisfaction (*satpol*). Among these, three factors are found statistically significant, which are plotted in Figure 14.8.

According to the results, neighborhood value sharing has positive effect but insignificant. Neighborhood safety as approximated by satisfactory police protection is irrelevant, which may be simply due to the fact that *satpol* is a poor proxy for neighborhood safety. For the national sample with both urban and rural households, neighborhood housing condition (*eaban*), subjective rating of neighborhood and neighborhood area income level are important determinants, as illustrated in Figure 14.8. Having abandoned or vandalized housing units in the surrounding area reduces the amount of home improvement dollars that the household

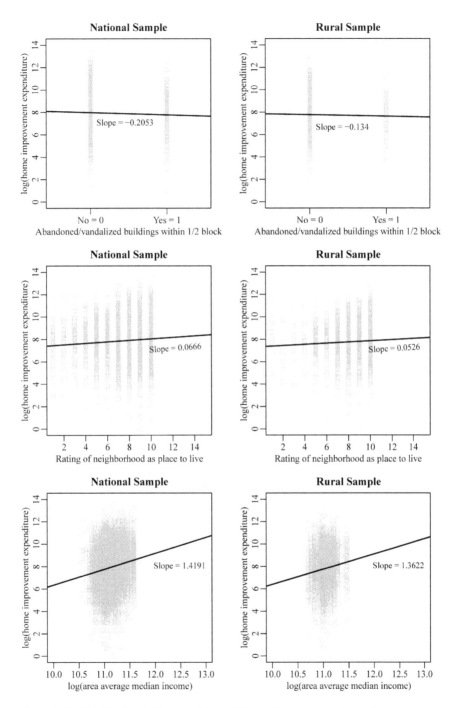

Figure 14.8 Neighborhood Characteristics and Home Improvement Expenditure

would invest. Higher neighborhood valuation and area income level increase the amount of home improvement investment as one would expect. For the sample with rural households only, neighborhood housing condition and subjective rating of neighborhood have the same expected sign, but become insignificant. Neighborhood income level is still an important determinant in the rural sample. Similar to household income level as a determinant, rural areas have a higher income elasticity of home improvement demand compared to their urban counterparts. In terms of magnitude, the area income elasticity is much larger than the household income elasticity. The high area income elasticity is actually consistent with some of the long-run income elasticities of housing demand found in the literature (e.g., Harmon 1988), which is around 1.

Environmental factors and public policy

Environment amenities and housing policies are exogenous factors that can potentially influence household housing and home improvement demand (Cho 2001; Wang and Chang 2013). The influence of environmental factors works through both the built environment and housing market. Due to limited observations on rural households with environment amenity related measures, we are only able to estimate a model for all households using national sample with two indicator variables: having open space within 1/2 block (*egreen*) and if the unit is a waterfront property (*wfprop*). The regression results indicate that, having open space nearby is not associated with home improvement investment in any significant way. One issue here is that the definition of open space in AHS questionnaire is very broad and subject to individual perception. Therefore, different households may have different definition and conceptualization for open space. Waterfront property, on the other hand, is a well-defined measure. As shown in Figure 14.9, waterfront property is positively and significantly associated with home improvement expenditure. However, the magnitude of the effect is smaller among rural households.

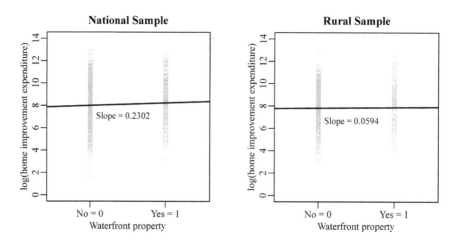

Figure 14.9 Waterfront Property and Home Improvement Expenditure

Policy impact on housing market is usually difficult to gauge, and varies across locations and demographic groups. Based on the AHS data, here we examine effects of four policy variables: if household received AFDC, TANF or other public assistance (*hhpqwelf*), if the household got a government loan/grant for alterations (*subfix*), if the household got a mortgage through government programs (*submor*) and if the household received a real estate property tax rebate last year (*txre*). The variables *hhpqwelf* and *txre* represent some sort of general public policy impact, while *subfix* and *submor* are directly related to home improvement activities.

The regression analyses indicate that general household welfare policy (*hhpqwelf*) has virtually no effects on home improvement expenditure. In other words, the potential income effects from this type of policies are less likely to spill over onto housing-related consumption. Government loans or grants for home improvement do have an expected positive impact among both urban and rural households, though the magnitude of the impact is smaller among rural households (Figure 14.10). State and local government-supported mortgage has a negative

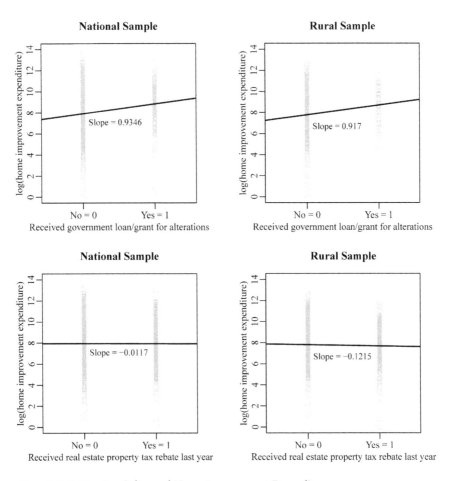

Figure 14.10 Housing Policy and Home Improvement Expenditure

impact overall, but it is insignificant among rural households. Such government mortgage programs do help to solve housing affordability issue financially, but there is not necessarily a strong enough income effect that would leave households extra financial resources to invest on home improvement. This is reasonable especially considering that most of households eligible for such mortgages are low-income families with limited access to credit. The real estate tax rebate has a marginal negative impact on home improvement expenditures (Figure 14.10). Similar to welfare policies, for households eligible for the rebate, the potential income effects from these policies are less likely to spill over onto housing related consumption. If these variables are found negatively correlated with income variables, then confounding issue could become a concern. In these cases, the interpretation of these policy variables and their impacts are limited without further methodological exposition.

Discussion

Rural housing is an important issue in many aspects through which it connects to other pressing policy agendas, such as economic resilience, early education and public health. For example, given that rural low-income households are more likely to own than to rent (Housing Assistance Council 1987), policies targeting rural home improvement can potentially reduce local inequality and solve other related socioeconomic issues. The housing market is often linked to economic resilience in structural ways, and economic resilience can be enhanced by a strong and efficient housing market (Catte et al. 2005). In rural communities, housing policies can be designed to limit displacement of "locals" and low-income households when facing economic shocks (Scott and Gkartzios 2014). Among which, home improvement investment is a practical way to maintain property value, though not necessarily to increase. Studies have revealed that, basic maintenances such as new siding or exterior painting are more important than major remodeling like a new kitchen in terms of resale return (Bahney 2015). As our results have shown, home improvement-related housing policies can be effective in leveraging investment in home maintenance and improvement. This implies that well-designed policies can play important roles in building rural economic resilience.

The policy impacts from supporting home improvement investment could go beyond the household level. In recent decades, rural housing development has caused serious environmental concerns regarding its impacts on ecosystems (Napton et al. 2010). The ecological literature has well established that rural housing development can affect biodiversity and reduce conservation values (e.g., Radeloff et al. 2010), especially sprawl development. If a supply-side substitution effect exists between home improvement investment and new housing development, then policies targeting home improvement could help to slow down land use change by reducing potential new housing development (Wang 2016).

Home improvement investment is crucial to both real estate asset value and living conditions in rural communities. While regional economic development could certainly encourage investment in home alternations and repairs, many factors may limit rural households allocating more resources to home improvement and lead to deterioration of living conditions and neighborhoods in the long run. The preliminary results established in this study can help to shed light on these aspects. From the quantitative analysis results discussed above we can learn that, first, rural households tend to have a higher income elasticity of home improvement demand compared to their urban counterparts. There are several potential explanations. It is possible that home maintenance or remodeling costs more in the rural construction market, for example, due to lack of economies of scale. It is also possible that on average rural households spend more money on landscaping due to larger lot size, which makes rural households more likely to allocate a higher proportion of extra income to home improvement – hence a higher income elasticity. On the other hand, it could be that rural households are simply more "rooted" and so they will enjoy the improvement for a longer period of time. This is very likely given that rural people tend to have a lower opportunity cost of time.

The policy implication of this result is that, the same policy is likely to have a stronger impact on rural households if the policy impact works through the income effect channel. Among the five categories of variables we have examined, many are important determinants of home improvement expenditure. Beyond the basic intuition that higher property value and more structures are usually associated with higher home improvement expenditure, some other policy relevant ones are: access to credit, mortgage rate, homeownership experience, education, marital status, neighborhood effects, environment amenities and home improvement-related housing policies.

A caveat to note is that, the analysis with rural households in this study is based on the sample from a limited number of PMSAs due to data availability. The results may not extend to a national representation of rural households. However, given that the AHS data is one of the best information collected on home improvement activities of American households, much inference can still be drawn to inform rural policymaking and public policy process in general.

Concluding remarks

The goal of this study is to empirically investigate the income elasticity of home improvement demand and factors that drive rural home improvement expenditure to vary cross-sectionally. The estimated income elasticity of home improvement demand for rural households is around 0.37, higher than their urban counterparts. That is, all things being equal, for every 1 percent increase in household income, it leads to an average of 0.37 percent increase in home improvement expenditure. For rural households that have farm-related annual income of $1,000 or more, the response is even higher and at 0.44 percent. From the empirical results, we have learned about the spatial structure of home improvement expenditure in the sense of an intra-metro urban/rural comparison. Beyond the basic intuition that higher property value and more structure are usually associated with a higher home improvement expenditure, through regression-based graphical analysis we have also identified some policy relevant determinants of home improvement investment: access to credit, mortgage rate, homeownership experience, education, marital status, neighborhood effects, environment amenities and home improvement-related housing policies. In future policy research, it is also necessary to bring a dynamic perspective to understand household home improvement decisions. Such a new framework could take into account both the housing market dynamics and the forward-looking behavior of households, which will provide policymaking with a more solid micro-foundation.

Appendix

Variable definitions

Table A14.1 Definition of Variables in Regression Analysis

Variable Name	Type	Description
age	continuous	householder age
baths	continuous	number of bathrooms in the unit
cellar	binary	if housing unit has basement, yes = 1
downpct	continuous	mortgage down payment percentage
eaban	binary	abandoned/vandalized buildings within 1/2 block, yes = 1
egreen	binary	open spaces within 1/2 block, yes = 1
elder	binary	if any household members 65 years or older, yes = 1
floors	continuous	number of floors in the unit
frstho	binary	if householder ever owned home before, yes = 1
garage	binary	if housing unit has garage, yes = 1
grad	continuous	householder education level, range is [31=less than 1st grade,47=doctorate]
hhpqwelf	binary	if household received AFDC, TANF or other public assistance, yes = 1
howh	ordinal rating	rating of housing unit as place to live, range is [1=worst, 10=best]
hown	ordinal rating	rating of neighborhood as place to live, range is [1=worst, 10=best]
ileak	binary	any inside water leaks in last 12 months, yes = 1
intr	continuous	mortgage interest rate
kidu18	continuous	number of children under 18 years
lmed	continuous	log-transformed area average median income
log(income)	continuous	log-transformed household income
lot	continuous	square footage of the lot, in acres
lprice	continuous	purchase price of unit and land, in $1000
married	binary	marital status of householder, married = 1
movedly	binary	if householder moved in last year, yes = 1
newc	binary	housing unit is a new construction in last 4 years, yes = 1
p_amtx	continuous	annual real estate tax payment as a percentage of housing value
p_pmt	continuous	monthly payment for mortgage as a percentage of housing value
per	continuous	number of persons in the household
poor	continuous	household income as a percentage of poverty line
rooms	continuous	number of rooms in the unit
satpol	binary	neighborhood police protection satisfactory, yes = 1
sharvals	ordinal rating	neighbors share the same values, range is [1=strongly agree, 4=strongly disagree]

(Continued)

Table A14.1   (Continued)

subfix	binary	if household got government loan/grant for alterations, yes = 1
submor	binary	if household got mortgage through government programs, yes = 1
txre	binary	if household received real estate property tax rebate last year, yes = 1
unit_age	continuous	age of housing unit as of 2013, in years
unitsf	continuous	square footage of the unit, in 1000 SQFT
value	continuous	current value of housing unit, in $1000
wfprop	binary	if housing unit is a waterfront property, yes = 1

Note

1 According to the U.S. Census, if a metropolitan area meets the requirements to qualify as a metropolitan statistical area (MSA) and has a population of one million or more, two or more PMSAs may be defined within it if statistical criteria are met and local opinion is in favor. In general, PMSA is smaller than MSA in terms of area.

References

Arnold, C. A. (1990). Ignoring the rural underclass: The biases of federal housing policy. *Stanford Law & Policy Review, 2*, 191–206.

Bahney, A. (2015). The top 5 home renovation projects that pay off (and what doesn't). Retrieved August 31, 2016 from www.forbes.com/sites/annabahney/2015/04/30/the-top-5-home-renovation-projects-that-pay-off-and-what-doesnt/

Carliner, G. (1973). Income elasticity of housing demand. *Review of Economics and Statistics, 55*(4), 528–532.

Catte, P., Girouard, N., Price, R., & André, C. (2005). The contribution of housing markets to cyclical resilience. *OECD Journal: Economic Studies, 2004*(1), 125–156.

Cho, C. J. (2001). Amenities and urban residential structure: An amenity-embedded model of residential choice. *Papers in Regional Science, 80*(4), 483–498.

Cromartie, J., & Bucholtz, S. (2008). Defining the "rural" in rural America. *Amber Waves, 6*(3), 28–34.

Dillman, D. A., & Tremblay Jr., K. R. (1977). The quality of life in rural America. *Annals of the American Academy of Political and Social Science, 429*(1), 115–129.

DiPasquale, D. (1999). Why don't we know more about housing supply? *Journal of Real Estate Finance and Economics, 18*(1), 9–23.

Dolbeare, C. N. (1999). Conditions and trends in rural housing. In J. N. Belden & R. J. Wiener (Eds.), *Housing in Rural America: Building Affordable and Inclusive Communities* (13–26). Thousand Oaks, CA: Sage.

Hansen, J. L., Formby, J. P., & Smith, W. J. (1996). The income elasticity of demand for housing: evidence from concentration curves. *Journal of Urban Economics, 39*(2), 173–192.

Hansen, J. L., Formby, J. P., & Smith, W.J. (1998). Estimating the income elasticity of demand for housing: A comparison of traditional and Lorenz-concentration curve methodologies. *Journal of Housing Economics, 7*(4), 328–342.

Harmon, O. R. (1988). The income elasticity of demand for single-family owner-occupied housing: An empirical reconciliation. *Journal of Urban Economics, 24*(2), 173–185.

Housing Assistance Council, Inc. (1987). *Rural housing and poverty monitor.* Washington, DC.

Ioannides, Y. M. (2011). Neighborhood effects and housing. In J. Benhabib, A. Bisin, & M. O. Jackson (Eds.), *Handbook of Social Economics* Vol. 1B (1281–1340). Amsterdam: Elsevier.

Knight, J. R., & Sirmans, C. F. (1996). Depreciation, maintenance, and housing prices. *Journal of Housing Economics*, 5(4), 369–389.

Krieger, J., & Higgins, D. L. (2002). Housing and health: Time again for public health action. *American Journal of Public Health*, 92(5), 758–768.

Lazere, E. B., Leonard, P. A., & Kravitz, L. L. (1989). *The other housing crisis: Sheltering the poor in rural America.* Washington, DC: Center on Budget and Policy Priorities and Housing Assistance Council.

Mulford, J. E. (1979). *Income elasticity of housing demand.* Report R-2449-HUD, RAND Corporation.

Napton, D. E., Auch, R. F., Headley, R., & Taylor, J. L. (2010). Land changes and their driving forces in the Southeastern United States. *Regional Environmental Change*, 10(1), 37–53.

Park, K. (2008). *Good home improvers make good neighbors.* Joint Center for Housing Studies, Harvard University, working paper W08–2.

Potepan, M. J. (1989). Interest rates, income, and home improvement decisions. *Journal of Urban Economics*, 25(3), 282–294.

Radeloff, V. C. et al. (2010). Housing growth in and near United States protected areas limits their conservation value. *Proceedings of the National Academy of Sciences*, 107(2), 940–945.

Scott, M., & Gkartzios, M. (2014). Rural housing: Questions of resilience. *Housing and Society*, 41(2), 247–276.

Seek, N. H. (1983). Adjusting housing consumption: Improve or move. *Urban Studies*, 20(4), 455–469.

Sirmans, S., Macpherson, D., & Zietz, E. (2005). The composition of hedonic pricing models. *Journal of Real Estate Literature*, 13(1), 1–44.

Topa, G., & Zenou, Y. (2015). Neighborhood and network effects. In G. Duranton, J.V. Henderson, & W. C. Strange (Eds.), *Handbook of Regional and Urban Economics 5* (561–624). Amsterdam: Elsevier.

Vallejos, Q. M., Quandt, S. A., & Arcury, T. A. (2009). The condition of farmworker housing in the Eastern United States. In S. A. Quandt and T. A. Arcury (Eds.), *Latino Farmworkers in the Eastern United States* (37–67). New York, NY: Springer.

Wang, Y. (1995). Permanent income and wealth accumulation: A cross-sectional study of Chinese urban and rural households. *Economic Development and Cultural Change*, 43(3), 523–550.

Wang, H. (2016). A simulation model of home improvement with neighborhood spillover. *Computers, Environment and Urban Systems*, 57, 36–47.

Wang, H., & Chang, C. J. (2013). Simulation of housing market dynamics: Amenity distribution and housing vacancy. In R. Pasupathy, S. H. Kim, A. Tolk, R. Hill, and M. E. Kuhl (Eds.), *Proceedings of the 2013 Winter Simulation Conference: Simulation: Making Decisions in a Complex World* (1673–1684). Piscataway, NJ: IEEE Press.

Zabel, J. E. (2004). The demand for housing services. *Journal of Housing Economics*, 13(1), 16–35.

Index

Note: Page numbers in **bold** indicate a figure on the corresponding page; page numbers in *italic* indicate a table on the corresponding page.

For Product Safety Concerns and Information please contact our EU
representative GPSR@taylorandfrancis.com
Taylor & Francis Verlag GmbH, Kaufingerstraße 24, 80331 München, Germany